Advance Praise for

1001 things
everyone should
know about
irish american history

"The 1002nd thing that everyone should know about Irish American history is that Edward O'Donnell has produced the most comprehensive, incisive, and engaging treatment of the subject ever attempted. He has mastered the difficult challenge of presenting the facts without ever slipping into pendantry or trivia. This will be an important reference work for years to come."　　　　—Peter Quinn, author of
Banished Children of Eve

"Edward O'Donnell's new book will be a lasting source of pleasure and edification for everyone interested in the history of Irish America. In a unique and highly engaging format, he gives us a rich and colorful portrait of one of America's most prominent ethnic groups. His grasp of the Irish antecedents is every bit as impressive as his command of the American context."　　　—Kevin Kenny, Boston College, author of
Making Sense of the Molly Maguires and *The American Irish: A History*

"Few people understand the Irish like Edward O'Donnell. Even fewer can explain Irish culture, history, politics, and religion with such wit, insight, and knowledge. Keep this immensely readable book handy, because you'll return to it time and time again."　　　　　—Terry Golway, author of *For the Cause of Liberty:*
A Thousand Years of Irish Heroes and *The Irish in America*

"O'Donnell's *1001 Things Everyone Should Know About Irish American History* will be the indispensable reference for anyone interested in the story of the Irish at home and in America. Readers picking up the book will find themselves dipping into one entry after another, as O'Donnell takes them on a fascinating journey from Cuchulain to the Celtic Tiger."　　　—Maureen Murphy, coauthor of *The Great Irish*
Famine Curriculum for the State of New York

1001 things
everyone should
know about
irish american
history

edward t. o'donnell

BROADWAY BOOKS / NEW YORK

Library of Congress Cataloging-in-Publication Data

O'Donnell, Edward T.
1001 things everyone should know about Irish American history /
Edward T. O'Donnell.—1st ed.
p. cm.
Includes index.
1. Irish Americans—History—Miscellanea. 2. Ireland—History—Miscellanea. I. Title: One thousand one things everyone should know about Irish American history. II. Title: One thousand and one things everyone should know about Irish American history. III. Title.

E184.I6 O36 2002
941.5—dc21
2001043198

FIRST EDITION

Designed by Donna Sinisgalli

ISBN 0-7679-0686-1
1   3   5   7   9   10   8   6   4   2

To my mother,

Madeline M. O'Donnell (b. 1926),

and my father,

Walter E. O'Donnell, M.D. (1923–2000)

acknowledgments

In the course of writing a book, one always incurs many debts. Such is the case here, and I have many people to thank for all their help and support. First, I wish to acknowledge the following people for their able assistance in the writing of this book: Paul Ruppert, Sarah Buscher, Elizabeth Toomey, Jennifer Bussey, Ellie Kuykendall, John Riddle, Carol Celeste, Robert Fay, Bridget Becker, Melanie Gold, Thomas Kertscher, Madaleine Laird, Hugh McAloon, Olivia Miller, Susan Olmstead, Sherril Steele-Carlin, and Mikel Weaver. Special thanks are also due to Terry Golway, Kevin Kenny, Maureen Murphy, and Dan Tobin for their advice, criticism, and input as I wrote the book. I greatly appreciate the patience and professionalism exhibited by the editorial team at Broadway Books, especially Jennifer Griffin, Luke Dempsey, Charlie Conrad, and Becky Cole. I also wish to thank my trusted agent, the great John Wright, who handled all the important details so I wouldn't have to.

I also am indebted to the wonderfully helpful people at the Museum of the City of New York, especially Eileen Morales and Marguerite Lavin, for their help in selecting pictures for the book. The same must be said for the people at the American Irish Historical Society, in particular Director Bill Colbert. I am also thankful for the assistance provided by the staffs at the Library of Congress, Boston Public Library, University of Notre Dame, General Services Administration, Concannon Vinyard, Hockey Hall of Fame, NASA, California Historical Society, Nebraska Historical Society, Nevada Historical Society, Institute of Texas Cultures, Tamiment Collection at New York University, Department of the Navy–Naval Historical Center, Bord Failte of Ireland, Nobel Prize Museum, Montana Historical Society, Pittsburgh Penguins Archives, George Meany Archives, The Lahey Clinic, and Johns Hopkins University Medical School Archives.

As this is my first book, I also want to take the opportunity to thank those people who have played a role in my development as a writer and historian. Fr. Anthony J. Kuzniewski, S.J., at the College of the Holy Cross in Worcester, Massachusetts, was the man who turned me on to the thrill and fascination of history. Professors Jim Shenton, Ken Jackson, Betsy Blackmar, Alan Brinkley, Eric Foner, Richard Bushman, Eric McKitrick, and Alden Vaughn continued this process in graduate school at Columbia University. I must also express my gratitude to Mr. Tom Caufield, a native of Ireland and my seventh-grade English teacher, for teaching me the essentials of writing. All those five-paragraph essays have surely paid off.

Finally, I owe everything to my wife, advisor, soul mate, and best friend, Stephanie Yeager O'Donnell. You make it all possible and you make it all worthwhile.

contents

People will not look forward to posterity

who never look backward to their ancestors.

—EDMUND BURKE

introduction

Just when it began, no one can say for certain. But for well over a decade now America has been experiencing an "Irish Renaissance" that shows no signs of flagging. Courses in the Irish language, Irish literature, Irish history, and genealogy now abound on college campuses across the country. Countless institutions have sprung up featuring Irish dance, music, art, and drama. Large-scale Irish fairs are once again an annual feature in cities with large Irish American populations, while hundreds of Irish shops from Connecticut to California sell Irish books, crafts, and bric-a-brac. The Irish dance sensation *Riverdance* and its successor *Lord of the Dance* have smashed attendance and video sales records worldwide. Famine monuments and Famine curriculum for public schools are now found in dozens of states. Frank McCourt's Pulitzer Prize–winning memoir *Angela's Ashes* and Thomas Cahill's *How the Irish Saved Civilization* have sold millions of copies. Certainly this includes a fair measure of green-beer commercialism that is downright embarrassing, but the overall tone reveals an admirable, earnest search among Irish Americans to discover, experience, and perpetuate their rich cultural traditions.

This book is a product of this trend. It is my answer to a question I've heard countless times in the past: Where can I find a book about the history of the Irish in America that is both accurate and accessible? My goal has been to write just such a book—a fun yet factual look at the people and events that have marked Irish American history. I've brought to this task an inclusive approach that recognizes that Irish America has always been characterized by an extraordinary diversity—from religion and politics to class and identity. My inclusive approach has likewise led me to chronicle not simply the triumphs of Irish Americans, but also their failures.

Finally, I like to think of this book as an American story as much as an ethnic one. The Irish were one of the first, but by no means the last, major immigrant group to come to America. Their successful struggle against poverty, exploitation, and hatred helped advance an ethos of tolerance that eventually became a central principle of democracy. We need only look at the ongoing conflict in Northern Ireland, or anywhere else in the world for that matter, to appreciate the importance—and uniqueness—of that American tradition.

Slainte!

Edward T. O'Donnell
Holden, Massachusetts
August 2001

PART 1

Ireland

Before 1850

ancient history

1. Ice Age During the Ice Age, which began approximately 2.5 million years ago and lasted until about 10,000 B.C., Ireland was covered by two major glaciers. They are responsible for much of Ireland's physical landscape today, most notably its rivers, valleys, and mountains, which by European standards are relatively short and round at the peak. The soil left behind by the glaciers (which began melting around 10,000 B.C.) left an otherwise rocky island with a layer of fertile topsoil that accounts for Ireland's long-standing agricultural traditions.

2. The First Inhabitants Ireland appears to have been unique among European nations in that Stone Age hunters never reached there. The most striking evidence supporting this theory is the remains of massive elk that boast a shoulder span of six feet and antlers eight feet across.

Ireland's first human inhabitants arrived during the Middle Stone Age (sometime around 8,000 B.C.), probably from Britain via a land bridge that stretched across the Irish Sea from Antrim to present-day Scotland. The trip may have been accomplished in small skin-covered boats called "coracles."

These people were few in number and lived as migratory hunters of wild pig, fowl, and fish, and gatherers of plants. As migratory people, they lived in small huts, produced no artistry (i.e., pottery), and did not engage in agriculture. Archaeologists have found mostly tools and small weapons made of flint, but little else.

Passage graves at Newgrange

With the land bridge eventually submerged by rising sea levels, Ireland's next inhabitants came in small boats from Britain or Europe, sometime around 6,000 B.C. in what is known as the Neolithic (or New Stone Age) period. They were the first farmers and herders and the first to establish substantial settlements. They were skilled in pottery, weaving, and tool making and evidence suggests they produced stone axes in large quantities for trade.

3. Passage Graves Of all the archaeological evidence found for the Neolithic period, none is more intriguing than the many burial chambers, or passage graves, found throughout the Irish countryside. Dating from approximately 3,000 B.C., these tombs consist of a burial chamber surrounded by a large mound of stone—some involving as much as 200,000 tons moved to the site. A single long passage adorned with decorative murals and stone carvings leads to the inner chamber. Scholars remain uncertain about the meaning of these designs, though they appear to have ritualistic significance associated with sun worship and the afterlife. It is also apparent that these were the burial grounds of kings. The greatest examples of these passage graves are found in the Boyne Valley, at Dowth, Knowth, and Newgrange in County Meath. According to Sean Duffy, author of *The Macmillan Atlas of Irish History*, "These are among the earliest examples of true architecture known anywhere in the world."

4. The Bronze Age Between 2,500 B.C. and 600 B.C., Irish metalworkers used the country's plentiful deposits of copper and other metals to produce bronze and copper tools (ax heads, sickles, pots, and craft implements), weaponry (spearheads and shields), and eventually jewelry. By 700 B.C. the Irish goldsmith craft reached its highest point of development, producing a wide array of jewelry and ornaments. Today, Ireland has more artifacts of gold from this period than any other European country.

5. Ierne The first known written reference to Ireland was made by Aristotle in the fourth century B.C., when he mentioned the islands of Ierne (Ireland) and Albion (Great Britain) in the Atlantic Ocean beyond the Pillars of Hercules (Strait of Gibraltar). But it was left to another Greek, the second-century A.D. Alexandrian geographer Ptolemy, to write the first detailed description of Ireland. For someone who never got within three thousand miles of Ireland, he provided a remarkably accurate description of the island, including the names of its main rivers, ports, and settlements, as well as the domains of important tribes. Since the Greeks never settled there, Ptolemy most likely got his information from accounts provided by mariners and traders.

The name Ierne most likely derived from the name of one of the island's larger tribes, the Erainn Celts who dominated the coastal region in present-day Cork. Their name probably came from the Celtic word for Ireland, *Eriu,* the forerunner to the modern *Eire.*

6. Hibernia Another early world power that never included Ireland in its far-flung empire were the successors to the Greeks, the Romans. The Roman governor in Britain, Julius Gnaeous Agricola, was invited by an ousted Irish chieftain to invade Ireland in A.D. 78 and seriously contemplated the idea until it was vetoed by Emperor Domitian. Archaeological evidence suggests that contact between the Roman Empire and Ireland was limited to trade. Perhaps the most important influence of Roman civilization on Ireland was the development of its oldest known form of writing, ogham, which preceded Old Irish. Used mainly between the fourth and seventh centuries, ogham was based on (though clearly distinct from) the Roman alphabet. Another contribution of the Romans was the term "Hibernia," the Latin variation of "Ierne."

Centuries later, when nationalists took to lionizing their homeland's once glorious past, they frequently mentioned that the Irish were the only people in Europe not to be conquered by the Romans.

7. The Celts Come to Ireland The Celts were an Indo-European people who originated in northeastern Europe as far back as 1,200 B.C. By 600 B.C. the Celts were a formidable presence in Europe, and by the third century B.C. they were encroaching on the Greek world. Indeed, the word Celt, like Ierne, derives from the name the Greeks gave to these much-feared barbarians, *Keltoi.*

The Celts reached Britain by about 400 B.C. and Ireland by 300 B.C. They most likely arrived in Ireland in small bands rather than as an invading horde. Many no doubt arrived from Britain, but linguistic evidence suggests that greater numbers came from Iberia (where the dialect of the Celtic language was different from that in Britain and similar to the one developed in Ireland).

The single most important fact regarding the Celtic cultural impact is that the Romans never conquered Ireland. The spread of the Roman Empire across continental Europe, through Gaul and into Britain, meant a steady erosion of a recently arrived Celtic culture. By contrast, the culture of Ireland's Celts had centuries to take root and flourish—nearly eight hundred years until the arrival of the first Christian missionaries and a thousand years before the Viking invasions. It is little wonder then that modern Irish culture continues to reflect this Celtic influence.

8. Celtic Ireland   Although the Celts shared a common culture and language, Celtic Ireland was divided into *tuaths,* or small tribes or clans. Clans were ruled by a chieftain or king. Below him was a small circle of privileged individuals (among them druid priests, judges, artisans, and harpists) and their families, the equivalent of a nobility. The majority of the *tuath* consisted of freemen, laborers, and slaves.

A central organizing principle of Celtic society was "clientship." That is, those of lower standing accepted the authority of their superiors in exchange for protection. In some cases, weaker kings became the clients of more powerful ones. Although this system did allow some kings to acquire significant power, probably none ever merited the legendary title "high king of Ireland."

Celtic kings did not inherit their titles; rather they were elected by the highest-ranking members of the *tuath.* Some Celtic kings grew very rich and powerful, having under them many lesser kings. Many of these lived in substantial defensive settlements called "ring forts," some of which still exist

in Antrim. These were not towns, however, for the Celts built none. For the most part they lived in simple dwellings as seminomadic dairy farmers. Cattle, not land (which was usually held in common within the *tuath),* was the most important possession and sign of power.

9. A Warrior People   The Celts in Ireland, and pretty much everywhere they went, were known as ferocious warriors. Perhaps the best description of the Celtic warrior comes from the Greek historian Diodorus, who wrote in the first century B.C., "Their aspect is terrifying. . . . They are very tall in stature, with rippling muscles under clear white skin. Their hair is blond, but not naturally so: they bleach it . . . They look like wood-demons, their hair thick and shaggy like a horse's mane." Just before battle they unnerved their opponents by whipping themselves into a prebattle frenzy, shouting, hurling insults, and rhythmically banging their swords and shields. Many also chose to fight completely naked. Virtually all accounts of Celtic warriors in action describe their almost ecstatic state of rage and fury. They also were widely known to collect the heads of their victims as trophies.

Some scholars have suggested that the strong Celtic be-

Ogham stone

lief in an afterlife may have contributed to their legendary fearlessness on the field of battle.

10. Celtic Language Celts spoke many similar dialects of an Indo-European language. Those who came to Britain and Gaul spoke what linguists term Brythonic Celtic, or P-Celtic. From it derive the modern languages of Welsh and Breton (and the now extinct languages of Pictish and Cumbrian). Celts who settled in Iberia and Ireland spoke Goidelic Celtic, or Q-Celtic, the ancient forerunner of Irish Gaelic, Scottish Gaelic, and Manx Gaelic.

11. Ogham Irish Celts, under the influence of Roman culture seeping in from Britain and the continent, developed a written form of the Celtic language in the fourth century A.D. Its alphabet consists of twenty letters (later twenty-five) formed by combinations of straight lines of varying length and position. More than three hundred ogham stones (upright stone pillars) dating from A.D. 350 to 600 have been found throughout Ireland, mostly in Munster. The stones appear to be memorial markers, as most of the inscriptions are the names of people and their lineage.

12. Gaelic Many people use the word "Gaelic" when they are referring to the native language of Ireland. Technically speaking, the correct term is "Irish Gaelic," or as most in Ireland say, "Irish."

Such specificity is needed because three forms of Gaelic currently exist—Irish Gaelic, Scottish Gaelic, and Manx Gaelic (spoken on the Isle of Man). All three derive from a common ancient Celtic dialect known as Goidelic.

The loss of the Gaelic language dates to the imposition of a harsh English colonial rule in the seventeenth century. By 1750, only a quarter of the Irish, mainly the people of the poorest and more remote counties in the south and west, spoke the language. By 1920, only about 20 percent had any knowledge of the language. But the Free State constitution established Irish as the official language of the Republic and made instruction part of the public school curriculum. Today, there are about 1,500,000 people (43 percent) out of Ireland's total population of 3.6 million who are familiar with Gaelic, with perhaps 80,000 of them considered fluent.

13. Druids The central figure of Celtic life was the druid, a kind of wiseman, teacher, judge, doctor, and high priest all in one. More than one scholar has compared them to the Hindu Brahmins of India, the highest figures in the caste system, who exercised social, legal, economic, and religious authority. Druids trained for up to twenty years, studying astronomy, ancient poetry, natural philosophy, astronomy, and the legends and myths of the Celtic gods. Accounts of these "wise men of the oak," as they were known, frequently mention their wearing distinctive white robes.

In their capacity as judges they wielded near absolute authority (including the power to issue sentences of death). "In all public and private quarrels," wrote Julius Caesar of the Celts of Gaul, "the priests alone judge and decide. They fix punishments and rewards, where crimes or murder have been committed or boundary and inheritance disputes arise." Their rulings reflected a powerful sense of morality. "We teach that the gods must be honored, no injustice done and manly behavior always maintained," explained one druid when asked to explain how they arrived at their verdicts. St. Patrick got much the same answer centuries later when a druid explained the foundation of their moral code as "Truth in the heart, strength in the arm, honesty in speech." Little wonder then that druids also possessed the political power to cast the deciding vote if the election of a chieftain was at an impasse.

Further evidence of the high place held by druids in Celtic society is demonstrated by the many exemptions they enjoyed from traditional obligations, such as military service or annual dues or tribute. As scholar Gerhard Herm writes in his history *The Celts*, "[T]he Druids were the authentic and most important representatives of the Celtic people, the embodiment of all that was unique to it."

14. Celtic Religion   One of the most important functions of the druids was that of priest. Druids were believed to possess the power of prophecy and the power to call upon the gods to intervene, both benignly and vengefully, in human affairs. Celtic religion combined mysticism and magic and also stressed a belief in the afterlife.

Druids and Celtic religion are often associated with nature worship. This is understandable and not altogether inaccurate. They believed oak trees were sacred (the word "druid" may come from the Greek word *drus,* for "oak") and the four principal days of the Celtic religious calendar *(Imbolc, Beltaine, Lugnasad,* and *Samain)* are tied to the changes in the seasons.

Scholars of Celtic religion have collected nearly four hundred names of different deities across Celtic Europe. Most appear to have been local deities, but some appear in multiple places. This enormous Celtic pantheon contained gods of every description, nature, and characteristic. Most, it appears, were regarded with fear, as evidenced by the consistently terrifying sculptures of Celtic gods found by archaeologists.

It was this religious tradition, backed by a powerful druid priesthood, that St. Patrick and other missionaries encountered when they began to arrive in the fifth century A.D. It took at least two centuries for Christianity to triumph over the druids, but strains of the latter's religious tradition persisted for over a millennium, if not longer. Christian missionaries wisely (from the standpoint of gaining converts) chose to Christianize many Celtic rituals. *Samain* on November 1 became Halloween and All Saints' Day, *Yule* in late December became Christmas, *Imbolc* in early February became Candlemas (later Groundhog Day), and the fertility rites of *Beltaine* on May 1 were melded into the adoration of Mary. Celtic deities were also Christianized by

transferring their powers and attributes to Christian saints.

15. Human Sacrifice   One aspect of Celtic religion that, thankfully, *did* disappear, and relatively quickly, was the practice of human sacrifice. It was still in vogue when St. Patrick arrived in the mid–fifth century A.D. Most likely it was done as a means to appease the angry Celtic gods.

Archaeologists in the 1950s discovered in ancient Danish bogs the perfectly preserved bodies of three men who had been ritually sacrificed. While they may or may not be Celts, a fourth body (known as Lindow Man to archaeologists) discovered in an English bog in 1984 is unquestionably a Celt, and probably an Irish one.

Of course, Celtic converts to Christianity never surrendered the *idea* of human sacrifice, since that is the essential meaning of Jesus' crucifixion.

16. Druids in History   Druids have experienced the ups and downs of historical revisionism. In the centuries following the conversion of Ireland to Christianity, druids were depicted as the occult leaders of a barbaric religion, often serving pagan kings. In the nineteenth century, however, they became the object of fascination in Europe, especially Britain (Winston Churchill, for example, joined the Albion Lodge of the Ancient Order of Druids in 1908). Many druidic societies were formed, some of which dabbled in the mysticism of druidic religion; others simply were social clubs that adopted the druid as a sort of mascot. The late twentieth century has seen a growing enchantment with and respect for druids and Celtic religious traditions. To be sure, some of this stems from the growing popularity of mysticism and the occult. But it also reflects a larger willingness to take more seriously Ireland's pre-Christian history.

17. Celtic Design   Most of the earliest Celtic artifacts (carved stone and metalwork) found in

Celtic design

bridge between the culture of pagan Ireland and the Christian Celtic traditions that developed after the arrival of St. Patrick.

18. Celtic Mythology   Fionn mac Cumhaill, or Finn MacCool, was the heroic leader of a company of soldiers (known as the Fianna) in the ancient Fionn Cycle of Irish mythology. MacCool's Fianna wandered about Ireland in the third century A.D. to battle evil, both human and supernatural. They were very much like today's comic book superheroes, possessing superhuman strength, speed, and agility. They are also classic Celtic warriors, firmly rooted in their natural surroundings and following a clear moral code of justice. In the early twentieth century, Irish nationalists drew upon this warrior tradition. In 1909, for example, Countess Markievicz founded Fianna Eireann, a nationalist youth organization. In May 1926, a group of nationalists led by Eamon de Valera founded the political party Fianna Fail, or "soldiers of destiny."

The Fionn Cycle of Finn MacCool stories are set during the reign of Cormac mac Airt, the legendary king of third-century-A.D. Ireland. Cormac was certainly a real, historical figure, who reigned in Tara for nearly forty years (227–66). But the Cormac of legend is a composite figure drawn from Celtic hero mythology and early Christian tradition. According to the legend, he was orphaned at birth and raised by wolves. His reign was marked by wisdom, bravery, and justice. Shortly before death, the story concludes, Cormac converted to Christianity. In addition to the Fionn Cycle, there are a number of writings attributed to Cormac, including the famous poem "Instruction of a King," a beautiful recitation of Celtic and early Christian morality.

Ireland date from the late Iron Age. The Turoe Stone, found in Galway, is among the most famous examples.

Celtic design as we know it today consists of a few elemental shapes, including spirals, interlacing, fretwork, and swastikas, woven together to create complex patterns. Figures of people, plants, animals, and instruments are sometimes included with these abstract designs, but always in a highly stylized form so as to conform to the overall scheme. For example, the arms of human figures are interlocked to form triangles while the bodies of animals flow into ribbonlike swirls that become part of an interlacing design.

Celtic artists developed endless variations on these design themes and executed them in every medium, from sculpture and metalwork to manuscript decoration. In the latter case, Irish monks in the seventh and eighth centuries used Celtic designs in their extraordinary illuminated manuscripts, especially the Gospels (see #34, "The Book of Kells"). Thus did Celtic design act as a

19. Medb   Another key figure in ancient Irish mythology is Medb, queen of Connacht. Her name (she's also known as Maeve), a derivative of the English word "mead," translates roughly as "she who intoxicates." She was a fierce and ambitious woman who possessed extraordinary powers, among them the ability to blind her enemies simply by gazing upon them.

Medb's invasion of Ulster (Tain Bo Cuailnge, "The Cattle Raid of Cooley") is the central story in the so-called Ulster Cycle of Irish mythology. Medb invades in order to gain a prized brown bull. Although the warriors of Ulster are immobilized by a mysterious affliction, Medb is thwarted in a series of epic battles with *the* towering figure of Irish mythology, the seventeen-year-old Cuchulain.

20. Cuchulain Cuchulain (also known as Cuchulinn or Cuchullin) is often compared to the Greek Achilles, both for his martial prowess and tragic early death. His legend comes to us from the Ulster, or Ulaid, Cycle of medieval Irish literature. Cuchulain was the greatest of the knights in the employ of Conor Mac Nessa, the king of the Ulaids of northeast Ireland, ca. 100 B.C.

According to the legend, he was born Sétante, the son of one Sualtaim and Dechtire, the sister of King Conor. Even as a child he possessed great size and strength, augmented by a gift of seven fingers on each hand, seven toes on each foot, and seven pupils in each eye. He was also strikingly handsome. According to the *Tain:*

Cuchulain

Truly fair was the youth that came there to display his form to the hosts, Cuchulain, to wit son of Sualtaim. Three heads of hair he wore; brown at the skin, blood-red in the middle, a golden-yellow crown what thatched it. Beautiful was the arrangement of the hair, with three coils of hair wound round the nape of his neck, so that like to a strand of thread of gold was each thread-like, loose-flowing, deep-golden, magnificent, long-tressed, splendid, beauteous-hued hair as it fell down over his shoulders. A hundred bright-purple windings of gold-flaming red gold at his neck.

Cuchulain was capable of performing superhuman deeds, often with the aid of the gods, who favored him. When angered, he took on the form of a raging monster, striking terror into the hearts of his foes. His most famous exploit (recorded in the *Tain)* was his single-handed defense of Ulster against the forces of Medb, Queen of Connacht. He was just seventeen.

Cuchulain fought for ten more years before meeting his demise, the victim of enemy trickery.

Cuchulain became a revered figure during the Gaelic Revival of the late nineteenth century, symbolizing both Ireland's rich cultural heritage and heroic warrior spirit. To commemorate the 1916 Easter Rising, a bronze statue of the famed warrior was erected in Dublin's General Post Office.

21. The First Christian Missionaries Contrary to popular belief, St. Patrick was not the first Christian missionary in Ireland, though he was certainly the most successful. Some evidence exists of missionaries traveling through Ireland by the late fourth century A.D., but they seemed to have enjoyed little success. The best-known missionary before Patrick was Palladius, sent by Pope Celestine in A.D. 431 to minister to "the Irish who believe in Christ." Many scholars believe that at least some of the deeds and accomplishments later attributed to Patrick were more likely those of Palladius (some contend that Patrick and Palladius were one and the same). There were others as well: Auxilius and Iserninus worked in the south of Ireland while Secondinas preached in the north and east.

22. St. Patrick   St. Patrick, or Patricius, as he was known in Latin, is the patron saint of Ireland. He is traditionally credited with bringing Christianity to Ireland, though it is more accurate to say that he was the *leading* figure among many missionaries engaged in that task.

No one knows for certain where Patrick was born, but based on his own account, it was most likely in southwestern Britain. In recent years many people have expressed delight in the "irony" that Ireland's patron saint was actually "English." The problem, of course, is that no one in the fifth century was what we would call "English." Rather, the people living in present-day England were Romanized Celts, or Britons. Patrick was thus a Celtic Briton who went by the name of Succat. Patrick's father was a low-level Roman official and a deacon. Patrick's grandfather had been a priest.

23. St. Patrick's Calling   At age sixteen, Patrick was captured by Irish raiders under the command of Niall of the Nine Hostages and taken to Ireland as a slave. For the next six years he labored tending sheep and pigs for one Miliucc near Mount Slemish in Antrim. Life as a herdsman was rough. Patrick barely survived, poorly clothed, without protection from the elements, and frequently near starvation. He sought consolation in constant prayer. Finally, his prayers were answered by a mysterious voice that said "Your hungers are rewarded: You are going home." Miraculously, he walked unharmed two hundred miles to the Wexford coast. There he managed to stow away aboard a ship transporting Irish wolfhounds to the continent. After reuniting with his family in Britain, he experienced a vision in which he was handed a letter inscribed with the words *"vox hiberionacum,"* or "Voice of the Irish," and heard people calling to him, "Come and walk among us once more."

It was not long before Patrick headed for Gaul to study for the priesthood. He was ordained about the year A.D. 430, and, haunted as he was by his years of captivity there, Patrick headed for Ireland.

24. St. Patrick's Mission   Patrick began his mission in Ireland sometime about A.D. 432, possibly as successor to Palladius, first bishop of Ireland. Although Christian missionaries had arrived before him, the Irish remained a pagan people. Patrick faced enormous dangers from local chieftains and bands of marauders, but especially from the druid priests, who correctly perceived him as a threat to their authority. "[E]very day," he wrote, "I am ready to be murdered, betrayed, enslaved."

Patrick concentrated his missionary efforts in the west and north of Ireland. He converted countless thousands during his mission and established, according to tradition, bishops throughout north, east, and western Ireland (everywhere, it seems, but Munster). Patrick, as primatial bishop, established his see at Ard Macha (present-day Armagh), symbolically a stone's throw from the seat of Ulster kings at Emain Macha.

When he died ca. A.D. 461 much of Ireland had been exposed to the teachings of Christianity. The process of conversion, however, took time, and as late as the seventh century, groups of non-Christian Irish continued to resist.

25. St. Patrick's Breastplate   One of the most important works attributed to Patrick is his prayer called "St. Patrick's Breastplate" for its alleged power to protect him from harm. It reads in part:

I arise today
Through the strength of heaven:
Light of sun,
Radiance of moon,

Splendor of fire,
Speed of lightning,
Swiftness of wind,
Depth of sea,
Stability of earth,
Firmness of rock.

I arise today
Through God's strength to pilot me:
God's might to uphold me,
God's wisdom to guide me,
God's eye to look before me,
God's ear to hear me,
God's word to speak for me,
God's hand to guard me,
God's way to lie before me,
God's shield to protect me,
God's host to save me
From snares of devils,
From temptations and vices,
From everyone who shall wish me ill,
Afar and anear,
Alone and in multitude.

[Source of translation, Thomas Cahill]

St. Patrick

Some scholars note that the language is more seventh century than fifth, and therefore question whether or not Patrick himself wrote the prayer. "On the other hand," as Thomas Cahill writes in his classic, *How the Irish Saved Civilization*, "it is Patrician to its core, the first ringing assertion that the universe itself is the Great Sacrament, magically designed by its loving creator to bless and succor human beings. . . . If Patrick did not write it (at least in its current form) it surely takes its inspiration from him."

26. St. Patrick's Legends Of the many legends associated with St. Patrick, two stand out. First, it is said that he drove the snakes out of Ireland. The problem with this story is that Ireland never had any snakes to drive away. Separated from England (where snakes of all sorts abound) and the con-

tinent thousands of years ago, Ireland emerged from the Ice Age snake-free. If St. Patrick were alive today, of course, he would have his spokesperson come forward to offer a slightly modified legend which stretched but did not break the limits of belief: "Since Patrick's arrival in Ireland no snakes have been sighted."

A second and more plausible legend is that he used the shamrock to explain the mystery of the Trinity (by comparing the three leaves with the Father, Son, and Holy Spirit). The legend is unverifiable, since Patrick doesn't mention it in his writings. Some have suggested it derives from an earlier Celtic tradition of using the shamrock as a metaphor representing a "trust in your soul," "belief in your heart," and "faith in your mind." Some missionary, if not Patrick himself, very likely

Christianized this concept. Few in Ireland seem troubled by these details, and the shamrock remains the Irish national symbol.

27. St. Patrick's Legacy Much of what we know about St. Patrick comes from his *Confessio*, a kind of spiritual autobiography. A unique mystical chant attributed to Patrick, called the *"Lorica,"* is preserved in the *Liber Hymnorum,* or *Book of Hymns.* A handbell that he is alleged to have used during Mass is on display in Ireland's National Museum.

And, of course, every year, on March 17, St. Patrick is honored in Ireland and throughout the world. The date, according to tradition, corresponds to the day of his death (ca. 493) at Saul, near Downpatrick in County Down. The style of celebration varies by country and even region. For centuries the people of Ireland marked the day as a solemn religious event, perhaps wearing green, sporting a shamrock, and attending Mass, but little more. Certainly there was no massive parade like the ones found in American cities like Boston, New York, and Chicago. These have the aura of proud pageantry about them, but sadly, much of St. Patrick's Day in America has been neither religious nor contemplative, but instead an excuse for excessive drinking. Fortunately, the revival of interest in Irish and Irish American culture has prompted parade organizers, church officials, and others to deemphasize drinking and encourage more appropriate activities, such as concerts and poetry readings.

Interestingly, as the American Irish move toward a more Irish form of celebrating March 17, the Irish in Ireland have begun to imitate their American cousins. St. Patrick's Day parades now occur in most major Irish cities. Differences still remain. Parades in Ireland tend to be more like Mardi Gras pageants than the more formal and earnest shows of ethnic pride found in America.

A more somber remembrance of Patrick occurs every year in Ireland, on the last Sunday of July. Thousands of pilgrims ascend—some bare-

foot and others on bloodied knees—the nearly half-mile-high mountain in the west of Ireland named Croagh Patrick. The devotional ceremony is in memory of the time in 441 when Patrick fasted there.

28. St. Columcille St. Columcille (also known as St. Columba) was the greatest of the Christian missionaries after Patrick. He was born into the clan which we know today as the O'Neills (the same clan that would later produce Brian Boru). He established monasteries in Durrow and Derry, not to mention many churches throughout the north.

The turning point in Columcille's life came in A.D. 561, when he was exiled to Iona (an island off the coast of Scotland) after encouraging an uprising against a powerful king in the north. Saddened to leave Ireland, he nonetheless made the best of his exile, taking twelve followers and establishing a monastery at Iona. It quickly achieved a wide reputation and received a steady stream of monastic applicants. To keep Iona from growing too large and to spread the faith, Columcille repeatedly sent out groups of monks to establish new communities. By the time of his death on Iona in A.D. 597, his monks had established sixty monasteries in Scotland. His successor, Aidan, continued his mission into northern England. As Thomas Cahill writes, "[J]ust as Cuchulainn had served as the model of prehistoric Irish manhood, Columcille now became the model for all who would earn the ultimate victory. Monks began to set off in every direction, bent on glorious and heroic exile for the sake of Christ."

29. The Spread of Christianity Sts. Patrick and Columcille were certainly the most important figures in the conversion of Ireland to Christianity, but they were by no means exclusively responsible for it. Innumerable anonymous missionary monks, priests, and bishops played a role as well. So, too, did the Christians from Britain and Gaul who arrived in Ireland in the sixth century not as missionaries but as traders and settlers. The conversion took hold only after about two centuries, but as late as the eighth century druids were still a visible, if rapidly diminishing, aspect of Irish society.

These Christian missionaries all seemed willing to blend Christianity with many of the traditions and practices of the Celtic religion. Thus we find many Christian holy places located at or near older Celtic religious sites, such as Cruachain, the ancient burial ground of kings mentioned so frequently in pre-Christian mythology. We also encounter evidence that some of the legends associated with early saints of Ireland, like Brigid, represent, to quote the *Oxford Companion to Irish History*, "the Christianization of a pagan goddess." This tactic was hardly an Irish innovation: Early Church fathers employed it throughout the Roman Empire, and it remains very much alive today among Christian missionaries in places like Africa and Asia. Perhaps this accounts for the contention that Ireland was the one nation to be Christianized without martyrdom.

30. St. Brigid Most of what we know about St. Brigid—known as the "Mary of the Gael"—comes from medieval biographies of the saints;

not exactly the most reliable sources. It is believed that she was converted by St. Patrick and after his death founded a monastery in Kildare around the year A.D. 500. Brigid comes across as an extraordinarily strong and self-reliant woman—very much like the Medb of Celtic legend—and some accounts say she was ordained a bishop and celebrated Mass. Not surprisingly, many scholars see numerous similarities between the stories of Brigid and the legends of Celtic goddesses, especially one named Brid. St. Brigid's day, February 1, corresponds with *Imbolc,* the Celtic feast of renewal and purification.

The most enduring image of Brigid, apart from the thousands of women bearing her name, is the St. Brigid's Cross. It comes from the story in which she converted a pagan on his deathbed by explaining redemption to him with the aid of a makeshift cross she fashioned from rushes lying on the floor.

31. Civilization Imperiled Ancient Greek and Roman civilizations produced an extraordinary canon of literature, art, science, and philosophy. This knowledge forms the basis of what we know as Western Civilization. Concepts like democracy, the rule of law, and respect for the individual; works of classical literature from Homer, Plato, Cicero, and Vergil; and the foundations of the disciplines of mathematics, engineering, and astronomy are part of this tradition. It's hard to imagine what our world would be like without these things.

And yet this irreplaceable canon of knowledge was nearly lost when the Roman Empire began to disintegrate in the face of invading Germanic tribes at the beginning of the fifth century A.D. In A.D. 409, the Roman army was forced to abandon Britain; and in 410 Alaric the Goth sacked the city of Rome. By 476 the last Roman emperor in the west, Romulus Augustulus, was deposed by a barbarian chieftain. The social stability, complex trade and communication networks, and high culture which flourished during

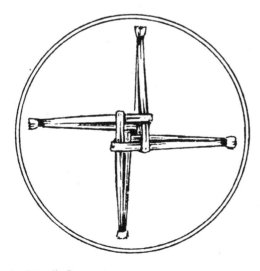

St. Brigid's Cross

the heyday of the Roman Empire crumbled. Schools were closed, libraries sacked, and people of learning killed or exiled. By the mid-500s most of Western Europe and much of the east had been reduced to small kingdoms ruled by Gothic invaders or their descendents.

32. Ireland's Golden Age: The Land of Saints and Scholars   While Europe was plunging into darkness, Ireland, which had never been part of the Roman Empire, was entering its Golden Age (mid-sixth to ninth centuries A.D.). While on the continent the glories of Roman civilization were disappearing, in Ireland they were beginning to take root. As men like Patrick spread Christianity, they preserved the compatible aspects of Celtic culture (i.e., righteousness and loyalty) and banished its barbaric aspects (i.e., slavery and human sacrifice). These changes ushered in a period of stability and relative peace and made Irish society a more than suitable refuge for those fleeing the barbaric devastation on the continent.

Central to this transformation of Ireland was the establishment by Patrick and those who followed him of dozens of monasteries throughout Ireland. These came to serve not just as places of piety and asceticism, but also (in a land with few large towns) education, authority, and commerce. Anyone desiring an education, the resolution of a dispute, or a place to buy and sell goods headed for the local monastery. Hundreds, and in some cases thousands, of ordinary peasants lived on monastic lands and their annual rents provided a strong financial base for the monasteries. Not surprisingly, some abbots grew to rival kings in power and authority.

Thus was Ireland prepared to serve as a refuge for the countless priests, monks, and scholars who fled there from a continent in ruins. Luckily for us, these refugees did not arrive empty-handed: They brought the books in which was written the literature, science, art, theology, and philosophy of the Roman world.

33. Civilization Saved, Stage 1   Irish monks took these books, mastered their content, and then painstakingly copied them over and over. Fortunately for posterity, they copied *everything*, not just the Bible and religious commentaries, but also works of pagan mythology, pre-Christian philosophy, and Latin and Greek literature. And they didn't merely copy these canons of Western Civilization; they created books that can only be described as extraordinary masterpieces of art and design.

34. The Book of Kells   Without question the single most important product of this period is the Book of Kells. This copy of the four Gospels (and other writings) in Latin features extraordinary drawings and designs rich in symbolism throughout the text. In some cases a single set of initials takes up an entire 13-by-9-inch page. The book includes full-page illustrations of biblical scenes such as the Temptation of Christ. The book is also noted for its script, which some scholars argue became the basis for everyday writing in Europe during the Middle Ages. One can only imagine how many years and how many monks it took to create such an extraordinary work of faith, artistry, sacrifice, and imagination. Its beauty and complexity have awed observers for centuries, including one Geraldus Cambrensis of the twelfth century, who concluded that the manuscript was "the work of an angel, not of a man."

It is not known for certain where the manuscript was produced. Some scholars attribute it to the monastery at Iona (founded by Columcille) while others believe it was copied at Kells after monks fled there from Iona following a Viking attack in 806. Other books of this type have been found all over Europe, a fact that demonstrates just how far the wandering monks traveled, reintroducing learning and literature.

Today the Book of Kells is kept on permanent display at the library of Trinity College in Dublin.

35. Civilization Saved, Stage 2   After generations of copying and mastering the collective knowledge of past European societies, Irish monks began to reexport it back to the European continent. This missionary impulse was born of the awareness among Irish monks that they themselves were the products of earlier missionaries from the continent. "Thus there was an impulse to travel towards that centre in which the great events they read about had taken place," writes Thomas O'Loughlin in the *Oxford Companion to Irish History.* "This was expressed religiously as the desire to pilgrimage for Christ, and act as teachers and missionaries." Irish monks, bearing faith, learning, and books, fanned out in all directions across Europe (and if you believe the legend of St. Brendan, west across the Atlantic). As Thomas Cahill writes, they "fearlessly brought ancient civilization back to its ancient home."

Irish monks established monasteries all across Europe. As they had in Ireland, these monasteries became centers of religious life, but also learning, art, and commerce. Irish monks were in turn followed by Irish scholars whose knowledge gained them top positions in the schools of European royalty, including Charlemagne and his successors.

36. Columbanus   The most famous itinerant monk in this recivilizing mission was Columbanus. Born in the mid-sixth century and educated at St. Comgall's monastery in Bangor, he headed for Gaul in 590, where he established several monasteries. When King Theodoric expelled him from Gaul for refusing to bless his illegitimate sons, Columbanus gathered a few monks and made for present-day eastern France and Switzerland, eventually establishing a monastery in A.D. 612 at Bobbio in northern Italy. He died in 615, but his monastery flourished and continued the pattern of sending out groups of monks to establish still more monasteries.

37. No Credit   So if the Irish played so critical a role in saving Western Civilization, why hasn't history given them credit? Simply put, the conquest and colonization of Ireland by the English meant the latter would write the history. Given their disdain for the Irish, it is hardly surprising that they chose to ignore this vital chapter of ancient history.

Invasions

38. The Viking Invasions   Viking raiders from Scandinavia began invading Western Europe in the last decades of the eighth century A.D. They first struck Ireland in 795, attacking island monasteries off the north and west coast of Ireland. Initially they focused on monasteries, recognizing that these centers of economic activity possessed substantial stores of food, finished goods, and potential slaves. As late as A.D. 835, Viking raids were mainly of the hit-and-run variety and focused primarily on the east and south coasts of Ireland. Rarely did raiders move more than twenty miles inland.

Thereafter, however, large Viking fleets arrived and staged more substantial attacks, pressing farther into the interior and establishing permanent settlements, including a *long-phort,* or "ship camp" at what is now Dublin in A.D. 841. The Vikings made Dublin into a major center of exchange and staging ground for raids in Britain. After 850, Irish kings began to mount successful attacks against these fixed Viking settlements. They recaptured Cork in 848 and Dublin in 902, though much of the coast remained under Viking control.

Twelve years after being thrown out of Dublin, Viking raiders reappeared off the Irish coast. They staged repeated attacks along the southern coast and retook Dublin in 917. From there they reasserted Viking control over a vast area some seventy miles south, west, and north of Dublin. Additional Viking towns independent of Dublin were established in Limerick (922) and Wexford (921). Dublin's Viking kings tried to ex-

The Battle of Clontarf

tend their control over these settlements, as well as those in Britain. After about A.D. 950, Viking control of Ireland began to wane, even as Scandinavian settlers became increasingly integrated into Irish life.

39. The Viking Influence on Irish Life Although the Vikings wrought a significant amount of havoc in their invasions and occupation of Ireland, their influence on Ireland was not entirely negative. In the course of a century and a half of Viking occupation, Ireland developed its first towns (Dublin, Waterford, Wexford, Cork, and Limerick), system of weights and measures, and coinage. The introduction of advanced ship designs and development of coastal towns greatly expanded Ireland's trade contacts with Europe, contacts that lasted long after the Vikings left.

40. Brian Boru and the Defeat of the Vikings If Irish and Irish American children grow up learning one bit of Irish history, it is that Brian Boru defeated the Vikings at the battle of Clontarf in 1014, thereby freeing Ireland from Viking rule. Unfortunately, the story is more complicated than that.

Brian was born (A.D. 941) into a royal family that had succeeded in consolidating its power as a result of the disruptions brought by the Vikings. Upon his brother's death in 976, he became ruler of a large kingdom in southern Ireland. By 997, his kingdom extended over the southern half of the island, and in 1002 he was recognized in both north and south as "high king" of all Ireland.

In 1014, the Vikings of Dublin and their allies revolted against Brian's authority. In the resulting Battle of Clontarf near Dublin, Brian led his army in victory over the Vikings, but was himself killed in the battle. For generations thereafter, many Irish kings tried to emulate Brian's feat of unifying Ireland under one ruler. None succeeded. Over the centuries, especially as Ireland suffered under British rule after the seventeenth century, Brian Boru became the central figure in the nationalist memory—the man who embodied the idea of an independent, unified nation.

41. Ireland After Brian   Brian Boru's successor was a member of the powerful O'Neills in the north. Although he retained the title of high king of Ireland, it was more symbolic than real, and on his death in 1022 an ensuing power struggle between rival kings left it unclaimed for a half century. Brian Boru's grandson, Turloch O'Brien, claimed the title high king in 1072 and was succeeded by his son Muirchertach O'Brien, who ruled from 1086 to 1119. Other high kings followed, but none could truly call himself the unchallenged ruler of Ireland and all relied heavily on alliances. In 1156, Muirchertach Mac Lochlainn of the O'Neills became high king. His chief ally was Dermot MacMurrough, the ambitious king of Leinster. And that, as they say, is where the trouble began in A.D. 1166.

42. Pope Adrian IV and King Henry II   Pope Adrian IV, as any good Irish nationalist will tell you, was the only English pope. That detail assumes importance in the nationalist mind because he was the pope who granted the request of King Henry II of Britain to conquer Ireland. Aha! The original English conspiracy (English pope + English King = invasion) against Ireland!

Yet this interpretation is a classic case of reading modern realities back into history. We need to remind ourselves that terms like "Ireland" and "England" did not carry nearly the same meaning in the twelfth century as they would later in the nineteenth and twentieth. Neither England nor Ireland were fully developed "nations" as we understand today. Furthermore, both were largely Catholic societies, so the Protestant-Catholic struggle that would later define the conflict between the two was simply absent. Indeed, Pope Adrian IV granted Henry's request in the hope that he would establish Catholicism more firmly in Ireland. Finally, it's worth mentioning that King Henry II was actually French and spent most of his life in France.

That much said, there is no disputing the fact that in 1155 Pope Adrian IV granted King Henry II of England permission to conquer Ireland.

43. King Dermot MacMurrough of Leinster and Strongbow   MacMurrough's strategic alliance with High King Muirchertach Mac Lochlainn backfired in 1166 when the latter died. Allies of the new high king, Rory O'Connor, ousted MacMurrough and sent him into exile. Vowing to return and reclaim his throne, MacMurrough headed straight for England, where he pledged loyalty to Henry II and received permission to raise an army. It was the joining of these two ambitions—Henry's of conquest and MacMurrough's of vengeance—that would soon lead to Ireland's centuries of trouble.

The leader of MacMurrough's army was Richard FitzGilbert de Clare, or Strongbow, as he was known. Like King Henry II, Strongbow was a French-speaking Norman. The Normans were the descendants of Viking raiders who settled in France in the ninth century A.D., and subsequently, under William the Conqueror, invaded Britain in 1066.

Strongbow had once been a prominent earl. But because he had cast his support to Henry's opponents during an earlier power struggle, he was frozen out of patronage and privileges when Henry ascended the throne in 1154. Eager to regain title and land in Ireland, he accepted MacMurrough's invitation to lead the invasion.

44. The Conquest Begins   MacMurrough returned to Leinster in 1167 with a small force and established a base of operations. In May 1169 the first invaders arrived and quickly took the city of Wexford. Strongbow arrived with an army of one thousand soldiers on August 23, 1170. Together he and MacMurrough seized the city of Waterford, populated at that time by Ostmen, the descendents of Viking settlers. As a reward, MacMurrough gave Strongbow his daughter Aoife in marriage.

45. An Important Clarification on the Conquest
It is important to pause here to clarify the often simplistic Irish nationalist version of the conquest of Ireland. Typically it is presented as a story where the English (some even go so far as to call them English Protestants—nearly four hundred years *before* the Reformation!) domination of Ireland began with the invasion of 1169. Instead, it is a rather more complicated and untidy history: A French king sitting on the throne of England sent an invading army to Ireland for the purposes of *promoting* Catholicism. Furthermore, the first people to defend Ireland from the Norman invasion were Ostmen, the descendents of the previous wave of Viking invaders.

46. The Norman Invasion Rolls On
MacMurrough and Strongbow, their alliance now cemented through marriage, wasted little time in moving on Dublin, which fell a few weeks later. From there, they overran Meath.

Henry II was pleased by Strongbow's success, but he

Dermot MacMurrough

did not trust his former rival. When MacMurrough died in May 1171, leaving Strongbow as sole heir to his kingdom, Henry moved decisively to take control of the operation. He arrived in Ireland with a large force on October 17, 1171. When Strongbow and several Irish kings (urged by their bishops, who viewed Henry II as a benevolent agent of the pope) immediately pledged their loyalty to Henry, the stage for continued conquest was set.

Here we see the problem in a nutshell: The disunity of Ireland's many kings and constant power struggles between competing dynastic families (accentuated by the lack of a standardized format for choosing a high king) made the job of the Norman invaders relatively easy. They had no need to divide and conquer—Ireland (in contrast to the kingdom of Scotland) was divided before their arrival.

47. The Treaty of Windsor and the Last of the High Kings　In 1175, High King Rory O'Connor, who had led an unsuccessful counterattack on Dublin at the outset of Strongbow's attack, signed the Treaty of Windsor. According to the terms of the treaty, he accepted Henry II as his overlord and reduced his status of high king of Ireland to merely king of Connacht. O'Connor did exercise some vague authority over the other Irish kings and was responsible for collecting from them tribute to be paid to Henry. O'Connor soon faced severe opposition, even in his own province, and was ultimately forced to abdicate in 1186. He died five years later in a monastery. There never would be another high king of Ireland.

the beginnings of english Rule

48. Slowly but Surely　Despite so auspicious a beginning for Henry II, the conquest of Ireland would take centuries to complete. In the late twelfth and early thirteenth centuries, bands of

Anglo-Norman invaders typically entered an Irish kingdom, established a small fort, and set about toppling the local king. Next, the band's leader divided the property among his warriors, who from that point forward worked to develop their holdings. This meant modernizing the agricultural system and importing needed labor from Britain. By the middle of the thirteenth century, Ireland had been transformed by this massive influx of Anglo-Norman people and ideas. New towns such as Kilkenny, Sligo, and Dundalk sprang up, and trade within and beyond Ireland boomed. As Sean Duffy put it so succinctly, "It was colonization rather than conquest which changed the course of Irish history after 1171."

49. Continued Resistance   Even as Anglo-Norman conquest and colonization spread across much of the eastern half of Ireland in the thirteenth century, with many Irish kings opting to accommodate their more powerful adversaries, other Irish kings put up fierce resistance. Those that did often paid a dear price. Brian O'Neill, for example, revived the title of high king (illegal under English overlordship) in 1258, but was defeated by the Anglo-Norman colonists and beheaded. Still, a few of the stronger Irish kings such as the O'Neills, O'Connors, O'Briens, and Mac-Carthys managed to withstand the Anglo-Normans. Many did so by importing hundreds of fearsome "gallowglass" (from the Irish for "foreign warrior") mercenaries from Scotland that greatly improved their military strength. Overall, the key result of this resistance was that it slowed the Anglo-Norman advance and kept intact some of Ireland's most important dynasties.

50. Edward the Bruce   The vulnerability of the Anglo-Norman colonial establishment (due to Irish resistance and infighting among some of the larger Anglo-Norman families) was revealed most fully when Edward the Bruce (d. 1318), brother of the Scottish King Robert I, invaded Ulster in 1315. He hoped to expel the Anglo-Norman col-

onizers and establish an independent Scots-Irish kingdom. After achieving some stunning victories early on, he was defeated and killed in battle at Faughart near Dundalk.

51. The Gaelic Recovery   The defeat of Edward the Bruce in 1318 did little to strengthen the British colonial position in Ireland. Indeed, it grew weaker for the rest of the fourteenth century for three reasons. First, fewer colonists arrived from Britain. Second, events such as the Black Death crippled the English economy, sharply limiting the Crown's ability to intervene in Ireland. Third, and most alarming to the Crown, the Anglo-Normans who had arrived in the 1200s rapidly became Anglo-Irish, intermarrying with the native Irish and taking on their language, dress, and customs. This was part of a larger revival of Irish culture in this period known as the Gaelic Recovery.

52. The Statutes of Kilkenny   The development of this Irish identity among the colonizing families in Ireland caused great concern to the British Crown. To reverse this trend, the British viceroy in Ireland pushed through the Irish Parliament the Statutes of Kilkenny in 1366. Its preamble neatly summed up the problem of British conquest:

> Now many English of the said land, forsaking the English language, fashion, mode of riding, laws and usages, live and govern themselves according to the manners, fashion, and language of the Irish enemies, and also having made divers marriages and alliances between themselves and the Irish enemies aforesaid . . . the English language, the allegiance due to our Lord the King and the English laws there are put in subjection and decayed, and the Irish enemies exalted and raised up, contrary to right.

Thus the Statutes explicitly forbade intermarriage between the Irish and the Anglo-Irish colonizers. Furthermore, the latter were prohibited from speaking the Irish language in conducting political, legal, or business affairs. They were also forbidden to wear Irish clothing, ride on Irish saddles, employ Irish poets or minstrels, use Irish greetings, or play hurling. The Statutes also defined what became known as the Pale of Settlement (from the Latin word *palus,* or fence post), a narrow strip of land little more than twenty miles wide in most places running north from Waterford to Dundalk on Ireland's eastern coast. According to the Statues, those living outside the Pale were henceforth considered "Irish enemies"; those inside, "obedient."

53. Growing Autonomy The Statutes failed to slow the trend of Anglo-Irish colonists becoming increasingly assimilated into Irish culture. A visit by King Richard II from 1394 to 1395 did gain greater recognition of his overlordship by some of the major Irish kings, such as the O'Neills, O'Briens, O'Connors, and MacCarthys. But Crown control remained minimal for the next half century. During that time, Ireland was, in effect, ruled by the three great earls—the Fitzgerald earls of Desmond and Kildare, and the Butler earls of Ormond. Together, they dominated the Dublin government (to the great distress of the more Anglicized settler population within the Pale) with little interference from the Crown.

54. Poynings' Law An Irish Parliament called at Drogheda in 1460 issued a unilateral decree of independence. Ireland, the decree argued, would no longer be subject to any law issued from the English Crown or Parliament unless it was first approved by the Irish Parliament. At the time, England was embroiled in the War of the Roses (1455–85) and could do little about it. However, after Henry VII brought the War of the Roses to a conclusion by defeating Richard III in 1485, he soon turned his attention to abolishing Ireland's self-declared home rule.

In 1494, Sir Edward Poynings arrived and called a Parliament at Drogheda (1494–95), which he induced to pass forty-nine statutes, the most important of which was the ninth, known as "Poynings' Law." It declared the Irish Parliament subordinate to the English government and required that all legislation in the former be first approved by the latter. Still, for all intents and purposes, Ireland remained beyond any meaningful Crown control well into the next century. Real authority was held by the three dominant earls of Kildare, Desmond, and Ormond.

55. Henry VIII For the first twenty-five years of Henry VIII's reign (1509–47), Ireland remained in the semiautonomous control of the Butler and Fitzgerald earls. But the onset of the Protestant Reformation in England in the 1530s added a new dimension to the struggle. When Henry VIII broke with the Church in 1534 and declared himself "the only supreme head of the church of England," the pope excommunicated him and many of Ireland's leading families sided firmly with the Catholic Church. The Earl of Kildare, "Silken" Thomas Fitzgerald, openly cast off his allegiance to Henry, arguing that excommunication had stripped him of legitimacy. Henry responded with force and in 1537 Fitzgerald and five of his uncles were executed in London. Four years later, Henry VIII declared himself "King of this land of Ireland, as united, annexed and knit forever to the imperial crown of the realm of England." Thereafter he made the assertion of English authority and the Protestant faith a priority of his reign, a policy continued by his successors. Thus was the nearly four-hundred-year-old contest between the Irish and English now transformed into one between Irish Catholic and English Protestant.

56. Discontent and Rebellion These differences grew increasingly pronounced under Henry's successors, Mary Queen of Scots (1553–58) and Elizabeth I (1558–1603). They sent new administrators, encouraged settlement by English colonists, and attempted the first significant plantations on land seized from rebellious lords. Native Irish and Old English grew disenchanted with the New English administration and resisted the newly established Protestant Church of Ireland, favoring instead the Counter-Reformation Catholic Church. Major uprisings, such as that of Shane O'Neill (1560–67) and the Desmond Fitzgeralds (1569–73, 1579–83), not to mention countless assaults on would-be planters, indicated seething resentment in the Irish countryside.

57. The Rebellion of Hugh O'Neill and Red Hugh O'Donnell

The greatest of these rebellions was led by Hugh O'Neill, the Earl of Tyrone, and his son-in-law Red Hugh O'Donnell, King of Tyrconnell. Although he'd worked closely with the English Crown, O'Neill eventually grew disillusioned by its heavy-handed policies, especially those that threatened his land. He began plotting a revolt in the late 1580s, building a formidable army, making contact with Catholic Spain, and forming a confederation of like-minded Ulster chieftains, most notably with Red Hugh O'Donnell. The rebellion (the Nine Years' War) began in 1593 and reached full bloom in 1595, the year O'Neill took the title "The O'Neill," suggesting a revival of the high king tradition. O'Neill and O'Donnell quickly scored victories against British troops advancing north into Ulster. The rebellion reached its high point in 1598, when O'Neill routed a British force (under the command of another brother-in-law) at the Battle of Yellow Ford. Flushed with success, O'Neill expanded his rebellion southward.

The tide, however, turned in 1600, with the arrival of Lord Mountjoy and a huge British force. Mountjoy, who benefited from superior numbers and cavalry, waged a relentless scorched-earth campaign to force the wily O'Neill into a head-on fight. That occurred in late 1601, when O'Neill and O'Donnell tried to meet up with a Spanish force of 3,500 at Kinsale. On Christmas Eve

Hugh O'Neill

1601, Mountjoy forced them into the open and defeated them in just three hours. The Spanish elected not to fight and quickly asked for terms.

Fearing execution by a vengeful Queen Elizabeth, O'Neill refused to surrender and kept up guerrilla raids for fifteen months. (O'Donnell died in 1602, possibly from poisoning.) After assurances of leniency, however, he emerged in March 1603 to sign a peace treaty. Hoping to calm the situation in Ireland, the Crown offered lenient terms. O'Neill was allowed to keep his head, land, and earldom, but lost his overlordship over Ulster's lesser chieftains. The title of high king, unsuccessfully revived centuries after Brian Boru, was now officially dead.

From the Plantations to Cromwell

58. The Flight of the Earls

In the years that followed O'Neill's rebellion, the restored earls of Ulster lived in a kind of limbo. They still possessed substantial land holdings and family ties, but they faced a growing tide of New English settlers and a hostile English administration. Some began to plot a renewed rebellion, again involving Spanish assistance, but in late 1607 they opted to flee (perhaps fearing their plot had been discovered). On September 4, 1607, O'Neill and 101 other earls boarded a French ship at Rathmullen in Donegal and sailed for the continent. They eventually landed in the Spanish Netherlands and from there proceeded to Rome, where they lived out their years on meager papal pensions. O'Neill died there in 1616.

59. Ulster Plantations   The English government was completely unprepared for so dramatic a move, yet they were quick to realize the enormous opportunity it presented. The fleeing earls were tried *in absentia* and convicted of treason, the penalty for which was forfeiture of their land. With 500,000 acres of land now in its possession, the Crown began a settlement program known as the Ulster Plantation. It had five goals: first, to increase popular loyalty to England by greatly increasing the non-Irish, Protestant population in Ulster; second, to "civilize" the native Irish who were considered barbaric papists; third, to improve the economy of Ireland and thereby increase Crown revenues; fourth, to prevent a hostile continental power from using Ireland as a staging ground for invading England; and fifth, to provide opportunity for landless nobles.

Crown officials identified three main groups (along with the Church of Ireland) eligible to receive land. Well-connected Scottish and English settlers received huge estates measuring from one to two thousand acres. As part of the deal, they were required to import English and Scottish settlers and build towns. The second group, English and Scottish servitors, or royal officials, also received large estates, as did a third group, the "deserving Irish." The latter group, largely Catholic earls who could prove their loyalty during the O'Neill rising, received only 58,000 acres, slightly more than 10 percent of the whole. The process of stripping the native Irish and Catholic population of Ireland of its land had begun in earnest.

Although it took a few decades to take hold, the Plantation of Ulster had a dramatic impact on the course of Irish history. Not only did it wipe out much of the province's native Irish leadership by eradicating the holdings of the 101 Irish earls who fled, it also in threw open the province to settlement by tens of thousands of English and Scottish Protestants. By the 1630s, in six Ulster counties, Protestants owned three million out of 3.5 million acres total.

60. The Ulster Rising of 1641   In response to their rapidly declining status, a number of Catholic landowners joined a rebellion led by Sir Phelim O'Neill in 1641. Although they were, for the most part, Ulster gentry, many of them "deserving Irish" who still possessed land, many were pressed by heavy debts and encroachments by the English administration in Ulster. They were also motivated by a continued loyalty to King Charles I, who was mired in the crisis that would soon explode as the English Civil War.

The landowners hatched a secret plot to seize Dublin Castle and extract concessions from the government. When it was foiled on October 23, 1641, O'Neill led the rebel forces south to generate a rising of the Catholic and Old English gentry against the Dublin administration. Quite unexpectedly, the limited protest of O'Neill and his followers erupted into a ferocious war of reprisal against the Plantation settler population, especially those living outside the province's fortified cities. Up to two thousand settlers lost their lives (not to mention hundreds of Catholics killed in reprisal). As refugees streamed southward, their tales of woe were magnified into fantastic stories of massacre. Before long, rumors reached England that papist conspirators had slaughtered tens of thousands of Protestant settlers. Stories of this kind in any era would have provoked an outraged response from England, but during 1641 and 1642 they took on apocalyptic dimensions in the eyes of Oliver Cromwell and his fellow Puritan zealots then working to topple Charles I. Thus did the Rising of 1641 draw Ireland into the English Civil War and eventually invite invasion by Cromwell.

61. The English Civil War   The English Civil War broke out in 1642 as a conflict between King Charles I and his supporters (the Royalists, or Cavaliers) and the supporters of Parliament (Puritans, or Roundheads). The latter had grown to resent the autocratic rule of Charles I. He had refused to allow Parliament to meet between 1629 and 1640. When it did convene in 1640, the members refused to grant the king any funds unless he agreed to scale back some of his powers and respect the rights of Parliament. He refused, and civil war ensued.

Oliver Cromwell, a leader of the Roundheads (so-called because of their short, bowl-cut hairstyle) in Parliament, led the Parliamentary forces to a series of victories over the Royalists. Charles I fled to Scotland, but was returned to England where he was beheaded on January 30, 1649. In his place, Oliver Cromwell was appointed Lord High Protector of England.

62. The Cromwell Invasion Parliamentary forces had already landed in Ireland in 1647. But it was the arrival on August 15, 1649, of twenty thousand troops under Oliver Cromwell, Lord Lieutenant General of the Parliament of England, that inaugurated a full-scale repression of Ireland. His purpose was unambiguous: to avenge the alleged massacres of 1641, repress Catholicism, and fortify Ireland against possible foreign invasion. He believed his mission to "carry on the great work against the barbarous Irish" was ordained by God.

It was this mind-set that justified the brutality that followed. In one instance, when the town of Drogheda refused to surrender to Cromwell in September 1649, Cromwell's soldiers stormed the city and put more than three thousand people, including civilian women and children, to the sword. Some weeks later, the town of Wexford did surrender but apparently not fast enough to suit Cromwell, and his soldiers slaughtered two thousand civilians. This campaign of terror had its desired effect, as most towns quickly surrendered to Cromwell's forces.

By the early 1650s, virtually all of Ireland had been conquered. The toll on human life was extraordinary, even by modern standards. Of Ireland's 1641 population of 1,448,000, 616,000

Oliver Cromwell

had died by 1652. Of those the great majority (504,000) were native Irish, mostly Catholic. Settlers and troops constituted the remaining dead (112,000). Thousands of surviving Irish rebels were transported to a life of slavery in the West Indies. Irish agriculture and livestock were devastated. "I am persuaded," wrote Cromwell, "that this is a righteous judgment of God upon these barbarous wretches."

63. Cromwell's Legacy In addition to the death and destruction visited by Cromwell and his lieutenants, Ireland under parliamentary rule experienced another massive transfer of property from the Catholic native Irish to Protestant English settlers. Under the 1652 to 1653 Acts of Settlement, most of Ireland's major Catholic landowners in the east were forced to surrender their property (upon penalty of death) and accept lesser holdings in the remote barren reaches of the province of Connacht. This policy, dubbed "To Hell or Connacht" by the Irish, led to a mass exodus of Irish Catholics to the lesser lands in the west of Ireland. Many never made it. Some eleven million acres of confiscated land was turned over to English "adventurers" (settlers) and soldiers. By 1660, Protestants would own 78 percent of the land in Ireland and the percentage was rising.

64. NEW YORK TIMES Columnist Maureen Dowd Observes

> When I first moved to New York, I called my mother to tell her I was going to stay in a residential hotel called the Oliver Cromwell.

There was a long pause, then tearful anger. "He encouraged his soldiers to throw babies up in the air and impale them on their swords as they came down," she snapped. I found another hotel. In Irish time, 1651 and 1981 were only moments apart.

—*New York Times,* May 20, 1998

65. The Restoration Cromwell died in 1658, and two years later Charles I's son, Charles II, was restored to the throne. Many Catholics viewed this development with hope. Charles II had a Catholic wife and they hoped he would remember the loyalty the Irish showed his father during the struggles of the 1640s. Unfortunately, what Charles II did remember about the 1640s was that his father had been beheaded. He was unwilling to make any move that might appear too solicitous of the Irish, though some families were restored to their land and the murderous persecution of priests diminished.

Irish Catholics found their man in Charles II's son, James II, who took the throne in 1685. James was a Catholic and made it clear that he planned to restore Catholics in Ireland to the power and prop-

erty they had once enjoyed—in short, to remake Ireland as a Catholic kingdom. He dispatched Richard Talbot, a Catholic born in Dublin, to serve as lieutenant general of the Irish army. Talbot quickly replaced Protestant army officers, sheriffs, judges, and magistrates with Catholics. These moves alarmed Protestants in England and Ireland and led to them to depose James II in 1688.

66. The Invasion of William of Orange When James II had a son in June 1688 and baptized him as a Catholic (ensuring that the next king would be a Catholic), his opponents took action. They invited James' son-in-law, William of Orange (so known because he was the son of the Prince of Orange in the Netherlands, and Mary, the daughter of Charles I), to seize the throne. He landed later that year with 14,000 troops and James fled to France. All that remained to complete the Glorious Revolution was the official proclamation of William and Mary as King and Queen of England, Ireland, and Scotland, and the defeat of the army being raised by supporters of James in Ireland.

James' right-hand man, Richard Talbot, Earl of Tyrconnell, had secured control of nearly all of Ireland (except the Protestant strongholds of Derry and Enniskillen) and had his army waiting. On March 12, 1689, James arrived with French officers and supplies. James convened an Irish Parliament in May that proceeded to abolish Poynings' Law and restore all rights and property to Catholics. Crown forces

The Siege of Limerick

began gathering in the north while the British navy secured Derry. William reluctantly arrived in June 1690 and the real fighting began. He met James at the Boyne River and defeated him on July 1, 1690. James then fled to France forever and William's army went about taking Munster and Connacht. Were it not for the daring exploits of Patrick Sarsfield, the top Irish commander, defeat would have come sooner. Still, William's army eventually defeated James' at Althone from July 17 to 24, 1691, and again at Aughrim on July 12, 1691 (with more than seven thousand killed). The war ended with the surrender of Limerick in October. Catholic Ireland had succumbed to Protestant England.

67. The Treaty of Limerick   The treaty that ended the war between William of Orange and James II contained generous terms for the latter's defeated supporters. Its key provisions were:

- Soldiers in James II's army were offered free passage to France (where the king now lived in exile).
- Those who remained in Ireland were allowed to keep their lands and to practice their trades and professions.
- Catholics were promised freedom of religion.

William supported these lenient terms because he wanted to end the struggle in Ireland (which cost lots of money and diverted military resources) so as to concentrate on his ongoing struggle against France. Irish Protestants, however, bitterly opposed the treaty's concessions to Catholics, and successfully watered down or removed key provisions from the final draft that was ratified in 1697. They also successfully pushed for a series of anti-Catholic measures known as the Penal Laws.

68. The Wild Geese   Defeated, as many as 16,000 Irish soldiers (including Patrick Sarsfield) accepted an offer (part of the Treaty of Limerick) of free passage to France, where they were eventually incorporated into the main army. Others went to Spain, Austria, Sweden, and Russia. Over time, the term "wild geese" came to refer to any Irish, soldiers and civilians, exiled after each of Ireland's periodic uprisings.

Under the Penal Laws

69. The Penal Laws   The events of 1688 to 1691 set the stage for complete subjugation of the Irish that had begun with the Ulster Plantation at the beginning of the century. Up to the 1690s, Catholics in Ireland had enjoyed far greater freedom of religion (relatively speaking, of course) than their counterparts in England. Now, having been stripped of most of their land and having been defeated militarily, they were at the mercy of a vengeful Parliament and Protestant population in Ireland.

Although King William personally opposed the Penal Laws, he capitulated under pressure. From 1695 to 1728 Parliament enacted a series of laws against the civil, religious, and economic rights of Catholics in Ireland. To summarize the most important ones, the Penal Laws (known at the time as "Popery Laws") made it illegal for Catholics to

- marry Protestants
- inherit land from Protestants
- buy land
- carry weapons
- teach school
- practice law
- vote in parliamentary elections
- hold public office
- practice their religion
- own a horse worth more than £5
- hold a commission in the army or navy.

A particularly devastating law forced Catholic landowners to divide their estates among *all* their sons (in contrast to the preferred practice of handing most or all of the land to the eldest) unless they converted to the Church of Ireland. This left them with a choice between two evils: abandoning their Catholic faith in order to save their holdings, or allowing them to be successively subdivided into oblivion.

Over time, some of these laws were either repealed or simply ignored. By the late 1700s, for example, Catholics were allowed to buy land and practice their religion. But the most debilitating statutes, those laws that denied Irish Catholics basic political, economic, and civil rights, were kept in full force until Catholic Emancipation in 1829.

70. The Protestant Ascendancy By stripping Ireland's majority Catholic population of most of its land and civil, religious, political, and economic rights, the British government empowered the roughly ten thousand Protestant families to whom land and titles were given. They became known as the Protestant Ascendancy, and they dominated Ireland's economy and politics well into the nineteenth century. They not only had the law on their side, but also a sizable police force (eventually called the Royal Irish Constabulary) and as many as twenty-five thousand British soldiers.

71. Grinding Poverty The great majority of Ireland's Catholic population were reduced to the status of tenant farmers, farm laborers, or servants. Some managed to lease farms, but they had to pay high rents. Evictions for failure to pay rent, or if a landlord decided to switch from crops to grazing cattle, were common.

This system of widespread tenancy encouraged larger tenant farmers to take on subtenants, usually very poor Irish Catholics. The latter typically farmed only a few acres of land on which they raised potatoes for their families and items like eggs, pigs, and butter for sale to earn the necessary cash to pay the annual rent. Their Catholic landlords, pressed by the need to pay rents to their

Protestant landowners, often showed little sympathy toward their less fortunate Catholic brethren, raising rents and ordering evictions when financial considerations demanded it. "Nevertheless," write Kerby Miller and Paul Wagner in *Out of Ireland,* "all Irish Catholics, comfortable 'strong farmers' and starving peasants alike, were united by religion and resentment against the Protestant Ascendancy."

72. Peasant Life Most Irish peasants lived in small huts haphazardly clustered into what they called *clachans.* The families living in *clachans* were often united in kinship and certainly in the traditions of the Gaelic culture they shared. It was here that, despite English efforts at eradication, the Irish language, storytelling, song, poetry, dance, music, and religion survived.

Peasant families were also tied by a system of collective farming known as *rundale,* which may have originated in ancient Ireland before the arrival of the Normans. By the eighteenth century, no doubt promoted by the forced subdivision of Catholic lands, the practice was widespread among the Irish peasantry. Extended families (occasionally more than one) living as joint tenants on a piece of land controlled a number of strips of land on which they raised their crops. Every so often, as needs and family composition changed (through death or marriage), family elders reallocated the strips. This system ensured an equitable distribution of land and created an incentive to work together for the good of the overall crop.

Like so many vestiges of ancient Ireland, the *rundale* system perished with the Famine.

73. Hedge Schools One of the results of the Penal Laws banning Catholic schools and teachers was the emergence of secret schools for the education of Catholic youth. Because so many were held outdoors, often behind barns or hedges, they came to be called "hedge schools." The name persisted even after instruction eventually moved into small schoolhouses or students' homes. By one estimate, as many as 400,000 Catholic children attended more than nine thousand hedge schools by the 1820s. Taught by itinerant instructors of varied training, students usually learned little more than the "three Rs." But some education was certainly better than none.

74. Edmund Burke Observes Not every member of the Ascendancy ignored the plight of the Irish peasantry. Edmund Burke, the son of an Ascendancy Protestant and Catholic mother, emerged in the mid-eighteenth century as one of the sharpest critics of British policy that drove the Irish into state of near slavery. In 1748, when he was just nineteen, he published the following harrowing description of Irish rural poverty:

> . . . as you leave the Town, the Scene grows worse, and presents you with the Utmost Penury in the Midst of a rich Soil. . . . Money is a stranger to them . . . As for their Food, it is notorious they seldom taste Bread or Meat; their diet, in Summer, is Potatoes and sour Milk; in Winter, when something is required Comfortable, they are still worse, living on the same Root, made palatable only by a little Salt, and accompanied with Water: their Cloaths so ragged, that they rather publish than conceal the Wretchedness it was meant to hide; nay it is no uncommon sight to see a half dozen Children run quite naked out of a Cabin, scarcely distinguishable from a Dunghill. . . . In this manner all the Peasantry, to a Man, live: and

Edmund Burke

I Appeal to any one, who knows the Country, for the Justness of the Picture.

75. Agrarian Protest With virtually no political, civil, or economic rights, Irish Catholic peasants had few ways in which to resist the exploitation of the Ascendancy. Sporadic outbreaks of violence against landlords, rent collectors, and estate managers occurred throughout the eighteenth century (indeed, it was a tradition that extended back centuries to the Norman conquest). But from the 1760s on, a new, secret, organized form of agrarian protest emerged. They adopted fanciful names such as the Whiteboys, Shanavests, and Molly Maguires, wore costumes to conceal their identities, and issued warnings and proclamations of their grievances (which ranged from high taxes and rents, to enclosure of land for cattle grazing, to evictions). Poor Protestants sometimes joined these movements or formed their own with names like the Oakboys and Hearts of Steel (the precursors to the Orange Order). When their demands were not met, these secret societies resorted to acts of sabotage (crop destruction, arson, and cattle maiming were common), beatings, and occasionally murder. Agrarian vigilantism lasted well into the nineteenth century, reflecting both the level of popular discontent among the Irish peasantry and their almost nonexistent power.

76. The Grattan Parliament The main political goal of the Protestant Ascendancy in the eighteenth century was to gain what Scotland had in 1707: political union with England. The Crown, however, did not see the need for such a union and refused to act on it. The crisis of the revolution in America, however, presented the Protestant "Patriots," as they were known, with an opportunity to press their case before a beleaguered Westminster government. Led by MP Henry Grattan (and backed by his Irish Volunteers citizen army), they secured in 1779 the removal of severe restrictions on Irish trade and in 1782–83 greater legislative independence for Ireland's

Henry Grattan

Parliament (by repealing the Declaratory Act of 1720 and modifying Poynings' Law of 1494). "Ireland is now a nation," said Grattan. "In that character I hail her and, bowing in her august presence, I say, *Esto perpetua.*"

77. The Catholic Relief Acts Many of the so-called "Patriots," including Grattan and Edmund Burke, recognized the futility (not to mention immorality) of depriving Irish Catholics of nearly all their rights. It made control of Ireland possible only by force and guaranteed discontent and future uprisings. Various Catholic Relief Acts were passed from the 1770s and to the early 1790s that removed Penal Law restrictions on land inheritance, education, professions (law), minor office-holding, and bearing arms. Still, Catholics in 1793 could not hold government offices or sit in Parliament. In 1795 William Pitt's effort to gain passage of full Catholic Emancipation was blocked by conservatives in Ireland and England.

78. Theobald Wolfe Tone and the United Irishmen
The failure of Pitt and other moderate Protestant reformers to secure full Catholic Emancipation opened the way for Irish radicals to seize the reform agenda. They were led by a charismatic son of a Dublin coachmaker, Theobald Wolfe Tone (1763–98). Although born into a Protestant family, Tone shunned organized religion in favor of deism. In 1791, he wrote *An Argument on Behalf of the Catholics of Ireland,* in which he stressed the need to unite Irish Catholics and Protestants to remove English control over Ireland (something that could only be accomplished if Catholics were granted full political rights). That same year he

played a leading role in establishing the Society of United Irishmen, a revolutionary body dedicated to establishing a nondenominational Irish Parliament.

But when the French Revolution (whose radicalism was a key source of inspiration for Tone and his followers) began to spin out of control in 1793, the British government began a campaign of repression against the United Irishmen and other potentially subversive groups. The Arms Act dissolved the Irish Volunteers (which the United Irishmen were actively trying to radicalize) and a Convention Act prohibited the holding of large public rallies. By 1794 British authorities arrested several key United Irishmen leaders and drove Tone into exile in the United States. From that point on the United Irishmen went underground and prepared for armed insurrection. Tone arrived in France in 1796, and secured promises of military assistance.

79. The Orange Order Violence between Catholic and Protestant groups began to escalate in the 1790s, especially in County Armagh, as the United Irishmen became more vocal in the call for equal rights for Catholics. Much of the violence was waged by Protestant gangs such as the Peep o' Day Boys, who attacked Catholics. Following a particularly violent clash known as the Battle of the Diamond, defenders of the Protestant Ascendancy established a secret society called

the Orange Order. Named in honor of Protestant William of Orange, it soon had lodges across Ireland. Since 1796, these Orange lodges have staged marches throughout Ireland, especially on July 12, the anniversary of the

Theobald Wolfe Tone

Battle of Aughrim (1691), at which William III triumphed over James II.

80. 1798: The Rebellion of the United Irishmen In December 1796, a great French fleet of thirty-five ships carrying twelve thousand soldiers, slipped past the British blockade and sailed into Bantry Bay. Aboard the flagship was Wolfe Tone. The weather was calm and conditions appeared perfect for a successful landing. But the fleet waited for the ship of General Hoche, the expedition's leader, and fate intervened. Before Hoche could arrive, a storm blew up and forced a retreat back to France. The one solid chance for a successful uprising was lost and so was the crucial element of surprise. British officials immediately commenced a campaign of infiltration and repression of the United Irishmen.

Despite these setbacks, the United Irishmen counted 280,000 loyal followers by 1798. The long-awaited uprising finally began May 23–24, 1798. But British intelligence had done their work well and knew in advance. Thomas Reynolds, a Catholic silk merchant–turned–informer provided them with ample warning. Many of the key leaders had been arrested even before the rising took place. British forces and rebels clashed in Curragh (May 25), Tara (May 26), and Curragh (May 29), with the rebels losing more than five hundred killed. Further rebel losses occurred at Antrim (June 7) and Ballynahinch (June 13). The rebels initially fared better in the south, but suffered defeats at New Ross (June 5) and Arklow (June 9).

The uprising touched off a wave of violence by Protestant and Catholic groups. Whipped into a frenzy by revived tales of the alleged massacres of 1641, local Protestant militiamen and vigilante bands terrorized and murdered Catholics. One militiaman (known thereafter as Tom the Devil) invented a gruesome torture called a "pitch cap" where the heads of suspects were covered with pitch and set on fire to coerce confessions. Bands of armed Catholics responded in kind with sectarian attacks on Protestants. In one case, two hun-

dred Protestants were herded into a barn in Scullabogue and burned to death.

The rebellion of the United Irishmen ended on June 21 with a skirmish at Vinegar Hill, eighty miles south of Dublin. The French finally arrived in August with 1,100 soldiers and were immediately seized by British forces. Among their number was Wolfe Tone, dressed in the uniform of a French colonel. He was convicted of treason and sentenced to die. Denied his request to be shot, Tone beat the gallows by committing suicide in his cell.

In the aftermath of the insurrection, 1,500 rebels were executed, whipped, or transported to Australia or the West Indies. All told, some thirty thousand people died. It was the bloodiest chapter in Irish history since the seventeenth century.

81. The Act of Union The uprising convinced most leading British officials that what Ireland needed most was not greater independence, but less. The model for binding Ireland in a union with England was the 1707 union between Scotland and England. At first, many Irish Protestants, led by Grattan, opposed the idea, and a good many Catholics, tempted by promises of full emancipation under the new union, supported it. In the end, however, the hostility of King George III and Irish Protestants to emancipation meant that the union occurred without Irish Catholics gaining a thing.

The Act of Union establishing the United Kingdom of Great Britain and Ireland took effect January 1, 1801. It abolished Ireland's Parliament and granted Ireland representation in Westminster (twenty-eight peers and four bishops to the House of Lords, one hundred MPs in the Commons).

Once the Act of Union became a reality, Irish Protestants dropped their hostility to it and became its most ardent defenders, especially when it became clear the Catholic emancipation would not be part of the deal. The Protestant Ascendancy realized that union with England guaranteed their privileged position in Ireland. For example, William Plunkett, who initially promised to "resist it to the last gasp of my existence and with the last drop of my blood," ended up joining the new government as solicitor general. It would be up to Ireland's Catholics to agitate for an independent parliament (home rule) until the 1870s, when Irish Protestants again joined the movement.

82. Robert Emmet's Rebellion The last gasp of the United Irishmen came in 1803 with a rebellion planned by Robert Emmet, the younger brother of United Irishmen leader Thomas Addis Emmet. Expelled from Trinity College in 1798 as a suspected rebel, he remained active in the cause, and in 1800 traveled to France to seek aid. He returned to Ireland in 1802 and began recruiting rebels and gathering weapons. He hoped to seize Dublin Castle to spark a popular revolt throughout Ireland (possibly with French assistance). When his Dublin arms cache blew up, he was forced to stage the revolt prematurely. Only a small group of rebels showed up on the evening of July 23, 1803, and they failed in their attempt on the Castle. They did, however, manage to hold a small section of Dublin before being routed by soldiers. In all, fifty people were killed, including two prominent government officials. Emmet escaped, but was captured a month later. Before he was hanged on September 20, he made a speech long remembered in Ireland and America:

Let no man write my epitaph. . . . When my country takes her place among the nations of the earth then, and not until then, let my epitaph be written.

Robert Emmet

With the passing of Robert Emmet the United Irishmen died, too.

Daniel O'Connell

83. Daniel O'Connell The single-most important and effective man in Irish political life in the nineteenth century was Daniel O'Connell. Born in Kerry in 1775, he was raised by a wealthy uncle, an upbringing that steeped him in the traditions and culture of Ireland. At sixteen, he was sent to school in France, where he witnessed the French Revolution firsthand and was eventually forced to flee back to Ireland. He studied law, and by 1800 had developed a thriving practice in Munster.

O'Connell began his political career in 1800, when he emerged as an outspoken critic of the Act of Union (interestingly, he was staunchly opposed to the Rebellion of 1798). In 1805, he took a leading role in the movement to repeal the remaining laws limiting the rights and freedoms of Ireland's Catholics. As his career as an activist developed, O'Connell committed himself to nonviolent agitation, a philosophy that derived from the scenes of horror he witnessed in revolutionary France and the remorse he felt after killing an antagonist in a duel in 1815. He thus would become the father of constitutional (as opposed to physical-force) nationalism.

84. The Catholic Association The key to O'Connell's success was his formation of the Catholic Association in 1823. It began as a small reform organization of landowners, merchants, and professionals, but was transformed into a mass grassroots movement with O'Connell's introduction of "Catholic rent." This said that anyone paying a penny per month could be a member of the Catholic Association. Local parishes all across Ireland became centers of Catholic Association agitation, and by 1825 O'Connell had a mass movement behind him. The contributions of the Association's 250,000 members topped £1,000 a week.

Daniel O'Connell at Repeal rally

85. Catholic Emancipation Worried by the growing strength of this populist movement, British authorities declared the Catholic Association illegal. But they were no match for the wily O'Connell, who promptly restructured the organization into a "public and private charity" dedicated to "public peace and tranquility as well as private harmony between all classes." It continued to raise money, and drum up support for emancipation in the countryside.

The turning point in the Catholic Emancipation crusade came in 1828, when O'Connell stood for election to Parliament in County Clare. At this point, Catholics who owned or leased land valued at forty shillings possessed the legal right to vote. Technically, there was no ban on their sitting in Parliament, though no Catholic had done so for over 150 years. The crisis came after O'Connell's victory, when he refused to swear an oath that referred to Catholicism as "superstitious."

Fearing another uprising in Ireland if O'Connell and subsequent Catholic candidates were prevented from taking their seats over the oath issue, Parliament relented. In April 1829 the last disabilities against Catholics were abolished. Not surprisingly, Daniel O'Connell thereafter was known as "The Liberator."

86. Repeal Movement Though he had just pulled off a revolutionary reform, O'Connell was not done. In his mind, Catholic Emancipation was merely the first step in a larger movement for greater Irish independence. He quit his law practice completely and devoted the rest of his life to politics. In 1832, he became the leader of a group of Irish MPs dedicated to repealing the Act of Union. Its goal was not outright independence—though some in the movement certainly favored it—but rather the restoration of the Irish Parliament and home rule. British officials, however, saw the Repeal Movement as a bid for Irish independence.

After languishing in the tangled Parliamentary politics of the era, the repeal campaign took off in 1841. By this time, the Repeal Movement was joined by a more radical organization known as Young Ireland, whose members promoted a heightened sense of Irish national identity. By 1843, O'Connell's "Repeal rent" totaled £48,000, and he began to stage mass rallies across the country. An estimated 750,000 people attended a spectacular "monster rally" (as they were known) at Tara, symbolic seat of the ancient high kings.

Fearing the growing power of O'Connell's movement (and remembering his success in the 1820s), British officials decided to act. O'Connell scheduled for October 8, 1843, what he hoped would be the largest monster rally yet at Clontarf near Dublin. Even as thousands began to arrive on October 7, the British government announced that the meeting would not be permitted. Fearing bloodshed if he pressed the matter, O'Connell (not unlike Martin Luther King, Jr., at the Pettus Bridge in Alabama in 1965) called off the rally. "Not for all the universe contains," he explained, "would I, in the struggle for what I conceive my country's cause, consent to the effusion of a single drop of human blood, except my own." The Repeal Movement fell apart after that. O'Connell was arrested for conspiracy and jailed from May to September 1844. Radical Young Irelanders, disillusioned by O'Connell's moderation, soon left the movement. O'Connell, now nearing seventy, began to suffer health problems.

Even though he lost in his bid for repeal, O'Connell must be remembered as the man who transformed the nationalist struggle in Ireland. As Henry Boylan writes in the *Dictionary of Irish Biography*, "he showed the people of Ireland, long used to defeat, that victory could be achieved, and that the power to achieve it was theirs, given the right leadership. It was a lesson that sank deep into the Irish consciousness."

But it would be a while before Ireland could act on this lesson, for within a year of O'Connell's release from prison, the country would be hit by a catastrophe of unfathomable proportions—the Great Hunger. For much of the next decade, the enormous challenge facing Ireland would not be independence, but survival.

The Famine

87. Origins of the Famine Ireland's agriculture had failed frequently in the century and a half leading up to the Great Hunger. Failures, some leading to significant death tolls, occurred in 1708–09, 1725–29, 1740–41, 1745–46, 1753, 1766, 1769–70, 1772–73, 1782–84, 1795–96, 1800–01, 1817–18, 1821–22, 1830–31, 1835, 1839, and 1842. The greatest of these occurred in 1740–41 (due to extremely cold weather), and produced a famine that killed as many as 400,000 people—a level proportionate to the Great Famine of 1845–52.

Ireland's Great Famine (1845–52) occurred as the result of many things. First, Ireland's population had doubled from four million in 1800 to over eight million in 1845, making it the most densely populated nation in Western Europe. Second, owing to British colonial policies, the vast majority of the population was so poor that they were dependent upon the potato as their main source of food. Third, starting in 1845, a mysterious blight destroyed successive potato crops between 1845 and 1852. Fourth, an indifferent British government failed to respond to the crisis, resulting in more than one million deaths and more than one million emigrants. It was the highest level of civilian suffering in Europe between the Thirty Years' War and World War I.

88. The Incredible Potato Remarkably, for a vegetable that seemed to define Irish peasant life before the Famine, the potato was native to South America, in the region of the Andes. Sir Walter Raleigh is credited with introducing the potato to Europe, planting them on his lands in Ireland in the 1580s. The potato took hold in Ireland for a number of reasons. The Irish climate is particularly well suited to potato growth. The potato also will grow almost anywhere—rocky soil, wet bogs, or on hills. Potatoes are also easy to cultivate and produce prolific yields—up to six tons on a single acre of land. Other advantages include their easy preparation (no milling as with grain), lack of disease (before 1845, of course), and extraordinary nutritional value. This last point is made clear by the many contemporary accounts of the Irish poor as being exceptionally strong and healthy. Irish males on the eve of the Famine were on average the tallest in Europe.

89. Growing Dependence upon the Potato At first, the potato was a food enjoyed only by the Irish gentry. But over the course of the 1600s, the British reduced the majority of the Irish people to the status of peasant farmers on small plots of rented land, who in turn devoted increased acreage to the growth of potatoes that they ate as a supplement to their diet of oats, grains, and dairy products. In the eighteenth century, as conditions for Irish peasants worsened, the potato became more and more of a staple crop, especially during the winter months. This trend continued until the eve of the Famine, when perhaps as many as 60 percent of the Irish people were solely dependent on the potato as their main source of food.

It must be pointed out, however, that on the eve of the Famine potatoes constituted just 20 percent of Ireland's annual agricultural output. Irish farmers of all ranks grew oats and grains alongside their potatoes. They also raised cows, goats, pigs, and chickens. Peasant farmers, however, ate very little grain, bacon, meat, or eggs. Instead, these products, along with some potatoes, were sold for cash to pay their rents.

90. "The Blight" The scientific name for what the Irish called "the blight" is *Phytophthora infestans* (literally, "late blight"). In simplest terms, it is a deadly fungus spread rapidly by spores in air or water. It originated in Mexico, appeared in America in the fall of 1843, and then made its way

to Western Europe by way of transatlantic ships. Irish farmers told of it striking overnight, leaving blackened leaves, a gooey inedible tuber, and a powerful stench.

The first reports of disease among the potatoes of Ireland came from the Botanic Garden in Dublin in August 1845. By September, the blight spread to farms in the northeast, eventually destroying one third of the potato crop. In 1846, the blight reappeared in June and spread at a rate of fifty miles per week to all thirty-two counties, destroying nearly 90 percent of the crop. Although the loss of just 30 percent in 1847 seems small, it was equally devastating because farmers had planted so few potatoes. Half the potato crop of 1848 fell to the blight. Between 1849 and 1852, smaller, localized outbreaks of the blight occurred, primarily in the south and west.

The blight was not confined to Ireland. Indeed, the first reports of the blight in Europe came from Belgium in June 1845. By September it appeared not only in Ireland, but also in parts of England, Scotland, France, the Netherlands, Germany, Scandinavia, and Russia.

91. The Response of the British Government At first, the Tory government of PM Robert Peel acted quickly. Peel had presided over food-relief efforts during crises in Ireland back in 1817 and 1822, and this time he ordered a scientific commission to investigate the causes of the blight; and in November 1845 secretly purchased £100,000 of Indian corn from America. In the spring of 1846, this corn was sold at cost to local relief committees who then sold it to the poor. Public works programs were established (mostly road building) which provided employment and wages to thousands. Peel's measures were successful in the short term. No one starved in the first year of crisis (August 1845–August 1846). But the potato failure of 1845 was small compared with those to come, and far greater measures would have to be taken to prevent mass starvation.

Unfortunately, in June 1846 Peel's govern-

Scenes of desperation at a Famine workhouse

ment fell in the wake of his successful effort to re-peal Britain's Corn Laws (tariffs on grain im-ports). He was replaced by a Whig administration headed by Lord John Russell. Russell, like Peel and many other British politicians, hoped to use the Famine crisis to reform and modernize Irish society, a society that they considered hopelessly backward. Russell would authorize relief, there-fore, but at a price. The cornerstone of his pro-gram (starting in the fall of 1846) was a vast system of public works.

92. Starving People Forced to Work Russell and other key British government officials, such Treasury Secretary Charles Trevelyan, advocated public works for ideological reasons. They sub-scribed to the free market ideas of Adam Smith, David Ricardo, and other classical economists who warned against government interference in

economic affairs. Free food distribution, they ar-gued, would damage the economy by artificially forcing down food prices, thus hurting farmers and shopkeepers. Public works, they stressed, would also help modernize Ireland by improving farms and roads.

93. The Nature of the Public Works Projects
Some small public works began in early 1846 as part of Peel's relief effort. Russell's much larger enterprise began that fall—at precisely the mo-ment when starvation and malnutrition from the second potato failure were taking hold. By March 1847, the programs employed 734,000 people (one out of every three adult males). Conditions were dreadful. Men were required to work twelve hours a day (6 A.M. to 6 P.M.), six days per week, at hard manual labor. The work carried on through the winter (an extremely cold one that

brought nine inches of snow), even though workers often had little more than rags for clothing.

While some projects of value were completed under the plan, many were useless, make-work tasks established because the British government could not bear the idea of giving away food without making people work for it. To this day one can travel the Irish countryside and see "Famine roads" leading nowhere, and "Famine walls" enclosing nothing. Worse still, the need to labor on the public works to survive meant that people had little or no time to plant crops. As a result, the harvest of 1847, while losing only 30 percent to the blight, was a fraction of its normal level.

Wages were a paltry two pence per day—far below market rates. To make matters worse, while wages were kept low, food prices were not controlled (in deference to free market ideology). Food sellers took advantage of the situation and prices soared. Thus, Russell's public works program set hundreds of thousands of starving people to work in deadly conditions at wages insufficient to buy them enough food to survive. As a result, women and children began to appear at public works seeking to earn desperately needed income.

94. Food Exports Amid Starvation

Much of the food unaffected by the blight was exported to the rest of Britain, Europe, and the United States. The same thinking that led British officials to resist calls for free emergency food distribution in 1846 also made them resolute "free traders" (hence their efforts to repeal the Corn Laws). They argued against stopping exports from Ireland on the grounds that it would damage the overall British economy and hinder Ireland's recovery. As a result, tons of oats, grain, dairy products, distilled alcohol, and livestock left Ireland while its people starved. As desperate people began to attack food convoys, British soldiers and police were posted as escorts.

While British officials argued that they could not violate the laws of free trade and the free market, they often did so when it suited their needs.

As historian Christine Kinealy has noted, when the Chinese refused to buy their opium, the British waged the Opium War (1839–42) to force them to comply.

95. The Lack of Alternative Foods

Before the Famine, Ireland had only rudimentary fisheries. Many fishermen were in fact farmers who fished to supplement their diet and income. Most fishermen used very primitive tackle and small boats called "coracles" that were incapable of plying deep waters where fish were more abundant. On top of this, the once plentiful herring population off the west of Ireland was greatly diminished in the 1830s. When the Famine struck, many fishermen pawned their fishing equipment to buy food, intending to buy it back the next year when harvests improved. Inland, sources of fish were unavailable, as most rivers and lakes were bounded by private property whose owners often refused to allow people to fish. Many Famine victims instinctively headed for the seashore in search of food and perhaps passage to America. There they found a coastline stripped bare of every crab, clam, and strand of seaweed.

Unable to eat the blight-ridden potatoes, afford expensive grain, or catch fish, the Irish ate pretty much anything they could find. First, they ate their seed potatoes—temporarily diminishing their hunger, but greatly limiting future plantings. After that, they usually slaughtered their pigs. Some took to bleeding their cows in order to drink the blood. As the crisis deepened in 1847 and after, people resorted to eating horses, birds, dogs, cats, mice, rats, frogs, and insects. When these sources disappeared, they turned to grass, leading to the numerous reports of the dead having green stains around their mouths. In 1849 there were even reports of cannibalism.

96. Black '47

Black '47 was the name given to the worst year of the Famine, 1847. No one knows how many died, but it is generally agreed that 1847 saw the greatest suffering and death. The near total loss of the potato crop in 1846, coupled with the punitive British policy of demanding work for food money, resulted in the death of hundreds of thousands.

97. Skibbereen Through a series of articles and letters published by eyewitnesses, this small town in County Cork came to symbolize the devastation and suffering of the Famine. One estimate claimed that in 1846 alone more than 10 percent (ten thousand people) in the area perished, with many more to follow in Black '47. For generations after, the town's name symbolized both the horror of the Famine and the role the British played in exacerbating it. As one nationalist song later put it:

> We may some day remember
> If we're wanted by the Queen
> That hundreds patiently lay down
> And starved in Skibbereen

98. How They Died Like all famines, most victims did not actually starve to death—they didn't live long enough to die of starvation. Disease, made deadly by the malnutrition and weakness caused by starvation, carried the great majority away. Most people died of fever, dysentery, and smallpox, but many others also succumbed to influenza, tuberculosis, measles, and bronchitis. In 1848 and 1849 Asiatic cholera, probably brought by British soldiers, took thousands more lives. Disease spread rapidly throughout Ireland as people hit the road in search of food, crowded into towns, and labored side by side in workhouses and on public works.

99. The Soup Kitchens Many things contributed to the eventual end of death by starvation and disease, including the end of the blight in 1852. But during the Famine, the single-most important step taken to alleviate the suffering occurred in the middle of Black '47. Faced with a mounting disaster of their own making, British officials abandoned the public works program and authorized the opening of soup kitchens to provide free soup to all. By July 1847, the kitchens were serving a simple yet nourishing soup called "stirabout" to three million people—37 percent of the population. These government soup kitchens demonstrated that the British government had the capacity, if not the will, to feed the starving masses of Ireland.

By the end of September 1847, the British, increasingly concerned about the cost of Irish relief and worried that the Irish might become dependent on the aid, declared the Famine to be "over" and terminated the soup kitchens. Their underlying goal was to shift all the costs of relief from the British government to individual Irish landlords under a provision called the Poor Law Extension Act.

100. The Poor Law Extension Act The original Poor Law had been passed in 1838. It divided Ireland into 130 districts known as "unions," each with its own workhouse, administered by a Board of Guardians. The Extension Act of 1847 made all future Famine relief the responsibility of the local unions. The cost of such an undertaking would be paid for by a tax, or "rate," levied on local landlords. Strict needs tests were established, lest any "undeserving" poor try to take advantage of the program. The physically infirm received aid, but often had to endure weeks of delay while their application was approved by Crown officials. All able-bodied men were required to work eight hours of hard labor before getting assistance.

The worst part of the Poor Law Extension Act was the so-called Gregory Clause. Also known as the Quarter Acre Clause, it prohibited anyone holding one quarter of an acre or more of land from receiving any assistance. Many smallholders who had managed to cling to their land for two years now faced a grim decision: Stay on the land and starve, or relinquish it in order to qualify for food. This policy revealed that the British government not only wanted to stop paying for Irish Famine relief, but that they also

Bridget O'Donnell and her children, 1849

sought to take advantage of the crisis by forcing Irish peasants off the land. Ridding Ireland of unnecessary farmers and their inefficient small farms was at the heart of the Russell government's goal of modernizing Irish society.

101. Starvation and Eviction

The effect of the Poor Law Extension and the Gregory Clause was renewed starvation and mass evictions. The Poor Law unions proved incapable of providing adequate relief while at the same time requiring starving people to perform hard labor in pestilential workhouses for food. The taxes on landlords to pay for this policy hit them hard, causing many to evict their tenants to avoid having to pay for their relief. Still thousands more (owing to the Gregory Clause) sold their land or terminated their leases in order to get food, causing still greater distress and homelessness.

Evictions increased in every year of the Famine up to 1850 and remained high through the early 1850s.

YEAR	FAMILIES EVICTED
1846	3,500
1847	6,026
1848	9,657
1849	16,686
1850	19,949
1851	13,197

All told, approximately 500,000 people were evicted from their homes during the Famine years, often in a cruel and callous manner. Frequently, landlords called in armed guards to serve eviction notices and keep the people away while men pulled down the houses and set them ablaze. Evicted tenants often built simple shacks called "scalpeens" along roadsides, often close to where they had once lived. Frequently landlords tore these down as well.

Some notable exceptions include the Edgeworths of County Longford and Henry Moore of Galway, both of whom nearly went bankrupt feeding their tenants. It should also be pointed out that some Catholic landlords resorted to evictions in order to save their farms.

102. Resistance

Resistance to eviction and other forms of injustice was common, especially in the early years of the Famine. Crime soared during the Famine, but mainly against property (usually stealing food). Crimes against individuals remained at pre-Famine levels. Occasionally, however, attacks against landlords, rent collectors, evictors, and police did occur. The most sensational of these was the assassination of Roscommon landlord Major Denis Mahon in late 1847.

103. The Young Ireland Uprising

In the years before the Famine, Daniel O'Connell's Repeal Movement had attracted the attention of a group of young, university-educated, Irish nationalists. Three of them, Thomas Davis, Gavan Duffy, and John Blake Dillon, founded a nationalist newspaper called *The Nation* in 1842. Week after week the paper espoused the views of this eclectic group of Catholic and Protestant activists who came to call themselves "Young Ireland." Inspired by similar nationalist movements on the Continent, they championed a new sense of Irish nationality, where a revived Irish culture would overcome the long-standing divisions between Catholic, Protestant, and Dissenter.

Within a few years, however, a rift developed between Young Ireland and old O'Connell. The lat-

Thomas Davis

ter grew increasingly leery of Young Ireland's enthusiastic nonsectarianism and their talk of outright independence (he favored home rule under the Crown). Young Irelanders for their part feared that O'Connell was too willing to compromise on the issue of repeal. The official break came in July 1846 when Young Irelanders rejected O'Connell's ultimatum that they renounce the use of physical force in their struggle for Irish freedom. Even though no one had called for armed insurrection, O'Connell's ultimatum prompted a walkout by members of Young Ireland (after Thomas Francis Meagher's stirring speech celebrating "the sword") and the subsequent formation of the Irish Confederation.

By early 1848, as the Famine ravaged the Irish countryside, a Young Irelander named John Mitchel called for open rebellion against British rule. He was convinced that the suffering of the Famine would produce a mass peasant uprising. In March 1848 he was joined by William Smith O'Brien, who called for the formation of an armed National Guard to defend Ireland against British repression. When Mitchel was arrested and transported to a prison colony in Australia in May, O'Brien decided to lead an armed insurrection.

In late July 1848, Smith O'Brien gathered a small, armed force in Tipperary. To their dismay, the anticipated mass uprising of embittered peasants failed to materialize—Young Irelanders had planned poorly and the Famine had wrought too much havoc. On July 29, 1848, a contingent of police clashed with Smith O'Brien's force in a cabbage patch. Two men died before the rebels fled in the face of military reinforcements. The rebellion of Young Ireland had ended almost as soon

as it began. Smith O'Brien and several others were arrested, convicted, and exiled to a penal colony in Tasmania.

Pathetic by the standards of Irish insurrections both before and after, the Young Ireland rebellion of 1848 did have a lasting impact. For one thing, it reestablished the physical force tradition of Irish nationalism to challenge O'Connell-style constitutional nationalism in the future. In addition, it allowed later generations of nationalists to point with pride to the fact that Ireland did not passively accept the oppressive policies of Britain during the Famine. Finally, the rebellion of 1848 produced a generation of exiled nationalists—in Australia, Canada, and the United States—who committed themselves to waging a more successful rebellion in the future.

104. "Souperism"   To this day the term "souper" is one of the supreme terms of derision in Ireland. It refers to the private relief workers who demanded that starving Irish peasants renounce their Catholic faith and convert to Protestantism as a qualification for receiving soup. One such group wrote in a Belfast newspaper that the Famine provided a great opportunity "for conveying the light of the Gospels to the darkened mind of the Roman Catholic Peasantry." While the actual practice of souperism appears to have been rare, the fact that it existed at all made it an important part of the bitter Famine legacy.

105. Total British Expenditures on Famine Relief   All added up, the British spent approximately £10,000,000 on Famine relief. More than half of this money came in the form of a loan for which repayment was due. Most of the money was spent on the punitive public works phase of relief in 1846 and 1847—ironically, the period of greatest mortality. Funding after that was sharply curtailed as a means of forcing Irish landlords to bear the cost of relief. Although the British press and government accused Irish landlords of shirking their duty, the latter actually spent £9,000,000 in poor relief.

Was this a particularly large amount of money? No, writes historian Christine Kinealy in her book *A Death-Dealing Famine,* not when one considers that fact that the Treasury expected repayment for approximately £5,000,000 of the funds. Moreover, in comparison to other large-scale expenditures by the Treasury, Famine relief seems quite small. For example, the Treasury expended £22,000,000 to compensate British slave owners when slavery was abolished in 1833. Shortly after the Famine, the British would spend £69,000,000 in the disastrous Crimean War.

106. Queen Victoria The story that Queen Victoria sent only £5 is false, but it stems from the fact that many saw her donation of £2,000 as a pittance compared to her wealth and indicative of British indifference. Many poor individuals and groups sent amounts that were far greater in proportion to their resources. Queen Victoria visited Ireland in August 1849, in part to demonstrate that the Famine was "over." She visited Cork, Dublin, Belfast, and Cobh (which was renamed Queenstown in her honor), but stayed far from the suffering. Many Irish mocked her visit by singing

Arise ye dead of Skibbereen
And come to Cork to see the Queen

107. Other Sources of Relief A General Central Relief Committee for All Ireland was organized in early 1847 to collect funds for relief. Among its leaders were Daniel O'Connell and the Young Irelander William Smith O'Brien. In the course of one year they raised more than £50,000 which they disbursed in more than 1,800 small grants. Like most relief agencies, it disbanded prematurely at the end of 1847. A second major organization was the British Relief Association. It, too, raised and distributed an enormous amount of money (£400,000) before disbanding in the summer of 1848. Its most notable achievement, the result of its chief agent Count Paul Edmund de Strzelecki (a Polish nobleman), were schools that fed 200,000 children a day in western Ireland. When Strzelecki appealed to the Treasury for money to continue the program, Charles Trevelyan refused.

108. The Role of the Quakers in Famine Relief The Quakers, or Society of Friends, took an early interest in the Irish crisis and provided some of the most important relief. As early as October 1846 they were serving free soup in Ireland, a policy later adopted by the British government. The many Quakers who went to Ireland to directly assist in the relief effort wrote some of the most important firsthand accounts of the suffering and lackluster British measures. At least eighteen Quakers died of disease and exhaustion while in Ireland. The Quakers also raised substantial sums of money (£200,000) both in Britain and the United States.

109. International Relief Efforts Besides the Quakers, private donations totaling more than £2,000,000 poured into Ireland from six continents. The first international donation came from India, a collection taken up by British soldiers, many of whom were Irish. Donations also came from the Sultan of Turkey and the Czar of Russia, as well as ex-slaves in the Caribbean and two Jewish congregations in New York City.

In America, the Senate passed in February 1847 a bill authorizing $500,000 in aid to Ireland and Scotland. When that was deemed unconstitutional, Congress approved the use of the warships *Jamestown* and *Macedonia* to bring privately raised supplies to Ireland and Scotland. The *Jamestown* (destined for Ireland) began loading in Boston on St. Patrick's Day 1847 and arrived in early April. More than one person in Ireland compared the swift action of the American government to the reluctant and inadequate measures taken by the British.

Perhaps the most interesting source of aid was American Indians. The Choctaw tribe sent $170 to Ireland through the Quakers. They were no strangers to oppression and starvation, having only recently (1831) been forced to travel the Trail of Tears to Oklahoma by President Andrew Jackson.

110. The Catholic Church Countless priests and nuns worked tirelessly throughout Ireland to relieve suffering and administer last rites to the dying. They were overwhelmed in these efforts and an untold number of them perished with the masses. The Irish Catholic Church raised money from abroad and expended a great deal of its own meager resources on relief. Pope Pius IX sent one thousand Roman dollars in January 1847 and issued an encyclical instructing Catholics all around the world to pray for Ireland and to raise money. This served to gain international attention for the crisis and brought in much-needed donations (totaling £400,000).

111. More Than One Million Emigrated As with the number who died, we will never know how many Irish fled the ravages of the Famine by emigrating. Some managed to sell a few possessions to buy cheap steerage tickets. Others with only a few pounds bought cheap tickets on ferries and coal barges to Liverpool. Many were given free tickets by landlords and British officials eager to rid Ireland of its "surplus" population. Most estimates suggest that between one and one and a half million left Ireland between 1845 and 1855. Of those who left, it is not known how many survived the passage.

For their destinations, some went only as far as London or Liverpool, either by choice or necessity. Others booked passage on ships to the continent, Australia, Latin America, and Canada. By far the greatest number—80 percent by most estimates—shipped out for the United States. Most of them landed in the principal ports of New York, Boston, Baltimore, and Philadelphia.

112. More Than One Million Died Because the British kept no mortality records during the

The Emigrant's Farewell

Famine, the exact number of deaths will never be known. But using the statistics from the 1841 and 1851 censuses, and factoring for emigration and birth rates, most historians agree that between one and one and a half million people died as a direct result of the Famine.

113. The Great Irish Famine in Comparison with Other Famines Unfortunately, in the century and a half since the Great Irish Famine, numerous other famines have wrought havoc all over the world. Many nations have lost greater numbers of people to famine, most notably China, which saw perhaps as many as thirty million people die between 1959 and 1960. But no nation has ever suffered as great a proportional loss of people as Ireland from 1845 to 1852, when more than 15 percent of the population perished (and another 15 percent were forced to emigrate).

114. The Role of Anti-Irish Racism Many British officials held negative views of the Irish as lazy and brutish. Charles Trevelyan, Permanent Secretary of the Treasury and central figure in determining British policy toward Ireland, argued, "The great evil with which we have to contend, is not the physical evil of the famine, but the moral evil of the selfish, perverse, and turbulent character of the Irish people." Free food, Trevelyan and others like him argued, would only reward laziness, foster dependency, and prevent Ireland's modernization.

115. The Role of Religion Many British officials saw the Famine as the work of God. Ireland, they argued, was a land of heretical "papists" whose sin and laziness had earned God's wrath. As Trevelyan put it, the Famine was "the judgement of God on an indolent and unself-reliant people." Yet they also saw the Famine crisis as a God-given opportunity to make fundamental changes in Ireland.

116. The Question of Genocide As horrific as the Famine was, "genocide" is probably too strong a term to use. So, too, is the word "holocaust." The use of both terms suggests an equivalence with the Jewish experience at the hands of the Nazis during World War II. Clearly some British officials, most notably Trevelyan, expressed attitudes that suggested genocidal thinking. But British policy was multifaceted and was influenced by many factors. The Famine began as the result of a unique natural disaster, but religious hatred, colonialism, racism, greed, and slavish adherence to economic ideology on the part of the British combined to transform it into an extraordinary human tragedy. Thus, the avoidance of terms such as "genocide" and "holocaust" when describing the Famine does nothing to diminish the fact that the British bear the greatest degree of guilt when it comes to assessing the Famine.

post-famine ireland

117. Population The most striking difference between pre- and post-Famine Ireland was population. In 1845, the year the Famine began, Ireland had an estimated population of 8.5 million. Six years later, it stood at just 6.5 million. And depopulation—a trend that made Ireland unique among all European nations—continued well into the twentieth century. by 1901, Ireland's population stood at 4.5 million and falling.

118. Emigration Chief among the reasons for this astonishing drop in population was emigration. Even as the economy improved after 1850, Ireland remained a place of high birth rate and limited economic opportunity. That, combined with the already firmly established tradition of emigration, made striking out for England, Australia, Canada, Latin America, and (overwhelmingly) the United States an irresistible option for the sons and daughters of Erin.

EMIGRATION FROM IRELAND BY DECADE	
1851–60	1,163,418
1861–70	849,836
1871–80	623,933
1881–90	770,706
1891–00	433,526
1901–10	346,024

Many an Irish nationalist would bemoan the fact that Ireland's chief export seemed to be its young and talented.

119. Socioeconomic Transformation One of the most significant legacies of the Famine is the impact it had on the socioeconomic profile of the country. The Famine decimated the cottier class, those tenant farmers who tilled tiny plots of land. In 1845, there were 628,000 farms of fewer than fifteen acres. Just six years later there were 318,000,

An Irish farm

and the number declined steadily for the rest of the century. Few dared ever admit it, but the Famine "solved" Ireland's chronic agricultural crisis.

120. The Position of Women If the position of more secure farmers improved in the aftermath of the Famine, that of women declined. Women in pre-Famine Ireland had never enjoyed much in the way of freedom or privilege, but they did occupy a key position in the family economy, performing farm labor and producing finished goods (usually textiles) for cash sale. After the Famine, however, Ireland's rural economy became more commercially oriented, shifting more and more from tillage to raising livestock. This trend, combined with a decline in demand for domestic manufactures, sharply reduced the social status of Irish women. Women also lost the freedom to choose their husbands as arranged marriages became a common practice among families struggling to maintain or augment their precious land holdings.

About 25 percent of Irish women never married, and as many as half of those who did married men ten years older than themselves (i.e., men who had delayed marriage in order to inherit their family land). Sadly, many Irish women in these circumstances found themselves simply exchanging their domineering father for a domineering husband considerably their senior.

Not surprisingly, Irish women turned to emigration as an escape. Virtually every other ethnic group coming to America (except Eastern European Jews) sent mostly young men. In contrast, more than half of the emigrants from Ireland from the 1850s to the 1920s were women.

121. A Larger Role for the Catholic Church Prior to the Famine, the Catholicism of a majority of Irish peasants was rather thin to say the least. The scarcity of priests and churches in the south and west of Ireland (a legacy of the Penal Laws) made attendance at Mass and reception of the sacraments rare events for many, but so, too, did the persistence of pre-Christian traditions that emphasized fairies, seasonal festivals, and magic.

The trauma of the Famine, however, dramatically weakened these traditions and opened the way for the Catholic Church to assume a dominant role in Irish life well into the twentieth century. For one, the Famine hit hardest the areas in Ireland where these beliefs were strongest. Moreover, the Church provided stability, solace, and leadership to those who survived the ordeal. In some cases, Catholic clergy also encouraged the rural Irish to believe that the Famine was God's punishment of them for clinging to pagan customs.

From the 1850s to the turn of the century, Ireland underwent a "devotional revolution." Hundreds of churches, schools, and charitable institutions were constructed and thousands of priests and nuns trained. Church attendance soared. By the late nineteenth century Catholicism had become one of the defining characteristics of Irish national culture and the nation's most dominant social institution.

122. Nationalism and the Bitter Memory of Famine Irish nationalists, especially the radicals involved in the Young Ireland movement, were

John Mitchel

quick to reject the "God's vengeance" theory of the Famine. For them, the Famine was *not* a natural disaster solely attributable to the potato blight. Rather, they interpreted the British government's handling of the crisis—the meager relief measures, forced labor, continued export of food, souperism, and the Gregory Clause—as evidence of a conspiracy to decimate the Irish population, enabling the British to retain dominance over the country. Young Irelander John Mitchel summed up this notion best when he wrote: "The Almighty, indeed, sent the potato blight, but the English created the Famine."

This legacy of bitterness made its way across the ocean to America. As one popular Irish American ballad went:

> [T]he day will come when vengeance
>   loud will call,
> And we will rise with Erin's boys to
>   rally one and all.
> I'll be the man to lead the van beneath
>   our flag of green,
> And loud and high will raise the cry
>   "Revenge for Skibbereen!"

For generations thereafter, Irish and Irish American nationalists would draw upon this grim memory to stoke feelings of rage and draw support to the cause of Irish freedom.

PART II

Coming
to America

the pre-colonial and colonial periods

Explorers and Exploration

123. The Voyage of St. Brendan Brendan was born around the year A.D. 500 in Fenit, County Kerry, and was educated in the great monasteries of the day. Ordained a priest, he traveled far and wide, establishing many monasteries. According to legend, Brendan also sailed across the Atlantic to the Americas, or what he called the "Land of Promise and of Saints." A written account of the trip, the *Navigatio Sancti Brendani*, tells of Brendan and his crew sailing from Dingle Bay and hopping from a series of islands ("God's stepping stones"), most likely the Hebrides, Iceland, Greenland, Newfoundland, and Nova Scotia. On their return voyage they took a southerly route via what might have been the Azores.

So did an Irishman discover America nine hundred years before Columbus and four hundred years before Leif Eriksson? No one knows for certain. On the one hand, many scholars have interpreted the *Navigatio Sancti Brendani* as a work of fantasy, even humor. On the other hand, a few scholars are not yet ready to dismiss the story as a mere fable. They point to the fact that the suggested route (via Iceland etc.) would have made sense. Furthermore, at least one person has successfully reenacted the Brendan voyage in a skin-covered *curragh* of the sort described in the epic, proving that it could be done. Ultimately, it's a question that will never be answered with any degree of certainty.

124. Mystery Hill and Other Tantalizing Evidence of Pre-Columbian Irish Exploration Ever since Europeans began to arrive in New England in the seventeenth century, people have discovered mysterious ancient ruins that some have suggested indicate the presence of Celtic voyagers in the New World long before Brendan. Beehive-like rock huts with underground passages at Mystery Hill in Salem, New Hampshire, for example, appear to some to bear a striking resemblance to the beehive structures found at the Celtic passage graves in Ireland (and others built later by druids and early Christians). Other structures bearing resemblance to ancient Celtic solar calendars, temples, and sacrificial altars have been found in places like Lowell, Massachusetts, and Stamford, Connecticut. Writings that appear to be ogham have been found etched into the walls in a Ridgefield, Connecticut, cave. As tantalizing as these and other finds are, most archaeologists dismiss the theory that these structures were built by ancient Celts and instead attribute them to American Indians (or a civilization that predated them) or colonists.

125. Did William Ayers Sail with Columbus? There is an unverified legend that one of Christopher Columbus's crewmen was a Galway native named William Ayers (also known as William Eris, William Harris, or in Spanish, Guillermo Ires). He allegedly sailed on Columbus's 1492 voyage and died at the hands of natives in Hispaniola. We do know that William was a real man, but it isn't clear that he was aboard one of Columbus's ships. His name appears on an early crew list, but the leading historian of

Christopher Columbus landing in the Americas, 1492

Columbus's crew, Alice Bache Gould, has deemed the list unreliable. Furthermore, she has found evidence that suggests Ayers was alive in Europe years after his alleged death in the New World.

The Irish in Colonial America

126. The Earliest Known Irish in America Certainly one of the earliest known Irishmen to set foot in the present-day United States was Richard Butler in the year 1584. Born in Clonmel, County Tipperary, in the 1560s, he traveled to England and found work as a page for Walter Raleigh, the future colonizer. He accompanied Raleigh's first expedition in 1584 that explored North Carolina's outer banks. Butler made a second voyage to the area in 1585 and spent several days exploring the territory with local Indians. It was this expedition that left behind the ill-fated settlement on Roanoke Island. Butler returned to Europe, where he took up privateering against Spanish and Portuguese ships. He was captured by the Spanish in 1592 and spent much of the rest of his life in a Spanish prison.

One of the men left by Butler on Roanoke Island was a fellow Irishman named Edward Nugent. Unfortunately, the only written reference we have to Nugent involves a particularly brutal incident. In his journal, Captain Ralph Lane wrote in 1586: "An Irishman serving me, one Edward Nugent, volunteered to kill Pemisapan, king of the Indians. We met him returning out of the woods with Pemisapan's head in his hands, and the Indians ceased their raids against the British camp." This and subsequent clashes between the colonists and local Indians provides the most likely explanation for the disappearance of the Roanoke settlement by 1590.

127. Sources of Early Immigration The Irish were among the earliest settlers in the European colonies that formed along the Atlantic coast in the 1600s. The great majority came as impoverished persons displaced by war, land seizure, and economic change. Some elected to go voluntarily, boldly striking out in search of new opportunities in the New World. Unable to afford the cost of passage, many signed on as indentured servants. Others were involuntary migrants—generally convicts, subversives, or the victims of upheavals brought on by the likes of Cromwell and William of Orange—sold into servitude and transported to the Americas. As trade between England and Ireland and the New World increased in the eighteenth century, so, too, would the rate of emigration from Ireland.

128. The Irish in Early Massachusetts Despite local hostility toward "heretics," Irish immigrants of many faiths found their way to Massachusetts in the early seventeenth century. Most came as indentured servants to work in the homes and on the farms of settlers in Plymouth Plantation and Massachusetts Bay Colony. A few Irish immigrants managed to become prominent members of society. George Downing, for example, arrived in Boston from Dublin in 1638 at the age of fourteen. He went on to graduate from Harvard College and marry the sister of Govenor John Winthrop.

129. Early Anti-Irish and Anti-Catholic Sentiment

As the number of Irish immigrants increased, many non-Irish colonists began to express anti-Irish hostility that originated in the Old World. In the 1650s, Richard Mather declared that the influx of Irish to Boston represented "a formidable attempt of Satan and his sons to unsettle us." In Virginia, Fr. Christopher A. Plunkett, a Capuchin friar born in Ireland, was imprisoned and exiled to Barbados along with several other priests by the colonial government from 1689 to 1690. In 1698, South Carolina levied a head tax on indentured servants from Ireland to discourage their immigration to the colony. In 1704, Maryland followed suit in order to "prevent the importing of too great a number of Irish Papists." In 1720, the government of Massachusetts expressed concern over the sharp rise in Irish immigration to the colony and announced that they would have to leave within seven months.

130. Ann Glover Hanged as a Witch

Along with many other Catholics in seventeenth-century Ireland, Ann "Goody" Glover was exiled to Barbados by Oliver Cromwell. After her husband's death, Glover came to Boston, Massachusetts, as a servant, around 1680. As an Irish Catholic widow who resisted conversion to Puritan ways, Glover was defenseless when her employer accused her of being a witch. Thrown in jail to await trial, Glover was interrogated by clergyman Cotton Mather. Although she spoke and understood English, "the court could have no answers from her, but in the Irish; which was her native language." Through a translator, she allegedly gave a confession, which should have prevented her execution. Nonetheless, Glover was hanged as a witch in 1688.

131. The Scotch-Irish

Starting in the later 1600s, migration from Ireland to America began to take on a recognizable pattern. While this migration to America included Irish Catholics, Anglicans, Quakers, and Baptists from every region of Ireland, from approximately 1680 to the Revolution, the overwhelming majority were Presbyterians from Ulster. They were the descendants of settlers brought in from the Scottish lowlands by James I to settle (and ideally pacify) confiscated lands in Ulster. By the end of the seventeenth century, they began moving to America to escape high taxes and soaring rents (known as "rack rents"). Between 1700 and 1820 they constituted 30 percent of all Europeans coming to America (50 percent between 1776 and 1820).

Drawn by the promise of free land, most Scotch-Irish headed for the western frontier. For the earliest arrivals, this meant the frontier of New Hampshire and Massachusetts. But poor farming and contentious relations with their eastern counterparts led many to move southward to western Pennsylvania by the 1720s and 1730s. As the number of Scotch-Irish arrivals continued to rise in the eighteenth century, they settled still farther to the south, all the way to Georgia. As they did, they established places like New Ireland (Maryland). These tough Irishmen played a crucial role in pushing westward settlement, a process that brought them into frequent conflict with Indians. Many prominent Americans, among them President Andrew Jackson and Davy Crockett, descended from Scotch-Irish settlers.

132. James Murray Writes Home

Like many an Irishman before him and since, James Murray of County Tyrone found America to his liking because of the combination of economic and political freedom it offered. In 1737, he took the time to write a letter home to his minister so that he might pass on the good word to his kin and friends:

> Read this letter, and look, and tell aw [all] the poor Folk of your Place, that god has opened a Door for their Deliverance; for here is ne [no] scant of Bread . . . Ye may get Lan [land] here for 10 pund a Hundred Acres for ever, and Ten Years Tell ye get the Money before they wull ask ye for it; and it is within 40 miles of this York upon a River Side that this Lan lies, so that ye may carry aw [all] the Guds in Boat to this York to sell, if ony [only] of you comes here. . . . Desire my Fether and Mether too, and my Three Sisters to come here . . . and I will pay their passage . . . I bless the Lord for my safe Journey here . . . this York is as big as twa [two] of Armagh. . . . There is servants comes here out of Ereland, and have served there [sic] time here, wha [who] are now Justices of the Piece.

133. Daniel Boone Daniel Boone (1734–1820), one of the most renowned American frontiersmen, was born in Pennsylvania to Quaker parents of Irish descent. He was an avid hunter, but is best known for exploring and settling Kentucky, despite resistance from the Indians. His first trip was in 1760 and by the mid-1770s he was working as an advance agent for the Transylvania Company. He helped build

Daniel Boone

the Wilderness Road, the principal route of westward U.S. migration between 1790 and 1840, and founded Boonesboro, Kentucky. He was a captain in the militia and served as a respected member of the Virginia Assembly. He settled in Missouri in 1779 and remained there until his death. His remains were returned to Kentucky twenty-five years later.

134. Indentured Servants Some Irish immigrants in this period arrived as skilled artisans. But for every skilled artisan or aspiring farmer, there were countless Irish who arrived in America as poor unskilled laborers. Unable to pay their passage, many signed contracts of indenture with ship captains, who in turn auctioned them off upon arrival in America. The contract bound the indentured servant to a term of service of four to seven years at the completion of which he or she received some land, money, or both. Some, like Daniel Dulany, were fortunate. He arrived in 1703, survived his indenture, studied law, rose to become a judge, attorney general, and a member of the colonial legislature and Governor's Council. Far too many others died before their term expired (especially if they landed in the disease-prone South), or survived to face a life of low-paid manual labor.

135. The Kellys on the Run The following advertisement appeared in the *Virginia Gazette* on May 16, 1777:

> RUN away from the Subscriber, in *Bedford* county on *Great Falling* River, an *Irish* Servant Man named MICHAEL KELLY, about five Feet five Inches high, with short black Hair, wears a cut brown Wig, a blue Broadcloth Coat, spotted Flannel Jacket, and a Pair of old patched Breeches. Also an *Irish* Servant Woman named MARGARET KELLY, Wife to the said *Michael.* She wore a blue Calimanco Gown and Petticoat. They both speak Irish, but neither of them are

known to speak English. I will give FIVE POUNDS on their being delivered to me, and FIFTY SHILINGS if they are secured in any Jail in this Colony, upon Information of the same given to WILLIAM HAYTH.

136. Notable Merchants and Entrepreneurs   Not all the Irish in colonial America arrived as penniless servants and stayed that way. By the mid-1700s prominent Irish merchants could be found in the major port cities. In New York, Charles Clinton, an immigrant from County Longford (and grandfather of De Witt Clinton) emerged as a prosperous merchant, as did Dominick Lynch, Robert Ross Waddell, Hugh Wallace, and Anthony Duane, father of James Duane (first mayor of New York City). In Philadelphia, wealthy merchants included George Bryan, Thomas FitzSimmons, Blair McClenachan, Stephen Moylan, and George Meade. William Patterson was a leading importer in Baltimore and helped found the Hibernian Society in 1803. William Hill established a successful ironworks in South Carolina.

137. Newspaper Men   One particular area where Irishmen achieved prominence was journalism. Hugh Gaine and Samuel Loudin established leading newspapers in New York, as did John Dunlop and Mathew Carey in Philadelphia. John Daly Burk established the *Polar Star*, Boston's first daily newspaper.

138. John Dunlop Extols American Opportunity   John Dunlop, publisher of the *Pennsylvania Packet*, wrote home to Ulster

Mathew Carey

to encourage more of his fellow Irishmen to come to America:

> The young men of Ireland who wish to be free and happy should leave it and come here as quickly as possible. There is no place in the world where a man meets so rich a reward for conduct and industry.

139. The Carrolls of Maryland   Without a doubt, the most prominent Irish Catholic family in colonial America was the Carroll family of Maryland. They descended from a once-prominent family, the O'Carrolls of the Barony of Ormond. The original Carroll to arrive in America was Charles Carroll, who immigrated to Maryland in 1688. He served briefly as the colony's attorney general, but England's Glorious Revolution soon led to a dismissal of Catholics from colonial offices. Charles' eldest son, Charles of Annapolis (1702–82), became a very wealthy landowner.

His son, Charles Carroll of Carrollton (1737–1832), went on to become one of the most well-known patriots of the Revolutionary era. He published pamphlets in 1773 decrying England's taxation policies, and in 1776 he proposed a resolution calling for colonial separation from England and her oppressive policies. Carroll became a member of the Continental Congress in July 1776, and was the first Roman Catholic to sign the Declaration of Independence. He was elected to the Constitutional Convention in 1787, and served as Maryland's U.S. Senator between 1789 and 1792. In 1828, he cofounded the Baltimore and Ohio Railroad and was said to be the wealthiest man in America at the time of his death in 1832.

John Carroll (1736–1815), cousin of Charles, became America's first Catholic bishop (see entry #511).

140. The First St. Patrick's Day Celebration   No one knows for sure when the first commemoration of St. Patrick's Day took place. One of the earliest references is to the establishment of the Charitable Irish Society, founded on St. Patrick's Day in Boston in 1737. Another early celebration took place in New York City in 1762, when an Irishman named John Marshall held a party in his house. Although little is known of Marshall's party, it is understood that his guests marched as a body to his house to mark St. Patrick's Day, thus forming an unofficial parade. The first recorded true parade took place in 1766 in New York, when local military units, including some Irish soldiers in the British army, marched at dawn from house to house of the leading Irish citizens of the city. Most celebrations of March 17, as indicated by John Marshall's example, were St. Patrick's Day dinners, hosted by individuals and benevolent organizations such as the Friendly Brothers of St. Patrick, the Knights of St. Patrick, and the St. Patrick's Society.

141. Early Irish Organizations in America
Beginning in the 1730s the Irish in America began to form fraternal and charitable organizations. Their purpose was twofold: to promote fraternity among the sons of Ireland living in the New World, and to provide charity to the least fortunate among them. The first recorded organization was the Charitable Irish Society, established on St. Patrick's Day 1737, in Boston. Its stated goal was "to aid unfortunate fellow countrymen, to cultivate a spirit of unity and harmony among all Irishmen in the Massachusetts colony and their descendents, and to advance their interests socially and morally." Other organizations include the Ancient and Most Benevolent Order of the Friendly Brothers of Saint Patrick, founded in New York in 1767, and the Society of the Friendly Sons of St. Patrick for the Relief of Emigrants from Ireland, founded in 1771 in Philadelphia. Significantly, most, if not all, of these organizations welcomed Irishmen regardless of their religion. Such differences would become important only in the nineteenth century.

142. Friendly Sons of St. Patrick The Friendly Sons of St. Patrick originated in Philadelphia on St. Patrick's Day 1771, when leading Irish businessmen came together to form an organization that provided fellowship for its members and charity for their less fortunate countrymen. When two members of the group relocated to New York City, they began the New York branch (1783), which remains active today.

The first members were natives of Ireland and their sons, mainly Protestant businessmen. They established traditions emphasizing their common Irish heritage that continue today, including the annual St. Patrick's Day Anniversary Dinner. However, the main activity of the group was to provide aid in the forms of money, food, shelter, and employment, to poor Irish immigrants. Members of the Friendly Sons have included U.S. Presidents George Washington, Theodore Roosevelt, and Richard Nixon, and New York mayors De Witt Clinton, James Duane, and William R. Grace.

Today, there are more than twenty Friendly Sons organizations across the country and their membership, now mostly Catholic, includes generations of Irish Americans far removed from the immigration experience. The St. Patrick's Day Anniversary Dinner continues to be the highlight of the year. The Friendly Sons also maintain their charitable focus, contributing funds to Irish American religious and community groups.

143. The Irish in Non-British Territories Many Irish came to North America in the service of Spain and France and settled in territories not yet under British control. One of the first on record is Irish-born Fr. Richard Arthur, sent to the Spanish town of St. Augustine in 1597. Nearly two hundred years later (1765), Irish-born Hugo O'Conor, a colonel in the Spanish army, was sent to Spain's New World holdings that became the states of Texas and Arizona. As the first Irish soldier to serve in the American West, O'Conor battled Apache and Comanche Indians and established the presidio and town of Tucson, Arizona. Similarly, Irish-born General Alexander O'Reilly was sent by Charles III in 1768 to restore Spanish authority after the Creole revolt that year. Philip Barry served as Spanish colonial governor of California from 1770 to 1775.

The Era of the American Revolution

144. Patrick Carr Falls in the Boston Massacre
An Irishman was among the first to shed his blood in the cause of American independence. Patrick Carr, an Irish-born journeyman leatherworker, was among the crowd fired upon by British troops on March 5, 1770. Carr died along with four others.

145. The Irish and the Declaration of Independence
Three of the fifty-six signers of the Declaration of Independence were Irish-born: James Smith and George Taylor, both of Pennsylvania, and Matthew Thornton of New Hampshire. Several others were of Irish origin. They include: Thomas Lynch, Thomas McKean, George Read, Edward Rutledge, and Charles Carroll (the only Catholic).

John Dunlop, the Irish-born publisher of the *Pennsylvania Packet,* had the honor of printing the first copy of the Declaration of Independence on July 4, 1776.

Charles Thomson (1729–1824), a former indentured servant from Ireland who went on to become a prosperous Philadelphia merchant, was secretary of the Continental Congress in 1776. In that capacity he was called upon to give the first reading of the Declaration of

Charles Carroll

Independence before Congress. He later had the duty of informing George Washington of his election as President.

146. George Washington Offers a Prayer of Thanks and Hope
George Washington offered this prayer to express gratitude for Ireland's support during the Revolution and the hope that Ireland might one day be free:

> Ireland, thou friend of my country in my country's most friendless days, much injured, much enduring land, accept this poor tribute from one who esteems thy worth, and mourns thy desolation. May the God of Heaven, in His justice and mercy, grant thee more prosperous fortunes and in His own good time, cause the sun of Freedom to shed its benign radiance on the Emerald Isle.

147. America's Revolution Inspires Ireland's Nationalists
The actions of American patriots, both in Independence Hall and on the fields of battle during the Revolution, inspired similar movements in France, Haiti, and Ireland. In the latter, Wolfe Tone's United Irishmen led a movement to establish an independent, democratic, and nonsectarian nation. Fired by the republican ideology of the American and French Revolutions, they hoped colonial Ireland would likewise throw off English colonialism and establish itself among the independent nations of the world. As Wolfe Tone wrote:

> I soon formed my theory . . . that to subvert the tyranny of our execrable government, to break the connection with England, the never-failing source of all our political evils, and to assert the independence of my country—these were my objects. To unite the whole people of Ireland, to abolish the memory of all past dissensions, and to substitute the com-

mon name of Irishman, in place of the denomination of Protestant, Catholic, and Dissenter—these were my means.

148. Shays' Rebellion Daniel Shays (1747–1825) was the descendant of Irish immigrants originally named Shea. In 1786, he led a rebellion of Massachusetts farmers against high taxes and imprisonment for debt. Similar rebellions took place in nearly all the colonies, but Shays' was considered the most serious. Massachusetts farmers were especially hard hit by bad harvests and declining prices and thus found the high taxes particularly onerous. Led by Shays, they took up arms and tried to seize an arsenal at Springfield. They also harassed politicians and merchants identified with the state government. The movement was eventually crushed by the state militia (Shays and the rebels were later pardoned), but it caused such alarm in the new nation that it gave momentum to the movement to abolish the Articles of Confederation and adopt a Constitution.

149. Irish Signers of the U.S. Constitution Meeting at a convention in Philadelphia in 1787, delegates from twelve of thirteen states (only Rhode Island sat it out) drafted the Constitution of the United States. Of the thirty-nine men who signed the document, four were Irish-born. They were Pierce Butler of South Carolina, Thomas FitzSimmons of Pennsylvania (one of two Catholic signers), James McHenry of Maryland, and William Paterson of New Jersey. Paterson played a particularly prominent role in the debates, as he was a lawyer with considerable political experience. Two other signers were sons of Irish immigrants—Daniel Carroll (the other Catholic signer) of Maryland and Richard Dobbs Spaight of North Carolina.

the nineteenth century

The Pre-Famine Irish

150. The '98ers Although many Irish came during the colonial period, the beginnings of recognizable and self-conscious Irish communities can be dated to 1798. The ill-fated rising of that year produced thousands of refugees to America, among them leaders like Daniel Clark, Samuel Parke, and John Binns in Philadelphia, and Dr. William James MacNevin, William Sampson, and Thomas Addis Emmet (brother of the legendary martyred nationalist Robert Emmet) in New York. Together they worked to develop a series of social, charitable, religious, and ethnic institutions dedicated to assisting their fledgling Irish communities, which grew rapidly after the end of the Napoleonic Wars in 1815.

151. The Alien and Sedition Acts In the 1790s, American public opinion was sharply divided over the French Revolution. Jeffersonians supported the Revolution, seeing it as an event in step with the spread of republican government begun in America in 1776. Those who identified with the Federalist Party, however, expressed horror at the radicalism and savagery of the revolution and therefore sided with England in its war with France; they likewise sided with England in its repression of the uprising of the United Irishmen (aided by France) in 1798.

That year, Federalists grew alarmed at the sudden influx of French and Irish refugees, whom they viewed as wild radicals. "If some means are not adopted to

William Sampson

prevent the indiscriminate admission of wild Irishmen and others to the right of suffrage," warned Federalist Harrison Otis Gray, "there will soon be an end to liberty & property." In response, the Federalist-controlled Congress passed the Alien and Sedition Acts. These were designed to discourage further French and Irish immigration by increasing the waiting period for naturalization from five to fourteen years, legalizing detention of subjects of enemy countries, allowing the expulsion of any "dangerous" alien, and by making it a crime to write or utter anything "with the intent to defame" the government. More than two dozen people were prosecuted under this last provision. The first was Irishman Matthew Lyon, a Vermont editor and politician who supported both radical republicanism and Thomas Jefferson.

The Acts were opposed by Jeffersonian Republicans, who won control of the federal government in 1800. Within two years, the Acts either expired or were repealed. Many historians point to this episode of Federalist-inspired anti-Irish hostility as the beginning of the Irish American identification with the Democratic Party.

152. The Earliest Irish in the West While large numbers of Irish immigrants settled in cities like Philadelphia and New York, several Irishmen and -women distinguished themselves in the early history of the West. Catherine O'Hare, for example, a native of Ulster, made history in 1802 when she bore, with the help of Indian midwives, the first known child of European descent west of the Rocky Mountains. One of the earliest contributors to the future city of Chicago was Irish-born John Whistler. In 1803, he oversaw the construction of Ft. Dearborn, and upon its completion served as its first commander. Joe Walker served as the first sheriff of Independence, Missouri, a town he helped found. He also surveyed the Santa Fe Trail and guided the first wagon train to California. Thomas Daugherty and Hugh Menaugh accompanied Zebulon Pike in 1806

during his exploration of the Rocky Mountains. Many of the best scouts in the early West were Irish.

153. Rising Immigration from Ireland Between the end of the American Revolution and the end of the War of 1812 (1783–1815), between 100,000 and 150,000 Irish immigrants landed in North America. Most were Ulster Presbyterians who came as farmers or artisans. Squeezed by high rents on their land and the collapse of the linen industry due to British free trade policy, more and more Irish looked to America as a place to begin anew. As economic conditions continued to worsen in Ireland, the numbers of immigrants soared. Upwards of one million Irish immigrants crossed the Atlantic between 1815 and 1845. Increasingly (especially after 1830), these immigrants were Catholics hailing from the south and west of Ireland. They were much poorer and brought fewer skills with them compared with their Ulster counterparts.

154. Liverpool–New York Trade One of the things making immigration to America in this period easier was the increased trade between Ireland and New York and Liverpool and New York. The growth in trade in the 1820s and 1830s encouraged emigration by lowering the cost of passenger travel. England, however, wanted to populate Canada rather than America with Irish immigrants and thus passed a series of Passenger Acts that made emigration to the latter far more expensive and inconvenient. For example, heavy surcharges increased the price of passage to New York to £4 to £5 versus just 15 shillings for transit to Canada. In addition, ships bound for Canada left from every Irish port, while most bound for America left from Liverpool. Still, limited opportunity in Canada led many an Irish family to book cheap passage to Canada and then walk to Boston. Such a trend accounts for the high percentage of Irish who settled in New England in the pre-Famine era.

155. John Doyle Observes John Doyle was part of the earlier pre-Famine immigration. He immigrated to America in the second decade of the nineteenth century and was among the many pre-Famine immigrants who arrived with some education, skills, and capital. In this letter of January 25, 1818, he confides to his wife that he is terribly homesick for Ireland, but at the same time upbeat about his prospects in his adopted homeland.

> As yet it's only natural I should feel lonesome in this country, ninety-nine out of every hundred who come to it are at first disappointed. . . . Still, it's a fine country and a much better place for a poor man than Ireland . . . and much as they grumble at first, after a while they never think of leaving it. . . . One thing I think is certain, that if emigrants knew beforehand what they have to suffer for about the first six months after leaving home in every respect, they would never come here. However, an enterprising man, desireous of advancing himself in the world, will despise everything for coming to this free country, where a man is allowed to thrive and flourish without having a penny taken out of his pocket by government; no visits from tax gatherers, constables or soldiers, everyone at liberty to act and speak as he likes, provided he does not hurt another . . .

156. The Formation of Poor Irish Enclaves In contrast to Doyle, more and more of the Irish who arrived in the 1830s and 1840s were poor, unskilled Catholics. Cast into rapidly expanding and industrializing American cities, these pre-Famine Irish Catholics found themselves forced to take the lowest-paid and hardest work. Unable to afford decent housing and seeking the comfort of fellow Irish immigrants, they crowded into run-down sections of East Coast cities like Boston and

Philadelphia and formed large Irish ghettos. Not surprisingly, rates of disease, crime, violence, and mortality among Irish immigrants rose to unprecedented levels. So, too, did nativism—the perception among native-born Americans that immigrants in general, and the Irish in particular, were a menace to American society.

Building Institutions

157. Creating a Support System To cope with the many stresses and strains associated with immigration and settlement in America, the emerging Irish communities in Boston, Philadelphia, New York, and elsewhere established networks of institutions that included newspapers, theaters, the emigrant aid societies, charity organizations, and fraternal societies. Catholic parishes with affiliated schools, orphanages, hospitals, and temperance societies likewise provided vital services and support for the newly arrived. (The Catholic parish is examined in detail in Part V: Religion.)

158. Irish Benevolent Societies Irish immigrants in the pre-Famine years established countless benevolent societies to bring together immigrants from Ireland and raise money for the poor. One of the first was the Hibernian Society of Charleston, South Carolina (1799). It was followed by the Hibernian Provident Society of New York (1801), Hibernian Society of Baltimore (1803), and Shamrock Friendly Association of New York (1816).

159. Irish Emigrant Aid Society To handle the problems of the growing number of poor Irish arriving in American port cities, many wealthy Irish merchants established Irish emigrant aid societies. One of the earliest was the Irish Emigrant Society opened in 1814 in New York to offer assistance to the newly arrived.

Because so many of the poor Irish were unable to leave the dangerous and unhealthful Eastern cities, emigrant societies often raised

Ticket to Irish Emigrant Aid Society ball

money to send them West. On one occasion, the Emigrant Society of New York petitioned Congress for a land grant in the West for the settlement of poor Irish immigrants. Opposition in Congress, and among Catholic clergymen who feared the Irish would lose their faith in the isolated wilds of the Midwest, ultimately doomed the project.

160. The First Irish Newspaper in America, THE SHAMROCK By 1810, the Irish community in New York had grown numerous enough to convince one exiled '98er, Thomas O'Conor, to begin publishing *The Shamrock*, or *Hibernian Chronicle*, the first Irish newspaper in America. Like *The Irish Echo* and other modern-day descendents, *The Shamrock* reported on events in Ireland and provided a public voice for the growing population of Irish in America, a feature increasingly important as anti-Irish sentiment began to rise.

161. The Ancient Order of Hibernians The Ancient Order of the Hibernians (AOH) originated with the rural secret societies of sixteenth-century Ireland. They had formed to protect Catholic interests against growing oppression. Among these early groups were the Defenders, whose motto, "Friendship, Unity, and True Christian Charity," eventually became the basis of the AOH motto, "Friendship, Unity, and Christian Charity." Little is known about these secret societies and their connection to one another, except that in the 1820s there existed in

England a group known as the St. Patrick's Fraternal Society. They were the ones who issued a charter in 1836 to a group of Irish immigrants in New York City. Meeting in St. James Church in Lower Manhattan, they established the first chapter of the AOH in America. A second soon opened in the coal-mining districts of Pennsylvania. It would be years before "Ancient Order of the Hibernians" became the accepted name.

The purpose of the AOH in America was similar to that in Ireland. In early nineteenth-century America, the Irish were the subject of much bigotry. The early chapters of the AOH were formed to preserve Irish culture, protect Church property, and provide assistance to Irish immigrants ("We Bury Our Dead and Visit Our Sick" went one motto). In the 1840s and 1850s the AOH was called upon frequently to protect Catholic churches from nativist mobs. (For more on anti-Catholic nativism, see entries #196, #220, #517, #524.)

162. Irish Theaters Like most nineteenth-century immigrant groups, the Irish established theaters. Irish immigrants flocked to them to see all manner of performances, from melodrama to song and dance. Often the productions were Irish or Irish American in theme, but not always. Most Irish theaters appealed to working-class Irish audiences, so the productions often dealt with immigration and urban life. One of the stock characters was the "stage Irishman," a lovable fool quick with a joke, ready to fight, sentimental about "dear old Ireland," and always searching for a drink. Over time, as an Irish middle class developed, the popularity of this stereotypical character declined in favor of more subtle humor by the likes of Harrigan and Hart.

Theaters, like saloons, were not simply expressions of Irish culture. They were also businesses. An Irish immigrant with a little money and a mix of luck and bravado could establish himself as a theater operator. His success depended on his ability to book popular talent and provide an attractive atmosphere. One of the earliest and most successful of these theater entrepreneurs was William Niblo. He purchased two theaters on Broadway in New York in the mid-1820s and reopened them in 1829 as Niblo's Garden. Combining beer gardens with performances, he became one of the city's most successful theater owners. Niblo's West Coast counterpart was Thomas Maguire, who rose from a hack driver in New York to become the owner of more than a dozen theaters in San Francisco.

163. Military Societies   One of the most popular forms of male fraternal activity in antebellum America was membership in a military society. Ostensibly formed to serve as units in the state militia, most military societies served mainly as social institutions. Meeting as often as once a week, they combined marching drills and shooting contests with drinking, eating, and singing. Most adopted flamboyant uniforms and heroic names.

Irish immigrants adapted readily to this practice, forming organizations like the Montgomery Guards, Hibernia Greens, and Irish Rifles in cities from Boston to New Orleans. They formed distinctly Irish units because they were usually denied membership in "American" companies. They also did so in response to rising anti-Irish violence. Conspiracy theorists often suggested the Irish were drilling in preparation to overthrow the American government for the pope and in the middle of the Know Nothing hysteria of the 1850s, the governor of Massachusetts disbanded several Irish units.

After the Civil War, the Irish took the tradition with them as they moved westward. Butte, Montana, had its Meagher Guards while Denver, Colorado, had several, including the Mitchel Guards. The high point of the year for most societies, apart from their annual banquet and contests, was the St. Patrick's Day Parade and, later in the nineteenth century, parades celebrating the Fourth of July.

164. The Saloon   Along with the Democratic Party and Catholic Church (and later the labor union), the saloon or tavern emerged as a central institution in Irish neighborhoods. This represented the perpetuation and adaptation of the Irish pub tradition in America. Gathering together for drink, storytelling, song, and, on occasion, plotting insurrection, was a tradition that went back centuries in Ireland. In the cities and towns of America, the saloon provided a place of refuge from the cruel world of poverty, discrimination, and sadness. Unfortunately, these were the very conditions that promoted excessive drinking, a curse found both in Ireland and America.

In addition to socializing, Irish saloons were important centers of political power. Saloonkeepers were businessmen (and women) and as such were important people in their communities. Often this translated into political power, at least on the local level (indeed, a popular joke said that the fastest way to break up a city council meeting was to burst in and say, "Pat, your saloon's on fire"). People in search of handouts, jobs, construction contracts, or favors frequently found them in the local saloon.

165. Thomas O'Connor Explains the Importance of the Saloon   In his compelling study of the Boston Irish, historian Thomas O'Connor explains the significance of the saloon in the Irish experience in America:

> In a country where they found themselves rejected and isolated, Irishmen looked upon the saloon as "the poor man's club," a natural transfer of the familiar pub that had always played such an important role in the social life of the Irish countryside. It was seen as one way of humanizing the cold, impersonal, and hostile urban environment in which the immigrants found themselves without work, without money, and without status. The saloon quickly became the social

center of most Irish neighborhoods. It was one of the few places where a poor, tired Irishman could go on his way home from work or job hunting, receive a warm welcome, rest his weary bones, forget about his problems, and experience a few hours of joy and laughter.

166. Volunteer Fire Companies Many Irishmen, like their American counterparts, joined volunteer fire companies. Like the military companies, these organizations were as much about socializing as they were about putting out fires. Members of these neighborhood companies often wore brightly colored uniforms and purchased fancy pumpers (which in some cases were only used for parades). Firemen were considered heroic figures, much like professional athletes today. Dozens of popular songs were written about them and many a Bowery play centered on the character known as "The Mose," an Irish fireman of Bunyonesque size and ability. One of the most popular series pro-duced by printmakers Currier and Ives was called *The Life of the Fireman.*

Yet fire companies were considerably more rough and tumble than those colorful portraits suggest. Since fires were public spectacles, fire companies vied for the honor of putting them out. If two companies arrived simultaneously at the scene of a fire, it was customary for them to brawl for control of the hydrant (while the building continued to burn). Some companies encouraged teenagers and young men who hoped to join the company to ambush rival companies on their way to put out fires, or to get to the fire first and physically seize control of the hydrant until the pumper arrived.

Volunteer fire fighting was an excellent way to make a name for oneself, and as a consequence many Irishmen joined as a means of launching a career in politics. Eight New York City mayors, for example, began their career in politics with service as volunteer firemen.

Because of the association between volunteer fire companies and machine politics, not to mention brawling and carousing, most cities professionalized their fire fighting systems in the 1860s.

167. The St. Patrick's Day Parade Although the practice of parading on St. Patrick's Day dates back to the colonial period, it was only in the mid-nineteenth century that the parade as we know it

New York City's
St. Patrick's Day
Parade, 1870

today took form. This occurred not simply because there were more Irish immigrants coming to America due to the Famine, but also because they faced a sharp rise in anti-Irish bigotry by those convinced they would never make good Americans. More than ever, the annual parade on March 17 would be a mixture of ethnic pride and immigrant defiance. By the 1850s, parades in cities like New York featured bands, county societies, and charitable organizations.

The Arrival of the Famine Irish

[See also the section on the Famine in Part I]

168. News of the Potato Crop Failure Arrives The earliest reports of agricultural distress in Ireland came in short notices in American newspapers. Among the first such reports was the following that appeared in the *New York Tribune* on October 4, 1845:

> We regret to have to state that we have had communications from more than one well-informed correspondent, announcing of the appearance of what is called "cholera" in the potatoes in Ireland, especially in the north. In one instance the party had been digging potatoes—the finest he had ever seen—from a particular field . . . up to Monday last. On digging in the same [field] on Tuesday he found the tubers unfit for the use of man or beast. We are most anxious to receive information as to the state of the potato crop in all parts, for the purpose either of allaying unnecessary alarm, or giving timely warning.

169. John Fraser Tells His Brother of the Famine While many of the Irish in America learned of the disaster unfolding in Ireland through newspapers, many received firsthand accounts in letters from friends and family. One such example is the following letter written in 1847 by John Fraser to his brother Fitzgerald Fraser in New York:

> My dear brother I suppose you have heard of the very great failure of Ireland[.] you cannot compare it to anything more properly than the seize of Jerusalem people are dying so fast with perfect hunger that we cannot attend to see them perfectly intered [sic][.] the crops failing in Ireland this season has left it in the greatest distress.

170. The Transatlantic Journey The Famine refugees who managed to get to port cities like Cobh boarded all manner of vessels headed for American and Canadian ports. Many of the ships were hastily converted cargo vessels that offered their passengers only minimal facilities. Conditions belowdecks were often abysmal and the provision of food and clean water inconsistent, leading to high rates of disease and death. Under the best of circumstances, an average transatlantic trip might take thirty days. In many cases, bad weather and poor seamanship led to trips as long as sixty days.

171. "Coffin Ships" Because of the high death rates on the transatlantic voyages, many of the vessels that carried Irish Famine refugees to the Americas were simply known as "coffin ships." During the Famine's worst year—Black '47—approximately 20,000 out of 100,000 emigrants perished at sea. Most were carried away by the diseases that ran freely in the reeking holds of the ships. Dr. J. Custis, a physician who traveled aboard six Famine ships, wrote that although he had witnessed the devastation of the Famine in the workhouses of Ireland, "it was not half so shocking as what I subsequently witnessed on board the very first emigrant ship I ever sailed on." As one priest observed, "it would be better to spend one's entire life in a hospital than to spend just a few hours in the hold of one of these vessels."

One notable exception to this saga of terrible suffering is the story of the *Jeanie Johnston.* Incredibly, it never lost a passenger or crewmember—either to disease or accident at sea—during its many voyages between 1848 and 1858 from Tralee (an area that eventually lost half its population during the Famine) to ports in America and Canada. Most likely this was due its humane captain and the owner's decision (rare among Famine-era ships) to have a doctor on board. A full-size replica of the *Jeanie Johnston,* completed in 2001 in Blennerville near Tralee, County Kerry, now serves as a working sailing vessel and floating museum.

172. Grosse Ille Even if Irish Famine refugees somehow managed to survive the perilous twenty-five- to fifty-day voyage to North America, thousands perished in port hospitals and quarantine stations. The most notorious of the latter was Grosse Ille, a quarantine station and makeshift hospital on an island in the St. Lawrence River near Quebec. Beginning in the spring of 1847, thousands of sick and weakened Famine immigrants began to arrive, and by year's end more than seventeen thousand of them lay buried in mass graves.

173. Shipwrecks Disease was not the only threat to human life aboard the coffin ships. Many Irish emigrants died in the more than sixty shipwrecks which occurred during the Famine years. The *Exmouth,* for example, foundered in 1847 just off the coast of Scotland, taking with it all but three of its 251 passengers. A few months later, the *St. John* fared only slightly better, losing at least ninety-nine passengers when it smashed on the rocks near Cohasset, Massachusetts. Hundreds came to see the wreck, including Henry David Thoreau. "I sought many marble feet and matted heads as the cloths were raised," he wrote, "and one livid, swollen and mangled body of a drowned girl,—

who probably had intended to go out to [domestic] service in some American family."

174. Heartless Crews On top of disease and disaster, immigrants faced still a third threat: abuse and mistreatment by callous crewmen. This took many forms, from overcrowding to violence, and occurred mainly on the shorter trips from Ireland to England. The worst incident occurred aboard the steamer *Londonderry* in the winter of 1848. Loaded with cargo and 174 immigrant passengers, the ship encountered a storm just off the coast of Donegal. Though most of the passengers were expected to make the journey on deck, the captain ordered them herded into one of the ship's three cabins. The next morning brought to light a horrifying scene: thirty-one women, twenty-three men, and eighteen children had been crushed or suffocated to death. The jury that found the captain and crew guilty of manslaughter noted that the cattle aboard the ship had received far more humane treatment than the people.

175. Castle Garden When America thinks of immigration, two images immediately spring to mind: the Statue of Liberty and Ellis Island. This is hardly surprising, given the fact that upwards of 16 million immigrants passed the Statue as they entered New York Harbor on their way to the inspection station at Ellis Island. One was surely a symbol of hope, the other a place of dread. Yet for the great majority of the millions of Irish who came to America, neither Lady Liberty nor Ellis Island played a role in their experience. The reason is simple enough: Most Irish immigrants arrived before the Statue (1886) and Ellis (1892) were built. The great symbol of Irish migration to America stands only a half mile away from these landmarks at the tip of Manhattan Island: Castle Garden.

Originally constructed in 1811 as a fort named Castle Clinton (named in honor of Mayor De Witt Clinton, a descendent of Irish immigrants from County Longford), it was converted

Castle Garden

in the 1820s into a public venue for celebrations, exhibitions, and entertainment. Thousands of New Yorkers routinely thronged to the Castle for gala welcoming ceremonies for arriving dignitaries—from President Andrew Jackson in the 1830s to Irish patriot Thomas Francis Meagher in the 1850s. By the mid-1840s the popularity of the site had grown such that a six-thousand-seat opera house named Castle Garden was constructed over the fort. In 1855, Castle Garden abruptly commenced its third unique historical phase, that of immigrant receiving center. Over the next thirty-five years more than eight million foreign arrivals were processed there (1.8 million Irish), a total second only to its successor, Ellis Island.

176. An Irish Priest Observes the "Runners"
Two things distinguished Castle Garden (and its counterparts in Boston, Philadelphia, Baltimore, and elsewhere) from Ellis Island. First, there was no rigorous inspection regimen (though immigrants were given quick health checks during periodic epidemic scares). Second, there were no measures taken to protect newly arrived immigrants from the wily con men who prowled Lower Manhattan in search of easy prey. Sadly, these men used their ethnic credentials—a good Irish accent, or better still, the ability to speak Irish—to ensnare their fellow Hibernians. As one Irish priest observed in the 1850s:

> The moment he landed, his luggage was pounced upon by two runners, one seizing the box of tools, the other confiscating the clothes. The future American citizen assured his obliging friends that he was quite capable of carrying his own luggage; but no, they should relieve him—the stranger, and guest of the

Republic—of that trouble. Each was in the interest of a different boarding-house, and each insisted that the young Irishman with the red head should go with him.... Not being able to oblige both gentlemen, he could oblige only one; and as the tools were more valuable than the clothes, he followed in the path of the gentleman who had secured that portion of the "plunder" ... the two gentlemen wore very pronounced green neck-ties, and spoke with a richness of accent that denoted special if not conscientious cultivation; and on his (the Irishman's) arrival at the boarding-house, he was cheered with the announcement that its proprietor was from "the ould country," and loved every sod of it, God bless it!

177. To the Cities As the great influx of Irish immigrants unfolded, many commentators searched for an explanation as to why an ostensibly rural people chose to remain in America's seaboard cities in such great numbers. Why did they not forgo the dreary, overcrowded slums in the East for the more healthful and economically promising regions in the Midwest and West? Some did, according to the editor of the *Irish-American.* "The pith and marrow of Ireland," he commented in 1849, "averaging between 100 and 5,000 dollars per family, have arrived within the past two years, in our seaboard cities. These emigrants do not stop in cities to spend their money and fool away their time. They go directly into the interior to seek out the best location as farmers, traders, and so forth." Other observers suggested that most Irish had no choice but to remain in the city. "Irish emigrants of the peasant and laboring class were generally poor," noted a visitor from Ireland in 1855, "and after defraying their first expenses on landing had but little left to enable them to push their way into the country in search of such em-ployment as was best suited to their knowledge and capacity."

It should also be pointed out that even if they had the resources, many Irish were unsuited for the kind of commercial farming found in America. Most Irish had been subsistence farmers where the cultivation of the potato required only a small plot of land and minimal agricultural knowledge or skill. By contrast, farming in America took place on relatively huge tracts of land (the Homestead Act of 1862 granted farmers 160 acres), required extensive knowledge of agrarian science, and was rapidly becoming commercialized and linked to Eastern markets.

Several historians offer a more glib explanation for the lack of Irish farmers in America: Because the land in Ireland had cursed them, they rejected the land in America.

Whatever the reason—and it's most likely a combination of all these factors—the end result was that the Irish immigrant experience in America was a fundamentally urban one. Whether by default or by conscious choice, the typical Irish immigrant settled in cities large and small. There they found not only jobs but also concentrations of other Irish immigrants and institutions like the Catholic Church and a political machine that eased their struggle.

178. How Many Came?

DECADE	NUMBER	% OF TOTAL IMMIGR.
1820s	54,338	35.8
1830s	207,381	34.6
1840s	780,719	45.6
1850s	914,119	35.2

Source: Roger Daniels, *Coming to America.*

The Struggle to Survive

179. A Warning to Would-Be Immigrants In 1849 the Irish Emigrant Society of New York published an "Address to the People of Ireland" warning them not to believe the wild tales of easy fortunes to be had in America:

> We desire, preliminarily, to caution you against entertaining any fantastic idea, such as that magnificence, ease, and health, are universally enjoyed in this country. . . . It is natural for persons who have adventured to leave home and to seek their fortunes in a foreign and distant country, to give highly coloured accounts of a success, which in reality, has been but the obtaining of a laborious employment; . . .

180. Little Irelands Everywhere the Irish settled, whether in huge cities like Boston and New York, or in factory towns like Lowell and Buffalo, they created ghettos often referred to by outsiders as "Irishtown," "Little Ireland," or "Little Dublin." Visitors to these neighborhoods frequently commented on how Irish they were in sound and ap-

pearance. "There are portions of New York," noted one visitor in 1860, ". . . where the population is as thoroughly Irish as in Dublin or Cork."

The Irish formed these ethnic ghettos partly out of choice. Living among their own kind provided social networks, job opportunities, churches, and charitable institutions. Yet "Little Irelands" were also as much a product of prejudice and poverty as they were ethnic affinity. Simply put, between their poverty and American hostility, the Irish were relegated to a few neighborhoods, usually near industrial sites and characterized by substandard housing and the lack of urban services like running water and regular street cleaning.

181. The Five Points Probably the most infamous Irish slum in America evolved in New York City—the Five Points. Named for a curious five-cornered intersection formed by the joining of three streets in Lower Manhattan, it achieved an international reputation by the 1840s as a neighborhood racked by poverty, crime, drunkenness, rioting, and disease.

A recent archaeological excavation in the Five Points area has called into question this portrait of unrelieved squalor and violence. Researchers have found abundant evidence of family life and hard work. These findings don't do away with the reality of the area's problems, but they do remind us that amid the troubles of urban life, residents struggled to live decent lives and care for their families. They also remind us that those who wrote about places like Five Points were more often than

Five Points

not predisposed to view the Irish as a backward, lazy, and violent people.

182. Charles Dickens Observes The one man who did the most to publicize and sensationalize the Five Points was Charles Dickens. During his tour of America in 1842, he stopped in New York. There, he was shown the splendor and wealth of Broadway. But he insisted on seeing the other side of New York life, and so with a police escort he toured the Five Points. His observations appeared in the book he wrote about his travels entitled *American Notes* (1842):

> There is one quarter, commonly called the Five Points, which in respect of filth and wretchedness, may be safely backed against Seven Dials, or any other part of famed St. Giles [a London slum] . . . These narrow ways, diverging to the right and left, and reeking everywhere with dirt and filth. Such lives as are led here, bear the same fruits here as elsewhere. The coarse and bloated faces at the doors, have counterparts at home, and all the wide world over. Debauchery has made the very houses prematurely old. See how the rotten beams are tumbling down, and how the patched and broken windows seem to scowl dimly, like eyes that have been hurt in drunken frays. Many of those pigs live here. Do they ever wonder why their masters walk upright in lieu of going on all-fours? and why they talk instead of grunting?

183. Pervasive Poverty Five Points was by no means the only scene of Irish suffering in America. No matter where they settled, large numbers of Famine-era Irish immigrants lived in poverty. This fact is borne out in the numbers of Irish turning up in poorhouses. In New York City, Irish immigrants accounted for 63 percent of

poorhouse admissions in 1855. In San Francisco from 1870 to 1900, the Irish made up 13 percent of the total population but constituted 35 percent of the admissions to the municipal almshouse.

The chief reason for Irish immigrant poverty was the lack of useful skills. Whereas only 28 percent of Irish immigrants arriving in 1826 were unskilled laborers, the number hit 60 percent in the 1830s and kept rising. Owning little or no land in Ireland, many arrived with little more than the clothes on their backs, having spent everything on passage. Doubtless, they possessed many skills, just not the kind that were in demand in an urban economy. (See also Work, Business, and Innovation in Part IX.)

184. Crime Anti-Irish sentiment was also inflamed by the prevalence of crime and disorder in Irish neighborhoods. In New York City, for example, 55 percent of those arrested in the 1850s were born in Ireland (the Irish constituted 25 percent of the population). One cannot attribute this to anti-Irish prejudice, given that 27 percent of the city's police force were Irish-born. Street gangs bearing such colorful names as the Plug Uglies, Kerryonians, and Whyos emerged at this time and were predominantly of Irish background. The story was much the same in Boston, Buffalo, Philadelphia, and New Orleans. Few Americans at the time were willing to see a connection between the extreme poverty and poor treatment of the Irish and the disproportionately high rate of crime and disorder among them. Instead, they attributed criminality and violence to the flawed Irish character.

185. Mental Strain Not surprisingly, the stresses and strains of adjusting to the harsh life in American cities led many Irish immigrants and their descendants to develop high rates of mental illness. Three out of four admissions to New York's Bellevue insane asylum in the 1850s were foreign-born and two thirds of them were Irish. The numbers in San Francisco for the period

1870 to 1900 paint a similar picture: Even though the Irish were just 13 percent of the city's total population, they accounted for 31 percent of mental illness admissions. The precise causes are hard to determine, but most experts point to the trauma of the Famine, grinding poverty, family strain, discrimination, and alcohol abuse as the key contributing factors.

186. The Problem of Alcohol Like their German counterparts, Irish immigrants brought with them to America a culture in which drinking was firmly rooted. For centuries they had equated drinking with socializing, celebrating, and mourning. Thus, when they arrived in American cities, Irish immigrants quickly established saloons and taverns. In Boston, for example, the number of licensed liquor dealers jumped from 850 in 1846 to 1,200 in 1849. Most of the new licensees were Irish. Unfortunately, excessive drinking that had long been a scourge in Ireland arguably grew worse in the harsh environment of the New World.

Part of the reason for the Irish trouble with alcohol lies not so much in *how much* the Irish consumed, but *how* they consumed it. Studies show that Italian immigrants drank the same amount as the Irish, but experienced significantly lower rates of alcoholism. The reason? Italians consumed their alcohol (mostly wine) as part of a meal, mainly in their home with friends and family. By contrast, the Irish consumed alcohol as recreation, more often than not in a drinking establishment separate from the home. Drinking in the male preserve of the tavern or saloon linked alcohol consumption to images of manliness and strength, a trend that promoted excessive consumption.

187. Fr. Theobold Mathew Fr. Theobold Mathew, the "Great Apostle of Temperance," founded the Cork Total Abstinence Society in 1838 to promote his antialcohol crusade. Although not particularly charismatic, the Capuchin friar became a national sensation, staging camp revival meetings that drew tens of thousands. His message was a mixture of Catholic piety, Protestant-style self-improvement, and strident nationalism (one of his slogans was "Ireland sober is Ireland free"). By 1840 the Society claimed that more than three million people—nearly half the population of Ireland—had "taken the pledge" to abstain from alcohol for life. Whiskey production in Ireland fell by more than 50 percent from the mid-1830s to the mid-1840s.

However, the rapid growth of the Society was followed by an equally rapid decline beginning in 1842. The reasons for this decline included Mathew's financial struggles, his shaky relationship with his church (most priests opposed his absolutism on the issue of drink), and the Famine, not to mention the deeply rooted tradition of drink in Irish culture. Fr. Mathew proved that it was relatively easy to get millions to take the pledge but quite another thing to get them to stick to it.

In 1849, Mathew traveled to America and spent two years spreading his message among the Irish there. He returned to Ireland in 1851 and died in 1856. By that time, Ireland's consumption of alcohol had returned to its level of the mid-

Fr. Theobold Mathew

1830s. Yet Fr. Mathew did succeed in establishing a total abstinence tradition in Ireland, which although a decided minority position, continues to this day.

188. Mortality Given these many stresses and strains faced by Irish immigrants in the mid-nineteenth century, it is not surprising to discover that Irish men tended to die at early ages. It soon became a truism to say one rarely saw a "gray-haired Irishman." This helps to explain why the strong Irish widow became such a fixture in Irish American life (and fiction). In his book on the Boston Irish, Thomas O'Connor noted that virtually all of the city's leading Irish politicians "lost their fathers at an early age and dropped out of school to earn money at menial jobs to help their working mothers keep the family together."

189. Rioting The incidence of rioting in America surged in the 1830s and more often than not, it seemed, the Irish were involved. On many occasions they were the victims of mob violence, as in Philadelphia's so-called Bible Riots of 1844 or the burning of a Marine Hospital (that housed sick immigrants, mostly Irish) on Staten Island in New York in 1858. At least as often, however, the Irish took a central role in the rioting. When abolitionists held rallies in the 1830s and 1840s, for example, they were frequently attacked by mobs of angry Irishmen who feared labor competition with free blacks. Clashes on July 12, the day Protestant Irish Orange parades took place, became annual events in cities like New York. The worst riot involving the Irish (indeed, the worst in all of American history) was the Draft Riot of 1863. The association of the Irish with rioting became so strong by mid-century that paving stones, often pulled up and hurled during riots, came to be known as "Irish confetti."

Explanations for the Irish penchant for rioting are varied. One reason is that urban rioting in general became more common in the antebellum period, a trend driven at least in part by sharpening class differences. In addition, the Irish brought with them to America a tradition of rural violence, sometimes called Whiteboyism, that legitimized extralegal acts of justice and retribution. Historians also point to the extreme poverty and discrimination experienced by Irish immigrants as a factor contributing to episodes of explosive rage, an explanation quite similar to the one put forth to explain rioting by African Americans in the 1960s and 1970s.

190. The Draft Riots The worst incident associated with the Irish was the New York City Draft Riots that occurred in July 1863. The poor performance of the Union Army and the unanticipated carnage produced by the war left the Lincoln administration desperate for soldiers. In March 1862, Congress authorized the first military draft in U.S. history. All male citizens (and immigrants who had applied for citizenship) aged twenty to forty-five were eligible to be drafted into the Union Army.

The draft proved to be extremely unpopular, especially among the urban poor, large numbers of whom were Irish. Many had been willing to fight when the war was simply about restoring the Union. But Lincoln's announcement of the Emancipation Proclamation in January had fundamentally changed the goals of the war. Working-class Irish in New York and other Northern cities had long been told by Democratic politicians that the greatest threat to their livelihoods (such as they were) was the abolition of slavery. It would result, they were told, in ex-slaves flooding Northern labor markets to compete with the poor Irish. Adding to their discontent was the fact that wealthy men could avoid serving in the army by paying a "commutation fee" of three hundred dollars (the annual wage earned by laborers) to the government, or by hiring a substitute to serve in their place. More and more, they argued, it was becoming "a rich man's war and a poor man's fight."

On Monday July 13, 1863, mobs of work-

The New York City Draft Riots, 1863

ers—mostly Irish—registered their opposition to the draft by tearing up New York City for four days. Although they focused much of their anger against symbols of the war like draft offices and institutions associated with the Republican Party, the rioters also assaulted African Americans, killing at least eleven.

191. HARPER'S WEEKLY Offers Some Perspective   It is important to remember that far more Irish Americans fought and died for the Union cause than participated in the riot. And when it came time to suppress the violence, Irish Americans played a leading role. As *Harper's Weekly,* a journal rarely friendly to the Irish, put it:

> It must be remembered in palliation of the disgrace which, as Archbishop Hughes says, the riots of last week have heaped upon the Irish name, that in many wards of the city, the Irish were during the late riot staunch friends of law and order; that Irishmen helped to

rescue the colored orphans in the asylum from the hands of the rioters; that a large proportion of the police, who behaved throughout the riot with the most exemplary gallantry, are Irishmen; that the Roman Catholic priesthood to a man used their influence on the side of the law; and that perhaps the most scathing rebuke administered to the riot was written by an Irishman—James T. Brady.

192. Relations with African Americans   The racial dimension of the Draft Riots, as well as many less spectacular incidents of antiblack violence by the Irish, indicate the existence of a high level of racism. Yet the relationship between Irish and black was complex to say the least. On the one hand, many Irish Americans, especially those living in large urban centers of the North, developed virulent antiblack sentiments. This occurred for several reasons. First, the Irish viewed black workers as competitors for low-paid work as laborers and domestic servants. As if to emphasize this perception, on several occasions in the 1840s and 1850s, factory owners and shipyard operators used free blacks as replacement workers during strikes by Irish workers. Second, the Irish flocked to the Democratic Party, which in the antebellum era was the party of the slave South. Democratic politicians and their newspapers took every opportunity to emphasize the inferiority of the slave and to depict abolitionists as godless radicals bent on bringing about social revolution.

Some historians, most notably Noel Ignatiev in his provocative book *How the Irish Became White,* have argued that adopting antiblack racism allowed the Irish to gain admittance into American society (albeit at the bottom). While his thesis is too simplistic (the Irish would be considered a lesser "race" into the twentieth century), its general conclusion is persuasive.

On the other hand, there were many significant positive aspects to the Irish and African American relationship. For one thing, as the two poorest and least liked groups, Irish and blacks frequently shared the same overcrowded neighborhoods. Not surprisingly, many cases of intermarriage between African American men and Irish women resulted. Recent research into music and dance have revealed a great deal of borrowing and blending of Irish and African styles and traditions.

193. Daniel O'Connell as Abolitionist Catholic Ireland's "Liberator" did not confine his condemnation of oppression to his native land. Active in the British and Irish antislavery movements and a friend of abolitionist William Lloyd Garrison, he drew a clear parallel between the enslavement of Africans in America and the oppression of his fellow Catholics in Ireland. While this view drew praise in Ireland, it was received rather coldly by the Irish in America, where the typical Irish immigrant looked upon abolitionism as a three-headed evil: First, they saw abolitionists as a hopelessly godless lot, enthused not only by abolition, but also free love, temperance, and women's

Daniel O'Connell

rights. Second, they feared that emancipation would mean labor competition with millions of freedmen. Third, Irish immigrants learned all too quickly the basics of American racist attitudes toward Africans.

Despite these formidable problems, O'Connell vowed to convert his Irish brethren in America to his way of thinking. In 1840, he joined seventy thousand Irishmen in signing "An Address of the People of Ireland to Their Countrymen in America." Unfortunately, despite great efforts by abolitionists to stir up popular support, the address fell on deaf ears. O'Connell, the Irish in America said, did not understand their adopted country and should focus on the troubles still plaguing his native land. For his part, O'Connell refused to retreat from his staunch abolitionism. "My sympathy is not confined to the narrow limits of my own green Ireland. My spirit walks abroad upon sea and land, and wherever there is oppression, I hate the oppressor . . ."

194. Frederick Douglass Voices His Frustration No abolitionist was more famous than Frederick Douglass. An escaped slave and superb orator, he traveled throughout the North as a living example of the African American quest for freedom. Like Daniel O'Connell (whom he met on a visit to Ireland in 1845), he was frustrated by the speed with which racist ideology infected the minds of Irish immigrants. He gave voice to what Ignatiev described as the process by which "an oppressed race in Ireland became part of an oppressing race in America." That is, despite the fact that both groups suffered from extreme exploitation and discrimination, the Irish possessed the one thing that African Americans did not: white skin.

Perhaps no class of our fellow citizens has carried this prejudice against color to a point more extreme and dangerous than have our Catholic Irish fellow citizens, and no people on the face of the earth have been more relentlessly persecuted and oppressed on account of race and religion than have this same Irish people. The Irish who, at home, readily sympathize with the oppressed everywhere, are instantly taught when they step upon our soil to hate and despise the Negro. They are taught that he eats the bread that belongs to them. . . .

The Irish-American will one day find out this mistake . . . but for the present we are the sufferers. Every hour sees us elbowed out of some employment to make room for some newly arrived immigrant from the Emerald Isle, whose hunger and color entitle him to special favor . . . a ceaseless enmity with the Irish is excited against us.

195. A British Historian Offers a Solution

Distressed over the poor relations existing between the United States and Great Britain, British historian Edward A. Freeman argued that the slavery controversy and Irish nationalists were to blame. He offered the following solution: "[T]he best remedy for whatever was amiss [between the U.S. and Britain] would be if every Irishman should kill a negro and be hanged for it."

Nativism, or Anti-Immigrant Sentiment

196. Sources of Anti-Irish Nativism

Nativism, or the organized hostility toward an immigrant group, is not simply a product of racism, bigotry, and intolerance. Americans in the mid-nineteenth century (and periodically thereafter) succumbed to nativism for the following reasons:

- Religious differences: The Irish were Catholics in a self-consciously Protestant nation. Catholicism left them loyal to the pope and subject to priestly manipulation, thus making them unfit citizens in a republic.
- Poverty: The Irish, understood to be lazy and thriftless, filled the slums of America's cities, merely adding to a growing problem of poverty.
- Crime: The Irish, understood to be prone to violence and lawlessness, filled America's jails.
- Drink: The Irish, whose culture considered drink a central part of social life, came to a nation in the midst of a great temperance crusade.
- Labor competition: The Irish, because they lived in poverty, were willing to work for less than native-born Americans and thus lower the latter's wages and steal their jobs.
- Racism: The Irish were ape-like, non-white, semihumans.

197. The Know Nothings

Fearing that the growing numbers of Irish and German immigrants posed a threat to the nation's economic and political security as well as cultural and religious identity, native-born Americans formed the secret Order of the Star-Spangled Banner in New York City in 1849; it soon spread to most other major American cities. Members were called "Know Nothings" because when asked about the organization, they maintained secrecy by saying "I know nothing." In the 1850s, as its membership and strength increased, the organization became more open and took as its official name, the American Party. It stood for sharply reduced immigration, prevention of voting and officeholding by the foreign-born, and an increase in the residency requirement for citizenship from five to twenty-one years.

In the early 1850s, as the two main political

parties began to split over the issue of slavery, the Know Nothing Party grew more prominent. Its candidates won many seats in state and local elections in 1852. Two years later, in the wake of the controversial Kansas-Nebraska Act, the Know Nothing Party gained additional adherents, winning control of the state legislature and governorship in Massachusetts and sending more than forty representatives to Congress.

But by 1856, the American Party was in steep decline. Like the Democrats and Whigs, it split over the slavery issue and was supplanted by another upstart political organization called the Republican Party. Its presidential candidate Millard Fillmore carried only Maryland in the 1856 election, while congressional strength dropped to twelve representatives.

198. Incidents of Anti-Irish Violence
Acts of violence against Irish immigrants can be traced at least as far back as the early 1800s, but they became more frequent and more violent as Irish Catholic immigration increased in the 1820s and 1830s. Anti–Irish Catholic riots broke out in Philadelphia in April 1822 and 1844, and in Boston in 1829. Mobs burned St. Mary's Church in New York in 1831 and an Ursuline convent in Charlestown (just outside of Boston) in 1834. Countless incidents like this frequently occurred on a smaller scale wherever the Irish were found in significant numbers. (For more specifics on some of these incidents, see entries #521 and #522.)

The Irish Out West

199. The West Was Best
Although the Irish who headed West did their share of suffering and dying, in general they fared better than their counterparts in the East. Historians cite several reasons for this fact, among them that western towns:

1. offered more opportunity for upward mobility for the unskilled compared to the industrial east;

2. lacked the powerful institutions like the Catholic Church and political machines that tended to delay assimilation;

3. lacked an entrenched native-born class capable of discriminating against them.

200. The Gold Rush
When word of the 1849 California gold strike arrived in the East, Irish Americans joined the tens of thousands who headed West in search of riches. Most ended up scraping by in the tough mining camps, but a few Irish managed to seize the opportunities presented. David C. Broderick (1820–59), for example, was born in Washington, D.C., moved to New York City when he was fourteen, and soon lost both his parents. Ambitious, he opened a saloon and soon became involved in Tammany Hall politics. When news of the gold strike reached him in 1849, he headed for California, where he made a small fortune in coining the metal. He reentered politics and gained election to the state senate, and earned a reputation as a major figure in the state's Democratic Party. Sadly, he died in the last legal duel in California.

John Conness (1821–1909) was born in Galway and came to the U.S. when he was twelve. Like Broderick, he was working in New York City when news of the gold strike arrived. He headed for San Francisco and after a try at mining, turned to selling dry goods to miners. He later went on to a political career in the California state assembly (1853–61) and United States Senate (1863–69).

David Broderick

201. Colonization Schemes Many leaders of the Irish communities in the Eastern cities advocated sending Irish immigrants to settle on Western lands. They hoped this would alleviate the dreadful conditions of the Irish slums and provide Irish immigrants, most of whom had lived as farmers in Ireland, a chance to take up farming again. James Shields, the future senator from three states, for example, founded the Irish colony of Shieldsville, Minnesota, in 1857, while General John O'Neill planted O'Neill, Nebraska, in 1872.

But most advocates of colonization schemes ran into three formidable obstacles. First, most of the Catholic clergy were staunchly opposed to such proposals. They feared the immigrants would lose their Catholic faith once set on isolated Western farms. This opposition receded (although not completely) after the Civil War and many clergy-assisted schemes were attempted. The Irish Catholic Benevolent Union, for example, tried two colonization schemes in the 1870s. But Kerrville, near Roanoke, Virginia, and Butler City in Pottawotomie County, Kansas, failed after only a few years.

Second, many of the intended beneficiaries of the program—slum-dwelling Irish immigrants—rejected the idea. Having already made a harrowing journey across the ocean, they were not interested in a second journey, no doubt involving blizzards, drought, wild animal attacks, and hostile Indians, to the unknown American interior. They would take their chances in the cities. The Irish Catholic Colonization Society of the United States (founded by prominent members of the clergy in 1879), for example, managed to establish successful settlements in Nebraska, Minnesota, and Arkansas, but failed to attract many Irish settlers.

Third, there was the problem of the Irish who did participate in the schemes. Many thwarted the goal of establishing self-sufficient Irish Catholic farmers by shunning independent farming in favor of farm labor for wages. Eventually, they left the settlements and found work in Western cities or with the railroads.

202. Fr. Thomas Hore Founds Wexford, Iowa In 1820, at the age of twenty-four, Fr. Thomas Hore of Wexford visited the United States. More than two decades later, as the Famine ravaged Ireland, he led 450 of his followers to New Orleans, planning to buy land in Arkansas and build a new community. When Arkansas did not welcome them, Hore instead took his people to St. Louis and then went on ahead to Iowa to buy three thousand acres of land. Upon returning for the group, however, he discovered that many had joined the California gold rush, while others were happy in St. Louis. Still, a dozen families followed Hore to Iowa, where they founded the new community of Wexford.

203. San Patricio de Hibernia Although most colonization schemes either never got beyond the planning stage, or failed after only a few years, several enjoyed success. Many Irishmen in the 1820s heeded the call of the Mexican government and headed for *Coahuila y Texas* to take advantage of offers of free land. The only condition for settlement was that newcomers had to be Catholic and conduct public business in Spanish. The Mexican government hoped such settlements would solidify its hold on the region.

In 1828, James McGloin and John McMullen received a large land grant for the settlement of two hundred families. The next year they brought Irish families from New York, establishing the Villa de San Patricio de Hibernia (town of St. Patrick of Ireland) on the Neuces River's north bank. The town became the county seat of San Patricio County, Texas, after Texan independence. In 1834, two more Irishmen, James Power and James Heweston, likewise established a settlement named *Refugio* (Refuge) on the Gulf of Mexico to which they brought dozens of Irish families. All told, approximately 150 Irish families settled in Mexican Texas between 1829 and 1834. As a rule, they tended to be better off than their fellow Catholic immigrants landing in Boston and New York.

204. The Donner Party In 1846, thousands of people headed West with hopes of securing land and opportunity. As members of the ill-fated Donner Party, the Irish American family of Patrick and Margaret Breen and their seven children could not have known that their own hopeful trip to California would become a three-and-a-half-month nightmare. Traveling through brutal winter conditions in the Sierra Nevada, the party of eighty-one, already diminished by six, suffered extreme hardship and starvation. In the end, only forty-five made it after resorting to cannibalizing the dead in order to survive.

Trapped by heavy snow, the Donner Party was finally discovered by rescue parties. The Breens were found in a hollow of snow twenty-four feet deep. Of the twelve recovered families, only two made it without losing any members; the Breens were one of them. They were described as being very generous, even sharing their food with others whose supplies were depleted.

205. Some Western Founding Fathers Many of the men and women who pioneered the development of the American West were Irish. John McLoughlin, for example, is known to history as the "father of Oregon." He arrived there in 1824 as an agent of the Hudson's Bay Company to manage its fur operations in the Oregon Territory. With no formal government there, McLoughlin effectively ruled the region until 1846.

Edward Creighton (1820–74) played a central role in developing the state of Nebraska. Born in Ohio to immigrant parents, he first worked as a wagon driver. Fascinated by the telegraph equipment he often carried, Creighton borrowed some money and went into the telegraph-building business. By the early 1860s he was building lines all across the Midwest, including parts of the first transcontinental telegraph line. Creighton grew rich on his shares in the Pacific Telegraph Company and later expanded into railroads and banking. As Omaha's leading citizen, he helped establish many lasting public institutions and charities.

Still another prominent figure in the West was Thomas Kearns (1862–1918), a hard-nosed adventurer born in Canada and raised in O'Neill, Nebraska. As a young man he headed for the mining district of South Dakota. Failing to strike it rich, he headed south to Tombstone, Arizona, and then on to Salt Lake City, Utah. In the early 1890s his Silver King Mine hit a huge vein of silver, making him a multimillionaire. He became the leading spokesman for Utah's non-Mormon population (not always with kind words for the Mormons) and served one term in the U.S. Senate. He later donated a considerable amount of his fortune to local Salt Lake City charities.

206. American Dublins Just as Irish immigrants have traveled to every corner of the U.S., they have given Irish place names to the towns they have settled. For example, there are nine Dublins across the country.

> **Dublin, California:** Best known for its prison, once home to junk bond king Michael Milken, it was settled by three Irish farmers in 1862 and is now an affluent suburb near Berkeley.
>
> **Dublin, Georgia:** Southeast of Atlanta, it is a tiny town founded by Jonathan Sawyer, who was either Irish or had an Irish wife.
>
> **Dublin, Indiana:** Historians speculate that either the town's founder was born in Dublin, Maryland, or the original surveyor of the town was Irish. Yet another theory is that the name came from "doubling in," i.e., pairing up horses to carry heavy equipment.
>
> **Dublin, Maryland:** There is no direct link between this north-central Maryland town and the Irish capital.
>
> **Dublin, New Hampshire:** Ten miles

from Keane, Dublin is a small village that was a summer home for Boston intellectuals and artists. Former residents include Amy Lowell and Mark Twain.

Dublin, Ohio: A typical suburb northeast of Columbus, Dublin manages to show its Irish pride in the shamrocks that appear on the cars of the Dublin police.

Dublin, Pennsylvania: Although situated in Bucks County, an area that saw a large Irish immigration (including many indentured servants) in the eighteenth century, the town's name came from two adjacent taverns called the "Double Inn."

Dublin, Texas: This small town in west-central Texas is notable for its strict alcohol laws and the nation's oldest Dr Pepper bottling plant. It might have been named for the Irish capital, or for early Texans "doubling in" their wagons to escape Indian raids.

Dublin, Virginia: This southwest Virginia town was settled by Samuel Caddle from Downpatrick, County Down, in 1774.

207. Sam Houston A hero of the War of 1812, Scotch-Irish Sam Houston (1793–1863) was a district attorney of Nashville, two-time Tennessee congressman, and one-term governor of Tennessee before he made his ultimate mark on history. Hounded by political adversaries in Tennessee, he moved to Texas, where he again became a leader, organizing the Texas army when the state declared its independence from Mexico in 1835. Houston developed a guerrilla strategy to use against the larger, professionally trained Mexican force, continually falling back before them until the conditions to strike were perfect. That moment came following Santa Anna's vic-

Sam Houston

tory at the Alamo (see entry #583). Houston's force overwhelmed the Mexican army in April 1836, thereby winning Texas' independence. He served as President of the independent Republic of Texas from 1836 to 1838 and 1841 to 1844. After Texas was annexed by the United States, he served as its senator (1846–59) and then governor (1859–61).

208. Kit Carson Born in Kentucky into a Scotch-Irish family, Christopher "Kit" Carson (1809–68) ran away as a teenager to join traders headed West. He learned trapping and trading, and was hired to guide John Frémont's government-financed explorations of the West in the 1840s. Carson later served in the Mexican American War under General Stephen Watts Kearny during his conquest of California. Carson earned a reputation as a courageous frontiersman fighter and was appointed Indian agent in 1854. During the Civil War, he led the First New Mexico Volunteers in fighting for the Union. Carson then remained Superintendent of Indian Affairs for the Colorado Territory until his death in 1868.

209. The Irish and Native Americans The history of the relationship between the Irish and Native Americans is a complex one. On the one hand, the Irish, especially the Scotch-Irish who settled on the frontier, developed a reputation as fierce and uncompromising Indian fighters. Perhaps this explains why a Scotch-Irish descendant, President Andrew Jackson, ordered the forced removal of thousands of Indians from the southeastern U.S. in 1831 (the Trail of Tears).

Later in the century, Irish American veterans of the Union Army would play a prominent role in the Indian Wars. One of the most prominent, Gen. Philip Sheridan, is remembered for his brutal assessment of the situation: "The only good Indian is a dead Indian."

On the other hand, several Irishmen distinguished themselves as advocates of Indian rights. In the early 1800s, Thomas McKenney became one of the first Americans to take up this cause. As the head of the Indian Trade Bureau and Bureau of Indian Affairs under four presidents (Madison, Monroe, Adams, and Jackson) he tried, often in vain, to get the federal government to live up to its treaty obligations. On of McKenney's lasting contributions, though, is the book *History of the Indian Tribes of North America*, published with James Hall in 1836. Famous Native Americans of his day are illustrated in beautiful lithographs, and he took special care to include information about all tribes.

Likewise, Thomas Fitzpatrick was an early advocate for Indian rights. Born in 1799, he immigrated to the United States when he was seventeen. One of the original mountain men who helped settle the West, he gathered a group of folks and led them to California on the first wagon train to reach that state. In spite of the fact that he initially fought many battles against Western Indians, he later became a key advocate for the Indians in Arkansas between 1846 and 1854. He succeeded in getting one of the first treaties for the Native Americans in 1851.

The Irish Down South

210. The Land of Celts? Although it is clear that many Irish immigrants settled in the American South during the colonial and antebellum periods, there is a small group of historians and sociologists who argue that the South has always been fundamentally "Celtic" in character, in contrast to the "Anglo-Saxon" North. Indeed, the central argument of this school of thought is that migrants to the South were "Celtized" while those in the North were "Anglicized." Some even go so far as to assert that this basic cultural divide explains the sectional crisis and Civil War, arguing that it was part of the same struggle that pitted Roundhead against Cavalier in the 1640s. The rebel yell of Confederate soldiers is thus seen as the revival of an ancient Celtic war cry.

It's an intriguing thesis that relies heavily on census surveys of last names and the cataloging of certain cultural traits (i.e., lawlessness, militancy, frankness, and hospitality) that form an underlying unity of the Celtic South. Unfortunately, the promoters of this interpretation include so vast a grouping of disparate peoples (from Connacht to western England) in their definition of "Celt" as to render the term meaningless. Their reliance on name surveys is likewise problematic, as anyone familiar with the prevalence of African Americans with Irish last names will attest.

211. The Statistics The Celtic South thesis aside, there can be no denying that many Irish did settle in the American South. The numbers, however, were far lower than in the Northeast and Midwest. By 1860, only 84,000 Irish-born lived in the South. Unlike Southerners as a whole, more than two thirds of the Irish lived in cities like New Orleans, Baltimore, Charleston, Richmond, Memphis, and Savannah, or large towns. Two basic factors explain the reluctance of the Irish to settle in the South. First, the great majority of the shipping (and the most affordable) went to seaports in the Northeast. Second, the North offered a greater number and variety of jobs than the South.

212. New Orleans By far the place of greatest Irish settlement in the South was New Orleans, not coincidentally the region's largest city. Even before the great influx of Irish in the 1830s, New Orleans had a large and significant Ulster Irish

Protestant population. Indeed, they celebrated St. Patrick's Day as far back as 1809. Starting in the 1830s, however, great numbers of poor Irish Catholics began to arrive. Many came as human cargo aboard cotton ships returning from Liverpool. By 1850, one fifth of the city's white population was Irish-born.

New Orleans welcomed the Irish for two reasons. First, they helped tip the racial balance in favor of a white majority. Second, they provided cheap and disposable labor in dangerous occupations in place of valuable slaves. As one Southerner explained when asked by a Northerner why so many Irishmen were employed in the risky work of loading huge bales of cotton onto ships, "Niggers are worth too much to be risked here; if the Paddies are knocked overboard . . . nobody loses anything."

213. Some Prominent Irish in the South Although most Irish immigrants settled in Northern states, leading Irishmen were to be found virtually everywhere across the South. Alexander Porter, for example, arrived in America as a refugee from the 1798 Uprising (his father had been killed in it). He grew up in Tennessee, but took the advice of a young Andrew Jackson and headed for the Louisiana Territory. He became a successful lawyer and then turned to sugar cultivation. He soon acquired a vast sugar plantation and emerged as a leading Southern Whig, eventually serving in the U.S. Senate.

County Louth–born Joseph Murphy established a wagon-building factory in St. Louis in the early 1840s. As the gateway to the American West, St. Louis drew a steady stream of pioneers and fortune seekers. Murphy made a small fortune building and selling more than 200,000 "Murphy Wagons" for Westward migration. Further east, Thomas Corcoran established a prosperous dry goods business in Washington, D.C. His son, William W. Corcoran, would later increase the family fortune several times over and use it to

endow the famed Corcoran Gallery. In Richmond, Virginia, John Dooley arrived in 1837 and opened a successful business as a hatter and furrier and became a prominent figure in business and politics.

214. The Irish Travelers Those familiar with the history of Ireland (or who saw Richard Harris in the film *The Field*) have no doubt heard of a group called the Travelers, or Tinkers. These "Irish gypsies," believed to be descendents of the Irish who lost their lands during Ireland's many upheavals, travel about Ireland in large caravans. They have a unique culture and speak a distinct language, Cant (a hybrid of several languages, including Irish). For as long as anyone can remember, Travelers have come into conflict with the settled communities they pass through. The latter accuse them of theft, drunkenness, noise, and littering.

One large contingent of Travelers arrived in Georgia sometime around 1865 and has remained a recognizable community ever since. They made their living trading mules and traveling throughout Georgia, Tennessee, and North and South Carolina.

Approximately five hundred families (two thousand people), descendents of these original migrants, currently live in Murphy Village, a settlement created in the 1960s under the guidance of Fr. Joseph J. Murphy to promote a more settled existence (most Travelers are Catholic). A second large Traveler community exists near Memphis, Tennessee. To this day, they remain insular communities, intent upon finding independent forms of work (barn painting and tool sales, for example), and maintaining their language, customs, and traditions.

The Later Nineteenth Century

215. The Numbers

DECADE	NUMBER	% OF TOTAL IMMIGR.
1860s	435,778	18.8
1870s	436,871	15.5
1880s	655,482	12.5
1890s	388,416	10.5

Source: Roger Daniels, *Coming to America.*

216. Onset of the "New" Immigration The decade of the 1880s saw the greatest number of Irish immigrants arrive in America since the 1850s. A total of 655,482 arrived in that decade compared with 436,871 in the 1870s. Despite this substantial increase in number, the percentage of Irish immigrants in the total immigration to America actually declined from 15.5 percent in the 1870s to 12.5 percent in the 1880s.

The onset of a new and massive immigrant flow from Eastern and Southern Europe explains this seemingly strange riddle. Whereas immigrants who arrived between 1820 and 1880 were predominantly from Western and Northern Europe, those arriving after 1880 came overwhelmingly from places like Russia, Poland, Italy, Greece, and the Balkans. Contemporaries soon took to referring to this new flow as the "new" immigration and the previous period as the "old." By 1920, the Irish accounted for just one in forty of the new arrivals in America.

217. Ellis Island and Annie Moore Ironically, even though only about one in twenty-five of the immigrants who passed through Ellis Island (1892–1954) came from Ireland, the first ever was a young girl from Cork named Annie Moore. Arriving on January 1, 1892—coincidentally her fifteenth birthday—Moore stepped off the *SS Nevada* to a new land and right into its history books. There to greet her as the first immigrant to enter the brand-new federal immigrant processing center in New York Harbor were city, state, and

Ellis Island

federal officials who presented her with a certificate and a ten-dollar gold piece.

Moore's story was typical of many Irish immigrants. Her parents had sailed for America earlier, leaving Annie and her two brothers in the care of an aunt. Once they were settled, they sent for Annie and her two brothers.

Institutions and
Organizations

218. Ancient Order of Hibernians Grows More Prominent After the Civil War, the Ancient Order of Hibernians (AOH) grew larger and more visible. Hundreds of chapters opened from coast to coast, in large cities and in small mining towns. Much of its focus was on charitable activities and promoting Irish culture. In cities like New York, the latter responsibility included organizing the annual St. Patrick's Day Parade.

Even though it was a staunchly Catholic organization, the AOH came under the scrutiny of the Catholic clergy for its support of physical-force nationalism in Ireland and alleged role in the Molly Maguire incident in the Pennsylvania coal fields in the 1870s (see #908). Many dioceses actually prohibited membership in the organization for a time, but the stamp of approval by several leading bishops in the late 1890s gave the AOH new life. Membership jumped from 53,000 in 1886 to 132,000 in 1908 (plus upwards of 55,000 women in the Ladies Auxiliary AOH).

By the turn of the century, the AOH turned its attention toward improving the public reputation of the Irish in America. It commenced a campaign against the "stage Irishman," threatening theaters with boycotts and urging members to avoid productions that featured such characters. In 1912, when John Millington Synge's play, *Playboy of the Western World,* debuted in America, the AOH denounced it as defamatory and organized protests. Similarly, the AOH campaigned to get Catholic parishes to deemphasize boxing in their youth athletic programs. Too many

Americans, they argued, associated the Irish with fighting and the preponderance of Irish fighters (and Italians, Jews, and Germans who took Irish names) only reinforced the stereotype.

219. Irish County Societies One organization that proliferated in the latter part of the nineteenth century was the Irish county society. Comprising members born in one of Ireland's thirty-two counties, they first appeared during the Famine period. But it was in the post–Civil War period that the county societies reached full bloom as social, cultural, and charitable organizations. By the 1890s, county societies not only sponsored a wide range of social events but also athletic competitions in Irish games like hurling. The latter reflected the influence of the Gaelic Revival in Ireland and America.

The Persistence of Nativism

220. Orange and Green Riots July 12 was never a good day as far as Irish Catholics were concerned, for it was the anniversary of King William of Orange's victory over Catholic King James II in 1691 at the Battle of Aughrim. Beginning in 1796, as tensions between Catholics and Protestants mounted, Protestant Orangemen began staging annual marches to mark the occasion. On several occasions, both in Ireland and in the U.S., riots broke out between Catholic onlookers and Protestant marchers. The latter claimed the marches were simply an expression of ethnic pride, while the former denounced them as exhibitions of triumphant domination.

The worst of these clashes took place on July 12 in 1870 and 1871 in New York. In 1870, a contingent of Orangemen staged a march up Eighth Avenue toward a park where they planned to hold a picnic. The parade was harassed all along the route by gangs of Catholic Irish who, along with three hundred Irish workmen, attacked it when it reached the park. Eight people were killed in the ensuing fracas.

The following year, the city's chief of police

banned the march, fearing violence. But the state's Republican governor overruled him and provided the state militia as an escort. Angry crowds again lined the parade route to harass the marchers. For reasons still unclear, the militia opened fire on the crowd, killing sixty-seven and wounding one hundred fifty.

221. Thomas Nast One of the most prolific and influential anti-Irish nativists of the 1860s and 1870s was Thomas Nast. Born in Germany in 1840, he immigrated to America and became a well-known illustrator and political cartoonist for such publications as *Frank Leslie's Illustrated Newspaper* and *Harper's Weekly*.

Anti-Catholic cartoon by Thomas Nast, 1871

The Orange Riot, 1871

While he is remembered today for creating the symbols of the Democratic (the donkey) and Republican (the elephant) parties, as well as the modern image of Santa Claus, Nast gained national fame for his harsh and derogatory cartoons of the Irish.

Nast was already famous when he began attacking Tammany Hall and Boss William Tweed in New York City from 1869 to 1872. The notoriously corrupt Tammany Hall was a symbol of rising Irish political influence and power in the city. Nast's anti-Tweed cartoons played a major role in bringing down Boss Tweed in a corruption scandal that erupted in 1871. Nast was particularly concerned about the rising influence of the Catholic Church in politics and the public

schools, and many of his cartoons were explicitly anti-Catholic.

222. The Myth of Mrs. O'Leary's Cow and the Great Chicago Fire   Some have argued that anti-Irish sentiment explains the story of Mrs. O'Leary and the Great Chicago Fire. According to popular legend, thirty-five-year-old Catherine O'Leary left a lantern burning in her barn in 1871. When it was kicked over by one of the cows, it started the fire that would engulf Chicago for a day and a half. Flames towered at five hundred feet, trees full of sap exploded, metal structures melted, seventeen thousand buildings disappeared, and more than three hundred people died.

Today, however, research indicates that Daniel Sullivan went to feed his cow in O'Leary's barn and dropped a match or lantern in the straw. In fact, in 1891, two reporters admitted to exaggerating, even fabricating, the story about Mrs. O'Leary. Unfortunately, the damage was done; she had been driven away and lived out her life as a recluse.

The extent of the fire can really be blamed on factors such as an inadequate fire brigade, nonenforced building codes, little rain, and powerful winds. In 1997, Chicago officially absolved Mrs. O'Leary of all blame.

223. American Protective Association   The 1880s brought a sharp rise in immigration to the U.S. and an increase in anti-immigrant hostility. In 1887, Henry F. Bowers established the nation's foremost anti-Catholic organization, the American Protective Association. Often derided as the American *Protestant* Association, it grew to half a million members by the end of 1893. Its main base of strength lay among middle-class Protestants in the Midwest. The group argued that Catholicism was incompatible with American institutions and government and revived many of the same policies proposed by the Know Nothings in the 1850s. The more extreme members spread rumors of papal plots and murderous conspiracies.

Like the Know Nothings, the APA soon faded, but not before provoking a near riot in Boston. In 1895, the local APA chapter sought permission to march in the city's July Fourth Parade. The Board of Aldermen denied permission on the grounds of public safety, but they were overruled by the state's governor. The march took place without incident, but during scuffles that broke out as the parade ended, a panicked APA member pulled a pistol and fired into the crowd, killing a Catholic man. No one was ever convicted of the crime.

224. The Irish in the Comics   In 1895, the American comic strip was born with Robert Outcault's "Hogan's Alley" in Pulitzer's *New York World.* Set in a classic Irish slum, the strip featured "The Yellow Kid," a moronic, if lovable, street urchin who always managed to get into trouble. Thus, Outcault not only put the comic strip on the map as a major popular literary genre, he also popularized the image of the Irish as charming buffoons. As historian William Griffin writes, Outcault "peopled this Hibernian environment with swarms of monkeylike urchins and hags bawling from tenement windows, with their 'wit' displayed through wildly distorted spelling and grammar." This was not a new idea, but simply an adaptation of the stereotypical "stage Irishman" character (see entry #674) to a new format (ironically, at the very moment that the Ancient Order of Hibernians was beginning its successful effort to rid the American stage of such a character).

Outcault's success brought many imitators. In 1900, Fred Opper, long famous for his ape-like depictions of the Irish on the covers of *Puck* magazine, started penning "Happy Hooligan." It lasted until 1932. By then the image of the Irish in comic strips—George McManus' "Bringing Up Father" (1913) and Frank Willard's "Moon Mullins" (1923) to name two—reflected their rising acceptance into mainstream American society.

225. Irish American Nativism   Even though they suffered greatly from discrimination, some Irish proved willing to discriminate against other, more vulnerable groups. During the depression years of the 1870s, the Chinese in California became the target of hostility and violence. The leader of the anti-Chinese movement was an Irish immigrant named Denis Kearney. He rose to prominence as head of the Workingmen's Party in large measure by fanning the flames of anti-Chinese racism among his largely Irish constituents. On several occasions workers attacked the Chinese settlement in San Francisco. Kearney's efforts culminated in Congress' passing the Chinese Exclusion Act of 1882, which banned all future immigration from China to the United States until World War II.

the twentieth century

The Irish on the Rise

226. Improved Economic Status In contrast to their lowly status in the mid-nineteenth century, Irish Catholics by 1900 had achieved an astonishing degree of upward mobility. By some measures, they had drawn equal to native-born Americans in terms of occupational distribution (see entry #921 for specific statistics). An Irish American middle class had emerged and more and more Irish could be found in the ranks of business, politics, and the professions.

227. "Lace Curtain" and Other Terms of Praise and Derision One of the surest signs of Irish upward mobility was the creation of several expressions to describe those who had "made it." In almost every case, these terms carried a double meaning, both recognizing an Irish family's success and deriding their pretensions to middle-class habits and appearances. The most widely known term is "lace curtain," but there were many others, including "two-toilet" and "cut glass." Working-class Irishmen also referred to their fellow ethnics entering office work and the professions as "narrowbacks"—i.e., weaklings. And as the Irish

The Kelly Family on the Irish Riviera, 1926

joined the ranks of Americans flocking to seaside retreats in the summer, many simple clusters of one-room cabanas and wooden cabins took on the self-deprecating nickname of the "Irish Riviera."

228. Super Patriots In keeping with their new-found economic success, many Irish Americans worked hard to demonstrate a love of Ireland and America.

> To call the members of the Hibernian race foreigners would be an anomaly, as they are an integral part of Americanism. The Irish have become an integral part of us, and even those of us who may be descended from passengers of the *Mayflower* can hardly look upon them as foreigners. Once here, the Irish have bound us so closely to that little isle whence they came that we can no longer look upon Ireland as a foreign country. . . . Everyone in the United States knows that the "Old Country" can refer only to the Emerald Isle . . . We feel that, after the United States, Ireland is the country in which we take the most interest. This very remarkable psychological state is due entirely to the Irishman's wonderfully passionate patriotism. . . . But the Irishman's love for his old home has never made him relegate America to a second place.
> —editorial in *Brooklyn Daily Eagle,* 1916

229. Hyphenated? As immigration to America surged in 1914 against a backdrop of rising tensions in Europe, President Woodrow Wilson and former President Teddy Roosevelt became leading voices in a rising chorus of criticism aimed what they called "hyphenated Americans." Theoretically the barb applied to all ethnic groups in America, but it was plainly aimed at the Irish and Germans, who were seen as having too great an affection for their homelands. In May 1914, for example, at the dedication of a statue in honor of Commodore John Barry, the Irish-born "father of the American Navy," Wilson praised him as an immigrant whose "heart crossed the Atlantic with him"—unlike so many others who "need hyphens in their names, because only part of them has come over." Irish Americans denounced these attacks as a resurgent Know Nothingism.

230. Immigration Restriction: The Irish Begrudgingly Admitted as Americans After decades of growing hostility toward mass immigration, Congress finally passed a sweeping immigration restriction law in 1921 (amended in 1924 and again in 1929). In essence, the law did two things: It sharply curtailed the overall number of immigrants admitted, and allotted each country a quote based on "racial" preferences. As a result, overall immigration dropped from 805,000 in 1921 to 294,000 in 1925. More important, many immigrant groups deemed "undesirable" saw their numbers plummet even more sharply. Italians, for example, who had averaged 158,000 arrivals per year before restriction, received an annual quota of just 5,802. For Greeks the numbers were slashed from an average of 17,600 arrivals per year to a quota of just 307.

And the Irish? What would be the status of this group still regarded with suspicion and contempt by many Anglo-American Protestants and still routinely depicted in popular culture as racially inferior beings? In a word, they were granted "preferred" status. In the 1924 version of the law, the Irish Free State received an annual quota of 28,567 (later reduced in 1929, along with most other groups, to 17,853). Ireland received such a high quota despite the fact that it sent an average of just 22,000 per year in the 1920s and a scant 1,300 per year in the 1930s.

The Irish, at least in the eyes of the quota makers, were finally welcome in America.

231. Well, Sort of: The Election of 1928 Few decades in American history have been so characterized by prosperity and optimism as the 1920s. Irish Americans, with rising levels of education, income, and membership in the professions, enjoyed the good times as much as any other group. For many of them, the man who embodied their rising fortunes was Al Smith, the boy from the mean streets of Manhattan who had risen to become a four-term governor of New York State. And in 1928, he was the Democratic nominee for President.

But behind the "roar" of the 1920s was a rising tide of cultural "reaction." Smith was popular among urban ethnics in the North, but elsewhere evangelical Protestants, prohibitionists, and anti-Catholics viewed him as the representative of big-city corruption and immorality. More ominous, membership in the Ku Klux Klan (now hostile to Jews and Catholics in addition to African Americans) soared to five million nationwide.

Smith also faced a larger problem: 1928 belonged to the Republicans. The popular image of Herbert Hoover as the grim man in the gray suit presiding over the onset of the Great Depression obscures the fact that in 1928 he was one of the nation's most accomplished and respected public servants. The public also identified his party with prosperity. Why, many asked, change horses now?

But if any Democratic nominee was destined to lose in 1928, he was not destined to lose in the *manner* that Al Smith did. Optimistic and jovial by nature, Smith was stunned by the cold response he received in the American Heartland. Vicious editorials and speeches by anti-Catholic demagogues hurt even more. The candidate urban

Al Smith campaigning, 1928

Americans saw as the epitome of the self-made man and bighearted public official was elsewhere viewed with fear as the proponent of popery, demon rum, foreign values, and Jazz-era depravity. Smith didn't lose the election of 1928 because he was Irish Catholic, but he lost *ugly* and lost *big* because of it.

Hoover garnered 58 percent of the popular vote (444 electoral votes) to Smith's 41 percent (87 electoral votes). Even his home state of New York went for Hoover, leaving Smith with victories in only Massachusetts and six Deep South states. His strong showing in the South had nothing to do with his policies and everything to do with the fact that sixty-three years after Lee surrendered to Grant, most Southerners still couldn't bring themselves to vote for a Republican.

Just as Smith's nomination in the summer of 1928 had thrilled Irish Americans, so his crushing defeat in November left them stunned and disillusioned. Maybe, many wondered, we haven't ar-

rived after all. It was a bitter experience many Irish Americans did not soon forget.

Odds and Ends

232. Wrong Way Corrigan Texas-born Douglas Corrigan (1907–95) was a welder by trade and an amateur pilot. Inspired by Lindbergh's famous 1927 Atlantic crossing, he bought a 1929 Curtis-Robin plane off a garbage pile. He modified and rebuilt the plane so that it could make the flight across the Atlantic. Officials at the Federal Bureau of Air Commerce, however, denied him the permit, citing his inexperience as a pilot and the dreadful condition of his airplane.

Determined to get his share of aviation glory, Corrigan hatched an ingenious plan. On July 18, 1938, he set off in his plane bound, he told his friends, for California. Instead, he pointed his plane northeast and soared out over the Atlantic. Twenty-eight hours and thirteen minutes later (five hours better than Lindbergh) he touched down at Baldonnel Airport near Dublin. "Just in from New York," he announced to the startled airfield attendants. "Where am I?"

When informed that he was in Ireland, Corrigan feigned shock. "You mean," he said, "this isn't California?" Word spread quickly about the wacky Yank who'd mistakenly made a 3,150-mile transatlantic flight without benefit of a radio or navigational equipment other than a compass. For two weeks he was Ireland's biggest celebrity and when he returned to the U.S. on August 4, "Wrong Way" Corrigan received a hero's welcome. His plan had worked to perfection. The bizarre nature of his feat earned him the fame he sought, and since the whole thing was an "honest mistake," he avoided prosecution for making an unauthorized flight.

After Corrigan earned a few dollars selling his story to magazines and Hollywood, he took up farming in California and disappeared from public view. He stuck to his story that his famous journey had been a mistake right up to the day he died. The sentimental still believed him. The rest understood his story for what it was: a brilliant bit of well-timed blarney.

233. Typhoid Mary Mary Mallon was born in 1869 in Cookstown, County Tyrone, and migrated to New York City when she was fourteen years old. Like so many Irish immigrant women, she took work as a cook in the homes of wealthy Americans. Her trouble began in August 1906 when typhoid fever broke out at a summer home in Oyster Bay, New York. The owner of the house, fearful that he would have trouble renting it the following summer unless it was given a clean bill of health, hired a sanitary engineer named George Soper to investigate. After finding none of the bacterium in the house's water system and kitchen, he inquired about the staff. It turned out that Mary Mallon had been hired only a week before the typhoid fever broke out and had disappeared soon thereafter. Determined to find her, Soper eventually tracked her down in March 1907, at a Park Avenue home where, not surprisingly, typhoid had just been reported. Mallon put up a fight but was arrested. Tests determined that she was a carrier of the typhoid bacterium, though was herself immune to it. City officials confined "Typhoid Mary," as the press now called her, to a public hospital located on a nearby island.

Three years later, after she promised to abstain from cooking, Mallon was released. But when typhoid fever broke out in a local hospital in 1915, officials found a staff cook named Mary Brown, who turned out to be Mary Mallon. She was sent back to the isolated hospital where she spent the next twenty-three years of her life, alone and bitter.

In all Mallon infected at least fifty-one people, and possibly as many as 1,400. She was not the only carrier discovered, nor was she the worst. But she unquestionably was the most infamous.

234. Bridey Murphy In 1956, Virginia Tighe claimed to be an Irishwoman named Bridey Murphy, who had been born in the nineteenth century. Under hypnosis administered by a man named Morey Bernstein, she "recounted" many details about her life in Ireland. "Bridey" told Bernstein about being married to a lawyer named Sean MacCarthy. She described Irish rivers and even the church she attended.

A reporter for the *Denver Post* got hold of the story, and Virginia became an overnight sensation. Bernstein wrote a bestselling book, a movie was made (*The Search for Bridey Murphy,* 1956) and songwriters penned tunes about Bridey Murphy.

In the end, it turned out that Virginia probably gained her intimate knowledge of Ireland from a woman named Bridey Murphy who lived across the street from her in Milwaukee. As a child Virginia heard Murphy tell many stories about Ireland and more than likely held them in her subconscious until they were drawn out under hypnosis. The Bridey Murphy hype eventually subsided and Virginia Tighe returned to obscurity.

235. The Unsinkable Molly Brown Margaret Tobin was born in 1867 in Hannibal, Missouri. She grew up poor and eventually made her way west to Colorado. There she met her husband, one of thousands of fortune seekers trying their hand at gold mining. Unlike most, he struck it rich.

Like many *nouveaux riches,* Molly yearned for acceptance in the highest social circles. That lifestyle accounts for her being aboard the ill-fated *RMS Titanic,* which struck an iceberg and sank in April 1912. Brown was among the more than five hundred passengers placed in lifeboats and rescued. Somewhere along the line, perhaps that very night, perhaps later after years of telling and retelling her story, she came to be known as the "Unsinkable Molly Brown." Sadly, she eventually lost everything and died in poverty.

Her house in Denver is now a museum of Victoriana that is visited by about 40,000 people a year.

236. Anne Sullivan Macy Much of Helen

Keller's fame resulted from the successful efforts of Anne Sullivan, daughter of immigrants from County Limerick, to teach the blind and deaf Keller to communicate with the world. Afflicted with poor sight herself, she met Keller in 1887, when Keller was seven and Sullivan twenty-one. After taming the unruly Keller, Sullivan employed a method of marking words on Keller's hands, eventually developing an extensive vocabulary. The two women remained companions even after Sullivan married. Sullivan gave Keller her cheerful spirit and perseverance as well as teaching her Braille and guiding her to understandable speech. The women's relationship is explored in the popular film, *The Miracle Worker*.

237. The Kewpie Doll   The Kewpie Doll was the creation of Rose Cecil O'Neill (1874–1944), a gifted artist who introduced the Kewpies in 1909 as a cartoon in *Ladies' Home Journal*. The Kewpies were androgynous, cherubic characters whose name derived from "Cupid." They proved immensely popular and soon commanded page-long adventures in women's magazines. O'Neill designed a hugely popular Kewpie Doll that she patented in 1913. All told, she earned over a million dollars in royalties before the Kewpie craze dwindled in the 1930s.

238. Tex Guinan   Mary Louise Cecilia Guinan (1884–1933) was one of Prohibition Era America's most celebrated nightclub operators. Her sobriquet, "Tex," came from her native state, where she once worked as a bronco rider. After a stint in Hollywood acting in several Westerns, she moved on to Broadway, before finally going into the nightclub business in 1924. At first she was simply the outlandish hostess at several well-known speakeasies, but success led her to open her own place, the glitzy Salon Royale, just off Broadway on West Fifty-eighth Street in Manhattan. Patrons sipped illegal booze and enjoyed music, showgirls, and Tex Guinan's flamboyant personality—"Hello, sucker" was her

trademark line. Arrested many times, she always won acquittal and became, in decidedly "wet" New York, a hero to those who detested Prohibition. Playing the part of the rebel to the hilt, she wore a necklace of miniature padlocks, one for each arrest. Guinan's eventual undoing came at the hands of another Irish American, Mayor Jimmy Walker. When one of his cronies was booted from the place, he shut it down. She tried to resurrect her glory in Chicago, and later on Long Island in New York, but it was never the same. Tex Guinan died in November 1933—two days before Prohibition was repealed.

the post-war era

From the Cities to the Suburbs

239. Rates of Immigration   Immigration to the U.S. from Ireland rose and fell with the fortunes of the Irish economy. A stagnant economy in the 1950s and 1980s, for example, produced surges in immigration. Conversely, during the 1970s and 1990s, Ireland's economy boomed and fewer Irish decided to leave. Most important, as early as the 1930s, the great majority of the Irish who chose to leave Ireland went to Britain, not the U.S.

DECADE	NUMBER OF IMMIGRANTS
1940s	26,967
1950s	57,332
1960s	37,461
1970s	6,559
1980s	ca. 40,000*
1990s	ca. 25,000*
* High rates of illegal immigration make it impossible to determine an exact figure.	

240. Irish Cultural Traditions   Expressions of Irish culture (albeit in many ways a very

Americanized version of it) could be found everywhere in large American cities in the late 1940s and 1950s. Many boasted several Irish radio programs and Irish newspapers. Irish cultural festivals *(feis)* and dance exhibitions *(ceili)* occurred throughout the year, sponsored by parishes, colleges, or fraternal organizations. Dance halls with names like Hibernian Hall and Innisfail dotted the landscape from Boston to San Francisco. Games involving traditional Irish sports like hurling continued to draw large crowds. The 1940s also saw the inauguration of a new Irish organization—the Emerald Society—first formed by Irish policemen and firemen and eventually spreading to other branches of the civil service.

241. Irish American Prosperity The trend toward upward mobility visible at the turn of the century grew more pronounced in the post-war years. Catholic colleges like Boston College, Georgetown, Notre Dame, and Loyola graduated

thousands of Irish Americans every year for careers in business and the professions. For the Irish in skilled trades, these were good years as well, with record levels of national prosperity translating into steady work and high wages. Overall, the Irish moved more slowly than any other pre-1890 immigrant group up the economic ladder, but the movement was nonetheless unmistakable.

242. The O'Neil Sisters In the spring of 1940 Daniel and Julia O'Neil decided to participate with their growing family in Boston's annual Easter Parade. The O'Neils were hardly wealthy, but Mrs. O'Neil was an accomplished seamstress. So, in the weeks leading up to the parade, she created matching outfits for her daughters. On Easter Sunday they caught the attention of a news photographer, who snapped their picture. The photo of several beautiful Irish Catholic girls walking in size order in matching outfits was sent out over a news service wire. Suddenly and unwit-

An Irish *Feis*

tingly, the O'Neils became the poster family of Irish American upward mobility, Catholic respectability, and solid family values. And every year it got better, as the family gave birth to one baby girl after another, each of whom took her place in her matching outfit every Easter. In all, the O'Neils had twelve children—the eldest was a boy, followed by ten straight girls, and then finally, another boy. They marched every year from the 1940s through the early 1960s and always made the papers. They also made public appearances and were interviewed on television. Everyone, it seems, loved the O'Neils. Considering that less than a century earlier, most Americans thought of the Irish Catholic family as hopelessly large and impoverished, Catholic America could not have asked for a better image.

243. The Ford-McDonnell Wedding Still another sign of changing times also occurred in the 1940s with the joining of two of the most prominent Irish families in America. On July 13, 1940, Henry Ford II married Anne McDonnell in a gala wedding enthusiastically covered by the press. The McDonnells were fabulously rich as a result of James Francis McDonnell's success as a Wall Street broker. It hadn't hurt that in 1916 he'd married the daughter of another Irish American tycoon, Thomas Murray (see entries #877 and #888). The family divided their time between their mansions in New York City and Long Island and considered themselves leading members of a set they called the FIFs—First Irish Families. Henry Ford II was the grandson of the great auto manufacturer, Henry Ford. The press covered it like a royal wedding, giving it weeks of coverage before the actual ceremony took place. One of the biggest prewedding stories was the announcement that Henry Ford II would convert (or reconvert, as Catholics liked to point out) to Catholicism so that the wedding could take place with the full blessing of the Catholic Church. Hundreds were invited to the event, which was held on Long Island. The famous radio priest, Monsignor

Fulton Sheen, performed the ceremony. The reception was one for the record books. As Stephen Birmingham wrote in his classic, *Real Lace*, "If it was not the wedding of the century, it certainly was the last of the great weddings in America before World War II." If the O'Neil sisters told America that Irish Americans were wholesome and respectable, the McDonnell-Ford wedding announced that they were rich and powerful.

244. The Election of 1960 Thirty-two years after Al Smith's humiliating defeat at the hands of Herbert Hoover, John F. Kennedy finally did what Irish Catholics once thought impossible—win the White House. Even though he'd won by the slimmest of margins (49.9 percent to Nixon's 49.6 percent), Irish Americans took his victory to mean one thing: They had arrived. As historian William

John F. Kennedy campaigning in Boston, 1960

V. Shannon wrote, "It removed any lingering sense of social inferiority and insecurity. To a people for whom politics had long been one of their chosen professions, the election of Kennedy was a deeply satisfying accomplishment in which every Irishman could take vicarious pleasure."

245. JFK Visits Ireland On the same evening that he delivered his famous address at the Berlin Wall ("I take pride in the words *'Ich bin ein Berliner' "),* John F. Kennedy flew to Ireland, the land of his immigrant forebears.

Kennedy toured the country for three days and everywhere was greeted by adoring crowds eager to see the unofficial king of the Irish Diaspora. He reveled in the emotion and symbolism of the moment.

Kennedy's most poignant remarks came at the end of his trip when he spoke in Dublin.

When my great-grandfather left here to become a cooper in East Boston, he carried nothing with him except two things: a strong religious faith and a strong desire for liberty. And I am glad to say that all of his great-grandchildren have valued that inheritance. If he hadn't left, I'd be working over here at the Albatross Company.

It was a classic statement on the Diaspora—one that acknowledged both the promise of America and the tragedy of Ireland.

The trip was a resounding success, so much so that Kennedy promised in his address before the Irish Parliament, "I certainly will come back in the springtime." No one on either side of the Atlantic could have known that he'd never get the chance.

246. JFK's Assassination JFK's assassination in November 1963 was a tragedy in which Irish Americans shared profound sorrow. They grieved for the lost man but also for the lost opportunity. The assassination cut short a life that many

thought symbolized the idealism of the postwar generation after just one thousand days in office. All they were left with was the almost saintlike aura that developed around the JFK memory, an aura that has endured despite later revelations of his many personal failings. No one summed up the grief felt by Irish Americans better than future Senator Daniel Patrick Moynihan when he said of the experience, "I don't think there's any point in being Irish if you don't know that the world is going to break your heart eventually. I guess that we thought we had a little more time. . . . Mary McGrory said to me that we'll never laugh again. And I said, 'Heavens, Mary. We'll laugh again. It's just that we'll never be young again.' "

247. Suburbanization The national trend after World War II was from the cities to the suburbs. Long before the problems of the inner city flared in the 1960s and 1970s, the Irish and their fellow Americans began heading for the greener pastures of the suburbs. Several factors facilitated this trend. The two most obvious were the postwar economic boom and the advent of the affordable automobile. The FHA and GI Bill provided millions with the opportunity to get a low-cost mortgage. The nation embarked on a massive highway construction program that opened up vast areas of land near cities to suburban development. Moving to the suburbs also made economic sense to many aspiring middle-class families because home ownership, unlike renting an apartment, allowed them to build up equity. Finally, there was the growing notion that the suburbs offered a better life—more room, better schools, and, truth be told, no minorities.

248. White Flight and Race Relations The typical trend in most American cities in the 1950s and 1960s was for Irish neighborhoods to be transformed into African American and Latino ones. This process, which usually began slowly and ended with a sudden mass exodus of Irish families, was not a simple story of white racism as the popular term "white flight" suggests. Many Irish

Catholic neighborhoods had developed over decades into tightly knit communities centered around parish churches and their many spiritual, social, and educational programs. As they grew in prosperity, Irish residents sought a middle-class lifestyle, but one *within* their insular, comfortable, familiar, homogeneous parish world. It is precisely this social and cultural outlook fostered by parish life that led many an Irish family to interpret the influx of African Americans as a threat to the world they had painstakingly constructed.

Thus, many urban middle-class Irish neighborhoods were buffeted by a multiplicity of forces, loyalties, and interests in the postwar years. Racism, from virulent to unconscious, was one of those factors, to be sure. Blacks moving into Irish neighborhoods often endured acts of vandalism and violence. But in many neighborhoods, community activists and liberal Catholic priests often tried to foster tolerance and brotherhood in their changing parishes. In the end they proved no match for the "panic peddling" and "block-busting" realtors who unscrupulously spread rumors of impending black incursion to drive down the prices of houses. Many were told, if they stayed, they risked the likely erosion of their one tangible asset (their home). If they sold early, they could protect that asset by reinvesting in the suburbs. Most working-class and lower-middle-class Irish families chose the latter. Between the push of fear and racism and the pull of the idealized vision of the suburbs, Irish Americans left their old urban neighborhoods for new ones just beyond the city limits.

249. South Boston and the Busing Question Of course, not all the Irish heeded the siren call of the suburbs. Indeed, the Irish in America headed for the suburbs at a slower rate than most ethnic groups. In the case of neighborhoods like South Boston, the Irish stayed both for reasons of loyalty and poverty. So when the city of Boston was ordered by Judge Arthur Garrity to desegregate its schools through a scheme to bus minority chil-

South Boston busing, 1971

dren to formerly all-white schools and white students to formerly all-minority ones, South Boston erupted in protest. So, too, did black neighborhoods like Roxbury. Neither liked the idea, especially when violence broke out. Still, the most vivid images of anger and violence were captured on camera in Southie. South Boston and its majority Irish Catholic residents came to symbolize post–Civil Rights era white backlash.

250. Thomas O'Connor Observes By the late 1960s, the Irish of Boston's neighborhoods no longer viewed municipal government in the same way their parents and grandparents once had—that is, as the provider of relief to the poor, the immigrant, the laborer, and the distressed.

Large numbers of middle- and working-class white ethnics—long the solid core of the Democratic party—now began to view the city government as their enemy. . . . [T]hey saw it as an overgrown establishment that was continuously oppressing them, taxing them, conspiring to take away their land and knock down their houses, telling them where to go, how to behave, how to dress, how to raise their standard of living. In anger and frustration, white neighborhoods rejected the B[oston] R[edevelopment] A[uthority]'s lure of better housing, cleaner streets, and better schools, in great part because they suspected that an alien liberal agenda would accompany these changes and ultimately threaten their family values, their religious ideals, and their working-class traditions.

251. Irish American Liberalism   Unfortunately, episodes like South Boston (and Senator Joseph McCarthy before it) helped strengthen and perpetuate the stereotype of Irish Americans as provincial, narrow-minded, and intolerant. While that characterization no doubt held true for a significant number of Irish Americans, study after study conducted by people such as Fr. Andrew Greeley of the National Opinion Research Center show that contrary to the stereotype, Irish Americans are wealthier, better educated, and more liberal on issues like gay rights and civil rights than any other white ethnic group except for American Jews.

The Waning of Irish Identity?

252. Tom Hayden Reflects on the Price of Assimilation

I was raised in an Irish-American home in Detroit where assimilation was the uppermost priority. The price of assimilation and respectability was amnesia. Although my great-grandparents were victims of the Great Hunger of the 1840s, even though I was named Thomas Emmet Hayden IV after the radical Irish nationalist exile Thomas Emmet, my inheritance was to be disinherited. My parents knew nothing of this past, or nothing worth passing on. When I asked my mother, "If I'm the fourth, who were the others?" she answered, "The first, the second and the third."
        —*The Nation,* May 18, 1998

253. Fading Institutions   As immigration from Ireland waned in the postwar period, and as Irish Americans took to the suburbs and sent their kids to college, many of the symbols and institutions of Irish identity began to fade. The many *feis* and *ceili* in cities like Boston, New York, Chicago, and San Francisco that used to draw huge crowds as late as the 1940s and 1950s became smaller and fewer in number. Hurling matches in New York that once filled a stadium now attracted crowds in the low thousands. Irish county societies saw their membership decline and many Irish language and step dancing programs ended due to insufficient enrollment. Irish radio programming was cut back and Irish newspapers folded. By 1970, the American Irish Historical Society in New York stood on the verge of bankruptcy and dissolution, with its treasury empty and membership in steep decline. It seemed as though the great melting pot effect—at once celebrated for its ability to blend different groups into an evolving American culture, and resented for the way it slowly but surely stripped away Old World traditions—had done its job. Irish Americans might regret the loss of their ethnic heritage, but it occurred as a result of their successful entry into middle-class America.

254. Daniel Patrick Moynihan Observes   In writing about the Irish in his classic (written with Nathan Glazer) *Beyond the Melting Pot,* Daniel Patrick Moynihan wrote of a fading Irish identity in the 1960s, a trend vividly symbolized by the decline of the once-proud American Irish Historical Society.

> This group was founded in New York in 1897 "to make better known the Irish chapter in American history." There was certainly a case to be made that the Irish had been slighted, and the Society set out to right this imbalance with some vigor. But little came of it. The membership was basically not interested in history; it was the imbalance of the present, not the past, that concerned them. When this was righted, the purpose of the Society vanished. Its *Journal* . . . has long ceased publication. The Society continues to occupy a great tomb of a mansion on Fifth Avenue, with a fine library that few seem interested in using, and splendid rooms where no one evidently wants to meet.

255. Fr. Andrew Greeley Disagrees   In contrast to the pessimism found in Moynihan's assertion that Irish identity was on the wane in America, Fr. Andrew Greeley predicted in 1981 that "there almost certainly will be a return to higher levels of self-conscious Irish identification." His words would prove astonishingly prescient.

The Irish American Renaissance

256. Resurgent Irishness   A genuine resurgence of interest in all things Irish, among Irish and non-Irish alike, began somewhere in the mid-1970s, though few people took notice until the 1980s. Many scholars point to the smashing success of *Roots*, the 1973 television miniseries about the African American search for ancestors, as the beginning of a nationwide effort among virtually all racial and ethnic groups to rediscover their heritage.

No European ethnic group has seen a greater

The Irish American Renaissance—a step-dance recital in Brooklyn, 2001

cultural revival than the Irish. Just consider the evidence: dozens of Irish studies programs established at colleges and universities nationwide; Famine curriculum for public schools adopted in dozens of states and Famine memorials everywhere; *Riverdance* and its successor, *Lord of the Dance,* smashing attendance and video sales records worldwide; an acclaimed six-hour PBS special, *The Long Journey Home* (1996) on the Irish American experience; Frank McCourt's Pulitzer Prize–winning memoir, *Angela's Ashes;* the list goes on and on. True, some of it is pure green-beer commercialism and some of it downright embarrassing (the 1999 television special *Leprechauns* is a case in point), but on the whole it indicates a positive, uplifting quest among Irish Americans to discover, experience, and perpetuate their rich cultural traditions.

257. William Griffin Explains the New Historical Consciousness

> Since 1970, however, there has been a "second spring" of Irish-American historical consciousness. The general surge of ethnic

awareness and the quest for identity and origins, especially among younger people, has combined with the renewed issue of Irish national unity to stimulate interest and enthusiasm. . . . Most hopeful of all are the abundant signs that Irish Americans, secure now in the American nation, are ready to look honestly at all dimensions of their role in making that nation. Their historical consciousness seems to have matured to the point where they are interested in facts rather than self-justification. They are ready to learn about the villains as well as the heroes.

—Historian William D. Griffin,
Book of Irish Americans (1990).

258. Daniel J. Casey Examines the Cultural Awakening in Irish American Literature

The truth is that the Irish Americans, like the Irish themselves, have only lately discovered the cultural archives they are heirs to. Until recently, it was rare to find, in Irish-American fiction, a sense of pride in a shared literary tradition that dates back to early Christian times. It was rarer still to find the genuine sense of humor that has characterized Irish literature down the days. But Irish Americans are now reading Yeats and Synge and Joyce and O'Casey and Beckett with new purpose, and they are finally beginning to shake the debilitating inferiority, self-pity, and guilt of three centuries of British and American casting.

—Daniel J. Casey, on Irish American
literature past and present, in *An Gael*,
Spring 1984.

259. The "New Irish" Immigration After 1980 In the early 1980s, Ireland's economy turned sour and a new wave of young Irish immigrants began flocking to America. Many came as educated opportunity seekers with proper legal documentation, but an even greater number arrived as

students or vacationers who stayed after their visas expired. Because of their uncertain status, most of these new Irish took jobs as "off-the-books" workers in construction, childcare, and restaurants and bars. By the late 1980s, the illegal Irish community in America numbered between forty thousand and one hundred thousand. These new Irish immigrants settled primarily in large American cities where they influenced the revival of interest in Irish culture.

260. Kevin Kenny Observes In his superb synthesis of the history of the Irish American experience, *The American Irish: A History* (Longman, 2000), historian Kevin Kenny notes that there was "considerable tension" between the established Irish American community and the new, more European, Irish immigrants coming in the 1980s and 1990s.

Much of this tension was generational, with the old regarding the new as rude, lazy and ungrateful. But there was also considerable cultural conflict, as neither side conformed to the other's definition of Irishness. Many of the young new Irish found native-born Irish Americans to be reactionary, puritanical and romantic in their conception of Ireland, while established Irish Americans found the newcomers disrespectful, irreligious and lacking in patriotism to both Ireland and the United States. On questions of gay rights in particular, the two generations disagreed bitterly.

261. The Problem of the Immigration Laws The boom in Irish immigration and the subsequent problem of thousands of Irish illegals exposed an unintended flaw in America's immigration laws. In 1965, Congress dropped the patently racist quota system established in the 1920s in favor of what was hoped would be a more equitable one. Ireland and all other nations were given a maxi-

mum number of twenty thousand spots per year. But the law explicitly favored immigrants with immediate family members already in the U.S. or those with special skills. Most would-be Irish immigrants lacked special skills and because Irish immigration had slackened since the 1920s, few possessed any immediate relatives to qualify for the family reunification preference. Legions of second and third cousins did not count. Thus, while one immigrant from Bangladesh might enter and subsequently sponsor the migration of twenty-five members of his immediate family, immigrants from Ireland—whose forebears had once come by the millions to build the country—were effectively locked out.

Irish and Irish American activists, with backing from powerful members of Congress like Senator Ted Kennedy and Representative Tip O'Neill, successfully lobbied for special immigration reforms designed to allow for more legal Irish immigration. The 1986 Immigration Reform and Control Act created forty thousand visas for immigrants from countries negatively affected by the new system adopted in 1965. Irish applicants received more than sixteen thousand of these "Donnelly visas" (named for the bill's chief sponsor). The Immigration Act of 1990 created forty-eight thousand "Morrison visas" (also named for its sponsor) for Ireland. While these two programs benefited thousands, far too many of the prized visas went to applicants in Ireland who never used them, or who quickly returned to Ireland after a brief sojourn in the states. Thousands of undocumented Irish already living in America remained in limbo.

262. A New Ireland   The most important development in the history of the Republic of Ireland since the 1920s has been the nation's astonishing economic transformation. In the mid-1960s, under Taoiseach Sean Lemass, Ireland's government began to encourage economic development with programs and policies designed to increase exports and attract foreign investment. In 1973, the Republic joined the European Common Market (today's European Union) and soon became eligible for billions of dollars in development funds. Slowly but surely Ireland's infrastructure was modernized and that, together with the country's highly educated population, positioned Ireland to be a major player in the new high-tech global economy of the 1990s and beyond.

The most significant development in Ireland's economy was its embrace of the computer industry. Tens of thousands of jobs were created annually as Ireland became the top producer of Europe's software and center of its technical support operations. Computer hardware manufacturing grew as well as companies like Dell and Gateway established factories in Ireland.

By the mid-1990s annual growth was averaging 7 percent and economists were referring to Ireland as the "Celtic Tiger." Perhaps most telling, Ireland in the 1990s experienced a net inflow of population, something which occurred only once before (in the 1970s) since the Famine. Incredibly, these arrivals were not merely returning Irish, but also immigrants and refugees from Eastern Europe and North Africa. After centuries of hemorrhaging its young and talented to the rest of the world, Ireland had become a desirable destination.

The impact of Ireland's booming economy goes far beyond the simple issues of jobs and income. Ireland's newfound prosperity has fueled a new, more optimistic outlook among the Irish. More and more they view themselves as European, rather than simply as Irish. This transformation in outlook has coincided with a sharp decline in the authority of the Catholic Church in everyday life.

263. Irish Lesbians and Gays   Few aspects of Irish American life seemed more immune to change than the annual St. Patrick's Day parades held in cities across the country. This was especially true of the parade in New York City, which maintained strict rules of behavior and banned symbols of modernity such as motorized floats. The only controversy in recent times associated with the event was the decision by the Ancient Order of Hibernians, the organization that runs the parade, to name Michael Flannery of NORAID as the Grand Marshall. But that flap was over questions of politics and ideology, not Irish identity itself.

Enter ILGO, the Irish Lesbian and Gay Organization. Their attempt to march in the parade in 1991 sparked a controversy that rages to this day. ILGO demanded inclusion in what they said was a celebration of Irish *ethnicity*. The AOH countered by asserting that the parade was a private, *religious* event, specifically Catholic, and that because homosexuality violated church teachings, they could not allow ILGO to march. The courts have consistently backed this interpretation.

Eight years after issuing its first challenge, ILGO has yet to win the right to march. Yet they have succeeded in some of their larger goals— shattering the image of the Irish in America as a one-dimensional community and forcing its members to confront the difficult questions of tolerance and inclusion that have marked American life for centuries. In the end, the answer may be found in, of all places, Ireland. What's been lost in the debate over the right of ILGO to march is the fact that groups similar to ILGO are allowed to march in parades in Ireland.

264. Look Who's Turning Up Irish   With Irish firmly established as "cool" in the 1990s, a good many unexpected people began turning up Irish. Among them, a large number of African Americans with Irish ancestors: Muhammad Ali, Gen. Colin Powell, Alice Walker, Martin Luther King, Jr., Derek Jeter, and Mariah Carey.

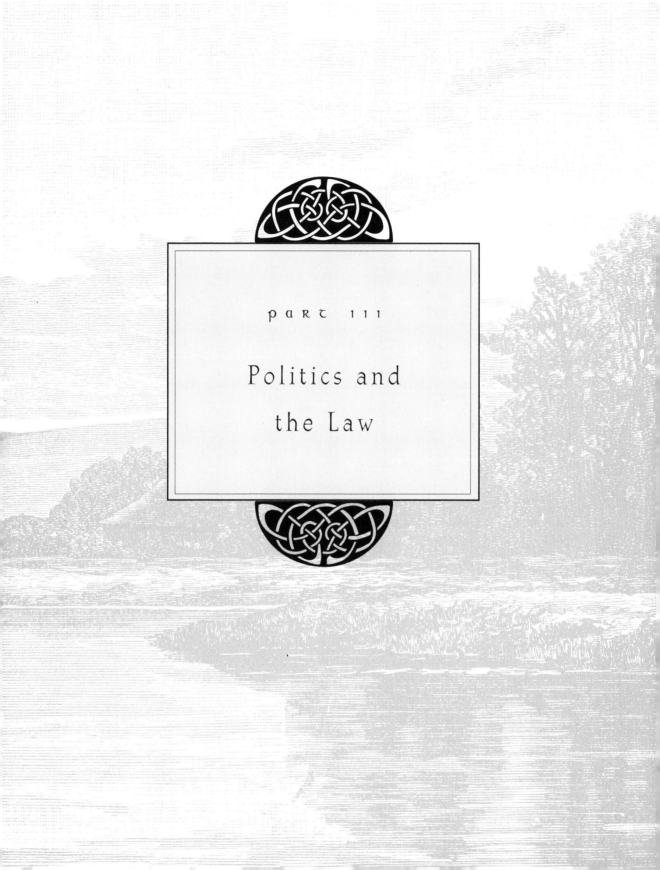

PART III

Politics and
the Law

265. Some Irish Leaders in the South Captain Florence O'Sullivan of Cork commanded a ship in the first fleet carrying English and Irish immigrants to the newly established settlement in Charleston, South Carolina, in 1670. He was soon named surveyor-general of the colony and served as commander of the militia. Sullivan's Island in Charleston's harbor is named for him. Two early proprietary governors of South Carolina were Irishmen Richard Kyrle who served in 1684 and James Moore who served from 1700 to 1703. Moore's son James became a royal governor of South Carolina in 1719.

In Virginia, Cork-born Daniel McCarthy rose to become a burgess in 1705 and speaker of the house (1715–20). In Maryland Daniel Dulany (1685–1753) arrived as an indentured servant and eventually became a judge and member of the colonial legislature.

266. The Irishman in New York—Thomas Dongan Born into a wealthy, landed family in Ireland in 1634, Thomas Dongan served in the British Army and later as lieutenant governor in Tangiers. In 1683, the Duke of York selected him to be New York's colonial governor. Upon his arrival, he called a representative assembly, which passed the "Charter of Liberties." It established representative government for the colony and guaranteed religious liberty.

In the wake of England's Glorious Revolution, which saw Dongan's benefactor, James II, deposed, Dongan returned to England in 1689. He succeeded his brother as the Earl of Limerick, but died in poverty in 1715 after his ancestral lands were confiscated.

267. The Irishman in Philadelphia—James Logan A native of County Armagh, James Logan (1674–1751) came to the colony of Pennsylvania as William Penn's secretary. After advancing through several political offices, he was elected mayor of Philadelphia in 1722. During his tenure as mayor, Logan allowed Irish Catholic immigrants to participate in the city's first public Mass. He later served as the colony's chief justice starting in 1731, and in the absence of a governor, became acting governor from 1736 to 1738.

Logan was also a natural scientist whose primary contribution to the emerging field of botany was a treatise that described experiments on the impregnation of plant seeds.

268. Other Early Irish Leaders In addition to the aforementioned, dozens of Irish immigrants emerged as important leaders in colonial America. George Bryan (1731–91), for example, arrived in Philadelphia in 1752 and became a merchant and a political leader who played a prominent role in the agitation that led to the American Revolution. William Johnson (1715–74) of County Meath immigrated to New York where, in recognition of his leadership during the French and Indian War, he was knighted and given one hundred thousand acres of land. Thomas Burke of Galway (1745–83) immigrated to North Carolina, became a successful planter, and a leader in the colony's move toward independence (indeed, he served as its wartime governor). James Sullivan (1744–1808) was governor of Massachusetts and John Sullivan fought with distinction in the Revolutionary War. John later served as governor of New Hampshire (1786–89); James served as Massachusetts state attorney general (1790–1807) and governor (1807–08).

Nineteenth-Century Movers and Shakers

269. James G. Blaine Already a successful newspaper editor in his adopted home state of Maine, James G. Blaine (1830–93) helped form the state's Republican Party, and served as its chairman (1859–81). After three terms in the Maine state legislature, Blaine served as a U.S. congressman (1863–76; house speaker 1869–75), and as a U.S. senator (1876–81). Several times a candidate for president, Blaine's personal conduct undercut his chances—he faced accusations of corruption and he failed to distance himself from unfortunate remarks a clergyman made about Democrats ("rum, romanism, and rebellion"), many of whom were Irish Catholics. Also secretary of state twice, during his tenure he organized the Pan-American Congress.

270. William Jennings Bryan After becoming a lawyer, William Jennings Bryan (1860–1925) moved from Illinois to Nebraska, hoping for better political prospects. He served as a U.S. congressman (1891–95), became a Democratic Party leader, and eventually served as Woodrow Wilson's secretary of state (1913–15). A fiery orator who represented farmers and labor and opposed big business and trusts, Bryan's political career is best known for his three unsuccessful presidential campaigns (1896, 1900, and 1908).

In 1925, Bryan prosecuted the Scopes "Monkey" Trial, during which defense attorney Clarence Darrow examined Bryan's fundamentalist biblical beliefs, highlighting Bryan's intellectual shortcomings. Bryan died in his sleep five days after the trial's conclusion.

271. De Witt Clinton Grandson of an immigrant

De Witt Clinton

from Longford, De Witt Clinton (1769–1828) was one of the most influential politicians in the early republic. He served as mayor of New York City from 1803–15 (except for 1807 and 1810). During this time he oversaw the creation and adoption of Manhattan's street grid (1811), a decision that sped development of the city and made it conducive to business. More important, Clinton was the visionary who proposed building a 363-mile canal across upstate New York to connect the upper Hudson River with Lake Erie. Unprecedented as a feat of engineering, the Erie Canal (1817–25) proved a stunning success and launched New York on its way to becoming the Empire State. For most of the nineteenth century, two thirds of the nation's imports and exports would flow in and out of New York Harbor.

272. Bourke Cockran Born in Sligo, William Bourke Cockran (1854–1923) immigrated to the United States when he was seventeen. Settling in upstate New York, he studied law and was admitted to the bar in 1876. Soon, he moved to New York City, where he began a successful career in public life, helped considerably by his gift for oratory. First elected to the House of Representatives in 1886, he served on and off

Bourke Cockran

until his death in 1923. Cockran was known for wielding considerable influence within the Democratic Party, serving as a delegate to the Democratic National Conventions of 1884, 1892, 1904, and 1920. He also took an active interest in the affairs of his homeland and at a 1916 rally in New York delivered a stirring speech denouncing the executions of the Easter Rising leaders.

273. Some Governors of Note Irish Americans made their way into the Governor's Mansion of many states in the nineteenth century. County Roscommon–born John G. Downey, yet another gold rush era success story, won election as governor of California in 1860. In 1863, Isaac Murphy was elected provisional governor of Union-occupied Arkansas and held power until 1868.

Bosses and Big-City Political Machines

274. An Observer Explains the Irish Affinity for the Democratic Party

> By a kind of instinct, the Irish have attached themselves almost universally to the Democratic party. They got the idea that it was the party of popular rights, the anti-aristocratic party, the liberal party. They at least know their friends. The Democrats always welcomed and guarded the rights of the foreigner. The Federal-Whig-Republican party always hated foreigners and wished to restrict their rights of citizenship.
>
> —Thomas L. Nichols, *Forty Years of American Life*, 1864.

275. Why Were The Irish So Successful in American Politics? Irish immigrants possessed a number of qualities that ensured their early success in municipal politics. First, they benefited from timing. The great tide of Irish immigration coincided with the granting of voting rights to all white male citizens and the rapid expansion of American cities. In addition, while some arrived speaking only Irish, the great majority spoke English—a decided advantage over their German counterparts. Large numbers of Irish immigrants were also familiar with democratic politics, having participated in Daniel O'Connell's grassroots movement for Catholic emancipation. In addition, strong cultural traditions of loyalty to village and clan were easily adapted to neighborhood and party.

276. The Political Machine A political machine is defined as a party organization, run by an autocratic "boss" or small group of men, capable of garnering sufficient votes year after year to maintain political and administrative control of a city, county, or state. They came into being in most large American cities in the early antebellum period, generally before the mass arrival of the Irish. The Irish, therefore, did not invent political machines, but they did become very adept at running them.

Several factors contributed to the growth of the political machine in the 1820s. First, most states abolished voting requirements, thereby opening up the political process to virtually all white men, including naturalized immigrants. Second, the 1820s marked the beginning of rapid urbanization. Most city governments were barely able to cope with the huge increases in population (due to mass immigration, which began at this time), the birth of mass transit, soaring crime rates, and widespread poverty. This created a power vacuum into which stepped the political boss and his "machine."

Political machines gained and retained power by providing charity and opportunity to the urban poor and a favorable business environment to commercial interests. The former took the form of handouts of food, coal, and clothing to needy families, or jobs on the city payroll or with a firm doing business with the city. "Ward heelers," as neighborhood party operatives were known, played a key role in tending to the needs of constituents in their neighborhoods. Commercial interests also benefited from the machine's prodevelopment style of government that encouraged the construction of schools, roads, sewers, parks, and playgrounds. Businesses that agreed to give generously to the machine's campaign funds, distribute bribes, hire workers sent by machine officials, and participate in kickback schemes received the lion's share of contracts for these projects.

277. Corruption and Charity   As the references to kickbacks and bribes indicate, machines were also known for their corruption, though it rarely involved the direct looting of the city treasury. Rather, machine corruption generally took the form of under-the-table payments. Often, machine politicians owned shares in businesses that not coincidentally gained lucrative city contracts. Boss Tweed in New York, for example, made more than a million dollars through city contracts awarded to his printing business.

Machines were also charged, not without reason, with corruption at the polls. Voting in nineteenth-century urban America was a rather rough-and-tumble affair. In many cities, machines manned the polls with "shoulder hitters" to encourage voters to cast ballots for their candidate and to fight off toughs in the employ of rival candidates. Since policemen and election officials who owed their jobs to political connections were in charge at polling sites, ballot stuffing (or the opposite practice of "counting out" an opponent) were common occurrences. So, too, was the use of "repeaters"—men expert in voting several times on election day, often posing as people who were in fact dead. There was an old saying in Boston: "The election is never over 'til all the votes are counted from St. Augustine's Cemetery."

Occasionally, reformers managed to defeat a political machine at the polls, but they invariably lasted only a single term. Vowing to fight corruption and police brutality might win votes on election day, but closing saloons on Sundays and laying off city workers (as reformers invariably did

in the name of morality and thrift) only led to political defeat a year or two later.

278. Cultural Defense   Another important aspect of the political machine's appeal was the cultural defense it offered its immigrant constituents. Nativism, or anti-immigrant sentiment, rose concurrently with the increased arrival of immigrants, especially the Irish. Democratic machines gathered the Irish vote by thwarting nativist ambitions and speaking out in favor of cultural and religious tolerance.

279. Tammany Hall   The most famous, or perhaps infamous, political machine in America was Tammany Hall in New York City. It originated in 1788 as a fraternal society—the Society of Saint Tammany, or Columbian Order—as an egalitarian alternative to the many aristocratic gentlemen's clubs founded at the time. Comprising mainly artisans and small merchants, the organization chose as their "patron saint" the Delaware Indian chief Tamanend (nicknamed Tammany) and employed Indian terms such as "sachem" for councilmember, "brave" for a rank-and-file member, and "wigwam" for their meeting hall. The latter accounted for the organization's popular name, Tammany Hall.

Initially, Tammany was a social and charitable agency not connected with politics. Tammany also had no original connection with the Irish and espoused an enthusiastic Americanism that took a dim view of foreigners. Most Irish New Yorkers in the early republic supported Jefferson, as his party was identified with opposition to the Alien and Sedition Acts (see entry #151) and support for France (by definition an anti-British posture). However, Aaron Burr and later Martin Van Buren transformed the society into their personal political organization and promoted an agenda that appealed to the growing number of poor Irish entering the city: universal manhood suffrage, abolition of imprisonment for debt, and tolerance of ethnic and religious minorities.

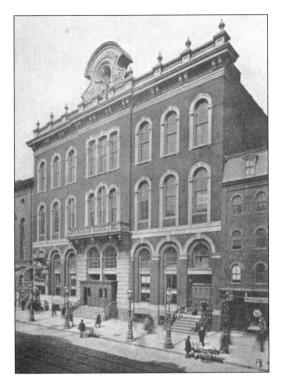

of Irish American city officials, among them the head of the Department of Public Works, Peter B. Sweeney, and Comptroller Richard B. Connolly. Known as the Ring, they conspired to bilk the city of millions of dollars through an elaborate series of kickbacks. The most notorious of these was the new New York County Courthouse (known to this day as the Tweed Courthouse), a project intended to cost $250,000, which eventually cost $13 million—a stunning 5,200 percent cost overrun! Tweed's undoing came at the hands of a disgruntled office seeker named James O'Brien, who handed over damning records to the *New York Times,* which began an exposé in July 1871.

281. The NEW YORK TIMES Exults   In the wake of the Boss Tweed scandal in New York City, the Republican Party demolished the Democrats in the election of 1872. The *New York Times,* a staunchly Republican newspaper that had long exhibited hostility toward Tammany and its Irish supporters published the following exultant editorial on November 7, 1872:

> [T]he rule of one class, and that the most ignorant class in the community, is over. The ignorant, unthinking, bigoted hordes which Tammany brought up to its support year after year are hopelessly scattered. Americans—truly so-called— are now determined to have some share in the government of this City, and will no longer leave it to be tyrannized over by our esteemed friends from the Emerald Isle. This is going to be an American city once more—not simply a larger kind of Dublin. The iron rod of our "oppressed" friend is broken.

282. Tammany's Comeback   The *Times* and those whose views it represented were wrong. Tammany was down, but it was far from out. Under the leadership of Tweed's successor, "Honest" John Kelly—the first of ten consecutive Irish Catholic

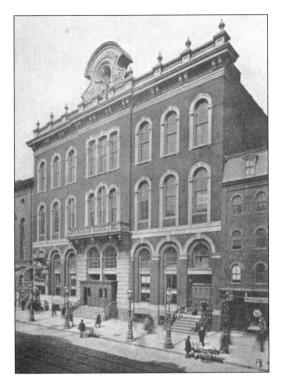

Tammany Hall

280. The Tweed Scandals   The head of a political machine was invariably known as the "boss." The most famous machine boss was William Tweed of Tammany Hall. Although not Irish himself (his background was Scotch Presbyterian), Tweed gained notoriety in the 1840s as the brawling foreman of his volunteer fire company Americus No. 6 whose Tiger logo eventually came to symbolize Tammany in political parlance and cartoons. Tweed assiduously cultivated the Irish vote in the Seventh Ward, handing out favors and reminding them he once lost an election to a Know Nothing. Tweed rose quickly through the ranks of the Tammany apparatus, becoming head of the Tammany General Committee in 1863. Known thereafter as "Boss" Tweed, he soon began making huge sums of money from printing firms he owned that had fat contracts with the city.

By 1870, Tweed had assembled a loyal cadre

John Kelly

bosses—Tammany emerged from the wreckage of the Tweed scandals a stronger and more influential force.

The key to Kelly's success was his respectable image and low-key style (in contrast to Tweed) and thorough restructuring of the Tammany organization. One contemporary remarked at Kelly's death that he had found Tammany a horde and left it an army. He created a tightly organized hierarchy (modeled, many mused, on the Catholic Church), of assembly district leaders, election captains, and ward heelers. Cementing this new system was Kelly's complete control of patronage and nominations. It was during his tenure that people began to characterize Tammany as a "machine."

Kelly's successor, Irish-born Richard Croker, solidified Kelly's accomplishments, though his brazen style stood in great contrast to Kelly's more polished image. He ran Tammany from Kelly's death until 1901 when, faced with mounting scandals and pending investigations, he retired to Ireland with a small fortune.

Charles Francis Murphy (1858–1924) succeeded Richard Croker in 1902 and became the most powerful boss in Tammany's history. The son of Irish immigrants, Murphy quit school at age fourteen and worked a series of jobs, saving money until he purchased a saloon. He eventually amassed four such establishments and made a significant percentage of his fortune. He soon became a member of Tammany Hall, and by 1892, Murphy became the leader of Manhattan's so-called Gas House District. His stature in the Tammany organization rose until, in September 1902, Murphy became the undisputed leader of Tammany Hall, a title he maintained until his sudden death in 1924.

In contrast to his predecessor Croker, the taciturn and teetotaling Murphy (his nickname was "silent Charlie") brought an air of respectability to Tammany Hall. He furthered this end by promoting a new crop of Tammany politicians—chief among them Al Smith—who moved the machine away from the Robin Hood methods of Boss Tweed and toward a Progressive Era style that rewarded the loyalty of the poor with reforms like factory safety and child labor laws. Thus, Murphy is credited with transforming Tammany into a political organization capable of drawing the votes of the ever-growing numbers of new immigrants from Eastern and Southern Europe, a feat that kept Tammany in power until the early 1930s.

283. George Washington Plunkitt Explains   Born to Irish immigrants, George Washington Plunkitt (1842–1924) rose to prominence as a member of Tammany Hall. He served in the state assembly, on the board of aldermen, and the state senate, and in classic Tammany fashion, earned a fortune. Although Plunkitt, like many of Tammany's members, was accused by opponents of political corruption, he denied the charges, drawing a distinction between what he termed "honest graft" (using one's political position to capitalize on inside information) and "dishonest graft" (accepting bribes or otherwise acting illegally). Plunkitt outlined many of his views on the politics of his day in a published series of interviews, *Plunkitt of Tammany Hall* (1905). During these interviews, Plunkitt summed up his life by stating "I seen my opportunities and I took 'em." He also explained why Tammany and political machines were so successful on election day:

> If a family is burned out I don't ask whether they are Republicans or Democrats, and I don't refer them to the Charity Organization Society, which would investigate their case for a month or two and decide if they were worthy of help about the time they are dead from star-

vation. I just get quarters for them, buy clothes for them if their clothes were burned up, and fix them up til they get things runnin' again. It's philanthropy, but it's politics, too—mighty good politics. Who can tell how many votes one of these fires brings me? The poor are the most grateful people in the world, and, let me tell you, they have more friends in their neighborhoods than the rich have in theirs.

284. Jimmy Walker and the Fall of Tammany Hall

By 1929, Tammany Hall seemed invincible. The stock market was booming, filling the city coffers with cash as never before and allowing for a long list of graft-producing municipal projects. The machine had just opened a brand new Tammany Hall on Union Square and its beloved rogue frontman, James "Jimmy" Walker (1881–1946), had just been reelected to a second term, defeating a would-be reformer Fiorello LaGuardia. Walker was the quintessential Jazz Era mayor—handsome, stylishly dressed, and openly accompanied by his mistress, showgirl Betty Compton. He was also funny, supplying the press with a steady stream of one-liners and wisecracks such as: "I'd rather be a lampost in New York than mayor of Chicago."

But Walker soon found himself in serious trouble. He had taken huge bribes and kickbacks from city contractors and now one judge Samuel Seabury was on his tail. Walker characteristically brushed off the investigation as just so much nonsense, but by 1931, with indictments pending, Walker abruptly resigned and sailed for Europe. By then the Roaring Twenties were bust and Tammany Hall would soon default on the mortgage for their new palace at Union Square. In 1933, that pesky reformer, Fiorello LaGuardia, mobilized the city's Jewish, Italian, and African American vote and swept into office. Tammany would remain a factor in city politics for another twenty years, but its long reign had come to an end.

Other Big-City Bosses

285. Frank Hague   Jersey City boss Frank Hague (1876–1956) was born on January 17, 1876, in "the Horseshoe" tenement area of Jersey City, New Jersey. The son of immigrant parents from County Cavan, Ireland, he entered public office in 1911, winning a race for city street and water commissioner. By 1917, Hague's political machine enabled him to gain the mayor's seat, which he held until his voluntary retirement thirty years later. Hague's machine also eventually made him the most powerful politician in New Jersey and a national Democratic Party leader. He retained power through a combination of intimidation of his political rivals and by providing his constituents goods—free food, fuel, and clothes, and employment help. After Hague's reign ended, he turned over his authority to his nephew, Frank Hague Eggers. Eggers lost the following election, and Hague was passed over for his customary spot on the Democratic National Committee.

286. James Michael Curley   Born in a South Boston Irish tenement to a father from Galway and mother from Connemara, James Michael Curley (1874–1958) overcame his impoverished childhood to dominate Boston politics for the first half of the twentieth century. Beginning in 1899, Curley held numerous offices: common councilman; alderman; state representative; U.S. congressman; and Massachusetts governor (1935–37). He liked being Mayor of Boston best, and eventually served four nonconsecutive terms (1914–17, 1922–25, 1930–33, and 1946–49). His flamboyant and combative style made him a favorite with the city's poor, whose cause he championed, and an enemy of Boston's Yankee elite, against whom he often railed.

Despite his electoral successes, Curley never managed to establish a true political machine. True bosses rarely served in high offices, preferring to exercise power from behind the scenes through hand-picked office holders. Boston's Irish were politically divided and Curley vied for power with three other powerful Irish chieftains, among them Martin Lomasney, John F. "Honey Fitz" Fitzgerald, and Patrick Kennedy.

Curley also represented, as historian Thomas O'Connor writes, one of two alternating styles of Irish politics that dominated the city for most of the twentieth century. The city's first Irish Catholic mayor, Hugh O'Brien (1885–89), and later Patrick Collins (1903–05), represented a "respectable" style, seeking peaceful accommodation with Boston's Anglo-Protestant ascendancy by downplaying ethnocultural issues and projecting an image (and reality) of fiscal restraint and propriety. In contrast, Curley was a brash "populist." Born into classic Irish ghetto poverty, Curley took his cues not from the downtown centers of financial, cultural, and political power but rather from the Irish-dominated wards. His election in 1915 ended decades of accommodationist Irish style. He was provocative, confrontational, flagrant, and beloved (at least by the Irish poor). His years as

James Michael Curley

mayor brought many benefits to working-class neighborhoods (paid for, noted Curley with unrestrained glee, by the wealthy who despised them). The price, notes O'Connor, was political warfare that hampered Boston's ability to focus on necessary municipal projects. The shenanigans associated with Curley also cost the city its share of New Deal money, even though Curley was an early and ardent supporter of FDR.

Edwin O'Connor drew on Curley's final mayoral campaign, which he lost, in the novel *The Last Hurrah* (1956). Curley published his autobiography, *I'd Do It Again* (1957), a year before his death.

287. John Francis "Honey Fitz" Fitzgerald   "Honey Fitz" (1863–1950) became the first American-born child of Irish parents to become mayor of Boston. Born to immigrants from County Wexford, Fitzgerald studied at Harvard until his father's death. After flirting with the insurance industry, he turned to politics. Soon the boss of Boston's Ward 6, Fitzgerald held numerous elective offices, including Boston Common Council member (1892), Massachusetts state senator (1892), U.S. representative (1895–1901), and mayor (1905–7, 1910–14). After his second term as mayor—the first four-year term for a Boston mayor—Fitzgerald held only one more elective office, in the U.S. House of Representatives (1919–21). His mayoral terms were marked by confrontation with the Yankee elites as well as other of the city's ward bosses, but he did provide increased services to his constituents, such as entertainment facilities and jobs. Ten years after his death, Fitzgerald's grandson, John F. Kennedy, became the first Irish Catholic president in United States history.

288. Ed Kelly   A much larger and more powerful citywide political machine emerged in the 1930s under Edward J. Kelly (1876–1950). Born in Chicago, he quit school at age twelve to work. Drawn to engineering, he studied on his own and took night classes while working for the city's water and sewer department. Chief engineer by 1920, he played a central role in some of the city's biggest infrastructure projects and befriended many influential members of the city's Democratic Party establishment. He was named interim mayor by Chicago's city council when an assassin trying to shoot President-elect Franklin Roosevelt killed Mayor Anton Cermak instead. Kelly proved an able and popular mayor who guided the city through the difficult times of the Great Depression. Elected in his own right in 1935, Kelly won again in 1939 and 1943. Working closely with Patrick Nash (their partnership was known as the Kelly-Nash machine), he drew enormous power from the forty thousand public jobs he controlled, not to mention the millions he doled out in the form of contracts for city improvements. He lost reelection in 1947 and retired from politics and philanthropy.

289. Chris "Blind Boss" Buckley

Christopher Buckley (1845–1922), the son of an Irish stonemason, moved to San Francisco in 1862. Introduced to politics while bartending, by 1873 (around the time he went blind), Buckley had become an influential member of the city's Democratic political organization. Although he never held public office, after Democrats swept the city elections in 1882, Buckley was the party's acknowledged leader and, although he never exercised the autocratic power of other city bosses, he wielded the most influence in San Francisco, controlling the selection of judges, mayors, and governors. Indicted in 1891 on bribery charges, which were later dismissed, Buckley's political influence quickly waned.

290. Tom Pendergast

The Pendergast machine in Kansas City was among the strongest in the nation before World War II. Tom Pendergast (1872–1945) was born into a large Irish Catholic family in Missouri. Through his older politically connected saloon-owning brother, he worked his way up the ranks through a series of patronage jobs in Kansas City. After a brief stint on the city council (1910–14), he left elective office to develop his political machine from behind the scenes. By the 1920s, he ruled Kansas City with an iron fist, controlling patronage and doling out bribes where necessary. He also grew rich by using his influence to gain lucrative public works contracts for his Ready-Mixed Concrete Company. One of Pendergast's greatest claims to fame is that he helped launch the career of Harry Truman, helping him get elected to the Senate in 1934. During the Depression, Pendergast used his connections with President Roosevelt to gain substantial New Deal funding, which he then used to serve the interests of his organization.

But scandal eventually caught up with him. When an investigation for widespread corruption, electoral fraud, and income tax evasion drew increased media coverage in the late 1930s, Pendergast lost his access to Roosevelt. Convicted on the tax charge, he served fifteen months in prison. By the time he was released, his machine had collapsed.

291. Other Bosses of Note

Irish political bosses emerged in smaller cities. For example, at the turn of the twentieth century, Dan O'Connell established in Albany, New York, one of the longest-running and most successful political machines ever built. It endured until the early 1990s. In New Orleans, John Fitzpatrick, known far and wide as the "Big Boss of the Third Ward," held many public offices, including mayor (1892–96). He headed an organization known as the Choctaw Club. Hugh McLaughlin ran the Democratic organization in Brooklyn (then an independent city), while in nearby Long Island City (part of present-day Queens) Patrick "Battle Axe" Gleason ruled with an iron fist. Farther north in Buffalo William F. Sheehan ran the local machine in the 1880s, while P. J. Somers won election as mayor of Milwaukee four times in the 1860s.

Some lesser bosses controlled small sections of big cities. Martin Lomasney, "the Mahatma," for example, was boss of Boston's Eighth Ward in the West End. In Chicago it was Michael "Hinky Dink" Kenna and John Coughlin who ruled Chicago's First Ward for nearly forty-five years from the 1880s to the 1920s. Big Tim Sullivan likewise dominated New York's Lower East Side for thirty years beginning in the 1880s.

292. Irish American Goo Goos   Not all big city Irish politicians were involved in machine politics. Several distinguished themselves as prominent reformers hostile to the machines. One such example was James Phelan. In the late 1880s and 1890s he led a good government movement in San Francisco that eventually brought down boss Chris "Blind Boss" Buckley. He later served three terms as mayor of San Francisco, beginning in 1897, during which he earned a reputation for good government and a commitment to the "city beautiful" movement. Phelan also served a term in the U.S. Senate from 1914 to 1920. His mansion, Villa Montalvo, which he willed to the state of California, now serves as a museum for his art collection.

His counterpart in New York was John Purroy Mitchel (1879–1918), the grandson of famed Fenian John Mitchel. His first stint in public service was as a special investigator of municipal corruption, a job that earned him a wide reputation as a reformer. Elected to the Board of Aldermen in 1909 on a reform ticket, in 1913 he defeated the regular Tammany candidate for mayor, Edward E. McCall. His administration was marked by energetic reform and, as a consequence, much controversy. Defeated by Tammany's John Hylan in 1917, he later joined the army air corps and was killed in a training accident.

Twentieth-Century
Movers and Shakers

293. Al Smith   Alfred E. Smith (1873–1944) was the son of a Teamster and factory worker. His father, Alfred E. Smith, Sr., was of Italian and German ethnicity. His Irish roots come from his mother, Katherine Mulverhill. Even though of multiethnic background, Smith always thought of himself, as did the public, primarily as Irish.

Smith grew up in the teeming immigrant quarter of New York City known as the Lower East Side. Although surrounded by scenes of abject poverty, the Smiths lived in modest, respectable, working-class comfort. That changed abruptly when Smith's father died. The tragedy forced the thirteen-year-old to quit school with only an eighth-grade education and work to help support his family. Work and socializing brought him into contact with the city's legendary Irish-dominated political machine, Tammany Hall. He soon joined the organization and developed a reputation as a skilled campaign worker and effective speaker. In 1903 he won election to the state assembly.

Smith represented a new era for Tammany Hall machine politics. In the days of Boss William Tweed in the 1870s, Tammany garnered the loyalty of working-class voters by performing Robin Hood–style charity. With money garnered through graft or kickbacks, they paid people's rent, passed out Christmas turkeys and bags of coal, and bought rounds of beer at the local saloon—all in exchange for votes on election day. By the turn of the century, however, Progressive Era politicians like Smith recognized the need to deliver social legislation.

As a result, Smith steered Tammany toward support for child labor laws, workers' compensation, tenement reform, and women's suffrage. His reformer credentials were confirmed in 1911 when, in the wake of the horrific Triangle Shirtwaist Factory Fire that killed 146 garment workers, Smith cochaired the investigative committee on factory safety.

Elected governor of the state in 1918 (and again in 1920, 1924, and 1926), Smith furthered his reputation as a reformer, signing into law numerous measures regarding rent control, public transportation, the rights of workers, and social welfare benefits. Many historians credit Smith's initiatives with laying the groundwork for

Al Smith with James Walker (left) and Florence Cohalen (center)

Franklin D. Roosevelt's New Deal during the Great Depression.

After nearly winning Democratic nomination for President in 1924, Smith succeeded in 1928. But he was soundly defeated by Republican Herbert Hoover in an election that featured ugly displays of anti-Catholicism. (See entry #231 for details about the 1928 election).

294. Joseph Patrick Tumulty After passing the bar in 1902, Joseph Tumulty joined Democratic politics. Tumulty came from Jersey City, where his Irish Catholic father was a grocer. Tumulty represented Hudson County in the state assembly then served as secretary to Governor and President Woodrow Wilson. Tumulty's Washington position involved power similar to today's chief of staff. He remained close to Wilson until 1917, when the two had a falling out—possibly due to the influence of a few anti-Catholic advisors who cooled the President's trust. Tumulty subsequently went into private law practice in Washington.

295. Joseph P. Kennedy Ambassador to Great Britain from 1938 to 1940 and the father of John F., Robert F., and Edward, Joseph Kennedy (1888–1969) was an American businessman who amassed a fortune and presided over an American political dynasty. He was born in Boston, son of Patrick Kennedy, a saloon owner and politician. He graduated from Harvard College in 1912 and married Rose Fitzgerald, the daughter of Boston mayor John F. "Honey Fitz" Fitzgerald, in 1914.

He began his career in business as a banker, before moving chiefly into investing in stocks, the film industry, and some say, bootlegging operations during Prohibition. He was one of the few big Wall Street investors to pull their money from the stock market in the summer of 1929 and thus escaped the Crash of '29 with his fortune intact. A major fund-raiser for President Franklin Roosevelt, he was named the first chairman of the U.S. Securities and Exchange Commission in 1934 and later chairman of the Federal Maritime Commission. In 1937, he was named to the prestigious position of Ambassador to England. But his isolationist views and defeatist attitude regarding England's chances against Nazi Germany, not to mention disparaging remarks about Mrs. Roosevelt, led to his recall in 1940.

With his own political career ruined, he turned his attention to his four sons. When his oldest son, Joseph P., was killed in World War II, he focused on John. Through his connections and family wealth, he assisted his son's political ascent to Congress and the White House. Sadly, he would live to see his sons John and Robert cut down by assassins. He died in 1969.

296. James A. Farley Grassy Point, New York, was not only the birthplace of James Aloysius Farley (1888–1976), but the birthplace of his political career as well. First elected town clerk in 1912, then chairman of his county's Democratic Com-

James A. Farley

mittee, Farley's political presence grew steadily. In 1932 he became chairman of the Democratic National Committee, the first in a string of Irish Catholics to occupy the post. Following his first successful presidential campaign, Franklin Delano Roosevelt awarded Farley the office of United States Postmaster General. Farley also led Roosevelt's first bid for reelection, after which he returned to his old position in the cabinet.

297. Ed Flynn Born into a middle-class Irish family in the Bronx, Ed Flynn (1891–1953) rose to become one of the most influential Irish American political figures from the 1920s to the 1950s. He earned his law degree at Fordham in 1912 and won election, with Tammany Hall's backing, to the state assembly in 1917. He later served as Bronx County Sheriff (1922–25). From 1922 to the time of his death he served as chairman of the Bronx Democratic organization. Known for his honesty and reform principles, he served as secretary of state and a trusted advisor to Franklin Roosevelt during the latter's term as governor of New York State. In 1940 Roosevelt tapped him to be Chairman of the Democratic National Committee.

298. Thomas Gardiner Corcoran Born in Pawtucket, Rhode Island, and educated at Harvard Law School, Thomas Gardiner Corcoran (1900–81) was one of several Irish American advisors in Franklin D. Roosevelt's inner circle during the New Deal. After five years of practicing corporate law in New York, Corcoran joined the Reconstruction Finance Committee in 1932. When Roosevelt began to take notice of his efforts, Corcoran was given a wider range of responsibilities than his official position as assistant general counsel allowed. He organized administrative agencies for various New Deal programs and assisted in drafting such legislation as the Fair Labor Standards Act of 1938.

299. David I. Walsh David I. Walsh (1872–1947) was born to Irish immigrants in 1872 and gradu-

David I. Walsh

ated from Boston University Law School in 1897. He began his political career as chairman of the Democratic Committee in Clinton, Massachusetts, and served in the state legislature before becoming Massachusetts' first Catholic governor (1913–15). Like Al Smith in New York, he pushed for social legislation, creating laws to protect the rights of workers. From state politics he moved to the national level as a U.S. senator from 1919 to 1924, and from 1926 to 1947. He was against U.S. membership in the League of Nations, but in favor of the United Nations.

300. Ken O'Donnell and Dave Powers Two prominent members of the cadre of Irishmen relied upon by President John F. Kennedy—sometimes called the "Irish Mafia"—were Kenneth P. O'Donnell and David F. Powers. Powers met Kennedy when the future president was campaigning for Congress in Boston and continued to work on Kennedy's behalf until his death, although he never held an official political position. O'Donnell came to the Kennedy fold through his friendship with Kennedy's brother, Robert, at Harvard. A witty, loyal confidant whose company Kennedy enjoyed and counsel he trusted, O'Donnell served as Special Assistant to the President for Kennedy's entire term. O'Donnell and Powers later published a book about their personal reminiscences, *Johnny, We Hardly Knew Ye.*

301. Some Governors of Note Several important Irish Americans served as state governors in the twentieth century. In California, for example, Edmund G. Brown (1905–96) won election as governor of California in 1958; his son Jerry

Brown (b. 1938) followed in his footsteps and won the office in 1974. In between Ronald Reagan held the office for two terms. In Massachusetts, David I. Walsh became the state's first Irish Catholic governor in 1912. He used the position as a stepping stone to higher office—the U.S. Senate—where he served from 1919 to 1947. Likewise, Al Smith became New York's first Irish Catholic governor in 1918, and served four terms before unsuccessfully running for president in 1928. Herbert Romulus O'Conor ran successfully for governor of Maryland in 1939 and held the office until he left for the Senate in 1947.

Irish American Political Machines in the Postwar Era

302. The Last Hurrah or Rainbow's End? In *The Last Hurrah,* his thinly disguised fictionalized account of the life of Boston's James Michael Curley, Edwin O'Connor endeavored to explain why political machines and master politicians that once seemed invincible disintegrated after World War II. It was, he explained, the natural consequence of the New Deal. The machine had originated and thrived for more than a century by meeting the needs of poor, powerless people. All they asked for in return was a vote. The birth of the welfare state in the 1930s meant that people would henceforth turn to the state, not the ward heeler, for assistance. Politicians like Curley and machines like Tammany had become obsolete by 1950, if not before.

Political scientist Stephen Erie, however, offers a different thesis. In his book *Rainbow's End,* he notes that some political machines were done in by the New Deal, but many were not. In fact, those bosses who made the transition to the new reality of federal money and civil service were able to build political machines that lasted until the 1970s. Erie argues that it was the curtailing of federal money to cities in the 1970s and 1980s that finished off the last of the machines.

303. Richard Daley, Sr. Richard Daley, Sr. (1902–76) is certainly one of the best examples of a political boss who built a powerful machine after the New Deal and World War II. As one of the last big city political bosses, he served as both mayor of Chicago and chairman of the Cook County Democratic Party for over twenty years. A native of the Irish-dominated South Side, Daley worked his way up from the Illinois state assembly to become a figure in national politics. His support of John F. Kennedy, to the point of delivering, many allege, thousands of votes from people who were dead, helped deliver a narrow victory in 1960 over Richard Nixon. Daley oversaw massive construction and urban renewal projects in Chicago, which pleased business interests and those who benefited from the jobs.

But Daley was staunchly antiunion and cool at best to civil rights issues that alienated workers and minorities by the early 1970s. Daley's intolerance for radicalism and challenges to his authority came to a head in 1968 when the Democratic National Convention convened in Chicago. Faced with antiwar protestors, the police responded with violent force that erupted into a riot. The incident remained a blot on Daley's reputation and his unflinching support for the police identified him as a member of the political old guard. In 1976, Daley was elected to his sixth mayoral term, but died soon after the election. The Daley legacy did not disappear with his death, however. His son, Richard M. Daley, Jr., is currently serving his fourth term as mayor of Chicago.

304. Kevin White Kevin White's tenure as Boston's mayor (1967–83) made him its first mayor to serve four consecutive terms. The son of two former Boston City Council presidents, White's early years in office were considered successful—he revitalized downtown Boston and attempted to ease racial tensions. His success led presidential candidate George McGovern to consider him as a running mate in the 1972 election. Boston's famous 1974 public school desegregation was met with prolonged and vehement protest from Boston's Irish and African American neighborhoods. Although opposing the desegregation plan, White's efforts to achieve peaceful resolution generally received praise. By the early 1980s, however, White's effectiveness was diminished by allegations of corruption within his administration. In 1983, he stunned the city by announcing that he would not run for reelection.

Irish American Presidents

305. Andrew Jackson The son of Irish immigrants from County Antrim, by age fourteen Andrew Jackson (1767–1845) had been orphaned and taken prisoner during the Revolutionary War. Nevertheless, he rose to become a military hero during the War of 1812 whose successes, especially in the Battle of New Orleans, earned him enduring popular support among Americans and two terms as president (1828–36). His election changed American politics because Jackson was the first president from west of the Appalachians, the first to appeal to the mass of American voters, and his election made the Democratic Party viable. Some see in Jackson a symbol that helped to reconcile the earlier Scotch-Irish immigrants with later, mostly Catholic, Irish immigrants.

Andrew Jackson

306. James K. Polk After practicing law in Tennessee, James K. Polk (1795–1849) entered politics, first in the state legislature and then in the U.S. House of Representatives (1825–39). Advancing the interests of Andrew Jackson, he eventually held the speakership (1835–39). He

James K. Polk

served one term as Tennessee's governor (1839–41), losing the two ensuing elections. A compromise candidate in the presidential election of 1844, Polk won with a four-point agenda: lowering the tariff, settling the Oregon boundary dispute with England, reestablishing an independent treasury, and annexing California. He accomplished all four goals and numerous others, but ruined his health in the effort. He sought no second term and died shortly after leaving office.

307. James Buchanan James Buchanan (1791–1868), whose father had emigrated from County Donegal, Ireland, held numerous political positions before becoming the United States' fifteenth president: Pennsylvania state legislator (1814–16); U.S. congressman (1821–31); U.S. senator (1834–45); secretary of state (1845–49); and minister to Russia (1832–34) and Britain (1853–56). With all his experience, however, as he assumed the presidency in 1857, Buchanan faced a nation quickly—perhaps inevitably—dividing over slavery. Buchanan offered only timid leadership in the face of growing national crisis and seemed content to let his successor deal with the questions of slavery and secession. By the time he left office in March 1861, the secession crisis was well under way and Civil War only a month away.

308. Ulysses S. Grant Ulysses S. Grant (1822–85), West Point graduate and Mexican War veteran, entered the Civil War in 1861, commanding the Twenty-first Illinois Volunteers. Although undistinguished until then, he proved one of the great generals in U.S. history, combining skill as a strategist, tactician, administrator, and organizer.

By 1864 he commanded the entire Union Army, forcing the Confederate surrender in 1865. President from 1869 to 1877, Grant's administrations were marred by scandals (not involving him personally) and bitterly partisan disputes over Reconstruction policies regarding the South.

In his retirement he and his wife traveled the world, including a visit to his paternal great-grandfather's home in County Tyrone, Ireland. Sadly, the early 1880s brought tragedy. Soon after Grant lost his life's savings to a corrupt investment house, he was diagnosed with terminal throat cancer. Distressed over the prospect of his young and healthy wife living out her days in poverty, he took the advice of his friend Mark Twain and wrote his memoirs. Completed just days before his death, Grant's *Personal Memoirs* became a bestseller and kept Mrs. Grant in comfort for the rest of her life. Still in print, the two-volume work is considered by many to be among the best narrative military histories ever written.

309. Chester A. Arthur   Named James Garfield's running mate on the 1880 Republican presidential ticket—through a deal between New York political boss Roscoe Conkling and Garfield's supporters—Chester A. Arthur (1829–86) unexpectedly became president after Garfield's assassination in 1881. One of Conkling's loyal lieutenants, Arthur had previously held the post of customs collector for the port of New York City. A defender of the spoils system, opponents feared that President Arthur would use the office to enrich and empower fellow Republicans. He quickly disassociated himself from Conkling, however, and spearheaded civil service reform. Suffering from Bright's disease, Arthur made a nominal and unsuccessful attempt at reelection, then retired.

310. William McKinley   Before being elected president, William McKinley (1843–1901) served fourteen years in the U.S. House of Representatives (1877–83, 1885–91), and spent two terms as Ohio's governor (1892–94).

Descended from Scotch-Irish immigrants, McKinley's fiscal conservatism led him to support high tariffs and the gold standard. During his presidency (1897–1901), the United States emerged as a world power. Victory in the Spanish-American War freed Cuba and left the U.S. with Puerto Rico, Guam, and the Philippine Islands. Elected to a second term in 1900, McKinley was shot on September 9, 1901, while visiting the Pan-American Exposition. He died four days later, leading to Theodore Roosevelt's becoming president.

311. Theodore Roosevelt   The twenty-sixth president of the United States, Theodore Roosevelt (1858–1919) remains today one of the most popular and highly regarded personalities in American history. Born into a distinguished New York family with Irish roots on his mother's (County Meath) and father's (County Antrim) side, he overcame a frail constitution as a youth to become a staunch advocate of the vigorous life. Active in politics soon after graduating from Harvard in 1880, he gained national recognition as New York City police commissioner (1896–97), assistant secretary of the navy (1897–98), and as a leader of the Rough Riders regiment that earned fame fighting in Cuba during the Spanish-American War. Elected vice president in 1900, he became president upon McKinley's assassination in September 1901. As president he pursued a progressive agenda, actively working to curb the power of big business ("trust busting") and signing many bills enhancing environmental conservation, workers' rights, and public health. He also pursued a vigorous foreign policy. Seen as a champion of the average man, he won reelection in 1904 by a landslide. He helped negotiate an end to the Russo-Japanese War and won the 1906 Nobel Peace Prize as a result. He chose not to run for reelection in 1908, but stormed back in 1912 seeking the Republican nomination. Denied, he ran for president as the candidate of the Progressive, or Bull Moose, Party. Defeated by Woodrow

Wilson, he remained active in public life until his early death in 1918.

312. Woodrow Wilson After a notable career as a university professor and president, Woodrow Wilson (1856–1924), the grandson of Scotch-Irish immigrants from County Antrim, entered politics in 1910 when he was elected governor of New Jersey. Success as a reformer there led to his election as president (1913–21). Wilson supported a progressive domestic policy, and saw passage of major social legislation, the establishment of the Federal Trade Commission and the Federal Reserve system, and passage of five constitutional amendments. Like many in his day, Wilson decried the presence of "hyphenated Americans"—including Irish Americans—and supported policies that encouraged rapid assimilation and a severing of ties to the Old World.

In the realm of foreign affairs, Wilson preferred to keep the U.S. neutral during World War I, but eventually led the nation into war. His lasting contributions to international relations were his Fourteen Points, among which was the call for a League of Nations, precursor to the United Nations. For these efforts, he won the Nobel Peace Prize in 1919. Irish Americans, however, came away from the postwar negotiations bitterly disappointed. While Wilson successfully pushed for the reestablishment of an independent Poland (part of Russia since the late eighteenth century), he opposed efforts by Irish nationalists to gain a similar independence for Ireland. Although of Irish ancestry, Wilson was a thorough Anglophile.

313. John F. Kennedy His election as the thirty-fifth president of the United States in 1960 marked a turning point in the history of the Irish in America. Born into a wealthy family, John F. Kennedy (1917–63) was the grandson of two of Boston's most powerful politicians, former mayor John F. "Honey Fitz" Fitzgerald and boss Patrick Kennedy. A graduate of Harvard, he served as commander of a U.S. Navy PT boat in the Pacific

during World War II. Elected to Congress in 1947, he moved to the senate in 1952. In 1953 he married Jacqueline Lee Bouvier. In 1960 he defeated by the slimmest of margins Republican Richard Nixon to become, at age forty-three, the youngest man elected president.

As president, his domestic program ("the New Frontier") called for tax cuts, increased federal funding for education, expansion of Social Security coverage, and the extension of civil rights. With the Cold War dominating international relations, foreign affairs assumed a large role in his administration. Kennedy was sharply criticized for the abortive Bay of Pigs Invasion of Cuba in 1961, but earned praise for his handling of the Cuban Missile Crisis in October 1962. The following year, Kennedy signed a nuclear test–ban treaty with the Soviets.

On November 22, 1963, Kennedy was shot and killed in Dallas, Texas.

314. Richard M. Nixon Born in 1913, Richard Milhous Nixon was the great-great-great-great-grandson of Thomas Milhous, who emigrated in 1729 from Timahoe, County Kildare. He served in Congress before becoming Eisenhower's vice president for two terms (1952–60). Nixon lost the presidency to Kennedy in 1960, but ran again in 1968 and won. Despite a term plagued by the Vietnam War and inflation, Nixon was overwhelmingly reelected. Nixon's second term began with a cease-fire in Vietnam, but ended in the disaster of Watergate. Facing impeachment, he became the only president in U.S. history to resign from office.

It should be pointed out that Nixon added to his Irish American credentials by marrying Patricia Ryan.

315. Ronald Reagan Ronald Wilson Reagan was the descendant of Michael Reagan, who came to the U.S. from Tipperary in 1853. His career spanned the film industry, California's governorship, and the White House. His presidency

Ronald Reagan

(1980–88) was marked by national prosperity, increased military preparedness, and vigorous anti-Communist efforts abroad. The latter, in combination with his diplomatic overtures to Soviet leader Mikhail Gorbachev, are seen by many as having played a key role in winning the Cold War. Critics, however, point to the massive federal debt piled up during the 1980s. Reagan survived an assassination attempt in 1981 and weathered the 1986 Iran-Contra scandal.

316. Bill Clinton Bill Clinton, born William Jefferson Blythe (he later took Clinton, his stepfather's name) is the descendant of immigrants from Ulster. He served five terms as the governor of Arkansas before entering the presidential race in 1992. His eight years as president were marked by the greatest peacetime economic boom in U.S. history. Prosperity and Clinton's centrist political agenda, emphasizing deficit reduction, free trade, and welfare and health care reform proved popular, but his administration also suffered from a series of scandals, especially over his attempt to cover up his relationship with White House intern Monica Lewinsky and his issuance of several last-minute pardons in the final days of his administration.

Congress

317. John C. Calhoun Although John Caldwell Calhoun (1782–1850) studied law at Yale, Southern politics soon became his life. He served as a state legislator in South Carolina from 1807 to 1810, when he was elected to Congress. Early in his career he advocated a strong national de-

John C. Calhoun

fense and federally funded domestic improvements. Calhoun was secretary of war (1817–25) before becoming vice president, a position he held until his resignation in 1832.

By the 1830s, Calhoun became a leading voice among Southerners who had come to believe that federal government initiatives—from the tariff to internal improvements—favored the North. During his years in the Senate (1833–50), he became a leading voice for states' rights, the perpetuation of slavery, and Southern nationalism.

318. Edward M. "Ted" Kennedy A graduate of Harvard and the University of Virginia Law School, "Ted" Kennedy was elected to the Senate in 1962 to a seat vacated by his brother John, who had become president. Four decades later he's still there, now one of the most senior members of the body. A liberal Democrat, he championed the 1964 Civil Rights Bill and the Head Start program in the 1960s; since then he's been a strong advocate for the rights of women, gays, refugees, immigrants, and minorities. He is the senior Democrat on the Health, Education, Labor and Pensions Committee in the Senate and is also a member of the Congressional Friends of Ireland. Although he long hoped to follow in his brothers' footsteps and run for president, his troubled personal life has rendered that an impossibility. Most notable was his role in an accident in the waters off Chappaquiddick Island in 1969 that resulted in the drowning of Mary Jo Kopechne, a campaign worker for his late brother Robert. Controversies and tragedies associated with younger members of the Kennedy family have also taken their toll on his public reputation. Still, he remains a favorite among liberal Americans, who see him as an effective advocate for their causes.

319. Robert F. Kennedy   U.S. senator and U.S. attorney general, Robert "Bobby" Kennedy was assassinated in 1968 in Los Angeles while running for the Democratic nomination for president. Campaign manager for his brother John F. Kennedy's bid for the Senate in 1952 and for the presidency in 1960, Bobby was appointed attorney general during John F. Kennedy's presidency. A graduate of Harvard and University of Virginia Law School, he was a tireless prosecutor against organized crime. He also was instrumental in the decision in 1962 to blockade Cuba during the missile crisis rather than resort to military action. With President Kennedy, he proposed the bill that eventually became the Civil Rights Act of 1964. Bobby resigned as attorney general after the death of his brother John, and voters in New York elected him as U.S. senator in 1964. In 1966, he called for negotiations to end the war in Vietnam and urged President Johnson to reduce, rather than increase, the war effort.

320. Huey Long   Huey Long became the head of a powerful political machine as governor of Louisiana before being assassinated just as he began a run for the presidency. After winning the governorship in 1924, Long made his mark on Louisiana through an aggressive program of building roads and bridges and extending the state university areas like the one in which he grew up. He used patronage to consolidate his power before driven out of office in 1929 on charges of bribery and gross misconduct. "The Kingfish," as he was known, stormed back a year later, however, winning election to the U.S. Senate. In 1935, he launched a bid for the presidency, only to be assassinated later that year in Louisiana.

321. Mike Mansfield   Michael J. Mansfield (1903–2000) was born in New York City, but moved to Montana to live with relatives when his mother died. He served in the military from 1918 to 1922, eventually returning to Montana to attend college and earn a master's degree. He joined the faculty of Montana State University teaching Asian and Latin American history and political science. In 1942 he won election to the House of Representatives and immediately earned a reputation as an expert in foreign affairs, especially regarding Asia. He won election to the Senate in 1952 and five years later was selected by Senate Majority Leader Lyndon B. Johnson to serve as majority whip. In January 1961, when Lyndon Johnson became John F. Kennedy's vice president, Mansfield became Senate majority leader. His mild manner and conciliatory approach earned him the respect of both Republicans and Democrats. He ran afoul of the Johnson administration when he changed his mind on Vietnam and urged U.S. withdrawal. Mansfield remained majority leader for sixteen years—still a record— and retired in 1977. He later served as Ambassador to Japan under Presidents Carter and Reagan.

322. John McCain   Born in the Panama Canal Zone in 1936, McCain grew up moving between naval bases in America and abroad. Both his father and grandfather were navy admirals, and McCain attended the U.S. Naval Academy at Annapolis, where he graduated in 1958. After training as a navy pilot, he volunteered for combat duty in Vietnam. He was shot down in October 1967, and spent the next five and a half years in prison camps. The injuries he sustained ruined his future as a pilot and prevented him from reaching his goal of becoming the third consecutive McCain to make admiral. He retired from the navy, moved to Arizona, and was elected to the House of Representatives in 1982. In 1986 McCain succeeded the legendary Barry Goldwater as senator for Arizona and won reelection in 1992 and again in 1998. In 2000, he challenged George W. Bush for the Republican nomination, winning several primaries before eventually losing the delegate tally to Bush. McCain's maverick style and straightforward way of speaking—even his famous temper—gained him an enthusiastic national following among moderates of both the Democratic and Republican parties.

323. Patrick McCarran Called the "perennial politician" by the *Las Vegas Review-Journal*, Patrick McCarran (1876–1954) was born to Irish immigrant parents on a farm in Nevada. He became a lawyer, county district attorney, and state supreme court justice. He ran twice for senate (1916 and 1926) before winning in the Roosevelt landslide of 1932. A staunch conservative, he often defied his Democratic Party. He supported Senator Joseph McCarthy in the latter's sweeping search for Communists, and sponsored the McCarran-Wood Act (1950) that required communists to register with the government. The McCarran-Walter Act (1952) tightened already tough restrictions on immigration. McCarran also played a key role in the development of Las Vegas and Nevada during the first half of the twentieth century.

324. Joseph McCarthy Few have made so large an impact in such a short time as Joseph McCarthy (1908–57), a back-bench senator from Wisconsin who for a few years seized the national stage with his terror-raising hunt for Communists inside and out of the U.S. government. Beginning with a speech in 1950, in which he claimed to know the names of hundreds of Communists inside the State Department, McCarthy embarked on a four-year finger-pointing campaign that struck fear throughout America—both fear that Communists might indeed have penetrated all parts of society and fear of being named as a Red. In no time, the term "McCarthyism" was coined and the previously unheralded senator was heading investigative committees and appearing on television.

McCarthy's demise finally came in 1954 in a hearing that pitted the Wisconsin senator against

Joseph McCarthy

the U.S. Army. Carried on national TV, the hearings showed McCarthy at his worst—a bombastic, unscrupulous, and cruel man willing to say or do anything to advance his career. The final blow came when Joseph Welch, counsel for the Army, asked, "Have you no sense of decency, sir? At long last, have you left no sense of decency?" In the end McCarthy's fall was as spectacular as his rise. The Senate voted to "condemn" his actions 67 to 22 and he quickly faded from prominence. His drinking grew heavier and his health quickly waned. He died on April 28, 1957, from complications due to alcoholism. He was only forty-eight.

McCarthy remains one of the most reviled figures in American history. Anyone who studies his life—even the staunch and principled anti-Communist—is bound to come away appalled by him. Yet McCarthy is too important a figure to be merely dismissed as an opportunistic demon. He didn't materialize out of thin air: He was the product of an intensely anxious era.

325. Eugene McCarthy Oratorically pithy and politically courageous, Eugene McCarthy (b. 1916) was born in Minnesota. First elected to the House of Representatives in 1948, he won a seat in the senate in 1958. He rose to prominence in the 1960s as a leading opponent of the war in Vietnam and in 1968 announced his candidacy for president. McCarthy shocked the political world with his strong showing in the New Hampshire primary, an event that prompted President Lyndon Johnson's stunning decision not to seek reelection. Robert Kennedy quickly stepped in to steal McCarthy's thunder as the leading antiwar

Democrat. McCarthy retired from the senate in 1970 and since that time has written and spoken on politics.

326. George McGovern　George Stanley McGovern (b. 1922) was born in Avon, South Dakota. He earned a Ph.D. from Northwestern University and then entered politics, serving four years in the U.S. House of Representatives before being elected to the U.S. Senate in 1962. Ten years later he won the Democratic presidential nomination, but his staunchly liberal agenda at a time of great national turmoil helped seal his fate against Richard M. Nixon. McGovern suffered one of the worst presidential election defeats in American history, losing even his home state of South Dakota, while winning only Massachusetts and the District of Columbia. Perhaps his consolation was that his sincerity and integrity were never questioned, whereas Nixon would be driven from office in 1974 in the historic Watergate scandal. McGovern lost his Senate seat in 1980 before running again for president in 1984.

327. Daniel Patrick Moynihan　Born in Tulsa, Oklahoma, Daniel P. Moynihan (b. 1927) grew up in New York City. Abandoned by his father when he was a baby, the family struggled to survive. From such a humble beginning he went on to become one of the last patricians in his field. His success as a student led him to pursue graduate studies after a stint in the U.S. Navy and earned his Ph.D. in 1961. He taught at Syracuse University, Harvard, and the Massachusetts Institute of Technology before taking a position in the Kennedy administration (he would later serve under Johnson, Nixon, and Ford). In 1965, his study, *The Negro Family: The Case for National Action,* elicited both praise and condemnation, both of which served to raise the obscure bureaucrat's public profile as an expert on social welfare policy. In 1976 he won election as Democratic senator from New York and served until 2001. His

retirement cleared the way for the historic Senate candidacy of First Lady Hillary Rodham Clinton.

328. Thomas "Tip" P. O'Neill　Tip O'Neill (1912–94), one of Massachusetts' great liberal politicians, was first elected to Congress in 1953, after four years as speaker of the Massachusetts house. He moved to the House of Representatives when John F. Kennedy was elected to the U.S. Senate. During thirty-four years of service he rose to become speaker of the house, where he championed the poor, unemployed, and ill. He was active on Irish political issues as one of the "gang of four" (O'Neill, Ted Kennedy, Pat Moynihan, and Hugh Carey). He is perhaps most famous for uttering the line, "All politics is local."

329. James Shields　James Shields (1806–79) is the only man ever to serve as U.S. senator from three different states. He emigrated from Ireland in 1826, settled in Illinois, and studied law. He won election to the state legislature before becoming state auditor and later a member of the Illinois supreme court (1843). He volunteered for military service during the Mexican-American War, earning a reputation as a courageous and inspirational officer. He later served with distinction as a general in the Union Army during the Civil War.

After the Mexican War, he was elected senator for Illinois (1849–55). He later moved on to the Minnesota Territory and encouraged Irish immigrants to settle there. When Minnesota became a state, he became one of its first two U.S. senators (1858–59). After his service during the Civil War, he settled in Missouri and was eventually drawn back into politics. He returned to the Senate a third time (for Missouri) but served only a year before dying in 1879.

Interestingly, early on in his career, Shields narrowly missed an opportunity to change the course of history—for the worse. While serving in the House of Representatives, Shields met Abraham Lincoln. Lincoln was a Whig and

Shields was a Democrat and the two clashed rhetorically. Tensions grew so high that they even scheduled a duel. Fortunately—given Shields' crack marksmanship—cooler heads prevailed.

Police, Lawmen, and FBI

330. The Irish Cop   Without a doubt, the most enduring image of the Irish in nineteenth-century America is that of the Irish policeman. As early as 1855, a quarter of New York's police force was Irish-born (and no doubt many more were Irish American). Even allowing for the possibility of a small amount of "honest graft," work as a cop promised only a modest living. It did, however, provide something that appealed to countless Irish workers seeking to avoid the harsh and quixotic realities of the industrial economy: security. And there was an additional, intangible, benefit: Becoming the most visible image of urban law and order was an excellent way to confront the negative stereotype of the Irish as criminals.

331. "Paddy Wagons"   The phrase "paddy wagon" originated in the mid–nineteenth century as a term to describe the wagon used by urban police departments to transport arrested persons from crime scenes to jail. But what exactly did it mean?

The New York City Police Parade, 1905

"Paddy wagon"

There's one school of thought that argues the name derived from the fact that such a disproportionately high number of Irish (paddies) were to be found locked inside on any given night. And another that suggests the name came from the fact that more often than not, the wagon was driven by a couple of paddy cops. To this day etymologists are uncertain about the origin of this term.

332. Inspector Thomas Byrnes   Thomas Byrnes (1842–1910) was born in Dublin, Ireland, in 1842 and emigrated to New York as a child. He joined the New York City Police Department in 1863 and worked his way up through the ranks. In 1883, after earning a reputation for solving high-profile crimes, including a three-million-dollar Manhattan Bank heist, he took charge of the task of organizing the NYPD's detectives. In 1888, he was promoted to chief inspector and four years later to superintendent of the department. By then, Byrnes had cultivated an international reputation as a detective. His critics, however, pointed out that only a man with strong ties to the underworld could solve such big crimes so quickly.

Indeed, the police in Byrnes' era played an instrumental role in managing (and profiting by) the city's various vice districts for their Tammany Hall benefactors. Byrnes was able to shrug off his critics until 1895, when a massive corruption investigation led to the appointment of Theodore Roosevelt as police commissioner. Rather than face the indefatigable reformer, Byrnes quickly announced his retirement. At his death in 1910, his estate was worth in excess of $350,000—an astonishing sum at that time, even for a high public official.

333. Bat Masterson Born Bartholomew Masterson (1853–1921), "Bat" adopted the name William Barclay Masterson early in his life. His mother, Catherine (McGurk) Masterson, was originally from Northern Ireland.

Masterson kicked around the West as a buffalo hunter, fight promoter, and newspaper man, spending a good deal of his time at the gaming table. On occasion, Masterson allowed himself to be coaxed into serving as sheriff of Ford County (where Dodge City, Kansas, was located). Disillusioned with the West he had once loved, he moved to New York in 1902, where he became a newspaper sports writer.

334. The Irish in the FBI The FBI originated from a force of special agents of the Justice Department created in 1908 during the presidency of Theodore Roosevelt. One year later it was named the Bureau of Investigation. Not surprisingly, given their affinity for police work, Irish Americans came to comprise a significant portion of the FBI's agents. As evidence, one can point to the case of Edwin C. Shanahan, who in 1925 became the very first FBI agent killed in the line of duty. Irish Americans also found their way into top administration posts within the agency. One of the agency's first directors was William J. Flynn, who assumed the title in 1919. He was succeeded in 1921 by another Irish American, William J. Burns. It was Burns who subsequently hired J. Edgar Hoover as assistant director.

Probably the most famous Irish American in the FBI was Clarence Kelley. Born in Kansas City on October 24, 1911, he attended the University of Kansas and Kansas City Law School before joining the FBI in 1940. His career as an agent lasted until 1961, when he retired and eventually took the job as chief of police in Kansas City. Kelley was tapped to replace the man who in many people's eyes (for better or worse) *was* the FBI—J. Edgar Hoover, who died in 1972. His tenure as head of the Bureau (1973–78) came during a time of great change in the organization. His management techniques were a welcome change from those of Hoover—he won several awards because of them, for his ethics in law enforcement, and for his contributions to bettering the outdated crime-fighting practices of the FBI. He left the FBI in 1978 and returned to Kansas City, where he formed Clarence M. Kelley Associates, Inc., a professional investigative and security consulting agency. He died in Kansas City on August 6, 1997.

The Other Side of the Law

335. Willie Sutton, Jr. William Francis Sutton, Jr. (1901–80), was called "Willie the Actor" because of the many disguises he used in his bank robberies. He grew up in Irishtown, a tough district in Brooklyn, New York. His childhood was marked by delinquency and violence. He faced his first murder charge at the age of twenty-one.

From the 1920s to the 1950s he was the nation's most infamous bank robber, stealing over $2 million during the course of his "career." He also displayed a talent for escaping from jail (three times). Sutton is best remembered for the answer he provided when someone asked why he robbed banks: "That's where the money is." Unfortunately, he never said it, as was made clear in his biography, but even today he's still credited with the famous line.

His last heist took place in Queens in 1950, a crime that landed him in prison for seventeen years. Upon his release in 1967, he headed for

Billy the Kid

Florida and died there in obscurity and poverty in 1980.

336. Billy the Kid

Most people know the notorious outlaw Billy the Kid as "William Bonney," but his real name was Patrick Henry McCarty (1859–81). His mother, who was born in Ireland, died when he was twelve, leaving him with his stepfather in New Mexico. He left home, and later was caught stealing clothes from a Chinese laundry. Thus began "the Kid's" life of crime.

In 1876, he was charged with killing three Indians in Arizona. Thereafter, he began a cattle-rustling spree throughout the Southwest and Mexico, leading a faction in New Mexico's notorious "Lincoln County War" over cattle. He was eventually captured in 1881, but not before killing Sheriff Jim Brady and several others. Sentenced to hang for Brady's death, he managed to escape (killing two deputies in the process). He remained at large until fatally shot later that year by Sheriff Pat F. Garrett in Fort Sumner, New Mexico.

337. Jesse James

Jesse James (1847–82) was one of the most notorious outlaws of the Old West. Born in Centerville, Missouri, he fought in the Civil War as a Confederate guerrilla. After the war, he returned home to Missouri, and began his life of crime with his brother, Frank. Their first bank robbery, in Liberty, Missouri, is believed to be the first daylight bank robbery during peacetime. They committed many more bank, train, and stagecoach robberies in and around Missouri before James was murdered in 1882 by a fellow gang member, Robert Ford, in exchange for a reward. Frank soon surrendered, stood trial, was released, and lived on the family farm until his death in 1915.

338. Owney Madden

Owney ("the Killer") Madden (1892–1964) hailed from Liverpool, England, but his family was of Irish stock. He led the notorious Irish gang the Gophers (pronounced "goofers") in the early part of the century. By the time he was twenty-one, he'd been arrested more than forty times. From 1915 to 1923, he served time for murder in the infamous Sing Sing, a penitentiary in New York State.

In 1923, Madden opened the famous Cotton Club jazz nightclub in Harlem, where Duke Ellington got his start. By 1932, Madden tired of the mob business (and the fact that most mobsters led very short lives), and he retired to Hot Springs, Arkansas, where he lived quietly until his death in 1964.

339. Bugs Moran

A notorious Chicago gangster, George "Bugs" Moran's (1893–1957) parents were Irish and Polish immigrants. Moran became the second in command of Dion O'Banion's North Siders gang, and ended up on the wrong side of Al Capone, who ordered the famed mass rubout known as the St. Valentine's Day Massacre. Moran may have relied on the "luck of the Irish" that day, as he missed being killed because he showed up late.

Moran's gang gradually lost power and prestige, and Moran moved to Ohio, where he began robbing banks. He was caught by the FBI in 1946, and died in Leavenworth Prison in 1957.

340. Dion O'Banion

Charles "Dion" O'Banion (1892–1924) grew up the Little Hell district on Chicago's North Side. He walked with a limp, and sang in the Holy Name Cathedral choir. Later, he became a singing waiter who crooned sentimental Irish ballads while picking his patrons' pockets. Gradually, he became the infamous leader of the North Siders gang. He learned early how to bribe officials and silence witnesses. Bootleg liquor and gambling were his big money makers. He covered up his activities by operating a flower shop. It amused him to provide funeral flowers for some of his gangster cronies who'd met their Maker. Eventually he ran afoul of John Torrio, one of Chicago's major crime bosses, and was gunned down in his flower shop.

On the Big Bench:
The Supreme Court

341. John Rutledge   John Rutledge (1739–1800), a descendent of Ulster immigrants, began practicing law in South Carolina in 1761. He was a member of the Continental Congress, and served from 1774 to 1776 and 1782 to 1783. During the American Revolution, he was involved in drafting South Carolina's state constitution. He later became governor of the state from 1778 to 1782. Rutledge's first term on the U.S. Supreme Court was between 1789 and 1791, when he resigned in order to return as South Carolina's chief justice. In 1795, President George Washington appointed him as chief justice of the U.S. Supreme Court. Because the Senate did not confirm his appointment, he only served for one term.

342. Roger B. Taney   At twenty-two, Roger Brooke Taney (1777–1864) was admitted to the Maryland bar and elected to the state legislature. In 1831, he was appointed attorney general by President Andrew Jackson. Taney was sworn in as chief justice of the Supreme Court in 1836. He is best known for writing the majority opinion in the *Dred Scott* decision (1857) that declared African Americans could never be citizens and therefore could never sue in federal court. That case was one of several key events that stoked the growing conflict between North and South.

343. Francis Murphy   The son of an Irish Catholic immigrant, Frank Murphy (1890–1949) was born in Harbor Beach, Michigan. After winning the mayoral election in Detroit in 1930, Murphy went on to serve as governor-general of the Philippines from 1933 to 1935. He was elected governor of Michigan after returning from abroad.

Murphy was another who benefited from the new opportunities available to Irish Americans during Roosevelt's New Deal. After being appointed attorney general in 1939, the pinnacle of Murphy's political career was his nomination to the United States Supreme Court the following year, where he sat for nine years until his death in 1949.

344. William Brennan   Eisenhower's 1956 appointment of William J. Brennan, Jr. (1906–97) to the Supreme Court was largely political. Seeking Catholic support for his presidential campaign, Eisenhower considered Brennan, an Irish Catholic with an impressive legal career, the perfect choice.   Brennan's work on the Court, however, revealed that he was a liberal, not a moderate.

William Brennan

Both liberals and conservatives agree that Brennan's stay on the bench was among the most influential in Court history. His philosophy was that laws exist to preserve the individual's dignity; without such dignity people are not truly free.

Because he often compromised in order to get a majority vote, many of his decisions represent the middle ground. His influence on the Court led to increased rights of the accused, affirmative action, abortion rights, the right to sue the government, reduced gender discrimination, and broader welfare laws. Brennan retired in 1990 for health reasons, and died in 1997.

345. Anthony Kennedy   Born in Sacramento, California, Anthony Kennedy (b. 1937) practiced law there for the first years of his career. In 1975 he was appointed as judge of the U.S. Court of

Appeals for the 9th Circuit and served from 1975 until 1988. In 1988, he was appointed to the Supreme Court by President Ronald Reagan. His nomination came after two other candidates had been turned down, and some saw this nomination of a relative unknown as practical move for Reagan. Kennedy is known as a conservative justice, who has become more moderate during his time with the Court.

346. Other Irish American Justices of the Supreme Court Several lesser Supreme Court justices had Irish origins. William Paterson, for example, was appointed by George Washington in 1793 and sat on the high court until 1806. Charles Evans Hughes (1862–1948) served from 1930 until his retirement in 1941. Pierce Butler (1866–1939) was nominated to the high court by President Harding and served from 1922 to 1939. Joseph McKenna joined the court in 1898 and remained there until 1927. James Francis Burns (1882–1972) served only from 1941 to 1942, leaving to take a job in the Roosevelt administration. Note: Justice Sandra Day O'Connor is frequently cited as being of Irish descent. Recently, her office released a statement explaining that, to the best of her knowledge, she is not Irish American.

Other Legal Eagles

347. Fr. Robert F. Drinan In 1970 Robert F. Drinan (b. 1920) became the first Catholic priest elected to the U.S. House of Representatives. Fondly remembered as "Our Father who art in Congress," Drinan served five terms before a pending revision of Canon Law forced him to retire in 1981. Drinan remained active in politics, battling on such issues as human rights, abortion, and world hunger. A distinguished legal scholar who has taught at Georgetown University Law Center since 1981, Drinan became chair of the American Bar Association's Standing Committee on Professionalism in 1996. Drinan is also a columnist for the *National Catholic Reporter*.

Thomas A. Emmet

348. Thomas Addis Emmet Born in Cork, Thomas Addis Emmet (1764–1827) was, like his brother Robert, a controversial figure in Irish politics. Admitted to practice law in 1791, Emmet defended political prisoners and in 1795 joined the Society of United Irishmen. Three years later, he was imprisoned for subversive activities and upon release, was forced to flee to New York. During his prison sentence he wrote about Ireland's history and politics, and in 1807, his *Pieces of Irish History* was published in New York.

Emmet soon became active in New York politics by joining the Democratic Party. He also earned a reputation as a gifted jurist and eventually became New York's attorney general. He argued many cases before the U.S. Supreme Court.

349. William Joseph Fallon If you were famous and in trouble in the 1920s, the man to call was attorney William J. Fallon (1886–1927). Born in New York City, he received his B.A. and J.D. from Fordham. From 1914 to 1916 he served as assistant district attorney for Westchester County, where he honed his courtroom skills. Fallon moved to Manhattan and opened a private law practice. He quickly earned a reputation as a superb criminal defense lawyer and before long had a throng of celebrities and, more commonly, mobsters beating a path to his door. He went on to become the most famous defense attorney in the 1920s. Legendary for his courtroom oratory, he earned the nickname "the Great Mouthpiece." Some of his clients included Arnold Rothstein, the mobster who fixed the 1919 World Series, Broadway producer David Belasco, and New York Giants manager John McGraw. In all, Fallon took on 126 cases and all of his clients walked, many by virtue of hung juries. Despite an acquittal, Fallon's reputation suffered irreparable harm when he was tried for jury tampering in 1924.

350. Charles O'Conor The son of an exile from the United Irishmen uprising of 1798, Charles O'Conor (1804–84) overcame poverty to become one of the most accomplished lawyers in nineteenth-century America. Admitted to the bar

Charles O'Conor

in 1824, he soon gained a reputation as an excellent attorney and eloquent speaker. One of his most sensational cases involved his successful defense of Mrs. Catherine Forrest against charges of infidelity brought by her husband, the famous actor Edwin Forrest, in a divorce case begun in 1851. He

later led the prosecution against William "Boss" Tweed (1871–72) in the wake of revelations of massive corruption. He also was part of the legal team that successfully defended former Confederate President Jefferson Davis against charges of treason. In 1872, a faction of the Democratic Party offered him the nomination for president—a first for a Catholic by a mainstream party—but he turned it down.

351. Paul O'Dwyer Born in County Mayo, Peter Paul O'Dwyer (1907–98) grew up in Brooklyn, New York. As a lawyer he made a reputation for himself as a tireless defender of progressive causes, from striking workers to African Americans struggling for civil rights. Some of his more renowned cases were those involving people accused of communist activities. Accusations that he harbored communist sympathies only seemed to

strengthen his resolve in fighting for the underdog. Active in the National Lawyers Guild, he became its president in 1947 and served on its national board from 1948–51. O'Dwyer also took a passionate interest in his home country and supported several nationalist initiatives. He also supported the state of Israel and even helped smuggle arms to the beleaguered nation in the 1950s. Active in local and national politics, O'Dwyer ran for political office several times, gaining election to the New York City Council.

352. William Sampson Born in Londonderry, Ireland in 1764, Sampson studied law and was admitted to the Irish bar. He joined the United Irishmen in the 1790s, and was exiled for treason after their failed uprising. He eventually arrived in New York where he continued his work as a lawyer, developing a reputation as one of the leading jurists in the young republic. He was known as an eloquent advocate of individual rights and for leading the movement to codify common law. Sampson is also remembered for his precedent-setting arguments on behalf of striking journeymen cordwainers and for the sanctity of the Catholic confessional. Apart from his success as a lawyer, Sampson also took a leading role in New York's growing Irish community. He also wrote a two-volume *History of Ireland* (1833).

353. Frank Walsh An attorney with a zeal for advocacy for the poor, St. Louis–born Frank Walsh was chosen by President Wilson to head the newly formed U.S. Industrial Relations Commission. Walsh investigated labor-management clashes from 1913 to 1918, and in 1918 was named cochairman with President Taft of the War Labor Board. Walsh was also an Irish nationalist who chaired the Commission for Irish Independence. He fell out of favor with Wilson when he pushed for U.S. recognition of the proclaimed Irish Republic. In 1936 he was chairman of the Catholic Citizen's Committee for Ratification of the Federal Child Labor Law.

354. Edward Bennett Williams Part owner of the Washington Redskins football team and owner of the Baltimore Orioles baseball team, attorney Edward Bennett Williams was also a politician who had access to every president from John F. Kennedy to Ronald Reagan. An Irish Catholic from Connecticut, he graduated from Georgetown University Law School in 1945 and became a successful trial lawyer who defended the constitutional rights of controversial Americans such as Jimmy Hoffa, Joseph R. McCarthy, and Adam Clayton Powell, Jr. A philanthropist, Williams provided for the work of Mother Teresa and other charities, and was a leader of the Knights of Malta in the United States.

Seekers of Social Justice

355. Maud Leonard McCreery The daughter of Irish immigrants, Maud Leonard McCreery (1883–1938) was born near Milwaukee, Wisconsin. In spite of her limited formal education, which ended after only one year of high school, McCreery became a powerful figure in Wisconsin's suffrage and labor movements. As a suffragist, McCreery started out as a volunteer in a campaign office, but soon found herself acting as a speaker, lobbyist, and founder of a local Political Equality League. After a bout of tuberculosis ended her career as a suffragist, McCreery switched gears and supported the labor movement as a union organizer and journalist.

356. Michael Harrington and Rachel Carson Americans generally hold two competing images of the 1960s. One is of tumult and excess, as exemplified by urban violence and the drug culture. The other is one of idealistic activism, most vividly exemplified by the civil rights movement and JFK's call to "ask what you can do for your country." Two of the most important contributors to this activist tradition were Irish Americans Michael Harrington and Rachel Carson. Their landmark books, both published in 1962, grabbed the nation's conscience and helped launch the War on Poverty and the modern environmental movement.

In *The Other America,* Harrington revealed to Americans enjoying unprecedented postwar prosperity the startling fact that as many as 40 to 50 million Americans—one fifth the nation—still lived in poverty. His passionate and eloquent plea on behalf of "the invisible poor" spawned a national debate on poverty and provided the inspiration behind Lyndon Johnson's War on Poverty in 1964.

In *Silent Spring,* Carson (a marine biologist by training) wrote powerfully about the detrimental effects of pesticides on the ecosystem. It prompted millions of Americans to stop and question the negative impact of modern technology and recognize the need for more responsible care for the earth's environment. As Jimmy Carter said at the ceremony awarding her a posthumous Presidential Medal of Freedom, the impact of her book was enormous. "Always concerned, always eloquent, she created a tide of environmental consciousness that has not ebbed."

357. Patricia Ireland Patricia Ireland (b. 1945) began her fight for women's rights in the 1960s when she discovered discrepancies in her insurance coverage. Her first victory came when the U.S. Department of Labor ruled in her favor, and she started her legal career doing volunteer work for the National Organization for Women, which she presided over for many years after being repeatedly chosen by the membership. She has worked tirelessly for the causes of poor women, lesbian and gay rights, African women, electing women candidates, and training people to fight antiabortion terrorists at clinics around the United States. A well-known and popular speaker, she has spoken all over the world.

358. Judge Arthur Garrity Judge W. Arthur Garrity's (1920–99) career included stints as an assistant U.S. attorney (1947–50), and as aide to

John F. Kennedy in campaigns for senator and president, and U.S. attorney (1961–66). But Garrity's most lasting impact came during his tenure as U.S. district judge with *Morgan v Hennigan*. Garrity's controversial decision on June 21, 1974, which ordered busing to desegregate Boston's public school system, sparked vehe- ment—at times violent—protest from Boston's Irish American and African American neighbor- hoods. It also brought denunciation from political leaders, protests outside his home, and death threats that necessitated protection from U.S. Marshals. During a 1998 interview, Garrity main- tained he would have done nothing differently.

PART IV

Nationalism

nationalism afteR the famine

359. Some Background Irish nationalism was never the same after the Famine. The failure of Daniel O'Connell's Repeal movement (1830s and 1840s) had discredited his policy of pursuing a purely parliamentary form of agitation (vs. physical force). Indeed, many nationalists came to reject the very idea of securing home rule within Great Britain and began to advocate a movement to gain Ireland's complete independence. They looked to the failed Young Ireland uprising (1848) for inspiration.

360. The Irish Tenant Rights League At the end of August 1850, nationalists and agrarian activists formed the Irish Tenant Rights League. Its goal was to gain for Irish peasants the "three Fs":

- fair rents: set by a board to prevent gouging of poor tenants by landlords
- fixity of tenure: protection from eviction
- free sale: the right of a departing tenant to compensation for any improvements made to the land.

Although the League folded by 1858, its main accomplishment was to link land reform (economic rights) with the nationalist cause.

361. The Fenians The first major nationalist organization to emerge after the Famine was the Fenian Brotherhood, founded by exiled nationalists (among them John O'Mahoney and Michael Doheny) in 1854 in New York City. The word "Fenian" was a reference to Finn MacCool and his band of warriors in the ancient Celtic myth of the *Fionna*. But to the public the Fenians called the organization the Emmet Monument Association. The name, a reference to the martyred United Irishman Robert Emmet, was designed to inspire the membership and provide a cover for its fundraising activities. The latter, intended to fund a future armed insurrection in Ireland, proved very successful, bringing in $500,000 from the U.S. and Canada between 1858 and 1866. By that time, the Fenian Brotherhood had established a full-blown

Fenian Congress, 1865

government in exile, centered in Philadelphia and consisting of a Senate, House of Delegates, and president.

362. The Irish Republican Brotherhood As the Fenian's took form in the United States, James Stephens, a participant in the failed Young Ireland uprising of 1848, founded in Dublin the Irish Revolutionary Brotherhood (later renamed Irish Republican Brotherhood) on March 17, 1858. Working in tandem with the Fenians in America (in fact, all involved called themselves Fenians), they planned for an armed uprising that would expel the British and lead to the establishment of a democratic Republic of Ireland.

363. The Fenian Invasions of Canada The Fenians were divided over the exact timing and nature of the future uprising. Many thought the American Civil War provided them with a superb opportunity. More than 144,000 men of Irish birth (and at least as many Irish Americans) served in the Union Army and many leading Fenians had dreams of enlisting them to invade Ireland as an army of liberation.

As part of their plan to mount an armed invasion of Ireland, American Fenians hoped to draw the United States into a war with Great Britain. They believed that with a major conflict on its hands, England would be powerless to suppress the nationalist uprising in Ireland, backed by the invading army of Irishman from America. "England's difficulty," said John Mitchel, "is Ireland's opportunity."

In October 1865, General Thomas W. Sweeney (still on active duty in the U.S. Army) was appointed Fenian Secretary of War and charged with drawing up plans for an armed invasion of Canada. Not everyone in the movement supported the idea; indeed, John O'Mahoney opposed it as impractical and reckless. Nonetheless, on May 31, 1866, six hundred armed Fenians under Colonel John O'Neill (of County Monaghan) crossed the Niagara River into Canada. There they seized Fort Erie and routed a surprised contingent of British troops and Canadian militia at Ridgeway. Despite this early success, when British and Canadian forces counterattacked on June 2, and O'Neill soon found himself outnumbered (his reinforcements had been stopped at the U.S. border). He retreated to the banks of Lake Erie and surrendered to the U.S. warship *Michigan.* Two additional expeditions, one occupying Pigeon Hill in Quebec (June 7) and another into New Brunswick to seize Campo Bello Island failed in similar fashion. Hundreds were arrested but released soon thereafter.

Four years later, with their organization in shambles due to British repression (the Fenians in Ireland staged a failed uprising in 1867—see next entry) and internal bickering over, among other things, the wisdom of staging the uprisings, American Fenians sought to revive the movement with yet another invasion of Canada. Led once again by Colonel O'Neill, the Fenian army made a second attempt to invade Canada on May 25, 1870, but never left U.S. soil. As two hundred Fenian soldiers gathered at St. Albans, Vermont, they were seized and arrested by federal marshals. It was probably for the best—newspapers had carried stories of the planned "surprise attack" and Canada stood ready with thirteen thousand soldiers on its border.

The failure of the Canadian invasions and the uprising in Ireland (1867) greatly damaged the Fenian movement on both sides of the Atlantic, leading to infighting and repression. The Fenians would remain active in the United States for many years to come, but their influence would soon be eclipsed by a new organization, Clan na Gael.

364. The Fenian Uprising in Ireland The Canadian disaster of 1866 was actually the second major setback for the Fenian movement. The year before, in the fall of 1865, British officials infiltrated the IRB and arrested a number of its key leaders: James Stephens, Charles Kickham, John

O'Leary, Thomas Luby, and Jeremiah O'Donovan Rossa. Although many in the movement argued that now was the time to launch the uprising, cooler heads prevailed for the time being. Hundreds more were arrested from 1866 to 1867, including John Devoy, one of the movement's rising figures. Desperate, IRB diehards finally responded with a poorly coordinated uprising in March 1867. It failed and led to further mass arrests and deportations.

The rising failed to spark a mass revolt to overthrow British rule, but they did succeed in stimulating nationalist sentiment throughout Ireland. This was especially true in the case of the Manchester Martyrs, three Fenians hanged for their alleged role in a daring rescue of two fellow Fenians that resulted in the death of a prison guard. Even members of the Roman Catholic clergy, leery of most radical nationalist movements, expressed sympathy for the martyrs.

365. Clan na Gael   Clan na Gael ("band of the Irish") was founded in 1867 by journalist Jerome Collins as a revolutionary nationalist organization committed to the forceful overthrow of British rule in Ireland. Unlike the Fenians, however, they were a secret, oath-bound society. While this fact hampered the Clan's growth somewhat, it also protected it from unwanted attention from British authorities. The movement spread across the country in the early 1870s as activists established revolutionary cells from New York to San Francisco. Ten years after its founding, with a dedicated membership of ten thousand, the Clan established formal ties with the IRB in Ireland through the creation of a joint Revolutionary Directory.

366. John Devoy   One of the key factors in the emergence of the Clan, was the arrival of John Devoy (1842–1928) in New York in January 1871. As a rising figure in the IRB in the 1860s, he was among the hundreds arrested in the British crackdown of 1866–67. Sentenced to long terms in

John Devoy

prison, they were given amnesty in late 1870 on the condition that they not return to Ireland until their sentences expired. Devoy and four others, among them Jeremiah O'Donovan Rossa, sailed into New York Harbor aboard the *S.S. Cuba* and were greeted with a tumultuous celebration.

Soon after settling in New York and acquiring a job at the *New York Herald*, Devoy joined Clan na Gael. He quickly assumed control of the Clan and oversaw its growth in size and influence in the 1870s.

367. O'Donovan Rossa, the Angry Exile   Another important figure in this period, also a member of the "Cuba Five," was Jeremiah O'Donovan Rossa (1831–1915). An active member of the IRB since 1858, he edited an influential Fenian newspaper *The Irish People,* and was arrested in 1865. After five harrowing years in jail (chronicled in his book, *O'Donovan Rossa's Prison Life),* he was released and traveled with Devoy to New York. There he joined Clan na Gael and started his own radical nationalist newspaper, the *United Irishmen.* In 1875, he started a widely publicized "skirmishing fund" to raise money for armed insurrection in Ireland. This incurred the wrath of Devoy and other Clan officials because it violated the organization's policy of shunning publicity and invited criticism from the Catholic clergy and middle-class Irish Americans who felt it only played up the "wild Irishman" stereotype. O'Donovan Rossa broke with Devoy and the Clan in 1880, but continued to raise money for the cause and fulminate against British repression for the rest of his life.

In his autobiography, *Recollections* (1898),

O'Donovan Rossa explained the mind-set of the exiled Fenian:

> Did I call myself an "exile"?—an Irishman in New York, an "exile"! Yes, another word, and all the meanings of the word, come naturally to me, and run freely from my mind into this paper. My mother buried in America, all my brothers and sisters buried in America; twelve of my children born in America—and yet I cannot feel that America is my country . . .

368. HARPER'S Provides a More Upbeat Assessment of Irish Nationalism

> Is there any nationality which has become so entirely a passionate romantic sentiment as the Irish? The largest halls will be crowded by the most rapt and enthusiastic audience to hear a fervid orator denounce the invader and despoiler, and prophesy that from her ruins and her desolation Erin will rise again triumphant. It is a faith even more actual and intense than that of the Israelites in their restoration. Traditionally they wait with their hearts turned toward Zion and the Holy City. One day, they say, all the tribes will be gathered again, and the chosen people shall be supreme. But they make no raids upon Palestine. They throw no banners to the breeze at the Hebrew headquarters in foreign cities. They do not march annually in solemn procession and shake metaphorical fists at abstract tyrants, and kindle with tearful enthusiasm as the legends of Tara and the Druidical hill, of Patrick and the monasteries are fondly repeated.
>
> —"Editor's Easy Chair," *Harper's New Monthly Magazine,* July 1872

369. The CATALPA Rescue

In early 1874, John Devoy received a letter from a fellow Fenian lan-

The *Catalpa* rescue

guishing in a prison colony in Western Australia. It painted a sad picture of forgotten heroes wasting away and pleaded with Devoy for help. "We ask you to aid us with your tongue and pen, with your brain and intellect, with your ability and influence. We think if you forsake us, then we are friendless indeed." Devoy felt pangs of guilt, but also sensed an opportunity to secure, as he put it to fellow Clan members, "the first victory gained over England in our day." In April 1875, the ship *Catalpa,* paid for and outfitted by Devoy, set sail for Australia. It arrived one year later and spirited away the six Fenian prisoners. News of the daring rescue touched off celebrations in Dublin and the men were given a hero's welcome upon their arrival in New York in August. It was a purely symbolic gesture and cost more money than Devoy or the Clan could afford, but the *Catalpa* rescue energized the nationalist cause on both sides of the Atlantic.

370. The Fenian Ram

John Holland was born in County Claire in 1840, and grew up to become a schoolteacher. In his spare time, however, Holland became a student of submarine technology. Although a few prototypes had been constructed by men like Robert Fulton, no one had ever built a workable submarine. Holland studied everything that was known about these earlier models, and began to design his own. In 1873 he arrived in America and settled in Paterson, New Jersey, where he continued to teach and refine his submarine design. But with no funding available, Holland could only dream of seeing his plans take form.

His fortunes changed dramatically in 1879, when he sought out John Devoy and proposed to build a submarine for the Clan that would be capable of sinking British ships at will. All they needed was funding. Devoy invested $23,000 in the project and in 1881 Holland's sixty-foot ship conducted its first successful test runs in New York City's East River. In the end, the *Fenian Ram*, as it was known, never saw action in the cause for Irish freedom. Nevertheless, Holland continued to work on his design and eventually produced a highly successful submarine which he sold to the U.S. Navy and several other countries. He is generally considered to be the father of the modern submarine.

Home Rule and Social Reform

371. Changes Under Gladstone   When William E. Gladstone became Prime Minister of England in 1868, few Irish nationalists thought he would be very different from his predecessors. He was, after all, widely known for his staunch support for the Ascendancy. The rise of militant Fenianism, however, convinced him that concessions were necessary if Ireland was to remain a peaceful part of the United Kingdom. In short order he pushed through three landmark acts.

- The Disestablishment of the Church of Ireland (1869): Irish Catholics (and Presbyterians for that matter) had long protested the law that required them to pay tithes to support a church whose membership was less than one eighth of the Irish population. Henceforth the Anglican Church of Ireland would be a voluntary religion with no special privileges.
- The Landlord and Tenant Act (1870): This law granted some Irish tenant

farmers one of the "three Fs" (see Irish Tenants Rights League), free sale, or compensation for improvements they made to their holdings in the event that they were evicted. The law also contained a provision that allowed tenants to purchase their holdings. It was the first of many significant land reform laws enacted between 1870 and 1903.
- The Ballot Act (1872): Irish tenant farmers could now vote secretly, thus freeing them from political manipulation by their landlords.

372. Isaac Butt and Home Rule   Gladstone's reforms helped revive constitutional nationalism—the moderate, nonviolent movement to regain an Irish Parliament, or simply, "home rule." In the 1874 election to Parliament, sixty pro–home rule MPs were elected in Ireland. They were led by a Protestant lawyer named Isaac Butt (1813–79). Immediately, they introduced a home rule bill that was soundly defeated, but the next year the movement was energized by the emergence of a younger, more dynamic voice—that of Charles Stewart Parnell.

373. Charles Stewart Parnell   Charles Stewart Parnell (1846–1891) was born in Avondale, County Wicklow, in 1846. A member of a wealthy, landed family, he was educated in England. Drawn to politics, especially the home rule variety, he won a seat in Parliament in 1875.

As a landlord and member of the Protestant Ascendancy, Parnell seemed at first an unlikely Irish nationalist. But he possessed a genuine sympathy for the plight of Irish Catholics and genuine hostility toward English domination of Irish affairs. The latter Anglophobia derived, in part, from the fact that his mother was an American and her father, Commodore Charles Stewart, had served in the U.S. Navy during the War of 1812 and sunk two British warships. His father also possessed nationalist sentiments.

Soon after arriving in Parliament he began delivering scathing speeches against English misrule in Ireland. "Why should Ireland be treated as a geographical fragment of England," he asked in 1875. "Ireland is not a geological fragment, but a nation." Parnell also used obstructionist tactics to hold up the general business of Parliament. By 1878 he was the undisputed leader of the Home Rule Party.

374. Michael Davitt   The late-1870s brought to the fore another leading Irish nationalist, Michael Davitt (1846–1906). Although born in the same year as Parnell, he came from the opposite end of the social spectrum. He was born in Mayo into a family of poor Catholic tenant farmers. Like so

Michael Davitt

many others, they survived the Famine only to be evicted. They migrated to England and found work in a Lancashire factory town. It was here that Davitt, at the age of eleven, lost his right arm in a factory accident.

In his late teens he joined the IRB and became its secretary in 1868, when he was only twenty-two. Arrested in the crackdown on the IRB following the Fenian Uprising, he served seven years of a fifteen-year sentence before being released in 1877. Eager to resume his nationalist activity, he immediately sailed for New York.

375. The Emerging Land Question   By 1878 John Devoy had come to the conclusion that the strategy of revolutionary Irish nationalism had to change. He knew full well that with just ten thousand members, Clan na Gael could hardly expect to overthrow British rule in Ireland by force of

arms alone. Moreover, by 1878 Devoy had become increasingly convinced that the nationalist movement needed to focus on more than the political goal of Irish independence. It must, he argued, address the fundamental social problem of Ireland: the landlord system that left the vast majority of people as tenant farmers paying high rents and living in fear of eviction. "I believe in Irish independence," he told an audience in 1878, "but I don't think it would be worthwhile to free Ireland if that foreign landlord system was left standing." Devoy's new thinking outraged hard-line physical-force nationalists, but it also opened the door to a remarkable nationalist alliance that would shake Ireland to its foundation in the years to come.

376. The New Departure   Devoy's new thinking now prompted him to seek an alliance that until recently would have been considered unthinkable: the joining of physical-force nationalists with Parnell's constitutionalists home rulers. In a telegram in October 1878, Devoy offered nationalist support to Parnell if he would champion land reform, refrain from criticizing the militants, and speak of Irish "self-rule" in more vague terms (i.e., not simply home rule) so as to attract supporters of total Irish independence. Parnell met with Devoy and Davitt on three occasions during 1878 and 1879 and expressed a general willingness to join what Devoy was calling the New Departure.

Just how much of Devoy's program Parnell agreed to support is unclear. Devoy believed, or at least allowed himself to believe, that Parnell had agreed to use home rule merely as a device for securing the complete independence of Ireland. In Devoy's mind, it would work like this:

- Parnell would launch a campaign to end British landlordism and the establishment of a program to transfer land to peasant ownership.
- The British government would refuse and respond with a crackdown.

- In the ensuing crisis, Parnell would demand Parliament grant Ireland home rule.
- When Parliament refused, Parnell would withdraw the Irish MPs to Ireland, where they would establish an independent Irish government.
- Britain's military response would be repulsed by the heavily armed forces of the IRB and Clan na Gael.
- Victorious, Ireland would declare itself an independent republic.

377. The Irish Land League The third element in the New Departure was the harnessing of growing tenant distress to the new nationalist effort headed by Parnell. Ireland in 1879 was in the throes of a terrible agricultural crisis marked by crop failure, falling prices, and rising evictions for nonpayment of rent. That spring Michael Davitt held a rally attended by fifteen thousand tenant farmers in Irishtown, County Mayo. Out of that event came the Mayo Land League which by October grew to become the Irish Land League with chapters across the country. Parnell, sensing an opportunity to enlist popular support for home rule, agreed to serve as the League's president.

378. The Land League in America Crucial to the success of the Irish Land League was the establishment of an American branch. Parnell arrived in America in January 1880 and commenced a whirlwind fund-raising tour through sixty cities and towns, culminating with an address before a joint session of Congress. Shortly after Parnell's departure, Irish nationalists gathered in New York City to form the American Land League. Within two years, activists established nearly one thousand American Land League branches across the country, from major cities like New York and Boston to the mining districts in Colorado and Butte, and raised over $500,000. No longer was Irish nationalist activism in America confined to a few thousand members of Clan na Gael. It had

become a mass movement, drawing support from upper-class professionals and poor factory workers alike. The latter were often drawn to the movement because they sought in the condemnation of landlord exploitation in Ireland, an effective critique of industrial capitalism in the United States.

379. Patrick Ford One of the most of vociferous champions of the Land League, especially its more radical aspirations, was Patrick Ford (1837–1913). Born in Ireland, he came to America as a child during the Famine. As a young boy, he worked in the offices of the radical abolitionist William Lloyd Garrison's newspaper, *The Liberator*. He served in the Union Army during the Civil War and in 1870 founded the weekly newspaper the *Irish World*.

Ford was a radical reformer and did much to challenge the stereotype of the Irish as socially conservative. He supported virtually every liberal cause, from currency reform, to women's rights, to land reform (he favored nationalization). Ford's brand of nationalism reflected this radical outlook. He viewed the Land League movement as a unique moment in history where the poor could smash land monopoly (and economic exploitation in general) and gain greater social equality. "[T]he struggle in Ireland," he constantly reminded his readers, "is radically and essentially the same as the struggle in America—a contest against legalized forms of oppression . . ." Through the *Irish World,* the largest-selling Irish American newspaper, he helped establish hundreds of Land League branches and collected more than half of the $500,000 raised. John Devoy, despite his own em-

Patrick Ford

brace of the land issue, deplored Ford and his extreme radicalism. But there was little he could do—Ford delivered the money.

380. The Connection Between Irish Nationalism and American Labor Activism
In the late 1880s, James Baggs, a New York City produce dealer, reflected on the popularity of the Land League among American workers:

> The greatest part of the vast sum of money sent through the *Irish World* was subscribed by the poor workingmen and workingwomen of America, who, in so doing, were impressed with the idea that they were doing a work that would benefit the people of Ireland, and the workers throughout the world as well.

381. The Land War
The Land League agitation started by Davitt and supported by Parnell and Devoy firmly linked the land question to the national question. As the League put it in its Declaration of Principles:

> The land of Ireland belongs to the people all of Ireland, to be held and cultivated for the sustenance of those who God decreed to be the inhabitants thereof. Land being created to supply mankind with the necessities of existence, those who cultivate it to that end have a higher claim to its absolute possession than those who make it an article of barter to be used or disposed of for purposes of profit or pleasure.

In a country where 70 percent of the land was owned by only two thousand people while three million tenants owned none at all, this was a powerful and popular message. The League called for the redistribution of property from landlords (who would be compensated) to tenants. To bring this about, tenants began to withhold their rents.

Some resorted to violence, destroying crops, maiming cattle, and in a few cases murdering landlords or their agents. The struggle became known as the "Land War" and its revolutionary potential sent chills through the Protestant Ascendancy.

382. Captain Boycott
Another tactic employed in the Land War was social ostracism. Anyone who aided the landlord by collecting rents or carrying out evictions found themselves cut off from social contact. This was especially true for those "land grabbers" who took over an evicted farmer's holding. As Parnell put it,

> When a man takes a farm from which another has been evicted, you must show him on the roadside when you meet him, you must show him in the streets of the town, you must show him at the shop-counter, you must show him at the fair and at the market-place and even in the house of worship, by leaving him severely alone . . . by isolating him from the rest of his kind, as if he were a leper of old, you must show him your detestation of the crime he has committed.

The most famous victim of this policy was the land agent for Lord Erne's Mayo estate, Captain Charles Boycott, whose name became a synonym for the practice. Shunned by the locals, he needed over one thousand British troops to harvest the estate's crops (at a cost of £10,000 to the government).

383. The Dynamite Campaign
Disaffected physical-force nationalists like O'Donovan Rossa, angered at Devoy's alliance with Parnell and the constitutionalists, embarked on a bombing campaign in England. The operations were funded by O'Donovan Rossa's "skirmishing fund" and began in January 1881 with the bombing of a military barracks. Many subsequent bombing attempts

were foiled by British detectives, but they had the desired effect of striking terror into the hearts of English citizens. Yet they also contributed to Gladstone's decision to adopt the sweeping program of repression against the Land League.

384. Coercion and Reform Gladstone responded to the Land War with both the carrot and the stick. In the case of the former, he had pushed through the second Land Act (August 1881), which granted tenant farmers the much sought after "three Fs" and established a loan program (up to 75 percent of the purchase price) to help tenants buy their land. The coercion came soon after, following Parnell's rejection of the Land Act as inadequate and issuance of a "no rent manifesto" that called upon all tenants to withhold their rents. Gladstone responded by outlawing the Land League and throwing Parnell and other League officials in the Kilmainham jail (October 1881).

385. The Kilmainham Treaty Gladstone's dual policy of land reform and coercion worked. After seven months in jail, Parnell and Gladstone struck a deal. Parnell and his followers would be released from jail in exchange for calling off the Land War. Additionally, Gladstone agreed to expand the Land Act to cover the thousands of indebted tenant farmers not included in the previous law. Moderate nationalists hailed the deal, but radical nationalists like Ford felt betrayed.

386. The Phoenix Park Murders Any hope of reviving the Land War disappeared only days after Parnell and Davitt left prison. A small group of Fenian extremists known as the "Invincibles," enraged at the British crackdown and the Land League officials' timidity, assassinated in Dublin's Phoenix Park Lord Frederick Cavendish, recently appointed chief secretary of Ireland, and Thomas Burke, the undersecretary. Now the enemies of Irish nationalism could dismiss the land agitation as a Fenian front for violent revolution. The

Charles Stewart Parnell

Phoenix Park murders, as at least one historian has pointed out, served as the Irish version of Chicago's Haymarket Riot of 1886 because of the conservative, antiradical backlash which ensued. John Devoy's goal of Irish independence, Parnell's crusade for home rule, and Ford's quest for social revolution appeared to be all but extinguished.

387. Parnell, the National League, and Home Rule In late 1882, Parnell completed his retreat from radicalism by transforming the Irish Land League into the National League, the organization committed to securing home rule. In response to the National League sending eighty-six home rule MPs to Parliament in the 1885 elections, Gladstone then stunned the British political system by casting his support for a home rule bill. Unfortunately, the move split his Liberal Party and the home rule bill went down to defeat.

388. The Fall of Parnell The home rule campaign of 1886 marked the high point of Parnell's career. Thereafter, he was beset by a series of problems. First, his health began to decline. Second, he alienated some of his more radical followers by opposing their efforts to revive tenant farmer activism (the so-called Plan of Campaign) as a protest against continued high rents and evictions despite the Land Act of 1881. Third, in 1887 he became the victim of a smear campaign led by the London *Times* that falsely accused (through forged letters) Parnell of sanctioning Fenian terrorism during the Land War. Fourth, and most devastating, his ten-year affair with a married woman, Katie O'Shea, became public during her divorce proceedings in 1890. Parnell, once dubbed "the uncrowned king of Ireland," was finished. Gladstone called upon him to resign, as did the Catholic bishops of Ireland. When he resisted, he only managed to split his party. He married O'Shea, but died suddenly in October 1891.

389. Nationalists in Disarray In the wake of the fall of Parnell, the Home Rule Party was left divided and in disarray. Across the Atlantic, Irish nationalism was similarly divided into warring factions. John Devoy's support for the New Departure alienated hard-line Fenians committed to armed insurrection and full Irish independence. The dynamite campaign that many of them supported likewise angered Devoy, who saw it as a pointless gesture that wasted resources, alienated public opinion, and invited British oppression. By the late 1880s, Devoy became involved in a power struggle for control of Clan na Gael with Alexander Sullivan, leader of the nationalists in Chicago.

While the hard-liners fought it out, a new moderate organization was established. The Irish National Federation of America was organized in 1891 in New York with Dr. Thomas A. Emmet (grandson of the eminent United Irishman exile) as president. They dedicated themselves to raising money for the National Party in Ireland led by Justin McCarthy. Eventually 150 branches were organized nationwide.

390. The Second Home Rule Bill When Gladstone and his Liberal Party returned to power in 1892, he immediately moved to introduce a second home rule bill (1893). This time he managed to get the House of Commons to pass it, only to have the bill resoundingly defeated by the Lords (419–41). It would be another twenty years (during which time the Conservatives held power) before a third home rule bill was introduced.

391. "Killing Home Rule with Kindness" After the failure of Gladstone's home rule bill, the con-

servative governments that succeeded him adopted a policy for Ireland which one of them described as, "killing home rule with kindness." By kindness, they did not mean respect for human rights or Irish self-determination. Rather, they meant land reform, which they hoped would mollify angry tenants and boost Ireland's overall economy.

The policy of "kindness" failed to kill the desire for home rule (or outright independence, for that matter). It did, however, dramatically advance the extraordinary transformation of rural Ireland. In 1903, Parliament passed the last of the Land Acts, the Wyndham Act. It offered landlords bonuses for selling their land to their tenants. Tenants, in turn, were given loans that they could take up to sixty-eight years to pay back. As expected, many landlords took the money and ran.

The results of this and earlier Land Acts (1870, 1881, 1885, and 1891), far less dramatic than political agitation, were astonishing. In 1870, the year of the first Land Act, only 3 percent of Irish farmers owned their own land. In 1906, land ownership among Irish farmers reached 29 percent. By 1918, the figure hit 64 percent. This "silent revolution" was one of the greatest peaceful (relatively speaking, of course) transfers of property in modern history. It is important to point out, however, that it stemmed not from "kindness" so much as from a desire to quell the persistent agitation of Ireland's tenant farmers. Moreover, it must be remembered, that it ultimately failed. Irish nationalism was not simply about land, but also about nationhood.

Cultural Nationalism

392. The Gaelic Revival Starting in the late nineteenth century, Ireland and America experienced what became known as the "Gaelic Revival." At the heart of it was the movement to revive the Irish language (see next entry), but it also involved efforts to stir interest in Irish history, art, dance, music, and literature. One of the most visible symbols of this revival was the proliferation of annual Gaelic festivals, known as *feis* (pronounced "fesh"), across the country. These usually featured competitions in dancing, writing, oratory, singing, and sports. By the 1930s and 1940s it was not uncommon for a *feis* in Chicago or Boston to draw as many as four thousand people.

393. Revival of the Irish Language

For Irish and Irish American nationalists, nothing so symbolized a distinct and venerable Irish culture than the Irish, or Gaelic, language. The fact that so few people of Irish birth or background spoke Irish—a direct result of British colonial domination—made its resurrection all the more meaningful. They hoped not merely for Ireland's political independence, but for cultural independence as well.

Before the 1870s a few efforts had been made to preserve and promote the Irish language in America. In 1856 a chapter of the Ossianic Society (based in Dublin) opened in New York City. The next year the first regular publication in America in the Irish language began with the establishment of "Our Gaelic Department," a weekly feature in the *Irish-American* (New York). But it was not until the early 1870s, with the establishment of the Philo-Celtic Societies in Boston and Brooklyn (with countless more following suit across the country in cities with large Irish populations) that a full-fledged movement began. This movement no doubt inspired the formation of the Society for the Preservation of the Irish Language in Dublin in 1876. Irish language scholar Michael Logan started the bilingual monthly magazine *The Gael* in 1881 that provided an important forum for Irish language literature. Many Irish American newspapers added Gaelic columns in the 1880s and 1890s as the Irish language revival hit full stride. In the 1890s, the Ancient Order of Hibernians established a Chair of Gaelic at Catholic University in Washington, D.C.

The revival of the Irish language continued well into the twentieth century. Irish American newspapers of the period are full of advertisements for Irish language classes and events. In 1916, the *Gaelic-American* ran advertisements for "The Galeophone Method." For fifteen dollars one received thirty-five phonograph records and a book of lessons "guaranteed" to produce a Gaelic speaker in no time.

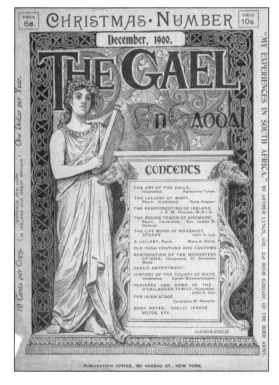

The Gael, 1900

394. Padraic O'Byrne

Many Gaelic columns consisted mainly of texts copied from old Irish manuscripts. However, by the 1880s many original works in Irish appeared. The most significant and prolific writer was Donegal-born poet Patrick O'Byrne, or simply Padraic, as he signed his work. According to Irish-language scholar Kenneth E. Nilsen, O'Byrne "can be regarded, along with Douglas Hyde, as an originator of modern poetry in Irish."

Patrick O'Byrne also contributed to a unique "first" for the Irish language. He translated the text for the first Irish language opera (written by Paul

MacSwiney of Cork), *An Bard argus an Fo,* or *The Bard and the Knight.* It was performed at Steinway Hall in New York City in November 1884. Subsequently, numerous plays in the Irish language were performed in New York and other cities.

395. Gaelic League

In 1891 an Irish-language enthusiast and poet named Douglas Hyde visited New York's Gaelic societies. Impressed with their effective promotion of Irish language and culture, he returned to Ireland and in 1893 helped establish the Gaelic League (and served as its first president). It was dedicated not simply to preserving the Irish language, but to reestablishing it as a living language, both spoken and written. By 1903 there were five hundred League branches established in Ireland. They held Irish-language classes, performances, and events. In 1899 it led the fight to block the removal of Irish from the curriculum at Trinity College in Dublin. Ten years later it succeeded in making Irish a compulsory subject at the National University of Ireland. Many prominent writers like William Butler Yeats were profoundly influenced by this language movement.

Initially the League was nonpolitical and enjoyed support from Protestants and unionists. But the political undertones of the language movement became clearer in the early twentieth century as the nationalist movement intensified. The fact that one of the primary founders of the League—Eoin MacNeill—would later become commander-in-chief of the Irish Volunteers illustrated the strong connection between cultural and political nationalism. By 1915 IRB influence in the Gaelic League was significant and many members participated in the Easter Rising of 1916. The British government outlawed the organization in 1919.

396. Douglas Hyde Stresses the Importance of the Irish Language

In order to de-Anglicize ourselves, we must at once arrest the decay of the language. We must bring pressure upon our politicians not to snuff it out by their racist discouragement merely because they do not themselves understand it. We must arouse some spark of patriotic inspiration among the peasantry who still use the language, and put an end to that shameful state of feeling—a thousand-tongued reproach to our leaders and statesmen—which makes young men and women blush and hang their heads when overheard speaking their own language.

397. Gaelic Athletic Association

In 1884 Michael Cusack established the Gaelic Athletic Association (GAA) in Tipperary. Earlier in life he had been an avid player of rugby and cricket, but he grew to dislike the elitism of the clubs associated with the sports. He also became convinced that the spread of English sports undermined Ireland's rising sense of nationhood and founded the GAA to promote Irish sports such as Gaelic football, hurling, and camogie (women's hurling). The obvious nationalist undertones of the GAA attracted members of the IRB, who soon came to dominate the organization. One of the rules of membership they adopted excluded anyone who played "imported games" or served in the police or army.

The GAA, like many nationalist organizations, fell on hard times (in the wake of the Parnell controversy) in the 1890s, but was revived at the turn of the century. Irish sporting events drew crowds as large as twenty thousand, prompting the GAA to build the sports facility which became known as Croke Park (named in honor of Archbishop Thomas William Croke, an early supporter of the GAA).

398. The Literary Revival

In the midst of the movements to revive the Irish language and promote a return to Irish sports, Irish literature and theater experienced an extraordinary period of creativity and innovation. Interestingly, most of

the leading figures—William Butler Yeats, John Millington Synge, Lady Gregory, and George Russell—were Anglo-Irish Protestants. Yet they discarded the class, religious, and political values of the Ascendancy in favor of a cultural nationalism that denounced British colonialism for hindering the development of native Irish traditions.

Yeats and the other literary revivalists were fascinated by ancient Ireland's past, especially the Celtic, pre-Christian era, and incorporated many of its themes and imagery into their works of drama and poetry. They also celebrated and romanticized the Irish peasant of the Gaeltacht as the possessors and nurturers of Ireland's non-British cultural traditions.

Yeats summarized the connection between Irish nationalism and the Irish literary revival: "No fine nationality without fine literature . . . no fine literature without nationality."

399. The Abbey Theatre

In 1899, the leading figures of Ireland's literary revival established the National Literary Society. Its goal was to support amateur actors and playwrights in producing a self-consciously national drama. In 1904, the organization opened the Abbey Theatre. It soon achieved a wide reputation for staging the works of the leading figures in Ireland's literary revival—William Butler Yeats, Lady Gregory, and John M. Synge.

There existed a significant divide within the Abbey Theatre between those dedicated to serious dramatic realism and those more motivated by explicitly patriotic and nationalist ideals. The best example of this divide was the reaction to John Millington Synge's *The Playboy of the Western World.* Born in County Dublin in 1871, Synge first studied music before settling upon the career in writing. The 1890s, while living in Paris, he met Yeats, who convinced him to move to the Aran Islands and write about the people that isolated, largely un-Anglicized region. Synge spent three years there, writing a book (*The Aran Islands,* 1907) and collecting stories which he incorpo-

Lady Gregory

rated into plays for the Irish National Theater. His first two plays, *The Shadow of the Glen* (1903) and *Writers to the Sea* (1904) provoked a hostile response from critics, who bristled at his celebration of earthy and sometimes crude peasant culture. The debut of his great comedy, *The Playboy of the Western World,* today considered a classic, sparked a riot outside the Abbey Theatre by protesters who considered its depiction of Irish characters derogatory and offensive.

400. A More Conservative Gaelic Revival in America

The outraged response to Synge's play was more the exception than the rule in Ireland. While Gaelic Revivalists continued to draw criticism from conservatives, they produced excellent and unique works that found a receptive audience. In America, however, the Gaelic Revival was of a more uniformly conservative character and intended mainly to boost Irish American self-esteem in an era of still strong anti-Irish bigotry. Consequently, America's Gaelic Revival was largely characterized by works of history, literature, and drama that celebrated a romanticized Irish past largely disconnected from the realities of Irish American urban life. In 1911, the Ancient Order of Hibernians, already in the midst of a campaign against the "stage Irishman" in popular drama, denounced the works of Yeats, Synge, and "other so-called Irish dramatists." Predictably, performances of Synge's *Playboy* sparked protests and riots in American cities.

401. Hibernocentrism

One of the products of the Gaelic Revival in America was the develop-

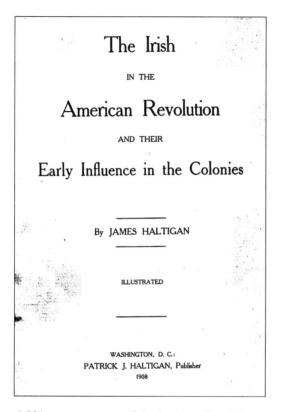

The Irish

IN THE

American Revolution

AND THEIR

Early Influence in the Colonies

By JAMES HALTIGAN

ILLUSTRATED

WASHINGTON, D. C.:
PATRICK J. HALTIGAN, Publisher
1908

A Hibernocentric view of the American Revolution

ment of what might be called a "hibernocentrist" view of Irish history—that is, the writing of histories of America and Ireland that sought to highlight the heroic and glorious contributions of Irish people to science, art, religion, technology, war, and civilization in general. Between the 1880s and 1920s, dozens of works of Irish history were published in the U.S., most expressing a distinctly hibernocentrist viewpoint. In one of the more vivid works of this genre, Martin Mulroy writes in *The Irish Discovery of America 1000 Years Before Columbus* (1906) that Irish Celts came to America "long before either the Italian or the Englishman had any notion of venturing from their native shores." For evidence, he cites St. Brendan's diary and accounts of seventeenth-century French missionaries who claimed to encounter Indians who spoke both Latin and Gaelic.

Hibernocentrism also extended to Irish American history and had the same goal in mind—to challenge the popular belief among Anglo-Americans that the Irish had arrived only recently in the United States and made few significant contributions. If they could prove that the Irish were among the earliest settlers in America and had made important contributions to American history—especially the American Revolution—they could effectively undermine anti-Irish sentiment.

402. A Hibernocentrist Observes

They [the Irish] appear to have been, from the most remote antiquity, *a polished people* and with propriety they may be called, *the fathers of letters!* Sequestered in a remote island giving laws to neighboring states, and free from foreign invasions for the certain space of two thousand and sixty years, they had time and leisure to attend to their history and antiquities; and they certainly exceeded all nations of the world in their attention to these points!

—Silvester O'Halloran, writing in the Foreword to William Dolby, ed., *The History of Ireland from the Invasion of Henry the Second to the Present Times* (1894).

403. Denouncing the "Scotch-Irish Myth" One of the inspirations behind this effort to tout the Irish role in the making of American history was the emergence of what Irish Catholics termed the "Scotch-Irish Myth." In the second half of the nineteenth century, a movement had developed among Americans of Protestant Irish ancestry to distinguish themselves from the growing number of Irish Catholics in America. Increasingly they began to refer to themselves as "Scotch-Irish," suggesting, not so subtly, that while their ancestors came from Ireland, their ethnic or "racial" strain was Scottish (i.e., that they

were descendants of Scots Presbyterians settled on the Ulster "plantations" of the late sixteenth and seventeenth centuries). If this were true, Irish Catholics would lose their claim to most of the "Irish" contributions to American history, since most of the early Irish in America were Ulster Protestants.

Not surprisingly, Irish Catholics denounced such a distinction as pure fiction. Irish was Irish and that was all there was to it. Any attempt to make distinctions between people of Irish ancestry was born of snobbery at best, bigotry at worst.

404. American Irish Historical Society The controversy over the "Scotch-Irish myth" in the 1890s led directly to the founding of the American Irish

The American Irish Historical Society

Historical Society. Many of the men who led the movement to establish the Society were active in the effort to refute the Scotch-Irish myth. In December 1896, they sent a letter to prominent Irish Americans across the country, inviting them to attend a meeting on January 20, 1897, in Boston. It read, in part:

> The American of English stock has his historical society, the descendants of the Dutch, Huguenot and Spaniards have associations which specialize the historical work of the bodies they represent, and we feel that the story of the Irish should be told before the mass of fiction and legend flooding the country under misleading designations has completely submerged the facts.

Those who attended the meeting that created the Society were Admiral Richard Worsam Meade, nephew of the Union Army hero at Gettysburg, the sculptor Augustus Saint-Gaudens, and then New York City Police Commissioner Theodore Roosevelt.

405. Michael J. O'Brien Without question the most prolific hibernocentric scholar of the period was Michael J. O'Brien. Born in Fermoy, County Cork, in 1869 he arrived in America at the age of twenty and took a job with the Western Union Telegraph Co. The job, which he held for the next forty-six years, required him to travel up and down the Atlantic Coast. Wherever he went, O'Brien poked around local libraries and archives, researching the history of the Irish and colonial America. Soon he began publishing his findings in the *Journal of the American Irish Historical Society* and continued doing so for more than twenty years. O'Brien was relentless and indefatigable, publishing countless articles and a dozen books, including *The Irish at Bunker Hill, The Pioneer Irish in New England,* and *A Hidden Phase of American History.* To the end, his goal remained the same: to refute the nativist contention that the Irish had made no worthwhile contributions to American history.

Toward Independence

406. The New Nationalism By the turn of the century Irish nationalists began to speak of a "new nationalism." It referred to the resurgence of a more radical Irish nationalism in the years following Parnell's fall and the defeat of the second home rule bill. Increasing numbers of nationalists became disillusioned with the pursuit of home rule and began to embrace the more radical idea of complete Irish independence from England (though not necessarily through violent means).

In addition to the Gaelic Revival, three events helped boost the new nationalism. First, in 1898 nationalists commemorated the centennial of Wolf Tone's 1798 rising, an event that rekindled the hopes of establishing an independent Irish republic. Second, in 1899 England plunged into the Boer War (1899–1902) in South Africa. Irish nationalists identified with the Boers' effort to resist British colonialism. Arthur Griffith, James Connolly, and other important nationalist leaders raised money for the Boers and launched a campaign to dissuade Irish men from joining the British army. Third, Queen Victoria's visit to Ireland in 1900 prompted a nationalist campaign calling for a boycott of the ceremonies and counterdemonstrations. Together these events heightened nationalist sentiment and brought before the public a new set of nationalist leaders.

407. John Redmond and the Irish Parliamentary Party Despite the rise of new nationalism, moderate Irish nationalism was far from dead. It, too, recovered in 1900 with the reunification of the Irish Parliamentary Party (which had split during the Parnell scandal) under John Redmond.

408. Nationalism Revived in America Divided and weak in the 1890s, Clan na Gael reunited in

John Redmond

July 1900 and commenced an effort to revitalize the militant, physical-force wing of Irish nationalism. John Devoy, elected secretary of the reorganized Clan, soon established a new newspaper, *The Gaelic American,* to promote its agenda.

Moderate nationalists likewise reorganized. In 1901, while on a fund-raising tour of America, John Redmond founded the United Irish League of America (UILA). Its purpose was to raise money for support of the Irish Parliamentary Party and home rule. Its moderate nationalism helped it garner financial support from moderate, middle-class Irish Americans not willing to associate themselves (and thereby risk their reputations) with physical-force nationalism. By 1910 hundreds of UILA branches managed to raise over £50,000 for the cause in Ireland.

409. Sinn Fein One of the emerging voices of new nationalism was that of Arthur Griffith. A journalist, he became an enthusiastic supporter of the GAA, Gaelic League, and IRB in the 1890s and developed a nationalist philosophy of self-reliance and self-determination that he eventually called *"Sinn Fein"* (Irish for "we ourselves"). Griffith was a moderate. He opposed physical-force nationalism and a complete separation from England. Instead, he called for a campaign of passive resistance in which Irish MPs would withdraw from Westminster to establish an Irish Parliament that would operate *within* the United Kingdom and remain under the Crown. As part of his program of self-reliance, Griffith also advocated an economic program based on high protective tariffs. On September 28, 1905, he founded the political party Sinn Fein and started a newspaper under the same name the next year. Sinn Fein wielded almost no political power before 1916, but it did exert a significant influence on Irish nationalist thought.

410. Radical Trade Unionism   Still another center of Irish nationalism was developing at the turn of the century in the form of a vibrant labor movement. Ireland's industrial workers were among the worst paid and worst housed in Western Europe. James Larkin, a Liverpool-born Catholic and radical socialist, became a leading figure in the effort to unite Irish workers—regardless of religion—and better their conditions. In 1908, he organized the Irish Transport and General Workers Union (ITGWU), which grew into a formidable labor union encompassing thousands of workers from any broad array of skills and trades. The ITGWU organized strikes and engaged in hard-nosed negotiations to win wage increases and improve conditions for workers.

Flush with this success, Larkin set his sights on the Dublin United Tramway Company, owned by William Martin Murphy, the richest man in Ireland. Murphy, a staunch conservative, vowed to destroy Larkin and the ITGWU. He established an employers' organization and then locked out twenty-five thousand workers by September 1913. The workers hung tough, but when their funds ran out and British Trades Union Congress withdrew financial support, the strike collapsed. Workers returned to their jobs with little to show for their sacrifice. Larkin headed for the United States to raise money for the ITGWU.

James Connolly, a fellow radical socialist and leading figure in the 1913 Dublin lockout, replaced Larkin as head of the ITGWU. Under Connolly, the link between trade unionism and radical nationalism was made explicit, especially in his role as commander-in-chief of the Irish Citizen Army, the socialist militia formed by the ITGWU during the Dublin lockout to protect workers from the Dublin police.

411. The Third Home Rule Bill   In 1910, the ruling Liberal Party suffered heavy losses at the polls. Though still in power, they once again had to rely on the support of Irish MPs. As before, this created an opportunity to gain passage of a home rule bill for Ireland. This time around, however, advocates of home rule would benefit from a major reform adopted by Parliament which curtailed the absolute veto power of the House of Lords (which had killed the home rule bill of 1892).

The third home rule bill was introduced in April 1912 and passed the Commons in January 1913. It was rejected in House of Lords a few weeks later, again approved in the Commons, and again rejected by the Lords in July. Under the new parliamentary system, the Lords could reject the bill one more time, but that would only delay its implementation, not kill it. Home rulers merely had to pass the bill a third time and it would take effect in the summer of 1914. Unfortunately, it was at this moment that the anti–home rule movement among Ulster Protestants developed into a formidable force behind a charismatic lawyer named Edward Carson.

412. The Ulster Volunteers vs. The Irish Volunteers   In January 1913 at the height of the home rule crisis, hard-line Ulster unionists pulled together several independent militia groups to form the Ulster Volunteer Force. Led by former British army officers, its membership soared to ninety thousand. In April 1914, the UVF successfully smuggled in twenty-five thousand rifles and three million rounds of ammunition purchased in Germany. The primary purpose of the UVF was to pressure Westminster into rejecting, or least modifying by excluding Ulster, the home rule bill by raising the specter of civil war.

In response to the formation of the Ulster Volunteers, Irish nationalists formed the Irish Volunteers in Dublin on November 25, 1913. The inspiration for the Volunteers came from an article written by Eoin MacNeill in the Gaelic League's newspaper calling upon nationalists to arm themselves in defense of home rule. Although ostensibly a pro–home rule organization, the Volunteers contained a strong IRB element (including Maurice Moore, Sir Roger Casement, Padraic Pearse, and Eamon de Valera), a fact that made John Redmond initially hesitant to support it. In less than one year, membership in the Irish Volunteers surpassed 160,000.

413. The Irish Citizen Army At the height of the Dublin lockout of 1913, the ITGWU formed the Irish Citizen Army to protect workers from the Dublin Metropolitan Police. The ICA did not disband after the lockout ended in January 1914, but continued to recruit members and drill in public parks. Under James Connolly it espoused both radical trade unionism and national self-determination. By 1916 it had a membership of 350 and began joint preparations with the IRB for the Easter Rising of 1916.

414. The Question of Partition In June 1914, as Ireland stood on the verge of civil war, the British government introduced a compromise proposal (the so-called Amending Bill) to allow the counties of Ulster a period of six years in which they could "opt out" of the home rule agreement. Originally Carson expressed vehement opposition to any home rule plan, but eventually accepted the idea of an Ulster exclusion when he realized that unionists in the south of Ireland were not prepared to fight for his cause. Similarly, John Redmond at first rejected any talk of partition, but soon supported the Amending Bill because it would most likely result in at least three Ulster counties agreeing to home rule (because of their large Catholic nationalist populations).

415. World War I In the midst of heated negotiations on the issue of home rule and partition, World War I broke out. Prime Minister Asquith put the home rule issue on ice, withdrawing the Amending Bill and passing a Suspension Act, which made the home rule bill (which would have become law automatically) inoperative until after the war. Carson, by threatening civil war, had won a reprieve for unionism. Although nationalists did not know it at the time, the last opportunity to achieve an independent, united Ireland had just passed them by.

416. Redmond Causes a Split Never an Anglophobe like Parnell, John Redmond called for the Irish people to support Great Britain in World War I. He did so out of the belief that such a demonstration of loyalty would lead to British support for home rule in Parliament. Radical Irish nationalists, particularly those in the IRB, denounced Redmond as a sellout. The result was a split within the formidable Irish Volunteers. The great majority of the 160,000 Volunteers sided with Redmond and formed a new organization called the National Volunteers. A small faction of radical nationalists, numbering only about three thousand, continued under the name Irish Volunteers. They slowly rebuilt their forces to fifteen thousand by 1916, at which point an IRB faction staged the Easter Rising.

417. O'Donovan Rossa's Funeral Although a towering figure in the nationalist cause in the 1870s and 1880s, O'Donovan Rossa had faded into obscurity and alcoholism by the 1890s. Yet militant nationalists in Ireland did not so easily forget him, and when he died in June 1915 they pounced on the opportunity to both honor a hero and stoke nationalist sentiment to still greater heights. They arranged for his body to be returned for a massive public funeral and burial in Ireland's

Jeremiah O'Donovan Rossa

Glasnevin Cemetery. Many an Irish and Irish American child would grow up memorizing, along with Robert Emmet's speech from the dock, the stirring words offered by Padraic Pearse that day:

> The fools, the fools, they have given us our Fenian dead, and while Ireland holds these graves, Ireland unfree will never be at rest.

418. Radicals in the IRB Plot a Rising Even before O'Donovan Rossa's electrifying funeral ceremony, a radical IRB faction within the Irish Volunteers began planning an armed insurrection. They did so without the knowledge of the Irish Volunteer commander-in-chief, Eoin MacNeill, who believed that insurrection would only be justified if England reneged on its home rule promise after the war. The radicals were impatient and motivated by the long-standing Fenian maxim that "England's difficulty is Ireland's opportunity." John Devoy and Clan na Gael pledged their hearty support to the initiative, as did the German ambassador in Washington, D.C. In January 1916, the plotters joined forces with James Connolly, commander-in-chief of the Irish Citizen Army, who had been planning his own uprising. Their master plan called for a general uprising in Dublin and the provinces (supported, it was hoped, by German arms) that if successful would force England, then overwhelmed with the war on the continent, to relent.

419. Countess Constance Markievicz Constance Gore-Booth (1868–1927) grew up a child of the Ascendancy. Born in London and educated near the family estate in Sligo, she met Queen Victoria when she was nineteen. An artist, she went to Paris in 1898 to study painting and there met Count Casmir Dunin-Markievicz, a painter and member of a wealthy Catholic Polish family. They married in 1900 and moved to Dublin in 1903 where she soon found herself drawn to the Gaelic League and Abbey Theatre. She became a staunch nationalist and in 1908 joined Sinn Fein. In 1913,

Countess Markievicz

during the Dublin lockout, she operated a soup kitchen for out-of-work laborers. She participated in the Easter Rising and was condemned to death. Her sentence was reduced to life in prison, but she was released in 1917 under a general amnesty. Soon after her release she converted to Catholicism and began a political career. In the 1918 general election she became the first woman elected to the British Parliament, but refused (in line with Sinn Fein policy) to take her seat. She served as a member of the first Dail Eireann (the Parliament of the Irish Republic—see entry #430), served two terms in prison, and sided with de Valera in opposing the Treaty. After the Civil War (and another term in prison) she continued to be active in Republican circles, joining de Valera's Fianna Fail party in 1926. She died in July 1927, shortly after winning reelection to the Dail.

420. Padraic Pearse As a child, Padraic Pearse (1879–1916) was deeply interested in the traditional language and culture of Ireland. He joined the Gaelic League as a teenager and in his early twenties became editor of the Gaelic League journal *An Claidheamh Soluis*. In 1908 he founded St. Edna's, a bilingual school dedicated to education in all aspects of Gaelic culture. Pearse's nationalism grew more radical with the times and by 1915 he joined the IRB and Irish Volunteers. That same year, he delivered his famed oration at the funeral ceremony of Jeremiah O'Donovan Rossa, ending in the memorable line, "Ireland unfree shall never be at peace." He was named commander-in-chief of the rebel forces for the Easter Rising and president of the provisional government.

421. The Easter Rising   Like all the insurrections before it, the Easter Rising was crippled by poor judgment and bad luck. The decision to stage the revolt on April 23, 1916, Easter Sunday, was both strategic (British forces might be caught by surprise on holiday) and symbolic (as in the Christian story of Easter, Ireland would be redeemed through the bloody sacrifice of its patriots). On Holy Thursday, April 20, the head of the Irish Volunteers, Eoin MacNeill, discovered the plot and urged them to cancel it. He was convinced that it was a futile gesture that could only harm Ireland's chances of gaining home rule or independence. The next morning, Roger Casement, returning by submarine from Germany to advo-

cate calling off the rebellion, was arrested. Later that day, the British seized a German ship loaded with arms destined for rebel hands. By Saturday, April 22, MacNeill issued an order canceling all Irish Volunteer military maneuvers for Sunday.

Despite these setbacks, Pearse and Connolly rallied a core of devoted nationalists and convinced them to stage the rising on Monday, April 24. The next morning, a force of fifteen hundred rebels (including about two hundred from Connolly's Citizen Army) seized the General Post Office and other strategic sites in Dublin. They pulled down the Union Jack and raised the Irish tri-color. From the balcony of the Post Office, Pearse read a "Proclamation of the Irish Republic" which included the following lines:

> The Irish Republic is entitled to, and hereby claims, the allegiance of every Irishman and Irishwoman. The Republic guarantees religious and civil liberty, equal rights and equal opportunities to all its citizens, and declares its resolve to pursue the happiness and prosperity of the whole nation and all of its parts, cherishing all the children of the nation equally, and oblivious of the differences carefully fostered by an alien government, which have divided a minority from the majority in the past.

422. The Rising Put Down   Connolly and other rebel leaders had convinced themselves that the British would not use substantial force against the rebellion out of a reluctance to destroy property and kill civilians. The British proved them wrong, shelling the city and moving in thousands of troops. In the six days of fighting between Easter Monday and the surrender on Saturday, April 29, 508 people were killed (300 civilians, 132 soldiers and policeman, and 76 rebels) and 2,520 wounded. Dozens of buildings were destroyed and Sackville (now O'Connell) Street was left a charred ruin.

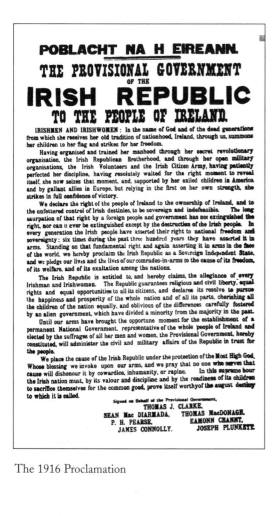

The 1916 Proclamation

423. The Initial Reaction   The initial popular response in Ireland to the Easter Rising was negative. Middle-class conservatives and the Catholic clergy were horrified by the violent and revolutionary character of the uprising. Many nationalists, led by Redmond, denounced the rebels as a misguided, fanatical minority that had greatly damaged the nationalist cause by antagonizing the British government. Still others criticized the rebels for endangering the lives of their husbands, brothers, and sons fighting in the British army in France.

Many of the rebel leaders expected such a reaction. During the last days of the uprising as their eventual defeat became obvious, Padraic Pearse predicted with great accuracy, "When we are all wiped out, people will blame us for everything, condemn us." Yet he also declared that "in a few years they will see the meaning of what we tried to do." In a word, the nationalist "blood sacrifice" Pearse so often wrote and spoke about in the years leading up to 1916 would eventually rouse the Irish people to fight for their freedom.

424. The Executions   In reality, it would take only a few days for the public to begin to change its mind. Despite pleas from leaders in Ireland and Britain for restraint, the British government reacted with white-hot rage. Martial law was declared in Dublin and then extended to all Ireland. The entire country was placed under suspicion, as though the uprising had the support of the masses. Thousands were arrested, bullied, interrogated, and jailed. Some were summarily shot. Stories of British soldiers gunning down unarmed civilians during the uprising soon came to light. The most infamous was the murder of the well-known pacifist and writer Francis Sheehy-Skeffington. While out on the streets of Dublin trying to stop looting, he witnessed a British soldier shoot an unarmed boy. To cover up his action, the soldier shot Sheehy-Skeffington dead.

Then came the secret trials and summary executions. On May 3 Thomas P. Clarke, Padraic

Pearse, and Thomas MacDonagh were led to the prison yard at Kilmainham and executed by firing squad. The next day Willie Pearse, Edward Daly, Joseph Plunkett, and Michael O'Hanrahan suffered the same fate. Over the course of the next week, Sean MacBride (May 5), Michael Mallin, Eamonn Ceannt, Con Colbert, Sean Heuston (May 8), and Thomas Kent (May 9) were similarly dispatched. Last to go were James Connolly and Sean MacDiarmada on May 12. Crippled from a bullet wound to his foot suffered during the uprising, Connolly had to be propped up in a chair before the executioners opened fire.

The summary execution of the fifteen rebel leaders produced an astonishing and immediate reinterpretation of the uprising in the eyes of the Irish public. In just ten days, the time it took for the firing squad to carry out its work, the people of Ireland came to see Pearse, Connolly, MacDonagh, Plunkett, and the rest as nationalist martyrs akin to Wolfe Tone. They came to view the Easter Rising as an event on a par with the heroic uprisings of 1798, 1848, and 1867. As historian Lawrence McCaffrey writes, "The British made Pearse's case: blood sacrifice did convert nationalist apathy into passion." Irish nationalism would never be the same.

425. Yeats Observes   William Butler Yeats, who himself had initially been horrified by the uprising, spoke for many when he penned the following lines in the wake of the executions:

> I write it out in verse—
> MacDonagh and MacBride
> And Connolly and Pearse
> Now and in time to be,
> Whenever green is worn,
> Are changed, changed utterly:
> A terrible beauty is born.

426. Casement Speaks from the Dock   Born into a strict Presbyterian family, Roger Casement (1864–1916) rose to international prominence as a humanitarian in the British colonial service for his reports exposing abuses of native workers by colonial powers in Africa and Latin America. He was knighted for his distinguished service in 1911 and retired two years later. By this time, through membership in the Gaelic League, he had been transformed into a passionate Irish nationalist. In 1913, he helped form the Irish Volunteers and the next year traveled to Europe seeking German support. In April 1916, he sent to Ireland a German ship loaded with arms and followed soon thereafter in a submarine. British authorities seized the ship and arrested Casement shortly after he landed. Charged with treason for his role in the Easter Rising, he was sent to England, tried, convicted, and sentenced to die.

Just before he was hanged for treason on August 1, 1916, Casement offered this eloquent justification of the nationalist cause:

> Self-government is our right, a thing born in us at birth, a thing no more to be doled out to us or withheld from us by another people than the right to life itself—the right to feel the sun or smell the flowers, or love our kind. It is only from the convict that these things are withheld, for crime committed and proven—and Ireland, that has wronged no man, that has injured no land, that has sought no domination over others— Ireland is being treated today among the nations of the world as if she were a convicted criminal.

427. Sinn Fein Reinvented   Soon after the founding of Sinn Fein in 1905, IRB activists joined the organization, seeing it as a possible alternative to Redmond's Irish Parliamentary party. As their influence within the party grew, they convinced Griffith to drop his idea of a semi-independent Ireland under the British Crown in favor of an unspecified form of government. IRB activists also helped make Sinn Fein a prominent opponent of British recruitment efforts in Ireland

after the outbreak of World War I. It was for this reason that in the aftermath of the executions, Sinn Fein was vaulted to political prominence as a party with impeccable anti-British credentials.

428. Eamon de Valera Spared   The one rebel leader who was spared death by firing squad was Eamon de Valera (1882–1975). What may have saved him was his American birth. He was born Edward de Valera in New York City to an Irish mother and Spanish father, but was raised by his mother's family in Limerick. Locked in a deadly struggle with Germany in 1916, the British government was unwilling to involve itself in a dispute with American officials.

Instead, he was sentenced to a lengthy jail term. Released in 1917 as part of a general amnesty, he became president of Sinn Fein. He and the party gained an enormous following in early 1918 when they led the opposition to the British government's imposition of conscription in Ireland. De Valera would go on to play a key role in the coming War for Independence and subsequent Civil War and would remain a force in Irish politics until his retirement in the mid-1970s.

429. The General Election of 1918   Despite being imprisoned in May, de Valera and seventy-two Sinn Fein candidates won seats in the British Parliament (out of 105 for Ireland) in the general election that December. Redmond's Irish Parliamentary Party, once the great hope of Irish nationalists, was left with just six seats.

For decades to come, hard-line nationalists would always refer to the general election of 1918 as validation of their insistence on an independent, united Ireland.

430. The Dail Eireann   None of the Sinn Fein MPs took their seats in Parliament, and instead convened on January 21, 1919, to establish the First Dail Eireann, or Irish Parliament, as the legislative body of an Irish Republic. The Dail affirmed the 1916 Proclamation of the Irish

Republic, declared Ireland's independence, and began creating several government institutions to replace British ones. The British government responded by declaring the Dail an outlaw institution (Sept 12, 1919).

431. The War for Independence Begins   On the same day of the Dail's creation, violence broke out between members of the Irish Volunteers (now increasingly referred to as the Irish Republican Army) and British soldiers and members of the Royal Irish Constabulary. On January 21 members of the Third Tipperary Brigade ambushed an RIC patrol, killing two. Unlike the Easter Rising, which involved a traditional military assault on strategic positions, the outgunned IRA adopted guerrilla-style hit-and-run tactics and quickly seized the initiative in the conflict.

432. Michael Collins   The man most responsible for the success enjoyed by the IRA against the British was Michael Collins (1890–1922). Born into a farming family in Cork, he grew to embrace the Irish nationalism of his father and schoolmaster (the latter a member of the IRB). At sixteen, he took a clerkship in London, where he learned finance and developed organizational and planning skills—all of which served him well after he joined the IRB. He participated in the Easter Rising, but was not recognized as a leader and thus spared execution. In 1919 the First Dail Eireann named him minister of finance. He also acted as director of intelligence, a position that made him a key figure in the buildup of the Irish Volunteers (soon recognized as the IRA). In these capacities he organized the acquisition and distribution of arms for the IRA and established an ingenious intelligence network that kept him informed of British operations. Collins also devised the successful guerrilla tactics employed with such effectiveness against the British army and Royal Irish Constabulary.

433. In Search of Recognition   In the midst of the

Fund-raising for freedom—Irish Republic bond

mounting violence, Michael Collins engineered de Valera's sensational escape from prison in April 1919. Unanimously elected president of the Dail, de Valera immediately set about gaining international recognition of the Irish Republic founded by Sinn Fein. He sent Sean O'Kelly to the Versailles Peace Conference, where the great powers were meeting in the aftermath of World War I. They had reason to be hopeful, because President Woodrow Wilson had declared national self-determination as one of his vaunted Fourteen Points. O'Kelly quickly discovered, however, that Wilson had no intention of upsetting his British allies by pushing for Irish independence.

In response, de Valera decided to tour the United States to arouse support for American recognition of the Irish Republic and gather financial donations from Irish Americans. Arriving in June 1919, he toured the country for eighteen months. During this time he drew widespread popular support and raised the astonishing sum of six million dollars. But he failed in his primary goal of achieving official recognition by the American government. His stay in America also resulted in a rift with the leaders of Irish American nationalism, John Devoy and Judge Daniel Cohalan, who resented his effort to organize Irish American support for the Republic independent of their control.

434. Friends of Irish Freedom   Back in March

Friends of Irish Freedom, 1916

1916, during the first of three "Irish Race Conventions" convened in New York City by Clan na Gael, a new nationalist organization was born, the Friends of Irish Freedom. Dedicated to seeing Ireland "cut off from England and restored to its rightful place among the nations of the earth," the FOIF played a major role in stirring up Irish nationalist sentiment in the U.S. and raising millions of dollars for the independence movement in Ireland. By the time de Valera arrived in June 1919, membership in the organization had surged to more than 250,000.

435. Irish American Convention, New York City, May 14, 1917

Resolved, that this assemblage of American citizens of Irish blood, loyal to the United States, and ready to defend her honor and interests, and recognizing that our Government is entitled to the best advice that Irishmen who understand the situation can give, urgently request the President and Congress to demand that England make good her promises in the only way possible in regard to Ireland, namely by according to the Irish people their indubitable right to be regarded as a sovereign people, and by granting to Ireland full national independence . . . and be it

Resolved, that we therefore submit to the President and Congress that America's entry into the war for democracy and civilization gives our government the right, and imposes upon it the duty, to demand from England that she settle the Irish Question permanently and finally . . .

436. The Black and Tans The guerrilla campaign waged by Michael Collins and the IRA took a severe toll on the Royal Irish Constabulary and British Army. By the end of 1919, dozens of RIC members and British soldiers had been killed and hundreds of RIC barracks destroyed. To counter this offensive, in January 1920 British authorities began to recruit a special force for deployment in Ireland made up largely of former British soldiers and sailors. Their name derived from their mixed uniform—dark green RIC shirts combined with tan British army pants. After a period of nominal training, Black and Tans were sent to Ireland and posted in RIC barracks (9,500 arrived by the end of 1921). As the fighting intensified, Black and Tans acquired a fearsome reputation for brutality and reprisal.

437. Tomas MacCurtain and Terence MacSwiney Two Lord Mayors of Cork, both members of the IRA, became victims of the conflict in 1920. Tomas MacCurtain, commander of a local IRA Brigade, was elected Lord Mayor in January 1920. He was assassinated in his bed on March 19. The coroner's report concluded that his murder "was organized and carried out by the Royal Constabulary." MacCurtain was succeeded in office by Terence Mac-Swiney. He was arrested five months later by the RIC and promptly began a hunger strike in protest. He lingered for seventy-four days and died on October 25, 1920. Both men were hailed as martyrs in

Terence MacSwiney

the cause for Irish freedom, and their deaths dramatically boosted popular support for the war being waged by the IRA. Many kept in mind MacSwiney's inspirational words:

> One armed man cannot resist a multitude, nor one army conquer countless legions; but not all the armies of all the empires of earth can crush the spirit of one true man. And that one man will prevail.

438. Bloody Sunday: Michael Collins Turns Up the Heat Michael Collins met the arrival of the Black and Tans with increased force. Scattered IRA men were organized into "flying columns"— mobile guerrilla units that struck without warning against British military installations and RIC barracks. Collins also orchestrated hit squads to kill British intelligence officers. On "Bloody Sunday," November 21, 1920, Collins' men staged a series of spectacular assassinations, killing thirteen (eleven of whom were British counterintelligence officers) and wounding eight. British forces retaliated in kind. Later that afternoon, a unit of the RIC burst into Croke Park in Dublin where thousands were gathered to watch a Gaelic football game. They opened fire on the crowd, killing twelve and wounding sixty. That evening three members of the IRA were arrested for their possible role in the assassinations died in police custody, allegedly trying to escape.

439. De Valera Returns After the successful fund-raising tour in America, where he garnered $5 million for Sinn Fein (but failed to gain U.S. diplomatic recognition of the Irish Republic), de Valera returned to Ireland (December 1920). He resumed his role as president of the Dail and quickly moved to rein in the IRA's guerrillas. He did so for two reasons. First, he believed that guerrilla action and assassination diminished popular support for the Irish Republic in sympathetic countries and thereby weakened chances for diplomatic recognition. Second, de Valera had grown intensely jealous of Michael Collins, and sought to reestablish himself as the head of the nationalist movement.

440. The Government of Ireland Act By late 1920, the coalition government of Lloyd George recognized the inevitability of the home rule government for Ireland. Unionists, however, stood resolute in their demand that six counties in Ulster (Antrim, Armagh, Down, Fermanagh, Londonderry, and Tyrone) be excluded from any such arrangement (they agreed to leave out the three remaining Ulster counties, Cavan, Monaghan, and Donegal, whose high Catholic populations led Unionists to fear they would present too much trouble). The compromise solution, known as the Government of Ireland Act, established two parliaments: one for the twenty-six counties in the South and another for the six counties of the North, both subordinate to Westminster. The act also established a Council of Ireland, made up of twenty members from each parliament, to meet regularly and discuss matters of mutual concern such as trade, tourism, transportation, and security.

The act passed on December 23, 1920. In the elections for the two parliaments that followed, Unionists won forty of fifty-two seats to the Northern Ireland Parliament. In the South, however, Sinn Fein boycotted the elections.

441. The Anglo-Irish Treaty Despite the Government of Ireland Act, Ireland remained in a state of war. Both Lloyd George and de Valera were eager for peace, and thus began protracted negotiations to arrange a peace conference in London. On July 11, 1921, both sides agreed to an immediate truce and arranged to meet in a peace conference in October.

In the weeks leading up to the conference, de Valera made a startling decision: He would not lead the delegation heading to London for negotiations. He claimed that his presence was needed

Michael Collins

in Ireland to keep radical nationalists in check. Critics of de Valera have long contended that he knew Britain would not accept a fully independent Irish Republic and decided to send Arthur Griffith and Michael Collins to take the blame for signing a treaty Irish republicans would find inadequate. In this way, de Valera would gain a semi-independent Ireland and see his rival, Michael Collins, destroyed by the ensuing controversy. Whether or not de Valera actually dreamed up such a scenario is unclear (though much evidence points in that direction), that is precisely how events transpired.

Griffith and Collins possessed experience in many fields, but not diplomacy. They soon found themselves caught between two extremes: Irish republicans who demanded nothing less than complete Irish independence and a British government controlled by Unionists determined to prevent independence. They were forced to make concessions or accept the resumption of war in Ireland.

Lloyd George proposed to grant Ireland dominion status as the "Irish Free State," but insisted on partition (separating the six counties in the northeast) and an oath of allegiance to the British monarch required of all public officials. Collins and Griffith countered with de Valera's proposal for an "external association"—essentially a loose affiliation involving no oath between Ireland and the British Commonwealth (as opposed to Irish membership *within* the British Commonwealth). George responded by offering to let the Irish draft a more acceptable oath of allegiance that would assert primary allegiance to the Free State over the Crown. When Irish delegates balked at a perma-

nently divided Ireland, George offered to establish a Boundary Commission that would assess the loyalties in the six northern counties before establishing a final border between North and South. He led them to believe that the Boundary Commission, after surveying the will of the people, would grant the counties of Tyrone and Fermanagh to the Free State, along with Derry City and the southern regions of Counties Down and Armagh. Implicit in this understanding was the belief that such a shrunken Northern Ireland would be economically impractical and thus lead, in the long run, to a united Ireland.

Negotiations dragged on until December 5, 1921, when Lloyd George demanded Collins and Griffith sign an agreement or face the resumption of war. The following day, after gaining a concession for the fiscal independence of the Irish Free State, Collins and Griffith signed the treaty creating the Irish Free State as a self-governing dominion within the British Commonwealth.

442. Michael Collins Describes the Dilemma

As de Valera had anticipated, even though Collins and Griffith signed what was the best deal possible under the circumstances, they would return home to face the torrent of criticism from republican hard-liners.

> Think—what I have got for Ireland? Something which she has wanted these past seven hundred years. Will anyone be satisfied at the bargain? Will anyone? I tell you this—early this morning I signed my death warrant. I thought at the time how odd, how ridiculous—a bullet may just as well have done the job five years ago.

443. The Split

Upon their return to Ireland, Collins and Griffith defended the treaty as the best deal possible under the circumstances. Sinn Fein leaders, led by de Valera, denounced the agreement as a betrayal of the Irish Republic

Arthur Griffith

established during the Easter Rising of 1916. Specifically, they opposed the treaty for leaving Ireland subject to British rule, as symbolized by the oath of allegiance required of all high-ranking public officials and creation of the governor-general, an official appointed by the British government with executive authority (rather limited) over all of Ireland. Interestingly, the status of Northern Ireland was not a major issue, since most republicans assumed the question would be settled favorably by the Boundary Commission.

Bitter debate raged in the Dail for weeks. On January 7, it ratified the treaty by a small majority, 64 to 57. De Valera resigned as president of the Dail and Griffith was elected to succeed him. The closeness of the vote indicated the unwillingness of a large faction of Sinn Fein and the IRA to accept the agreement, and set the stage for the Civil War that began six months later.

444. The Irish Civil War

Protreaty members of Sinn Fein established a Provisional Government and a regular army under the direction of Michael Collins. Although they would have preferred total independence from Great Britain, the majority of the Irish population supported the treaty (indicated by the fact that 80 percent of Irish voters in the elections of June 1922 supported protreaty candidates).

Staunch republicans within Sinn Fein and the IRA, however, remained bitterly opposed. Despite the efforts of the Provisional Government to disband them, individual IRA units remained active throughout Ireland and became known as Irregulars. They counted among their number many of the heroes of the War for Independence, including Rory O'Connor, Harry Boland, Erskine Childers, and Cathal Brugha. Conflict finally erupted on June 28, 1922, when government forces under Michael Collins attacked the headquarters of the Irregulars in Dublin. Outnumbered, outgunned, and divided by infighting, the Irregulars were on the run by mid-August, confined to guerrilla strikes like those used in the War for Independence. The Provisional Government adopted harsh measures of repression, most notably mass internment and the death penalty. By December, protreaty forces had, for all intents and purposes, won the Civil War. At de Valera's urging, the IRA declared a cease-fire on April 30, 1923, and on May 24 ordered its men to dump their arms and return to civilian life.

All told, the Civil War claimed the lives of 927 people, including seventy-seven executed by the government (far more than the twenty-four rebels shot by the British during the War for Independence). Its real significance was the lasting divisions it established in Irish political life for generations to come.

445. Assassination of Michael Collins Of the hundreds killed in the Civil War, one death stands out as symbolic of the fratricidal nature of the conflict: the assassination of Michael Collins. The man largely responsible for forcing the British to the negotiating table was gunned down on August 22, 1922, in an ambush by Irregulars opposed to the Treaty. Many historians have speculated that Collins' chief rival, de Valera, may have had a hand in his death. He certainly benefited from it.

The Irish Free State

446. The Constitution of the Irish Free State On December 5, 1922, the Dail ratified the Constitution of the Irish Free State. In keeping with the terms of the Anglo-Irish treaty, it established the Free State as a dominion within the United Kingdom and required an oath of alle-

giance to the British Crown of all members of the Irish Parliament. The office of governor-general was created to represent the interests of the Crown. Finally, the treaty named the *Oireachtas* (made up of the Dail, the Senate, and the governor-general) as the legislative body of the Free State, while an executive council, headed by a president chosen by the Dail, was given full executive powers.

447. The Free State Under William T. Cosgrave The first president of the executive council of the Irish Free State was William T. Cosgrave (1880–1965), a long-time activist in the nationalist cause. A participant in the 1916 Easter Rising, he was released in the general amnesty of 1917 and won election to the first Dail Eireann. He served as minister for local government. He supported the Anglo-Irish Treaty and when in August 1922 Arthur Griffith died suddenly of a heart attack and Michael Collins was assassinated, he took over as head of the Provisional Government.

Under the Constitution of the Irish Free State, Cosgrave was appointed president of the executive council (an office he held until 1932). In 1923, shortly after assuming the presidency, he founded a new political party, Cumann na nGaedheal (Irish for "Community of Irishman"), which dominated Irish politics until the early 1930s.

Under Cosgrave and his right-hand man, Kevin O'Higgins, the Irish Free State evolved into a conservative society dominated by the Catholic hierarchy, prosperous farmers and shopkeepers, and former unionist Protestants. As Lawrence McCaffrey writes, the inclusive, progressive Irish nationalism which inspired the Easter Rising of 1916 gave way to one that was "narrow, provincial, and exclusive, discouraging economic modernization, social reform, intellectual creativity, and cooperation between north and south." These developments pleased the more conservative elements of Irish society, but caused distress among many nationalists, especially Socialists, trade unionists, and leaders of the Gaelic Revival. Indeed many who sided with the antitreaty forces after 1922 did so not so much for their devotion to republicanism, but rather as a protest against the conservative social, political, economic, and cultural policies enacted by the Free State government.

448. The Boundary Commission During the furor that erupted over the 1921 treaty, little attention was paid to the issue that would later come to define the nationalist cause for most of the twentieth century: partition. This can be explained, in part, by the faith many republicans placed in the promised Boundary Commission (a provision of the 1921 treaty). It was assumed that since the Commission was charged with establishing a boundary closely in line with the wishes of the population, it would assign large sections of the lower North (which contained Catholic, pro–Free State majorities), including County Tyrone and Fermanagh, Derry City, and the southern regions of Down and Armagh, to the Free State.

But when the commission began deliberations in late 1924, it soon became clear that its chairman, a South African judge, would not agree to any reduction of the six-county Northern Ireland. Economic and geographic considerations, he and the Northern Ireland representative argued, would take precedence over popular will. Cosgrave's government tried to salvage something from the mess, but only managed to extract a British concession canceling the Free State's financial obligation to the British debt. Ever thereafter Sinn Fein republicans blamed Free State leaders for signing on to the permanent partition of Ireland and focused their anger and activism against the border and the British government that maintained it.

449. Sinn Fein and the IRA in the Wilderness In the wake of the Civil War, de Valera and the antitreaty republicans boycotted Irish politics, insisting that the Free State government was invalid and that the second Dail, elected in 1920, remained the only legitimate government of Ireland.

450. The Return of de Valera De Valera soon decided that antitreaty republicans could achieve their goals only through participation in Irish politics. In 1926 he broke with Sinn Fein and formed a new political party, Fianna Fail (Irish for "Soldiers of Destiny"). In the general election of June 1927, Fianna Fail candidates outpolled Sinn Fein by a wide margin (26.1 percent versus 3.6 percent; forty-four seats versus five seats). Reluctantly, they accepted the despised oath of allegiance and took their seats in the Dail. From that point forward, the party made steady gains, until 1932 when it won a plurality of seats in the Dail and, in coalition with the Labour Party, formed a government with De Valera as its prime minister.

451. Toward a Republic For the next sixteen years (1932–48), Fianna Fail controlled the government of the Free State. Step by step, de Valera transformed Ireland into a republic. In 1933, he abolished the oath of allegiance from the Irish constitution and reduced the influence of the governor-general. Three years later, he seized the opportunity presented by the constitutional crisis in England over King Edward VIII's abdication to eliminate the office of governor-general and reduce the authority of the Crown in the Irish constitution.

In 1937, de Valera introduced a new constitution that replaced the name Free State with *Eire* and established the offices of president

Eamon de Valera

(mainly symbolic) and prime minister, known as *taoiseach* (Irish for "chief"). The new constitution passed in the national referendum with 57 percent of the vote. The closeness of the vote and the fact that nearly a third of eligible Irish voters refused to vote indicated how divided Ireland remained fifteen years after the conclusion of the Civil War.

452. The Economic War   De Valera also made good on his campaign promise of 1932 to end payment of "land annuities" to the British government. These were the payments made by Irish farmers for loans granted by the British government under the Land Acts of 1891 to 1909 that allowed them to buy their land. Once in office, de Valera continued to collect the payments, but put them toward government expenditures in Ireland instead of turning them over to the British government. Britain retaliated with high tariffs on Irish goods, especially cattle and dairy produce. De Valera's government responded with punitive tariffs of its own. This "Economic War" lasted six years, ending in the spring of 1938 on terms favorable to Ireland.

- Britain surrendered the so-called "treaty ports" which it controlled as part of the 1921 treaty.
- The Irish government paid a final lump sum of £10 million to settle the land annuity question.
- Both governments repealed the high tariffs.

453. De Valera's Flawed Vision   Despite his achievements in moving Ireland toward the status of independent republic, de Valera's legacy in these years had two major flaws. First, he pursued a romantic and wholly unrealistic plan of economic development. Ireland, he believed, ought to shun industrial development and foreign investment and remain a land of small farmers and producers. The result was a nation burdened by high levels of unemployment, poverty, and emigration. Second,

de Valera rejected the idea of separation of church and state. As a consequence, the Catholic Church wielded more direct authority over the people of Ireland than it did over any other European nation.

454. Life in the North   For Irish Catholics living in the six northern counties, the decades after partition brought a steady worsening of their situation. Their political rights were undermined by the abolition of proportional representation, gerrymandering and the granting of extra votes for the owners of business properties. By the late 1920s most areas with Catholic majorities came under political control of the Protestant minority. The city council of Derry city, for example, had twelve Protestants and eight Catholics, despite a clear Catholic majority in the population.

The economic and civil rights of Northern Ireland Catholics were sharply curbed by private acts of discrimination (Protestants controlled most business and thus most employment), public acts of violence (working-class Protestant gangs frequently drove Catholics from shipyards and factories), or public policy (Protestant-controlled-government agencies denied Catholics employment in public jobs or a fair allotment of housing and other services). As a result, Catholics in Northern Ireland suffered from far greater rates of poverty and unemployment than their Protestant counterparts.

There were many poor Protestants in the North, but like poor whites in the Jim Crow American South, they rejected any notion of class unity. It was a classic case of the pecking order: Poor marginalized Protestants maintained a sense of dignity by keeping poor Catholics below them.

455. The Royal Ulster Constabulary   One of the most vivid symbols of Catholic oppression in the North was the Royal Ulster Constabulary (RUC), created in 1922 to replace the Royal Irish Constabulary (1836–1922). Originally plans called for one third of the RUC's members to be

Catholics, but that number barely reached one fifth in 1923 and steadily declined thereafter to about 10 percent by the late 1960s. The RUC were augmented by the so-called B-Specials, an elite, all-Protestant unit allegedly created to counteract terrorism, but largely used to terrorize the North's Catholic population. Catholics in Northern Ireland quickly came to see the RUC and B-Specials as hostile agents of Ulster Unionist oppression. Not surprisingly, the RUC would be at the center of controversy in the late-1960s and 1970s when Catholics began organizing for their civil rights.

456. World War II and Neutrality　When World War II broke out in 1939, de Valera's government announced a policy of strict neutrality. This made sense for two reasons. First, the small, fragile Irish state, like Switzerland and Portugal, hoped to avoid the devastation of war. Second, since England was a major combatant in the war, a declaration of neutrality by Ireland—still technically part of the British Commonwealth—served as a powerful affirmation of de Valera's policy of moving Ireland toward the status of independent republic. The British Prime Minister, Winston Churchill, denounced de Valera's decision, but later tried to tempt him (unsuccessfully) with an offer of ending partition in exchange for opening Ireland's ports to the British navy. The anger of some Western leaders was offset somewhat by Ireland's quiet tilt toward the Allies during the war. In addition, nearly a hundred thousand Irishmen left Ireland for Britain during the war (passage to America was too dangerous) to work at factories, docks, and railways. More than fifty thousand Irishmen served in the British army during the war.

Nonetheless, de Valera's portrayal of Irish neutrality in the strictest possible terms led to a number of uncomfortable incidents, including de Valera criticizing the presence of American GIs in Northern Ireland, and his extremely controversial decision to personally deliver a message of condo-

lence to the German ambassador in Dublin following the news of Hitler's death. "So long as we retained our diplomatic relations with Germany," de Valera explained, "to have failed to call upon the German representative would have been an act of unpardonable discourtesy to the German nation." It may have been proper in terms of diplomatic niceties, but the visit proved a public relations scandal that de Valera would never quite live down.

457. Northern Ireland During the War　Northern Ireland, still very much part of the United Kingdom, played a significant role in World War II. England depended heavily upon its factories and shipyards to produce vital war supplies. This, of course, invited German attack. Nazi air raids in April and May 1941 killed seven hundred in Belfast and left one hundred thousand homeless. In violation of Irish neutrality, German bombers struck Dublin in May 1941 and killed thirty four. Germany's hasty apology was accepted.

458. The Republic of Ireland Act　In 1948 Fianna Fail's sixteen years of uninterrupted power came to end with the election of a coalition government formed by Fine Gael (successor to Cosgrave's Cumann na nGaedheal party), Labour, and Clann na Poblachta, a staunchly republican party made up of many ex-IRA men. On September 7, 1948 the new government's taoiseach, John A. Costello, announced while attending a Commonwealth conference in Canada that Ireland would soon declare itself a Republic. The Republic of Ireland Act was passed December 21, 1948, and took effect April 21, 1949.

De Valera's constitutional changes in the 1930s brought Ireland to the doorstep of declaring itself an independent republic. But he resisted that last step, believing that maintaining Commonwealth ties with Northern Ireland through a symbolic link with Britain (external association) increased the long-term chances of a united Ireland.

459. American Friends of Irish Neutrality De Valera supported the founding of American Friends of Irish Neutrality in November 1940. The organization worked to cultivate American support for Irish neutrality, or at least to answer those who criticized the policy. More importantly, the AFIN successfully lobbied the Roosevelt administration to pressure Britain not to invade Ireland, something it was fully prepared to do as a security measure.

460. The Ireland Act Just as de Valera had feared, the Republic of Ireland Act prompted a retaliatory gesture by the British government. The Ireland Act of 1949 pledged continued British support for Northern Ireland's existence as a separate entity. "[I]n no event will Northern Ireland or any part thereof ceased to be part . . . of the United Kingdom without the consent of the Parliament of Northern Ireland." Thus, in one of the countless ironies of Irish history, the declaration of the independent Republic of Ireland had the unintended effect of making partition more permanent.

461. Grappling with Social Problems The coalition government of 1948 to 1951 not only differed with de Valera on matters of state, they also made a laudable attempt to address the many social problems plaguing Irish society. Minister for Health Dr. Noel Browne, waged a highly successful war on tuberculosis, one of Ireland's great scourges which claimed three to four thousand lives every year. He hired a staff and built hospitals and by 1957 annual deaths due to the dread disease dropped below seven hundred. A second, more ambitious program, known as the Mother and Child Scheme, proposed to tackle Ireland's high infant mortality rate by offering free medical care and education to all mothers and children to age sixteen. It was defeated after an all-out public relations blitz by the Irish Medical Association and the Catholic hierarchy attacking it as Socialist and antifamily. The failure to enact the Mother and Child Scheme represented a major setback for public health in Ireland. It also stood as a dramatic example of the conservative character of Irish society and the powerful place of the Catholic Church within it. "[T]he Roman Catholic Church," the *Irish Times* noted with regret in the aftermath of the controversy, "would seem to be the effective government of this country."

462. The IRA Reawakens: The Border Campaign Having set aside their weapons in the spring of 1923, the IRA remained on the fringes of Irish political life for the next decade. They experienced a small upsurge in popularity in the early 1930s with the electoral victory of de Valera's Fianna Fail party, but remained an army in name only. The IRA went underground after de Valera banned the organization in 1936. A short-lived bombing campaign in Britain in 1939 grabbed headlines (and killed seven), but failed to produce a boost in popularity or membership. Thereafter the IRA shifted its focus to Northern Ireland, but was nearly wiped out by 1944 in a joint effort waged by the British, Irish, and Northern Ireland governments. Following the end of World War II, former IRA members reestablished the organization and committed it to uniting Ireland by physical force.

In late 1956, they launched Operation Harvest, or what popularly was known as the Border Campaign. Armed groups of IRA gunmen infiltrated the North and attacked British army and RUC positions and government offices. Their goal was to embolden nationalists in the North and South and touch off a wider uprising. Initially the attacks excited nationalist opinion in the South, but it proved shallow and short-lived. Most Irish opposed physical force nationalism. Furthermore, the Border Campaign had the effect of arousing and uniting Protestant Unionist opinion in the North and prompting harsh measures of repression (including internment) by governments on both sides of the border. After 341 incidents in 1957, the Border Campaign withered to just twenty-seven in 1959. In February 1962, citing lack of public support, the IRA declared the Border Campaign over. Because the campaign focused on military and political targets, the death toll is relatively low: six RUC, eight IRA, two members of a rival republican organization, and two republican civilians.

463. Signs of Hope in the 1960s   The failure of the IRA's Border Campaign was due in part to the great changes taking place in Ireland in the late 1950s and 1960s. Although poverty, poor health, emigration, and economic stagnation remained problems for decades, Ireland in this period underwent positive economic, social, and cultural transformation. In politics, Eamon de Valera moved to the periphery in 1959, taking up the largely ceremonial position of president (where he remained until 1973). Under Taoiseach Sean Lemass the Republic expanded its social programs, most notably free public education. An improved economy led to rising standards of living and a decrease in emigration. In the arts there was a rebirth of interest in traditional Irish music.

As the Republic of Ireland became more and more a modern European nation, the issue of partition diminished in importance. Sensing the opportunity for improved relations, Lemass and his counterpart in the North, Prime Minister Terence O'Neill, staged high profile visits to each other's section of Ireland in 1965. The prospects for peace and reconciliation, many believed, looked quite promising.

The Troubles

464. Rising Tension   Yet even as official diplomatic relations between North and South warmed, the situation within the North began to rapidly deteriorate. The growing Catholic middle class in the North had by the mid-1960s begun to chafe at the province's discriminatory policies that confined them to limited job opportunities, poor housing, and unequal political power.

465. Rev. Ian Paisley   As Catholics in the North grew restive, so, too, did the Protestant majority that feared the loss of their privileged status. They reacted with outrage to Prime Minister O'Neill's visit to the Republic in 1965 and began to organize against what they perceived was a tilt toward unification with the Republic.

One of the leading voices of reactionary Unionism was that of Presbyterian minister Rev. Ian Kyle Paisley. Well before 1965 he had established himself as the North's leading anti-Catholic cleric. In 1962, for example, he was arrested in Rome for protesting against the Second Vatican Council. In 1966 he denounced "O'Neillism" as a surrender of "Protestant supremacy" and founded a political organization named the Ulster Constitu-

Rev. Ian Paisley

tional Defense Committee, a paramilitary group called the Ulster Protestant Volunteers, and a fiery Unionist newspaper known as the *Protestant Telegraph*. From that point forward, Paisley would play a decisive role in organizing Northern opposition to any and all initiatives for Catholic civil rights or closer ties with the Republic.

466. The Civil Rights Movement   In January 1967 a coalition of liberals, labor unionists, radicals, and republicans came together to form the Northern Ireland Civil Rights Association (NICRA). They were committed to bringing about an end to the state-sponsored policies of discrimination against Catholics living in the North:

- An end to gerrymandering that created a small number of all-Catholic political districts and thereby diluting Catholic voting power (Nationalists in the North never had more than 19 of 52 seats in the N.I. Assembly).

- An end to job discrimination that left Catholics with an unemployment rate more than double that of Protestants.
- An end to housing discrimination that left Catholics in dismal, segregated public housing projects.
- An end to the Special Powers Act that gave the Royal Ulster Constabulary sweeping powers of arrest and detention, as well as the authority to prohibit public assembly or parades.
- Reform or abolish the RUC that was rightly seen (with just 11 percent of its members Catholic) as the enforcement arm of Protestant domination.

NICRA activists took their inspiration from Rev. Martin Luther King, Jr.'s peaceful movement for justice in the United States, even to the point of singing "We Shall Overcome" at their protest marches.

One vital point regarding the civil rights movement in Northern Ireland cannot be overemphasized. It was comprised of people committed to social justice, not nationalists dedicated to bringing about a united Ireland. Many in the movement surely supported the idea of a thirty-two-county republic, but they steered clear of such divisive issues and concentrated instead on getting a fair deal for Catholics living in the North.

467. The Troubles Begin While killings attributed to the Troubles can be traced as far back as 1966, the first significant clashes took place in mid-1968. In June NICRA activists organized protest marches in response to a case of blatant anti-Catholic discrimination in the awarding of housing units in Caledon, County Tyrone. On August 24, a march of 2,500 NICRA protesters in Dungannon erupted in violence when 1,500 of Rev. Ian Paisley's Ulster Protestant Volunteers confronted them. Far worse violence occurred on October 5 when five-hundred NICRA members defied a government ban and staged a march in

Derry. They were assaulted by RUC units at the Craigavon Bridge, leaving seventy-seven nationalists and eleven policemen injured.

468. People's Democracy Three days after the violence at the Craigavon Bridge, students at Queens University in Belfast met to form a political party and activist organization called the People's Democracy. Among them was Bernadette Devlin, a young activist who would soon win election to Parliament.

In late 1968 NICRA responded to peaceful overtures from O'Neill's government and agreed to temporarily halt the protest marches. But the more radical People's Democracy brushed aside this initiative and on January 1 began a "Long March" from Belfast to Derry (modeled after King's march from Selma to Montgomery). It involved only a few dozen students, but took on great significance when it was ambushed on January 4 by Protestant counterdemonstrators outside Derry. The RUC was present, but did little to stop the violence against the marchers. And when the marchers retreated to the Catholic section of Derry, the RUC followed, sparking widespread violence.

469. Political Realignment in Northern Ireland The crisis in Northern Ireland produced a political split in the Unionist ranks between moderates and hard-liners. Northern Ireland Prime Minister Terence O'Neill, uncertain as to what course of action to take, called for elections to the Northern Ireland Parliament in early 1969. His party suffered a major loss at the polls to hard-line Protestant politicians who were galvanized by the nationalist challenge to Unionist supremacy.

The Nationalist Party, traditional party of the Province's Catholics, also suffered a setback. They were challenged by a new crop of young and talented candidates from several small parties, some of which would eventually unite to form the Social Democratic Labour Party (SDLP).

In April of 1969 the nationalist community

British Troops in Northern Ireland

of the North won another victory. Bernadette Devlin, a twenty-one-year-old civil rights activist, took advantage of Unionist disarray and won a seat in the British Parliament. The youngest woman elected to the House of Commons did not mince words in her victory speech: "I was elected by the oppressed people of Ulster, and I shall work for them."

470. Unionist Concessions Prime Minister O'Neill became convinced that concessions to some of the demands of civil rights activists were necessary if civil war was to be avoided. Shortly after Devlin's election, he approved a measure abolishing the North's skewed electoral system in favor of one person, one vote. Other reforms would follow in the next few years, including removal of housing allocation from local control, adoption of antidiscrimination employment laws, and a reorganization of local government. While these represented positive steps by moderate Unionists, they were perceived as too little, too late by the nationalist community.

471. The Marching Season The situation in Northern Ireland remained tense throughout the spring and summer of 1969. Clashes between demonstrators and police grew more frequent with the onset of the "marching season," the time

of year (mainly June to August) when Protestant Orange societies stage annual marches commemorating past victories over their Catholic rivals. One of the most important takes place on July 12 in commemoration of William of Orange's defeat of James I in 1691. Another is held on August 12 to celebrate the closure of the gates of Derry by young apprentices just before the arrival of James I's forces in 1689. While Unionists defended the marches as expressions of cultural pride and tradition, Catholics denounced them as nothing more than exhibitions of domination.

472. Battle of the Bogside The march of the Protestant Apprentice Boys through the Bogside, the Catholic section of Derry, on August 12, 1969, touched off an explosion of pent up Catholic anger. "Northern Ireland Catholics," writes Jack Holland, "sensing change was in the air, were aroused from their stupor; they were no longer content to sit back and be spectators at a display of Protestant hegemony designed to humiliate them." Crowds (MP Bernadette Devlin among them) set up barricades and pelted marchers with rocks and bottles. The police responded with tear gas and batons and a full-scale riot ensued. For three days the "Battle of the Bogside" raged, eventually touching off rioting in Catholic Belfast. The police responded with live ammunition, killing six and wounding hundreds. Fires gutted hundreds of homes. In a dramatic, televised speech, the Republic's Prime Minister Jack Lynch said the government of Northern Ireland was "no longer in control of the situation" and that "the Irish Government can no longer stand by and see innocent people injured, and perhaps worse." Units of the Republic's armed forces, he ominously declared, would be positioned along the border.

473. The Arrival of British Troops More than five hundred British troops were already in Northern Ireland by the spring of 1969, but the rioting in August convinced London that a more substantial force was needed to restore order and keep the warring parties apart. On August 15, as smoke still billowed from the riot ravaged Catholic ghettos of Derry and Belfast, six thousand British troops arrived. Their ranks would swell to nine thousand by October and continue to rise thereafter.

Significantly, Northern Ireland Catholics who would soon view the troops as the ultimate symbol of British oppression, at first greeted them as welcome protectors. Convinced that the RUC was hopelessly pro-Unionist, Catholics hoped the soldiers would serve as a neutral force in the conflict. For a few weeks Catholic women offered tea and cookies to the soldiers. It was a "honeymoon" that did not last long.

474. The IRA Reborn Curiously absent from the scene in 1969 was the IRA. Since the cessation of the Border Campaign in 1962, the organization had atrophied into little more than a small cadre of disillusioned, aging Marxist revolutionaries. Its political wing, Sinn Fein, was similarly a shadow of its former self. Indeed, many a nationalist wondered aloud where the IRA was during the clashes of 1969. A typical graffiti message on the walls of Belfast summed up the popular impression of the once towering presence in Irish life: "IRA = I Ran Away."

Then in January 1970 the IRA split into two factions. The official IRA consisted of members who favored moving away from violence toward a more political course of action that stressed social issues alongside the nationalist quest for a united Ireland. The Provisional IRA, or Provos as they were called, dismissed politics as a sell-out and vowed to continue the militant campaign to unite the thirty-two counties. On the surface, the breakup of an already moribund organization suggested its days were numbered.

The arrival of British troops, however, gave new life to the IRA. Hard-line activists within the Provisional IRA saw it as an opportunity to transform the current civil rights movement into a full-blown nationalist crusade to throw the British out of Northern Ireland entirely and bring about a united Ireland. They sent IRA units into Derry and Belfast to provoke confrontations with British soldiers. The latter seemed all too willing to comply and by July 1970 British soldiers had begun house-to-house searches in Catholic areas. Confrontations left four Catholics dead and swept away the image of the British soldiers as neutral protectors in the conflict.

475. NORAID The Irish in America reacted to these events unfolding in Northern Ireland with outrage. They held rallies, wrote to Congress, and protested in front of the British embassy. They also gave money to various groups pledged to aiding the nationalist cause. One such group was the Irish Northern Aid Committee, or NORAID, founded in the wake of the Battle of the Bogside by IRA veteran Michael Flannery. From the outset the organization claimed the funds it raised went to peaceful purposes like relief to families of interned IRA suspects or victims of Unionist violence. Yet most informed observers believed its purpose was to provide the new IRA with a steady supply of cash and arms.

476. The Irish National Caucus Father Sean McManus arrived in the United States in 1972, one of the bloodiest years in Northern Ireland's history (467 people killed). At the time there existed several Irish American activist organizations concerned with the situation there, most prominently NORAID, a group accused of channeling gun money to the IRA. But McManus, born and raised in Northern Ireland's County Fermanagh, had seen enough of violence and sectarianism. He also recognized the pivotal role Irish America could play in bringing about a lasting peace to the troubled six counties. So seventeen months after he arrived, in February 1974, Fr. Sean established the Irish National Caucus.

The INC was different in that it was nonsectarian and nonpolitical. More important, it was dedicated to getting Americans, especially those in Congress, to see the Northern Ireland conflict as a human rights issue. While clashes involving paramilitaries, the British Army, and the RUC grabbed the headlines, the Catholic population in the North suffered systematic discrimination in housing and employment. In 1984, the INC introduced the McBride Principles, a set of fair employment practice guidelines to judge the eighty or so publicly held corporations in Northern Ireland. Private and public investors, especially state and municipal governments, were urged to avoid doing business with or investing in companies not in compliance. This initiative not only put substantial economic pressure on businesses in Northern Ireland—to date sixteen states and forty cities in the U.S. have adopted the McBride Principles as part of their investment policies—but also succeeded, as the *Washington Post* put it, "in getting Congress to see Northern Ireland as a human rights issue." Once framed in those terms, resolving the Northern Ireland conflict became a legitimate, even necessary, focus of American diplomatic influence.

477. The American Ireland Fund

In 1976, Anthony O'Reilly, head of H. J. Heinz Co., and Dan Rooney, owner of the Pittsburgh Steelers, co-founded the Ireland Fund. It was dedicated to raising money for programs that supported peace and reconciliation in Northern Ireland. In 1987, after a decade of successful fund-raising, the Ireland Fund merged with the American Irish Foundation to form the American Ireland Fund. Since that time, it has raised over $100 million and opened chapters in several countries around the world. It has funded over one thousand individual projects ranging from arts and education programs to peace and reconciliation initiatives.

478. Hume Forms the SDLP

In 1970, civil rights activist John Hume and Gerry Pitt (a Belfast Socialist) drew together several Northern Ireland opposition groups to form the Social Democratic Labour Party. Committed to peaceful tactics and constitutional nationalism, the SDLP positioned itself as more than a sectarian party. In addition to calling for civil rights for Catholics, it also advocated a wide range of social reforms designed to benefit a cross section of Northern Ireland society, Protestant and Catholic. Hume and the SDLP leadership also sought to allay Unionist fears by downplaying the call for a united Ireland and arguing that it would only occur with the consent of a majority of the people of Northern Ireland.

479. Internment

Three events in 1971 combined to bring about the British policy of internment (jailing of IRA suspects indefinitely without formal charges). First, the IRA killed its first British soldier in February 1971 followed by several more in subsequent weeks. Second, hard-liner Brian Faulkner was elected as the new Prime Minister of Northern Ireland. Third, violence steadily escalated during the summer marching season.

In response, the British adopted a policy of internment (specifically Section 12 of the Special Powers Act) on August 9, 1971. That morning British soldiers carried out sweeps through thousands of Catholic homes across the North and arrested hundreds. Massive riots broke out in Derry and Belfast. Thirteen were killed and hundreds of homes destroyed. Thousands of Catholic refugees streamed across the border into the Republic. Internment would last until late 1975.

480. January 30, 1972: Bloody Sunday

Internment and the resulting violence outraged Northern Ireland Catholics, including many previously not overly sympathetic to the civil rights movement. Catholic MPs boycotted the Northern Ireland Parliament at Stormont, while others withdrew from their posts in local governments. Upwards of twenty thousand refused to pay their rent or taxes.

Civil rights activists hoped to capitalize on this rising tide of popular discontent. They announced plans for a mass protest march to take place in the Bogside district of Derry on January 30, 1972. All marches had been banned since

Protesting the Bloody Sunday killings

convened Bernadette Devlin, who was speaking in Derry when the shooting started, physically assaulted Maulding when she was denied the opportunity to speak.

481. Direct Rule Imposed In the aftermath of the Bloody Sunday massacre, the Faulkner government in Northern Ireland was given an ultimatum by Britain: transfer law and order responsibilities to the British and end internment or face the dissolution of the Northern Ireland Parliament. Faulkner refused and on March 22, 1972, the Stormont Parliament was abolished and direct rule from London established. A new office, Secretary of State for Northern Ireland, was established. Britain's goals were to gain Catholic support for direct rule (as they once had supported the introduction of troops) and restore order. It failed at both.

482. Spiraling Violence The shocking death toll of 173 in 1971 soon paled in comparison to the carnage of 1972 and beyond. The IRA stepped up its campaign of violence, exemplified in the July 21 bombings in Belfast that killed nine people. Unionist extremists responded in kind with bombings and assassinations. By year's end 467 people were dead. The IRA was now a force to be reckoned with. "From a small band of neglected old men," writes Jack Holland in *Hope Against History*, his account of the Troubles, "the IRA in Belfast had become, by early 1972, stronger than at any time in its history, with hundreds of new recruits and many thousands of supporters." The

August 1971, but the local RUC commander decided that the best policy would be to allow the march to occur. The organizers could be arrested later. He advised the commander of British troops in Northern Ireland that the RUC would handle the detail.

The British Army commander, however, acting on orders from high-level authorities (to this day unknown), prepared to confront the marchers. Toward 4 P.M., after the relatively peaceful procession of some fifteen thousand (there was some stone throwing by Catholic youths at security forces) gathered in "Free Derry Corner" to hear some speeches, members of the First Battalion of the Parachute Regiment moved in and opened fire. In twenty horrifying minutes, the paratroopers fired more than one hundred shots. Thirteen unarmed marchers were killed—most shot in the back and several at point-blank range—and eighteen wounded. A fourteenth victim died later.

Protest poured in from around the world, but the response of the British government, especially its Home Secretary Reginald Maulding, was a contemptuous snarl about a nationalist "riot" and soldiers firing in "self-defense." When Parliament

British army presence reached its all-time high of twenty-one thousand soldiers.

483. The Sunningdale Agreement

In the face of mounting crisis, Britain called a summit of the heads of Northern Ireland and the Republic of Ireland, along with leaders of the main political parties in the North (SDLP, Alliance, and several Unionist). Meeting in Sunningdale, England, they hammered out an agreement outlining a new government for Northern Ireland that called for:

1. A power-sharing executive made up of representatives from the major parties
2. A seventy-eight-seat Northern Ireland Assembly determined by proportional representation
3. A Council of All Ireland consisting of twenty members from the Parliaments of the North and South to have authority over economic and security issues.
4. An agreement that the status of Northern Ireland could only change if approved by popular referendum.

The third point represented a major concession by Unionists, the fourth a major concession by nationalists.

The new government took power in January 1973 and Unionist opposition mobilized immediately. In Parliamentary elections in February, Loyalists won eleven of Ulster's twelve seats in Westminster. The eleven called for an immediate repeal of the power-sharing government. Tensions continued to mount (as did violence) until the Ulster Workers Council called a general strike on May 14. Daily life in the North ground to a halt and on May 28 the power-sharing government collapsed. In between, on May 17 UVF bombs in Dublin and Monaghan killed thirty-three in the bloodiest day of the Troubles. London reimposed direct rule.

484. Increased Sectarian Savagery

As the UVF bombings indicated, the form of violence had shifted by 1973 from targeting combatants—British soldiers, UVF members, and Unionist paramilitaries on the one hand and IRA soldiers on the other—to killing innocent civilians. This newer, more atavistic form of violence resulted in both the IRA and its Unionist counterparts losing whatever moral high ground they once occupied. In the Republic, where only a few years earlier Jack Lynch had threatened to use force to protect Catholics in the North, the government began to crack down on IRA activity. Still the killing continued: 247 died in 1975; 297 in 1976.

485. The IRA Bombing Campaign

In early 1974 the IRA decided to expand its war against Britain by commencing a bombing campaign in England itself. In February 1974, an IRA bomb destroyed an army bus, killing twelve (nine soldiers, plus three civilians, including two little children). In July they hit the Tower of London, killing one woman. In October the IRA bombed a pub in Guilford frequented by off-duty British soldiers, killing four soldiers and two young women. The worst incident took place in Birmingham on November 21 when bombs in two pubs killed twenty-one. Ten Irish men (known as the Guilford Four and Birmingham Six) were quickly arrested, beaten, interrogated without a lawyer present, tried, and convicted. They would spend sixteen years in jail before British authorities admitted they were innocent and released them.

486. The Peace Movement

In 1976 there emerged out of the despair in Northern Ireland a peace movement led by two Catholic women, Mairead Corrigan and Betty Williams. The spark behind the movement came when Corrigan's sister lost three children in a car accident caused when an IRA man was shot driving away from soldiers. She joined with Williams to organize peace marches involving both Protestants and Catholics. As they grew in size and gained significant media coverage, many hoped the protests might unify the moderate masses of both camps and isolate the extremist gunmen. In 1977 Williams and Corrigan were awarded the Nobel Peace Prize, but the movement soon faded.

487. The Hunger Strikes Until 1979, IRA prisoners held in Long Kesh (a k a "the Maze") were treated as "special category" (i.e., political) prisoners. They were allowed, among other things, to wear civilian clothes and to move freely within certain parts of the prison. But in the wake of the killing of Lord Louis Mountbatten and his fourteen-year old grandson (not to mention eighteen British soldiers) aboard his fishing vessel, the government of Margaret Thatcher announced a suspension of the special category status. IRA prisoners staged a series of protests, including the so-called "dirty protest" where they wore only blankets instead of prison uniforms and smeared their excrement on the prison walls. A compromise was reached in early 1981, but only after several men staged a hunger strike.

That agreement quickly fell apart and on February 28, 1981, one of the IRA leaders, Bobby Sands, commenced a hunger strike. As he wrote in his diary on the first day of his hunger strike, he took this action to draw attention to the oppressive policies of the British government:

> I am standing on the threshold of another trembling world. May God have mercy on my soul. . . . I am a political prisoner. I am a political prisoner because I am a casualty of a perennial war that is being fought between the oppressed Irish people and an alien, oppressive, unwanted regime that refuses to withdraw from our land.

This time the Thatcher government refused to budge. As fate would have it, an MP from Counties Fermanagh and Tyrone died shortly after Sands began his strike. Sands was nominated to run for the seat and he won on April 10, 1981. It was a bril-

liant and successful ploy for international attention and sympathy. Still Thatcher remained unmoved.

Sands died on May 5, and received one of the biggest funerals in Irish history. By then, in accordance with a carefully orchestrated plan, several other men had joined the hunger strike. One by one they died—ten including Sands—until the strike was suspended in August. It came at an excruciating price, but the hunger strike turned the world's attention to the problem of Northern Ireland. More specifically, like the Bloody Sunday massacre a decade before, it galvanized Irish American public opinion and sent donations to NORAID and other groups to record heights.

488. The Prisoners Declare Victory

> Far from discrediting our cause, British intransigence, which created the hunger strike, has given us international political recognition, and has made the cause of Irish freedom an international issue, has increased support at home and abroad for Irish resistance, and has shown that the oppressed nationalist people and the political prisoners are one.
> —from the official statement issued by the prisoners of Long Kesh announcing the end of the hunger strike

489. New Ireland Forum In 1983, John Hume prompted Taoiseach Garret Fitzgerald to form the New Ireland Forum with the goal of resolving the ongoing conflict in Northern Ireland. The New Ireland Forum had two goals: to entice Britain back into negotiations and to diminish the appeal of Sinn Fein and the IRA. After hearing testimony from a wide range of perspectives, the New Ireland Forum issued a report in 1984 that put forth three possible solutions to the conflict:

1. A unified Ireland with equal rights for all minorities.
2. An Ireland ruled jointly by Dublin and London.

3. A federal Ireland with the four provinces enjoying substantial autonomy.

490. The Anglo-Irish Agreement After balking at the report and its proposals, the Thatcher government eventually agreed to the Hillsborough Conference in 1985. There Thatcher and Fitzgerald signed the Anglo-Irish Agreement establishing:

1. An Intergovernmental Conference where Irish and British representatives could meet to discuss issues of mutual concern.
2. An advisory role for the Republic on matters in Northern Ireland
3. An agreement that the thirty-two counties of Ireland could some day be united, but only if agreed to by popular referendum.

Predictably, the Anglo-Irish Agreement was denounced by extremists on both sides as a sellout. But moderates like Hume saw it as a symbolic, but important step toward peace. "When history is written," Hume later wrote, "the Anglo-Irish Agreement will be seen to have been the first major step in the current peace process."

491. Gerry Adams Steers the IRA in a New Direction Born in 1948 in the Ballymurphy district of Belfast, Gerry Adams was one of many new recruits drawn to Sinn Fein and the IRA when the Troubles exploded. Coming from a long line of republican activists, Adams had come of age in the segregated, confined world of Northern Ireland's Catholics. He joined Sinn Fein as a teenager and became a prominent activist working against discrimination in hiring and housing. He served two terms in prison before being chosen as Sinn Fein's president in 1986.

By this time Adams had become convinced that the IRA would never achieve its goal of a united, independent Ireland through violence

Gerry Adams

alone. The British government showed no sign that it was preparing to surrender control of Northern Ireland any time soon and the IRA did not enjoy widespread support within a nationalist community grown weary of war. Adams proposed the IRA break with orthodox republican ideology and recognize the government of the Republic. In practical terms, this meant authorizing Sinn Fein candidates to contest elections and if elected, take their seats in the Irish Parliament.

A September IRA army convention endorsed Adams' proposed new course. In November, delegates to a Sinn Fein convention likewise endorsed the plan. Sinn Fein's Martin McGuinness summed up the new departure:

> We must accept the reality that sixty-five years of republican struggle, republican sacrifice and rhetoric have signally failed to convince the majority of the people in the twenty-six counties that the Republican Movement has any relevance to them . . . . By ignoring that reality we remain alone and isolated on the high altar of abstentionism, divorced from the people.

492. The Downing Street Declaration John Hume continued to prod both the Irish and British governments to work for peace and in 1993 British Prime Minister John Major and Irish Taoiseach Albert Reynolds signed a statement that was soon dubbed the Downing Street Declaration. The joint statement reaffirmed their government's commitment to resolving the conflict and to letting the people of Northern Ireland decide the ultimate question of unification. Reynolds also pledged to work to eliminate the parts of the Republic's constitution that laid claim to the six counties. Finally, they pledged their support to hold negotiations that included all political parties in the North, including Sinn Fein, if they renounced violence.

493. Sinn Fein Enters Political Mainstream Sinn Fein's response to the Downing Street Declaration was to affirm its support for the proposed peace process, but to reject the particular elements of the accord. For example, it rejected the idea of a six-county referendum to decide the North's future, stating that only a thirty-two-county referendum would represent the legitimate opinion of the Irish people.

Hume took Sinn Fein's support for the peace process as a positive development and worked to convince Sinn Fein Leader Gerry Adams to participate in the process. The key to that, of course, was an IRA cease-fire, which Adams managed to gain on August 31, 1994. Loyalists announced a cease-fire of their own on October 13. Peace advocates and optimists were thrilled. More experienced hands recognized the long road that lay ahead. A cease-fire would only get Sinn Fein into the talks, not guarantee a resolution.

494. The Framework Document In February 1995, after many delays, negotiations between the British and Irish governments produced a blueprint for a lasting peace settlement. The Framework Document, as it was called, was strikingly similar to the Sunningdale Agreement of 1973 in that it called for a Northern Ireland Assembly and a joint North-South body, and it reaffirmed the right of the people of the six counties to determine their future status. Although hard-liners on both sides rejected it as inadequate, unlike Sunningdale the province did not dissolve into violence after it was made public. But the document was merely an outline, not a detailed settlement, and tough negotiations remained ahead.

495. St. Patrick's Day at the White House Over

the protests of the British government, President Clinton rewarded Sinn Fein for their cease-fire by granting Gerry Adams a visa in March 1995 to enter the U.S. on a speaking tour and fund-raising mission. Clinton went a step further by inviting Adams to a St. Patrick's Day celebration at the White House. It was a big gamble on the part of Clinton, for if the IRA resumed its killing, he would face a tirade of criticism from the skeptics. Believing that a new era was at hand, he decided to give the peace process a boost by making a grand gesture.

496. The Vexing Question of Decommissioning The burst of optimism that followed the paramilitaries' cease-fires in 1994 gave way to unease by early 1995. The government of John Major had agreed to allow Sinn Fein into all-party talks on the status of Northern Ireland if the IRA declared a cease-fire. Now in the early months of 1995, Major added a new demand: the IRA had to agree to disarm, commit to a specific program for making it happen, and make a token "good faith" gesture of disarmament, or in the parlance of Northern Ireland, decommissioning. The IRA rejected the new conditions out of hand. Not only were these extra conditions, but they were unacceptable in their own right. Sinn Fein's Martin McGuinness testily reminded Major's government that, "the British army had not defeated the IRA—that the IRA had not surrendered—and that the British government could not even remotely expect Sinn Fein to deliver that surrender to them." Decommissioning might occur in the future, the IRA was saying, but only as a voluntary decision made by the IRA alone, as part of a negotiated settlement, with no suggestion whatsoever of defeat or surrender.

497. The People of Ireland Warm to the Peace Even as the leaders of the various factions bickered over the peace process, the people of Ireland, especially those in the North, embraced the first sustained peace in years. As a goodwill gesture,

British authorities scaled back the presence of British troops, ending street patrols in some areas and removing many of the checkpoint barriers that had become a dismal aspect of the Northern Ireland landscape since 1969. Tourism and cross-border travel and trade increased at a rapid pace as people on both sides of the divide seemed eager to build ties that would secure the peace. The highpoint of cease-fire optimism came when President Clinton visited Ireland in late 1995. In both the Republic and the North he was greeted by throngs of cheering well-wishers eager to see the American President and the man who had done so much to bring about the current peace. President Clinton and First Lady Hillary Clinton would later describe their Ireland trip as one of the most delightful moments of their first term in office.

Senator George Mitchell and Bill Clinton

Toward Peace

498. Senator George Mitchell When President Clinton began casting about for a person to serve as impartial mediator of the Northern Ireland peace talks, several names came up for consideration. But it took little time to realize that the best man for the job was recently retired Senator George Mitchell (b. 1933) of Maine.

Adopted as a child, he knew only that his biological father's parents came from Ireland. After being educated at Georgetown University Law School, he worked for the Justice Department as a trial attorney. He went on to become a United States Attorney and United States District Judge before being named to fill a vacated Senate seat in 1980. His leadership and negotiation skills brought him increased recognition from his Senate colleagues who elected him Senate majority leader. He served in that capacity from 1988 until his retirement in 1995.

President Clinton initially asked him to serve as his economic advisor on Ireland and to help arrange a conference to encourage U.S. investment in Ireland. But in late 1995 the British and Irish governments requested Mitchell be named as chairman of a committee charged with reaching an agreement on the vexing issue of paramilitary decommissioning.

Mitchell accepted the assignment and on January 24, 1996, his committee issued a report outlining the conditions for participation in the upcoming all-party talks. The Mitchell Principles, as they were known, called for all parties to renounce violence and commit themselves to democracy and decommissioning. Actual decommissioning by paramilitaries would not be a precondition to admission of parties like Sinn Fein to the talks. Rather, the Mitchell Principles called upon the various groups to begin negotiations about decommissioning *during* the all-party talks.

499. Renewed Violence Prime Minister Major, however, continued to demand some form of decommissioning take place, *prior* to Sinn Fein's entry into the talks. After months of stalemate and growing discontent among its hard-liners, the IRA broke its cease-fire. On February 9, 1996, the IRA detonated a massive bomb near London's Canary Wharf. It killed two, injured more than one hundred, and caused $140 million in damage.

It proved a poorly calculated gamble to force concessions from the British government.

500. The Process Gets Back on Track

Despite the broken IRA cease-fire (the Loyalist paramilitaries maintained theirs), the peace process continued forward. In June 1996, all-party talks began with the parties that had pledged themselves to the Mitchell Principles. Missing was Sinn Fein, barred from the talks because of the resumption of IRA violence and its refusal to condemn it. The door remained open, however, to its inclusion in the future.

501. Sinn Fein Returns

The potential for a negotiated settlement in Northern Ireland improved dramatically in May 1997 when British voters ousted the conservative government of John Major in favor of Tony Blair's revamped Labour Party. In Northern Ireland, Sinn Fein polled its highest vote percentage ever as Gerry Adams and Martin McGuinness both won seats. Peace advocates saw the vote as a nationalist endorsement of Sinn Fein and the strategy of negotiation over the militarism of the IRA. The Blair government wasted no time in courting another IRA cease-fire.

On July 20, 1997, after receiving assurances by the Blair government that Sinn Fein would be allowed into the all-party talks and that a deadline for a settlement was set for April 9, 1998, the IRA issued a statement formally announcing another cease-fire. Six weeks later, as promised, Sinn Fein's representatives were allowed to enter the talks.

502. The Good Friday Accord

With former Senator George Mitchell acting as chief negotiator, the all-party talks resumed with the goal of reaching a settlement by April 9, 1998. It was not an easy process. Extremists on both sides denounced the talks. The threat of renewed violence became a reality when a rash of killings and beatings between December and February left several Catholics and Protestants dead. For a time both

Sinn Fein and the Ulster Democratic Party (UDP) were suspended from the talks when their respective paramilitary organizations, the IRA and UFF, were linked to the killings. Both were eventually readmitted.

As the April 9 deadline loomed, the talks grew more intense. Finally, after several marathon sessions which included Prime Minister Blair and (by telephone) President Clinton, a deal was reached in the early morning hours of Good Friday, April 10, 1998. The symbolism of the date was lost on no one.

The agreement consisted of the following main points:

1. Decommissioning of all paramilitary organizations within two years.
2. Establishment of a 108-seat Northern Ireland Assembly elected on a proportional representation basis and given full legislative powers over Northern Ireland (thus ending more than twenty-five years of direct rule from London).
3. Establishment of a Northern Ireland Executive (essentially a cabinet) consisting of twelve offices headed by representatives of the main parties.
4. Establishment of a North/South Ministerial Council made up of ministers from the Republic of Ireland and Northern Ireland to make recommendations on matters of mutual concern like tourism, security, and the environment.
5. Establishment of a Council of the Isles consisting of ministers from the parliaments of Britain, Ireland, and the new assemblies established in Scotland, Wales, and Northern Ireland to meet twice a year.
6. Reform of the Royal Ulster Constabulary (RUC) based on recommendations proposed by a commission.

7. Speedy release of those imprisoned for paramilitary activity.
8. Affirmation of human rights, democracy and equality.
9. A referendum in the Republic of Ireland on abolishing Articles 2 and 3 (which lay claim to the six counties of the North) from its Constitution.
10. A referendum in the North and South of Ireland accepting or rejecting the Good Friday Agreement.

503. The Referendum and the Election The day after the agreement was signed, Taoiseach Bertie Ahearn set the tone for the days ahead: "Today's agreement is a victory for peace and democratic politics. We have seized the initiative from the men of violence. Let us not relinquish it."

On May 22, 1998, the people of Northern Ireland and the Republic headed to the polls to vote on the Good Friday Agreement. There was never any doubt that it would pass by an overwhelming majority in the Republic. The big question was whether it would pass in the North and if so, would it pass by a sufficiently large majority (i.e., with enough support by Protestant Unionists) to qualify as a mandate? To the great relief of all who supported the peace process, 71 percent of voters in the North and 94 percent in the Republic (including 55 percent of Protestants) approved the agreement. The people of Ireland—Protestant and Catholic, Unionist and Nationalist—had spoken and the message was plain for all to see: we want peace.

Elections for the new government were held one month later on June 25, 1998, and resulted in the following allotment of Assembly seats:

Ulster Union Party: 28 seats
Social Democratic Labour Party: 24 seats
Democratic Union Party: 20 seats
Sinn Fein: 18 seats
Alliance: 7 seats
Other Unionist Parties: 7 seats

David Trimble, head of the UUP, became the new government's First Minister; Seamus Mallon of the SDLP took the position of Deputy First Minister.

504. The Extremists Isolated Predictably, extremists in both camps denounced the agreement as a sell-out to the other side and vowed to prevent its implementation. After their vigorous "Vote NO" campaigns failed to defeat the referendum, they turned to violence. For ultra-Unionists, this meant using the always-explosive marching season as an opportunity to provoke a crisis and rally the forces of Unionism. In July, when British authorities denied members of the Orange Order the right to march through the Catholic section of Drumcree, the latter refused to leave, vowing to stay indefinitely until allowed to march. Tensions reached a crisis point until members of a Loyalist mob torched the nearby home of a Catholic woman married to a Protestant man. The parents managed to escape, but their three boys were killed in the blaze. Extreme Unionism collapsed under the weight of international condemnation.

Weeks later their republican counterparts suffered a similar fate. On August 15, 1998, a splinter group of extremist republicans known as the Real IRA detonated a five-hundred-pound bomb on a crowded street in the city of Omagh. The blast killed twenty-nine—the single worst act of violence in the history of the Troubles—including seven children. Even Sinn Fein, normally inclined to justify IRA violence (or at best to apologize for "mistakes"), joined the world in condemning the barbaric act. As Jack Holland writes in *Hope Against History*, "It became obvious that what was left of the tradition of violent republicanism was completely discredited."

505. Implementation As everyone familiar with the history of diplomacy knows, peace *plans* are not the same thing as peace itself. Implementation of a peace plan is never an easy undertaking. Such has been the case in Northern Ireland since the Good

Friday accord was signed. The effectiveness of the new governing bodies has been greatly undermined by countless crises, suspensions, and resignation threats, mainly over the issue of weapons decommissioning by the Unionist and Republican paramilitaries and the reformation of the Royal Ulster Constabulary. Low-level violence by paramilitaries continues to occur and each summer's "marching season" brings renewed opportunities for conflict. Still, one thing is certain about Northern Ireland: Since the 1997 cease-fire, the people have grown accustomed to peace and the vast majority are unwilling to countenance a return of the gunmen.

506. The Larger Question The key question regarding the fate of Northern Ireland was posed by William Butler Yeats nearly a century ago—Will the center hold? Specifically, can a society so wedded to sectarian hatred and violence remake itself into one that celebrates tolerance and cooperation? There are two ways to look at it. A pessimist would argue that violence and hatred are so deeply engrained in Northern Ireland society that Nationalists and Loyalists will never stop fighting. An optimist would argue just the opposite: that *because* so much blood has been shed in Northern Ireland both sides are prepared to stop and enjoy the fruits of toleration and peaceful coexistence. We can only hope the future proves the latter correct.

PART V

Religion

catholicism

The Colonial Era

507. How Many Catholics? Tens of thousands of Catholics, perhaps more, arrived on the shores of America in the seventeenth and eighteenth centuries. Some came as transported criminals, others as aspiring merchants. The great majority, finding almost no Catholic churches or clergy and abundant hostility to "popery," converted to some form of Protestantism, usually Baptism or Methodism. The weakness of institutional Catholicism in Ireland (a result of the Penal Laws) and the lack of Irish women in America (leading to marriage to Protestants) also contributed to this process. One historian has estimated that there were twenty-five thousand Catholics in America at the end of the American Revolution, despite the fact that seventy-five thousand to one hundred thousand Catholics had emigrated since 1700. Many examples of this trend support this contention. James Sullivan, a Protestant who served as governor of Massachusetts in 1807, was the descendant of Catholic refugees from the 1690s. In New York City, many prosperous Catholic merchants worshipped at Trinity Church (Episcopal) until the city's first Catholic church, St. Peter's, opened in 1785.

James Sullivan

508. Early Anti-Catholic Laws As the number of Irish immigrants increased, many non-Irish colonists began to express anti-Irish hostility that originated in the Old World. In the 1650s Richard Mather declared that the influx of Irish in Boston represented "a formidable attempt of Satan and his sons to unsettle us." Fr. Christopher A. Plunkett, a Capuchin friar born in Ireland, was imprisoned and exiled along with several other priests to Barbados by the government of Virginia in 1689–90. In 1698 South Carolina levied a head tax on indentured servants from Ireland to discourage their emigration to the colony. In 1704 Maryland followed suit in order to "prevent the importing of too great a number of Irish Papists." In 1720 the government of Massachusetts expressed concern over the sharp rise in Irish immigration to the colony and announced that they would have to leave within seven months.

509. Secret Priests Many colonies tolerated Catholics, so long as they did not practice their religion. Some like New York actually passed laws banning priests from the colony, expelling them for a first offense and threatening them with execution if they returned a second time. In 1741, in the midst of a perceived slave revolt many believed was instigated by Catholic slaves, New York City officials hanged a man they suspected of being a Catholic priest (he turned out to be merely a zealous Protestant minister).

Due to this hostility, many priests resorted to secret visits to colonies. New Yorkers in the late 1700s spoke of a Fr. Farmer who occasionally made a clandestine visit to celebrate Mass and baptize children from the more tolerant colony of

Pennsylvania. How many other "secret priests" carried out similar works no one knows.

510. Fr. Whelan Reports on the Early Church in New York City

Fr. Charles Maurice Whelan, an Irish Capuchin friar, became the first resident Catholic priest in New York City in 1784. The community he describes below would found St. Peter's Church in 1785, the first Catholic church in New York State.

> The Catholics in these parts are very poor, but very zealous. For the greater part they are Irish. As such they would not be able to build a church nor even to rent a place for saying mass. However, a Portuguese gentleman has given them a part of his house for that purpose, and I hope that divine Providence will provide us with another place by next May, since said gentleman cannot let us use his house any longer.

511. John Carroll, America's First Catholic Bishop

John Carroll (1736–1815), cousin of Charles Carroll the signer of the Declaration of Independence, was born in Maryland. He attended school and the seminary in Europe and became a priest in 1761. He returned to the colonies in 1775 and went on to play a leading role in establishing the American Catholic Church. In

1784 Pope Pius VI named him the head of the American mission. Four years later, he used a portion of his own land in Georgetown and established Georgetown University. In 1789, Rome established Baltimore as

Bishop John Carroll

the nation's first Catholic diocese and Carroll as its first bishop (he was installed a year later). In addition to providing leadership to the fledgling American church, Carroll also oversaw construction of the Basilica of the Assumption of the Blessed Virgin Mary in Baltimore and the first cathedral in America, completed in 1818. He was made an archbishop in 1808.

The Antebellum Church

512. The Arrival of the Unchurched

In 1815, Catholics in America numbered approximately ninety thousand. Most were not Irish. Rather they, or their ancestors, emigrated from England, France, Spain, and other European nations. Living mostly in cities along the eastern seaboard, they worshipped in a handful of churches served by a small number of priests.

All that changed when the migration of Irish Catholics to America boomed after 1820 (see Part II). As waves of Irish (and German) immigrants pushed the total number of Catholics in America to 1.6 million by 1850, the fledgling Catholic Church was overwhelmed. Not only were these new arrivals numerous and poor, but many of the Irish called themselves Catholics while knowing next to nothing about the faith. These "unchurched" Irish, many of whom had never attended Mass and could not make the sign of the cross, were the product of the Penal Laws which sharply curtailed the free practice of Catholicism, especially in the remote regions of the west of Ireland. Studies indicate that only a third of Ireland's Catholics attended Mass regularly in pre-Famine period. So on top of all their duties, the clergy in America faced a monumental task of transforming these people from Catholics in name to Catholics in practice.

513. The Irish Takeover of the American Catholic Church

As waves of poor, unchurched Irish Catholics entered America, clerical leaders pleaded with Church leaders in Ireland and Rome to send more priests and nuns. As late as 1830 most clergy in the American Catholic Church were English or French. After that date, however, the Church clergy became decidedly more Irish.

514. The Irish Influence on American Catholicism   Irish priests and bishops tended to be more conservative and authoritarian than their French, English, and German Catholic counterparts and their growing numerical superiority pushed the American Church firmly in that direction. They also tended to share a negative view toward the many reform movements that were all the rage in antebellum America. The very idea of social reform, as opposed to individual redemption, collided with the strong, fatalist outlook of Irish peasant culture. Whether it was the temperance crusade, abolitionism, women's rights, public education, or antipoverty initiatives, most Irish clergymen viewed them as just so many variations of evangelical Protestantism that preached the wrongheaded idea that society, rather than just individuals, could be reformed. And more often than not, these same reformers tended to be nativists hostile to "popery."

Two Styles of Leadership

515. "Dagger John" Hughes   The embodiment of this trend toward an authoritarian clergy and hostility to evangelical Protestant reform was John Hughes (1797–1864), bishop of New York. Born in County Tyrone, he came to the U.S. in 1818 and soon entered Mount St. Mary's seminary in Maryland. Ordained in 1826 he soon achieved a national reputation as a fiery pro-Catholic polemicist, engaging in several high-profile "debates" in the pages of leading Protestant and Catholic newspapers. His detractors took to calling him "Dagger John" because of his personality and the fact that he always drew a daggerlike cross under his signature.

He was made bishop of New York in 1842 (and archbishop in 1850). He became a leading

Archbishop John Hughes

figure in the reshaping of the American Catholic Church along Irish lines— that is a militant brand of worship that emphasized obedience, piety, regular worship, and reception of the sacraments—backed by an authoritarian clergy. Central to this plan was a program of institution building designed to insulate Catholics from the corrupting influences of American culture. This included not just parish building, but the establishment of a vast system of parochial schools, hospitals, and orphanages, plus separate fraternal societies to compete with American ones. On more than one occasion, Hughes mused that it might be more important to build a parochial school first, followed by the parish church. This outlook was understandable, given the hostile environment of his era. However, critics then and in subsequent generations have argued that in the long run Hughes' model of defensive Catholicism hindered the full participation of Catholics in American life until the mid-twentieth century.

516. Bishop John Timon Provides Some Contrast   Not every Irish bishop was as conservative or defensive as Hughes. A few bishops in the antebellum period, most notably John Timon (1797–1867) of Buffalo, pursued a more ecumenical policy. Born and ordained in the same years as Hughes (1797 and 1826), he first established himself as a highly successful missionary in the American West. In 1847 he was named the first bishop of Buffalo, New York. For the next two decades he worked to build bridges between Catholicism and Protestantism. He placed considerably less emphasis on building a vast, separate

Catholic institutional network of schools and hospitals and became a strong supporter of efforts to send Irish Catholic immigrants to western lands (a practice Hughes condemned as guaranteed to result in a loss of the faith). Timon's views represented the minority of the Irish clergy in America and by the time of his death in 1867, it was clear that Hughes' vision had won out.

The Problem of Anti-Catholicism

517. Sources of Anti-Catholicism As a nation comprised mainly of Protestants of European ancestry, America possessed a strong tradition of hostility toward Catholicism. Some focused on the questions of dogma and doctrine and declared Catholicism a superstitious religion based on false ideas about the nature of faith, good works, saints, and transubstantiation. Others feared the power of the pope. As head of the papal states and possessor of an army, they viewed him as an autocratic leader and an enemy of republican government. Moreover, given the fact that Catholic dogma declared that all good Catholics owed complete allegiance to the pope, did that not disqualify Catholics as potential republican citizens? Wasn't it possible, even likely, that the priests would control the votes of Catholic immigrants in America and thereby bring down the republic? Perhaps, wrote Samuel F. B. Morse (of telegraph fame) in his two books, *The Foreign Conspiracy Against the Liberties of the United States* (1835) and *The Imminent Dangers to the Free Institutions of the United States Through Foreign Immigration* (1835), the pope was sending legions of seemingly helpless Catholics to America for the purpose of overthrowing the government.

518. Rev. Lyman Beecher Explains the Catholic Menace Lyman Beecher was one of the most prominent preachers in mid-nineteenth century America. He was widely respected and had his sermons, including those that warned of the Catholic menace, published in papers across the country.

> The Catholic Church holds now in darkness and bondage nearly half the civilized world. . . . It is the most skillful, powerful, dreadful system of corruption to those who wield it, and of slavery and debasement to those who live under it.

519. THE AWFUL DISCLOSURES OF MARIA MONK One of the bestselling forms of literature in the antebellum period were books that told sensational tales of priests, nuns, and Catholic plots to overthrow the government. Rebecca Reed's *Six Months in a Convent* (1835) and Samuel B. Smith's *The Downfall of Babylon, or the Triumph of Truth over Popery* (1833) were just two examples of the genre. By far the most famous of these books was Maria Monk's *Awful Disclosures.* Published in 1836 as the firsthand account of one Maria Monk and her ordeal in a Montreal convent, it sold more than three hundred thousand copies. The book told of her conversion to Catholicism and entry into the convent where, she soon learned, nuns were required to submit to lustful priests. Any children resulting from these liaisons were immediately baptized, strangled, and buried in the convent basement. She fled to New York, she claimed, to save the life of her child.

For a while Monk was a star performer on the nativist lecture circuit, sponsored by a committee of concerned Protestant clergymen. But she was eventually exposed as a fraud (her mother revealed that she had never been in a convent and had run away from home with her boyfriend, the likely father of her child). By the time her second out-of-wedlock baby was born, her backers abandoned her. So, too, had her agent, who absconded with all the money from the sale of the book. Monk subsequently disappeared into a life of poverty. Years later she was arrested for theft while working in a brothel, and died in prison.

More than one historian has noted that

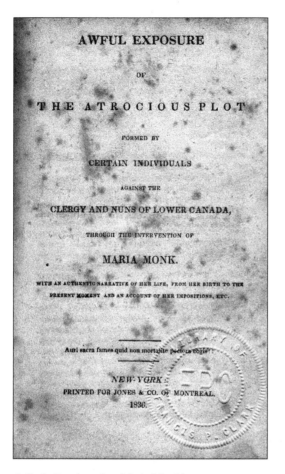

AWFUL EXPOSURE

OF

THE ATROCIOUS PLOT

FORMED BY

CERTAIN INDIVIDUALS

AGAINST THE

CLERGY AND NUNS OF LOWER CANADA,

THROUGH THE INTERVENTION OF

MARIA MONK.

WITH AN AUTHENTIC NARRATIVE OF HER LIFE, FROM HER BIRTH TO THE
PRESENT MOMENT AND AN ACCOUNT OF HER IMPOSITIONS, ETC.

Auri sacra fames quid non mortalia pectora cogis!!

NEW-YORK:
PRINTED FOR JONES & CO. OF MONTREAL.
1836.

A Catholic rebuttal to Maria Monk's story

Monk's book was the *Uncle Tom's Cabin* of the Know Nothing movement.

520. The Story of Fr. William Hogan

William Hogan was born in Ireland and became a priest before emigrating to America around 1810. Assigned to St. Mary's parish in Philadelphia, he proved himself a popular priest. But he soon ran afoul of Bishop Henry Conwell, who resented his popularity and disapproved of his vigorous social life. When Hogan resisted Conwell's attempts to rein him in, Conwell suspended him. The trustees of St. Mary's rushed to Hogan's defense and Conwell soon had a full-blown schism on his hands. He eventually excommunicated Hogan in 1821 and then, like many American bishops in the 1820s, wrested control of the parish from the lay trustees.

Following his excommunication, Hogan managed a circus, studied law, and married twice, before reemerging in the 1840s as a leading voice of anti-Catholicism. He went on the lecture circuit, wrote belligerent essays in popular journals, and published in 1854 a book entitled, *Popery as It Was and as It Is*. The general tone of the latter is conveyed in the following statement: "I am sorry to say, from my knowledge of [Roman Catholic priests] . . . that there is not a more corrupt, licentious body of men in the world."

521. Burning of the Charlestown Convent

One of the earliest incidents of rising anti-Catholicism was the burning of the Ursuline convent in Charlestown, Massachusetts (just outside of Boston). Rumors had been swirling around town that Protestant girls were being held against their will inside the convent (which also served as a school, ironically, to many children of wealthy Protestant families). Other rumors told of a secret plot by Irish Catholics to overthrow by force of arms the American republic and turn it over to the pope.

On the night of August 11, 1834, a working-class mob of native-born Americans attacked the convent and school and burned it to the ground. No one was killed in the incident and wealthy Bostonians rushed to condemn it as the work of delinquent laborers and ruffians. In the trials that followed, all accused rioters were eventually acquitted. Bishop Benedict Fenwick's efforts to recover damages were likewise unsuccessful. Fenwick and his successors left the burned remains of the convent untouched for forty years as a grim reminder of the nativist intolerance.

Not surprisingly, when Bishop Fenwick decided to establish a Catholic college a few years later, he built the College of the Holy Cross (1843) in Worcester, Massachusetts, forty miles away—just to be on the safe side.

522. The Philadelphia "Bible Riots" and Other Anti-Irish Clashes The incident in Massachusetts was certainly not the last of its kind. Outbreaks of violence against Irish Catholics erupted in Boston, Baltimore, New York, and most notably, Philadelphia in 1844. In this last case, the issue was not sensational rumors about Catholic convents, but rather a very real struggle over the curriculum in the local public schools. More specifically, the fight centered on which bible would be used for reading and instruction. Catholics objected to the use of the Protestant King James version (which included annotations and commentaries at odds with Catholic teaching).

In early May, a Protestant mob attacked the Irish neighborhood of Kensington, burning Irish homes, a convent, and two churches. A second riot broke out in July when a mob attacked the militia guarding a Catholic church in Southwark. A total of eighteen were killed—mostly members of the nativist mobs shot by the Irish and militia.

When rumors of a similar outbreak of violence against the Irish in New York reached the ears of Bishop John Hughes, he wasted little time in sending a message to the newly elected nativist mayor. "[I]f a single Catholic church is burned in New York," he warned the mayor, "the city will become a second Moscow." These were chilling words for those who remembered that only thirty years earlier Moscow burned to the ground before Napoleon's invading legions. The message was clear: All that we ask is to be left alone; but if provoked we will fight back and the results will be grave. As a precaution, the bishop called upon the men of the Ancient Order of Hibernians to establish a twenty-four-hour guard over St. Patrick's Cathedral. Fortunately, the mob never materialized.

523. Protestants Learn to Proselytize in Irish Many nineteenth-century evangelical Protestant groups were intent on converting as many Catholics as possible. They set up missions in Irish slums and tried to lure potential converts with offers of food and shelter in exchange for listening to a sermon. Generally these initiatives were resounding failures. To improve their chances of success, several Protestant groups sent Irish speakers (mostly converts themselves) out into the streets to preach. Their level of success is unknown, but a number of contemporary accounts noted that whereas an English-speaking proselytizer was most often ignored or insulted by his intended audience, an Irish-speaking one invariably drew a crowd.

524. The Enduring Problem of Anti-Catholicism In 1887, Henry F. Bowers founded at Clinton, Iowa, an anti-Catholic organization that sought to revive the spirit of the Know Nothings. A quasi-secret society, the American Protective Association played upon the fears of rural Americans concerning growing visibility, power, and influence of Catholics in the nation's cities. Derided by Catholics as the American *Protestant* Association, it became extremely popular in the 1890s, especially after the economic depression that began in 1893. At its height the APA boasted a membership of between five hundred thousand and two million members. It soon faded with the return of prosperity after 1897, but it stood as a reminder to Irish Catholics that anti-Catholicism still ran strong in American culture.

Building a Catholic World and Identity

525. Parish Life The parish became the center of most Irish Catholic neighborhoods in the nineteenth century. It provided weekly religious services to meet the spiritual needs of its members, but also the key sacramental events that marked the life of a Catholic: baptisms, first communions, confirmations, marriages, and funerals. Parishes also offered a multifaceted network of overlapping institutions designed to foster unity and a deeper Catholic identity. In addition to the parochial school, a typical parish had several religious and fraternal societies to dissuade Catholics from joining secular organizations like the Masons or Odd Fellows.

526. Catholic Institutions   Compelled by the belief that American Protestant culture was hostile to Catholicism, most Catholic bishops and clergy in nineteenth-century America worked to build a vast network of charitable agencies such as hospitals, orphanages, almshouses, asylums, and homes for single mothers. Here again the goal was to provide Catholics with an alternative to non-Catholic institutions, many of which were seen as places of anti-Catholic bigotry (hospitals, for example, that refused access to Catholic priests for visits) and Protestant proselytizing. Priests and nuns thus performed works far beyond their religious duties, serving as teachers, healthcare providers, arbitrators, and administrators.

527. The Case of the Orphan Trains   One Protestant institution that drew the loudest condemnation from the Catholic clergy was the Children's Aid Society in New York City. Founded in 1853 by Charles Loring Brace, the CAS was committed to saving children who were orphaned or living in unfit homes. The goal was to remove the children from the harmful environment of the slum and place them in the homes of respectable families. Starting in 1854 and running until 1929, the CAS sponsored so-called "orphan trains" that carried 250,000 children to the Midwest, where they were placed with adoptive families. In some cases, the children found loving families, in others they were treated like servants. Some children benefited enormously from the program and went on to successful lives as a result. John Brady and his friend Andrew Burke, for example, grew up to become the governors of Alaska and North Dakota. Other children merely ended up in Midwestern jails rather than Sing Sing.

Upper-class New Yorkers hailed Brace for his humanitarianism, Archbishop John Hughes denounced him as a kidnapper, for the great major-

ity of the children taken by the CAS were Irish Catholic and most ended up in Protestant homes. To combat this effort, Hughes organized the Catholic Protectorate and other agencies designed to harbor children in need and to place them in Catholic families.

528. The Valiant Work of Irish Catholic Nuns   It must be stressed that without the presence of an army of Catholic nuns, a majority of whom hailed from Ireland, none of this church and institution building could have taken place. It wasn't enough for the bishop or pastor to raise money and build buildings. Every school, orphanage, hospital, and home for wayward girls required trained personnel to staff them. Nuns brought experience, dedication, and a capacity to work extremely hard. Almost as important, they cost next to nothing to employ and thus allowed for the construction of vast complexes of educational and health-related institutions.

529. Catholic Colleges   In addition to building a parochial school network, the Church also worked to establish a network of colleges throughout the U.S. to provide upwardly mobile Catholics with higher education within a Catholic environment. It was also hoped that such colleges would serve as recruiting grounds for future priests. Older Catholic colleges like Georgetown (1791) and St. Louis University (1818) grew while newer ones like Fordham (New York, 1841), Villanova (Philadelphia, 1842), Notre Dame (South Bend, Indiana, 1842), College of the Holy Cross (Worcester, Massachusetts, 1843), St. Joseph's College (Philadelphia, 1851), and St. Mary of the Lake (Chicago, 1846) were established.

The goal of the Catholic college was twofold: to train young men for the priesthood or the professions. Regarding the latter, Archbishop Hughes offered that Fordham was founded so "that the Catholic parents of this diocese and elsewhere, who could afford it, should have an opportunity of educating their sons with safety to their faith and

Notre Dame campus, 1848

morals, and yet as to qualify them to take an honorable part in the more elevated walks of public and social life."

530. St. Patrick's Cathedral New York City already had a cathedral named in honor of Ireland's patron saint, but it was rather small and located in the heart of the city's "Little Ireland" district. Archbishop John Hughes envisioned a bigger cathedral, in a more central location. Modeled after the great European Gothic cathedrals, this new St. Patrick's Cathedral would stand as a proud symbol of Irish Catholic power in the city and in America.

So in 1858, with money pledged by the city's wealthy Catholics, Hughes presided over a groundbreaking ceremony commencing its construction. Many New Yorkers dubbed the project "Hughes' folly" when they learned it would be built way uptown on Fiftieth Street and Fifth Avenue amid undeveloped, grass-covered lots. They also criticized the Church for building an expensive building when so many Irish Catholics lived in poverty. But Hughes wanted a prominent symbol of Catholicism and knew the city would grow northward to meet it. After many delays (including the Civil War), the new St. Patrick's

opened in 1879. To this day it is the largest Catholic cathedral in the United States and the eleventh largest in the world.

531. The "Devotional Revolution" Given the lack of religious education and habits of churchgoing found among Irish Catholics, the hierarchy on both sides of the Atlantic commenced a broad program later dubbed by historians as "devotional revolution." Its goal was to impose a more uniform practice of the faith while instilling a more intense attachment to it. Cardinal Paul Cullen in Dublin and Archbishop John Hughes led the way in establishing an emphasis on regular attendance at Mass, confession, and reception of Holy Eucharist. They also encouraged a wide range of devotional practices—everything from the use of missals, catechisms, and rosary beads to participation in pilgrimages, retreats, and novenas. Vestiges of pre-Christian traditions still popular among the Irish peasantry—i.e., fertility festivals thinly disguised as saints' days and raucous wakes—were slowly quashed. As the Irish in America embraced the devotional revolution, Catholicism became an increasingly central part of their Irish American identity.

532. Knights of Columbus A private society for Roman Catholic men, the Knights of Columbus was founded by Irish American priest Michael J. McGivney and several laymen in 1882 in New Haven, Connecticut. It had several goals. First, as a fraternal society it was designed to provide friendship and care to needy members and their families. This would be accomplished by establishing an insurance fund to pay for the funeral of a deceased member and provide his family with short-term financial support. Second, the Knights as an organization was dedicated both to defending Catholicism from its attackers and championing the belief that American democracy and Catholicism were uniquely compatible. In 1914 the Knights established a Commission on

Fr. Michael J. McGivney

Religious Prejudices to investigate and expose incidents of bigotry.

Tellingly, the group's name was chosen in honor of Christopher Columbus, a figure who was both an American hero and a Catholic. It indicated in a very explicit way the desire to provide their members with a Catholic equivalent to the Puritans' Plymouth Rock.

The Knights experienced rapid growth in the 1890s, fueled by a combination of rising patriotism spurred by the Spanish-American War, enthusiasm generated by the four hundredth anniversary of Columbus's arrival in the New World, and anti-Catholic bigotry as promoted by the American Protective Association (see entry #223). By 1905 the organization had chapters in every state. The organization's profile rose dramatically as a result of its voluntary work and fund-raising during World War I. It would continue to grow in membership and influence well into the twentieth century.

The Church in the Later Nineteenth Century

533. Continued Irish Dominance The hierarchy of the Catholic Church in America grew even more Irish as the nineteenth century progressed. Irish priests and bishops had an advantage due to the numerical superiority of the Irish in the American Church. The fact that they spoke English and overwhelmingly favored the devotional revolution made them ideal candidates for bishops in the eyes of Rome. By 1900 two out of every three bishops in America were Irish-born or Irish American.

St. Patrick's Cathedral, New York City

534. Liberals vs. Conservatives As the Catholic Church in America grew larger, stronger, and to a certain extent, more confident in the late nineteenth century, it confronted several major questions, the answers to which would shape the character of the Church for most of the twentieth century. Should Catholics be allowed to join labor unions, especially more radical ones like the Knights of Labor? Should bishops work to develop a dialogue with Protestant religious leaders? Should Catholics endeavor to enter fully into American life, or must they remain somewhat apart as a means of preserving their faith?

In seeking to provide answers to these questions, the hierarchy found itself divided. One group of bishops, the liberals, were led by Cardinal James Gibbons (1824–1921) of Baltimore, Bishop John Ireland (1838–1918) of St. Paul, Minnesota, and Bishop John Keane of Richmond, Virginia (1839–1902). They supported the right of workers to join unions, pursued an ecumenical course regarding Protestants, and called for the full participation of Catholics in American life. These "Americanists" were opposed by a core of conservative bishops led by Archbishop Michael Corrigan (1839–1902) of New York City and Bishop Bernard McQuaid (1823–1909) of Rochester, New York. The latter condemned all forms of radicalism, including labor activism, and promoted a vision of the Church as an embattled institution at odds with much of the ethos of American society (i.e., individualism and democracy).

In the end, after much struggle, the liberal wing won out.

535. The Enduring Question of Parochial Schools The emphasis on the parochial school as a fundamental component of American Catholicism grew even stronger in the years following the Civil War. Even though the great majority of Catholic children attended public schools, conservative members of the hierarchy were committed to the parochial school as a matter of principle. As Archbishop Michael Corrigan of New York put it in 1892:

> The American episcopacy does not oppose the public school, but only asserts that Catholics should be educated under the surveillance of the Church, that is, in parochial schools; if the State does not want to help us, it does not matter; we will continue to sacrifice ourselves, as for fifty years we have done, but we will not give our Catholics up to the atheistic teacher, to the neutral school.

By the 1880s, some conservative bishops tried to adopt a policy whereby parents who failed to send their children to parochial schools would be denied the sacraments. Liberal bishops, however, eventually defeated the proposal, but not the idea that parochial schools should be built whenever possible.

536. The Question of Labor Unions As more and more Irish became active in the labor movement in the 1870s and 1880s, many conservative members of the American hierarchy grew alarmed. Radical doctrines such as anarchism, Socialism, and Communism, argued these clerics, were hostile to the Church and antithetical to its teaching on private property, the family, and civil authority. Thus, just as Irish American labor leaders faced great challenges in the Gilded Age from powerful industrialists and unresponsive, often hostile, government, they also had to contend with a potentially devastating fight with the American Catholic Church.

The largest and most influential labor union in the nineteenth century was the Knights of Labor, an industrial union headed by Irish American Terence Powderly (see entry #909). As a secret labor organization, replete with binding oaths of allegiance, the Knights came under considerable scrutiny from Church officials. So too did its set of rather utopian social goals. A devout

James Cardinal Gibbons

Catholic, Powderly lifted the ban of secrecy in 1881 and moderated the oath in order to avoid clerical condemnation of the union. When the Cardinal of Quebec condemned the Knights in Canada and threatened its members with excommunication, Powderly doubled his efforts to convince American Church leaders of the compatibility of Knights membership and fidelity to Church teachings. Several liberal bishops, especially Gibbons of Baltimore, were sympathetic to the Knights: "We must prove that we are the friends of the working classes," argued Gibbons in a letter to the Vatican. "I would regard the condemnation of the Knights of Labor as a signal calamity to the Catholic Church of America." Fortunately, Gibbons' view prevailed in Rome and contributed to Pope Leo XIII's encyclical *Rerum Novarum* (1893) which upheld the rights of workers to form unions.

537. The Case of Fr. Edward McGlynn Edward McGlynn (1837–1900) was born in New York City to Irish immigrants from Donegal. He entered the priesthood at a young age and was sent to Rome for his seminary training and ordination. Upon his return he served in several parishes before becoming pastor of St. Stephen's, the largest and poorest parish in New York City. Starting in the 1860s, McGlynn built a reputation as both a tireless advocate of the poor and an independent priest who sometimes defied the directives of his archbishop (he refused, for example, to build a parochial school). This gained him the undying admiration of his parishioners, who called him their "soggarth aroon" (Irish for "precious priest"), and the watchful eye of the conservative hierarchy.

As work among the poor came to dominate his labors, it began to weigh heavily upon his mind:

I had begun to feel life made a burden by the never-ending procession of men, women and children coming to my door begging not so much for alms as for employment; not asking for food, but for my influence and letters of recommendation, and personally appealing to me to obtain for them *an opportunity of working for their daily bread.* I felt that, no matter how much I might give them, even though I reserved nothing for myself, even though I involved myself hopelessly in debt, I could accomplish nothing. I began to ask myself, "Is there no remedy? Is this God's order that the poor shall be constantly becoming poorer in all our large cities, the world over?"

After reading Henry George's *Progress and Poverty,* a widely hailed book published in 1879 that examined the cause of economic inequality in American life, McGlynn became a confirmed radical. He became an enthusiastic supporter of the Irish Land League, especially the more radical wing led by Michael Davitt, and in 1886 he openly campaigned for Henry George as a Labor Party candidate for mayor of New York City. Archbishop Michael Corrigan, a leader among conservative Catholic bishops, first suspended and then excommunicated McGlynn. McGlynn was eventually reinstated in 1892, but was transferred to an isolated upstate parish where he died in 1900.

The Twentieth Century:
The Confident Church

538. The "Brick and Mortar" Priest In the early twentieth century, as the Catholic Church grew in size and collective wealth, parish priests in many dioceses came to be judged by their ability to build. In new parishes and old, these "brick and mortar" priests built a massive network of Catholic institutional infrastructure. No longer was it enough to build a parochial school. Youth activity centers, function halls, and athletic fields and complexes increasingly became the norm.

Bishops likewise launched ambitious programs to build networks of hospitals, nursing homes, high schools, colleges, seminaries, and convents. All of this was made possible by extremely high rates of church attendance and weekly collections, not to mention an optimistic sense of mission.

539. Militant, Separatist Catholicism The driving impulse behind this massive building program was a new, more assertive form of Irish American Catholicism. As the story of New York's Archbishop John Hughes clearly indicates, not every nineteenth-century Catholic bishop was nonconfrontational. Nonetheless, most tried to earn the respect and cooperation of non-Catholics, especially those who dominated business and political power. But with the turn of the twentieth century, Catholic bishops began to pursue a more militant form of leadership. It was born of a contradictory set of beliefs: first, that Protestant American society was fundamentally hostile toward Catholics (hence the need to establish a separate Catholic subculture); second, that Catholics were now so numerous and increasingly powerful in business and politics that they could confidently demand respect and voice their opinions (i.e., Catholics were as American as any group). In the words of historian Paula Kane in writing about the Boston archdiocese, this was a "triumphalist, separatist Catholic subculture" which was "sacred but equal, separate but integrated."

Central to this emerging Catholic world was the establishment of separate fraternal and social organizations for Catholics of every age. Organizations like the Boy Scouts and institutions

such as the YMCA were to be replaced, if at all possible, by the Catholic Boy Scouts and the CYO (Catholic Youth Organization). More than ever before, in many dioceses and parishes, Catholic bishops urged, even demanded, that parents send their children to parochial schools. For adult Catholics, the typical church offered dozens of organizations and events to compete with those available in the wider, secular society—everything from the Holy Name Society and Knights of Columbus to bingo night and regular dances.

540. The Ku Klux Klan Perhaps in response to this growing assertiveness, the Ku Klux Klan (revived in 1915) broadened its scope of paranoid hatred to include Catholics (and Jews) as well as African Americans. The new Klan of the 1920s was popular in the North, especially the Midwest, as well as the South and saw its membership rise to five million by 1929. They revived the traditional antipathies toward Catholics (that loyalty to the pope made them unfit Americans) and warned of their growing political and social power. The Klan was particularly strong in Indiana and therefore the University of Notre Dame came under consistent rhetorical attack. On one occasion, Klansmen arriving at South Bend to attend a Klan rally were beaten by an angry posse of Notre Dame students. This rising tide of anti-Catholicism helps explain the vicious character of the 1928 presidential campaign in which much was made of Al Smith's Catholicism (see entry #231).

Reformers, Radicals,
and Reactionaries

541. Fr. John A. Ryan Starting in the early twentieth century, Fr. John Augustine Ryan (1865–1945) became America's most vocal Catholic advocate for social reform. He believed ardently in social morality, which included fair wages, a more equal distribution of wealth, protection for women and children, social security, and public housing.

Beyond the theoretical, Ryan planned legislation and programs to promote his ideology. The Socialist writer Upton Sinclair called Ryan the "Catholic miracle," although Ryan maintained that his positions were rooted in Catholicism, not Socialism. Ryan believed in Franklin Delano Roosevelt's New Deal and remained a lifelong supporter of the president, and served on various government panels.

Ryan also took high-profile stands against two very different, prominent Catholics. When Margaret Sanger took on the Catholic Church in her crusade for birth control, Ryan took the lead in criticizing her beliefs based on traditional Catholic teaching. Later in the 1930s, Ryan took on the "radio priest," Fr. Charles Coughlin for his anti-Semitism and pro-Fascist critique of Roosevelt's New Deal.

542. Fr. Edward Flanagan   Fr. Edward Flanagan (1886–1948) was born in County Roscommon, Ireland, and first traveled to the United States to earn an undergraduate degree. He was ordained in Austria in 1912 and returned to America to pastor an Omaha, Nebraska, parish. Moved by the plight of homeless and orphaned boys, he opened Father Flanagan's Boys Home in 1917. Filling a need, it expanded rapidly, and was renamed Boys Town in 1922. Within fifteen years Boys Town had been incorporated and added additional facilities across the state. Flanagan died in 1948 while on an overseas fund-raising trip for Boys Town. His story was made famous in the 1938 movie *Boys Town,* starring Spencer Tracy.

543. The Catholic Worker Movement   Born in Brooklyn, Dorothy Day (1897–1980) grew up in Chicago. After a brief stint in college she moved to New York City in 1916 where she immersed herself in the radical scene there. She became an activist in all the leading rights issues of the day, especially women's rights and birth control, and became a regular correspondent for left-wing publications such as the *Call* and the *New Masses.*

Impregnated by one of her many lovers, she had an illegal abortion. Soon thereafter she married another lover, but was soon divorced.

Day's life began to change dramatically in 1926 when she found herself pregnant again. This time she had the baby. The baby's father was an atheist, but Day had her baptized a Catholic. Soon thereafter she became a Catholic herself.

In 1933 she met Peter Maurin, a gifted French immigrant who shared her mix of radical politics and spiritual longing. In May of that year they founded the *Catholic Worker* newspaper, the cornerstone of what became the Catholic Worker Movement. "We started publishing the Catholic Worker," remembered Day, ". . . in May, 1933, with a first issue of 2,500 copies . . . By the end of the year we had a circulation of 100,000 and by 1936 it was 150,000." The paper articulated the founders' commitment to combining leftist politics, pacifism, and concern for the poor with the Catholic faith. Soon the Catholic Worker movement began to open houses and food kitchens to offer direct help to the poor and vulnerable.

In addition to Day, the Catholic Worker Movement attracted many Irish Catholics, among them Aemon Hennacy, who became a leading activist in Chicago and later Salt Lake City.

544. Fr. Charles E. Coughlin   The great-grandson of an Irish laborer, Charles E. Coughlin (1891–1979) was born in Hamilton, Ontario, Canada. Ordained as a priest in Toronto in 1916, Coughlin joined the Diocese of Detroit in Michigan in the early 1920s. At the invitation of local radio station WJR, Coughlin began hosting *The Golden Hour of the Shrine of the Little Flower* in 1926. With an audience numbering in the millions, Coughlin took advantage of his growing popularity by expounding upon various social and political issues. In addition to founding the weekly newspaper *Social Justice* in 1936, Coughlin's Union Party supported a presidential candidate that same year (North Dakota congressman William Lemke). His increasing dependence on anti-

Fr. Charles Coughlin

Semitic rhetoric during the early days of World War II embarrassed the Catholic Church and enraged government officials. After his radio show was canceled and his newspaper banned from military installations in the early 1940s, Coughlin retreated to a quiet life as a parish priest in Royal Oak, Michigan.

545. Legion of Decency The Legion of Decency was established in the 1930s by the Roman Catholic Church to advocate for more wholesome motion pictures. Its board reviewed films, condemning those it considered indecent and encouraging Catholics to pledge not to patronize theaters showing these movies. In 1934, pressure from the Legion of Decency and other groups led to the creation of the Production Code, a set of strict content guidelines followed by major movie studios for more than twenty years. Headed by Irish American Catholic Joe Breen, the Production Code Authority did not permit scenes including any sort of sex, violence, crime, or vulgarity.

Growing Acceptance and Influence of Catholicism

546. The Catholic World As in the past, the Catholic parish after World War II was much more than a mere place of weekly worship; only now they were more prosperous than ever before. Parishes continued to form a small, familiar world at the core of many Irish Catholics' identity—precisely what Archbishop John Hughes had in mind a century before. Even if the children attended public school, a Catholic family was plugged into a multifaceted network of Catholic Youth Organization programs, fraternal organizations (Knights of Columbus), religious devotions (Holy Name Society). Most parishes sponsored a full calendar of social activities, from periodic fairs, to dances, to weekly bingo. Journalist Mark Russell put it best when he once quipped: "I was twenty before I realized Protestants played basketball."

547. The Hollywood Priest Something happened in Hollywood in the late 1930s that forever changed the way America perceived its Irish Catholic citizens. Indeed, it forever changed the way Irish Americans viewed themselves. To be sure, a generation earlier George M. Cohan had done much to present a positive, superpatriotic image of Irish Americans. But in the early days of Hollywood, the most vivid image of Irish America was that of the thug, a role personified by James Cagney in *Public Enemy* (1931). Toward the end of the 1930s, however, that image began to change.

The most astonishing transformation was the image of the Irish Catholic priest. Until recently the symbol of a sinister, foreign culture, he was now presented as the embodiment of American virtue and manhood. The trend began with the 1938 film *Boys Town,* for which Spencer Tracy won an Oscar for best actor. By 1944, exactly one hundred years after the streets of Philadelphia ran red with the blood spilled during the anti-Catholic "Bible Riots," the film *Going My Way* took three Academy Awards, including best actor (Bing Crosby), best supporting actor (Barry Fitzgerald), and best director (Leo McCarey). It was followed by other upbeat depictions of Irish Catholic parish life such as *The Bells of St. Mary's* (1945) and *Fighting Father Dunne* (1948). Clearly these films relied heavily on stereotypes, but stereotypes of a very different sort from earlier eras.

548. Rev. Fulton Sheen No one embodied the new American appreciation for the Catholic priest more than Rev. Fulton John Sheen (1895–1979).

Archbishop Fulton Sheen

Francis Cardinal Spellman

Born Peter Sheen in El Paso, Illinois, he was ordained as a Roman Catholic priest in 1919. His eloquent and engaging Lenten sermons at New York City's St. Patrick's Cathedral led to tremendous popularity among that city's Catholics. From 1930 to 1952 Sheen hosted a radio show called *The Catholic Hour*. He moved on to television in 1952, when he became the much-loved host of a weekly thirty-minute program called *Life Is Worth Living*. The program regularly drew an audience of millions. In 1953 he was named TV's "most outstanding personality of the year." His messages, full of wise advice on living the Catholic faith, always ended with the blessing "God loves you." He also spoke forcefully on the evils of Communism and urged his listeners to pray the rosary for the people living under Communism.

A power struggle with Cardinal Spellman led the latter to deny him permission to appear on television. Sheen was named bishop of Rochester, New York, in 1966 a position he held until his retirement in 1969. He spent the last ten years of his life writing and speaking in New York City. He wrote a number of books on life and the Catholic faith, including *The Power of Love* (1965) and *Guide to Contentment* (1967).

549. Cardinal Francis Spellman   Another highly influential Catholic cleric, albeit of a very different sort, was Francis Cardinal Spellman (1889–1967), head of the New York Archdiocese. Born in Massachusetts, he was ordained in Rome and served the papal secretariat from 1925 to 1932, translating papal communications into English. He then returned to the United States, where he served as auxiliary bishop of Boston. In 1939 he was named Archbishop of New York and quickly became a national figure during his service as military ordinary (bishop of the armed forces) during World War II. Spellman was widely recognized for his religious conservatism, American patriotism, and staunch anti-Communism, and his pronouncements on these topics were carried in the national media. Elevated to Cardinal in 1946, he remained in the national spotlight until his death in 1967.

550. Other Bishops of Note   Spellman was by no means the only high-profile Irish American bishop. For example, Archbishop Dennis Dougherty, a staunch conservative who forbade his flock to watch Hollywood movies, presided over Philadelphia until 1960. William Cardinal O'Connell and his successor, Cardinal Richard J. Cushing, presided over the Archdiocese of Boston from 1907 until 1970. Their counterparts in Los Angeles were Timothy Cardinal Manning and his successor, Roger Cardinal Mahoney. John Patrick Cardinal Cody oversaw Chicago from 1965 to 1982 while Robert Emmett Cardinal Lucey presided over San Antonio.

551. John Courtney Murray   John Courtney Murray (1904–67) was a Catholic priest whose writings on religious freedom and the relationship between church and state exerted a profound influence on the faithful in and out of the Catholic Church. He was born in New York City to a Scottish father and Irish mother (Margaret Courtney). At the age of twenty-nine, he entered the Catholic priesthood and was ordained in 1937.

That same year he accepted a position of professor of theology at the Catholic seminary in Woodstock, Maryland. He wrote widely on the subject of church-state relations, eventually drawing the ire (and censure) of Rome for his argument that the American-style separation of church and state was both compatible with Catholic teaching and a model for other societies. His book *We Hold These Truths: Catholic Reflections on the American Proposition* brought him national attention (and his photo on the cover of *Time* magazine) and helped to dispel concerns over whether Catholics were fit for national office during the election of John F. Kennedy. He later served as an advisor to the Second Vatican Council in Rome and helped write the Declaration on Religious Freedom.

552. The Persistence of Anti-Catholicism

Even as Catholics became more numerous, more established, and more influential in the mid-twentieth century, anti-Catholicism continued to rear its ugly head. To be sure, the Maria Monk and Ku Klux Klan variety had largely disappeared. It was replaced, however, by a more refined form of anti-Catholicism wrapped in the respectable mantle of sociology and psychology. As Kevin Kenny writes in *The American Irish,* "In the 1940s, many American intellectuals still tended to believe that Catholicism was fundamentally antithetical to democracy, because its alleged authoritarianism and absolutism could not be reconciled with American political practice and philosophical thought." Paul Blanshard's bestselling book *American Freedom and Catholic Power* was only one of many works of this era that stressed the incompatibility of Catholicism and American values.

Offsetting this latent suspicion of Catholics as un-American was the emergence of the Cold War. In the 1940s and 1950s, no group in America would be more readily associated with anti-Communism than Catholic Americans. Communism was a godless, evil force to be resisted—through military service, prayer vigils for the "captive nations" of Eastern Europe, and dis-

association with all forms of radicalism. This fact explains the wide support Catholics, from Cardinal Spellman on down, gave to Senator Joseph McCarthy when he launched his anti-Communist crusade in 1950. It further explains why the Knights of Columbus led the successful campaign to have the phrase "under God" added to the Pledge of Allegiance in the 1950s. With credentials such as these in a tense Cold War atmosphere, it became harder and harder to question Catholic loyalty and patriotism.

1960s: Challenges to the Faith

553. Vatican II

In 1959 Pope John XXIII announced that he would convene an Ecumenical Council to foster a spiritual renewal in the Church and a reconsideration of its position in the modern world. Specifically this entailed updating numerous aspects of Church teaching and practice to meet the conditions and realities of the modern era. While the council made many weighty theological decisions, the impact of Vatican II on the lives of everyday American Catholics took the form of changes in the liturgy. The Latin Mass was replaced by Mass in English and lay participation, at least in theory, was encouraged. Longstanding practices like meatless Fridays that had set Catholics apart and helped form their identity were discarded.

Many Catholics greeted these changes with enthusiasm, while others came to regard them as extreme. The latter generally liked the Mass in English, but came to miss the rituals like meatless Fridays and regular praying of the rosary. More liberal Catholics, on the other hand, criticized Vatican II for not going far enough. Old teachings on priestly celibacy and the role of women remained largely unchanged. When Pope Paul VI issued the encyclical *Humana Vitae* in 1968 affirming the Church's opposition to birth control even among married couples, their alienation grew still greater.

554. The Tumultuous 1960s Rock the Church

Vatican II was only one of several developments in the 1960s that rocked the once-solid Catholic Church. The increased suburbanization of Irish Catholics led inexorably to the weakening of the old urban parish. Try as they might, Catholics in the suburbs would never be able to recreate the conditions that upheld the classic parish of old. People were too spread out in the suburbs and too likely to move in a few years. Catholics of the 1960s, increasingly assimilated, educated, accepted, and well-off, didn't need the parish as much as their parents and grandparents once did.

On top of this socioeconomic change was the emergence of the so-called "counterculture" of the 1960s. While there is no way to measure how many Irish Catholic youth subscribed to the new thinking, its influence was surely significant. It challenged the core values that lay at the heart of Irish American identity: patriotism, piety, chastity, respect for authority, and traditional roles for women.

The most evident indicator of the crisis in the American Catholic Church was in the decline in regular attendance at weekly Mass and the even steeper drop in the number of Catholics entering religious life. Whereas (according to Gallup) 75 percent of Catholics attended Mass regularly in 1957, only 54 percent did by 1975. Religious vocations also dropped dramatically. In 1965 the number of nuns hit its all-time high at more than 181,000, but by 1980 the number stood at 127,000. The same trend was true for priests: 49,000 seminarians in 1964 versus 13,000 in 1980.

555. The Berrigan Brothers Oppose the Vietnam War

One issue in particular divided the American Catholic Church: the Vietnam War. In the early years of the war (1965–67), American Catholics, like a majority of Americans, supported military action in Vietnam. For Catholics, anti-Communism had become an almost inseparable part of their American Catholic identity. They viewed American efforts to thwart Communist

Fr. Philip Berrigan

expansion around the world in almost missionary terms.

But as the war expanded in 1967 and the death toll began to rise, many Catholics, especially younger ones, began to question the wisdom and morality of American involvement. Two of the leading voices of Catholic antiwar sentiment were the Berrigan brothers. Daniel Berrigan (b. 1921) and his brother Philip (b. 1923) grew up in upstate New York and became priests (Daniel a Jesuit and Philip a Josephite) in the early 1950s. Deeply committed to social activism, civil rights, and pacifism, they staged several sensational antiwar protest actions. In 1967 Philip led a group of protesters who poured blood on draft records in Baltimore; seven months later Daniel likewise joined protesters in seizing draft records from an office in Catonsville, Maryland, and burning them with napalm. A fugitive after the incident, Philip was eventually captured by the FBI. Although he served jail time, his action inspired others to act for peace. Both brothers have remained active in social justice causes since the war's end, including initiatives to protect the environment, stop the arms race, and dismantle the military-industrial complex.

556. Anti-Communism

If the Berrigan brothers represented one wing of Irish Catholic America, clerics like Cardinal Spellman acted as the voice of traditional, patriotic, anti-Communist Irish America. Since the beginning of the Cold War in the mid-1940s, Spellman had become one of the most outspoken proponents of aggressive containment. He supported the Korean War and Senator Joseph McCarthy in his crusade against domestic Communism. In his mind, and in the minds of many Irish Americans, Vietnam was simply the next chapter in the story of America's global struggle with the godless forces of Communism. Lack of success in the war and growing opposition to it failed to dampen his enthusiasm. Despite growing condemnation of the war from his fellow bishops and the Pope, Spellman traveled to Vietnam to demonstrate his unwavering support for the war. "It looks as if Cardinal Spellman is in Vietnam," sneered one frustrated priest, "to bless the guns which the Pope is begging us to put down."

557. John Tracy Ellis Observes the Troubled Church

That the all-pervading secularization of national life has caused an inevitable corrosion of religious values affecting Catholics as well as all other Americans is generally admitted. And to that external circumstance there has been added a serious loss to the Church's membership. Like co-religionists in other countries, Catholics in the United States have experienced the mounting stress and strain that have accompanied changes in the liturgy and in other features of their religious life sanctioned by Vatican Council II.

—Historian John Tracy Ellis, writing in *American Catholicism* (1969)

558. Fr. Andrew Greeley

One Catholic who has dedicated his life to examining the values, concerns, and opinions of American Catholics is the noted sociologist, priest, and writer Fr. Andrew Greeley. In his career he has shown himself to be a renaissance man with interests in several interrelated fields. Since 1960, as a member of the National Opinion Research Center and a faculty member at the University of Illinois, the University of Arizona, and the University of Chicago, he has produced a vast body of research and analysis in groundbreaking studies of the changing world of ethnic America and contemporary issues facing

the Catholic Church. His far-ranging research has covered priests, Catholic schools, abortion, and sex, among other topics. He was one of the first priests to study the feminine aspects of God.

Fr. Greeley's other passion, writing novels, have gained him a wide following (twenty million copies sold). But his inclusion of rather unpriestly subjects like sex and infidelity has earned him the wrath of more traditional Catholics. All of the proceeds from Greeley's novels go to various charitable and social causes.

The Catholic Church Today

559. A Changing Church

Irish Americans constitute a large, though declining share of the nation's Catholics. Many polls and surveys indicate that among those who consider themselves practicing Catholics, especially those of the baby boomer generation and beyond, a majority support the Church's teachings on faith (i.e., transubstantiation of the bread and wine) and basic morality, but choose to ignore teachings like the prohibition on birth control. On more controversial issues like abortion rights, married priests, and female ordination, polls likewise indicate that a growing core of Catholics support these issues, or hold moderate views on them.

The attitudes of the American Catholic hierarchy, still disproportionately Irish American, are generally more conservative and traditional. This reflects the profound impact of Pope John Paul II's tenure. The conservative pontiff has named hundreds of bishops and cardinals since 1979, most of them chosen for their adherence to conservative Catholic teaching.

560. Anti-Catholicism: The Last Respectable Form of Bigotry?

In the mid-1980s, sociologist Fr. Andrew Greeley posited that even though Catholics were among the wealthiest groups in America, visible at the highest levels of business and politics, they still faced a pervasive undertone of anti-Catholicism. In the post–civil rights era, noted

Greeley, anti-Catholicism was "the last respectable form of bigotry." It was still permissible, he argued, to refer to Catholics as narrow minded and predisposed to racism, sexism, and authoritarianism.

protestantism

561. The Statistics In several polls and surveys conducted in the 1970s and 1980s, researchers discovered what at first seemed an astonishing fact: A majority of Americans who identify themselves as Irish also identify themselves as Protestant. For a nation (and an ethnic group for that matter) that had grown so accustomed to conflating Irishness with Catholicism, this announcement was greeted with disbelief. Among some Irish Catholics, the reaction was anger.

The explanation for the find is actually quite simple. Ultimately, it is a question of timing, more than numbers. Huge numbers of Irish immigrants came to America in the colonial period (indeed, 30 percent of all immigrants from Europe arriving between 1700 and 1820 came from Ireland) and the great majority of them were Presbyterians from Ulster. Of the many thousands of Catholics who came in the seventeenth and eighteenth centuries, most appear to have converted to some form of Protestantism. The Protestant descendents of these early Irish arrivals have been multiplying ever since. In contrast, the great migration of Irish Catholics began only in the 1830s (during which time, of course, many Protestant Irish continued to come). The poll conducted by the National Opinion Research Center makes this point clear: in the 1970s, only 41 percent of Irish Catholics were fourth generation or more as compared to 83 percent of Irish Protestants.

Irish Contributions to American Protestantism

562. Francis Makemie Born in County Donegal, Ireland, in 1658, Francis Makemie (1658–1708) is regarded as one of the founders of the Presbyterian Church in America. After being ordained, he traveled to the colonies as a missionary and began preaching in Virginia, Maryland, and the Carolinas in 1683. He married and settled in Maryland, where he founded two churches. Although Makemie was licensed to preach under the 1689 Toleration Act (which granted freedom to Nonconformist Protestants), he and his fellow pastors were subjected to arrest and opposition from the government. Despite these difficulties, he and other Presbyterian ministers formed the first American presbytery in 1706.

563. Philip Embury The founder of the Methodist Church in America, Philip Embury (1728–73) was born in County Limerick, Ireland, in 1728 and licensed as a lay preacher there. He came to the colonies in 1760 and, prodded by local Methodists in need of a leader, began preaching in 1766 to a small congregation that met in his home. The growth of this Methodist meeting eventually led to the construction of the first Methodist church in America: Wesley Chapel (named for John Wesley, the father of the sect) in New York City. Embury delivered the first sermon heard in the new church in 1768.

564. Alexander Campbell Alexander Campbell came to the United States from Armagh, Ireland, in 1809. Born in 1788, the son of a Scottish Presbyterian minister, Campbell followed in his father's footsteps and founded (with Barton Stone) the Christian Church, which later broke into three denominations: the Christian Church (Disciples of Christ), the Churches of Christ, and the Christian Churches and Churches of Christ. The church split because of differences of opinion regarding the authority of the New Testament. The largest of the denominations, The Disciples of Christ, boasts over 1.5 million members today. He also founded Bethany College in West Virginia and was an abundant writer. Alexander Campbell died in 1866.

PART VI

The Military

Tradition

565. Irish and Irish American Soldiers Irish soldiers, especially Scotch Irish, constituted between one quarter and one third of the Continental Army. That included nearly 1,500 officers of Irish ancestry, among them twenty-two generals and more than a dozen sea captains.

Shortly after the conclusion of the peace between England and the United States, Lord Mountjoy spoke in Parliament of the reasons why England lost:

> America was lost through the Irish emigrants. . . . I have been assured on the best authority that the Irish language was commonly spoken in the American ranks.

566. Col. John Stark, Hero of Bunker Hill John Stark was born in Londonderry, New Hampshire, in 1728, after his mother and father came to the United States from Ireland in 1720. He spent most of his life in the military and became an early hero in the Revolution for his gallant performance at the Battle of Bunker Hill. It was in this setting that he rallied his men with the famed words "live free or die, for death is

Col. John Stark

not the worst of evils," a slogan which lives on today as the state motto of New Hampshire. Colonel Stark later fought at Trenton and Princeton, and under his leadership, the British were defeated at Bennington, Vermont, in August, 1777. Though he had resigned the service earlier that year, he accepted the post of brigadier general. His successful repulse of Burgoyne's attempted retreat at Saratoga was a major factor in bringing about the British surrender. Stark died in 1822.

567. The Evacuation of Boston, March 17, 1776 When the British Army evacuated Boston on March 17, 1776, George Washington was unable to resist the temptation to recognize the day's significance in the eyes of so many of his soldiers. He named John Sullivan the officer of the day and made "St. Patrick" the password for those on guard duty. To this day, March 17 is a state holiday in Massachusetts, though few of the state's residents seem to be aware that it is in commemoration of "Evacuation Day."

568. Gustavus Conyngham Gustavus Conyngham (1747–1819) may not be as well known for his exploits on the high seas as Scotsman John Paul Jones, but he arguably accomplished a good deal more. Born in 1747 in Donegal, he came to Philadelphia at age sixteen and became an accomplished seaman. When the Revolution broke out, he joined the rebels as a raider and in 1777 his ship *Revenge* wrought havoc on British shipping in the seas in and around Britain. In 1778 he shifted his focus to the West Indies and continued raiding British ships. In all he captured sixty ships for the patriot cause. He was later captured twice and forced to endure a harrowing stay in prison. Following the war, perhaps due to his cantankerous personality, Conyngham was not given a commission in the United States Navy and he resumed work as a private sea captain. This rather inglorious end to his military career prompted the great maritime historian Samuel Elliot Morison to call him, "the most successful commerce-destroyer in the United States Navy and the most unfortunate."

569. Stephen Moylan Born in Cork, Stephen Moylan (1737–1811) arrived in Philadelphia in 1768. Within a few short years he became a wealthy merchant active in shipping. He cast his lot with the rebels in 1776 and spent considerable amounts of his own fortune outfitting privateers to harass British ships. He became the Continental Army's first mustermaster and later served as George Washington's secretary, followed by a stint as quartermaster general. When the latter assignment proved too difficult, he entered the army as a cavalry officer. He quarreled with Casmir Pulaski, the Polish officer in charge of the American cavalry and was eventually court-martialed. Acquitted, he returned to the field and served to the end of the war. He remained a friend of Washington until the latter's death.

570. Henry Knox Henry Knox (1750–1806) was born in Boston to immigrants from Northern Ireland. Knox was proprietor of the London Book Store in Boston until he joined a local artillery company at eighteen. In 1775 he brought fifty cannon—much needed artillery—from captured Fort Ticonderoga, thus saving them from British capture. He was promoted to brigadier-general after he directed George Washington's famous 1776 Christmas night trip across the Delaware River. Washington appointed Knox the first secretary of war under the United States Constitution. Fort Knox, Kentucky; Knox County, Maine; and Knoxville, Tennessee, all bear his name.

571. John Sullivan John Sullivan (1740–95) was born in Summersworth Parish, Maine. He became the first lawyer in Durham before being commissioned as a major in the militia in 1760. As relations between America and Britain eroded in the early 1770s, Sullivan joined the ranks of the Revolutionaries. In 1774 he led an attack on Fort William and Mary to secure munitions for the rebel cause. Some of the gunpowder seized was later used at Bunker Hill. Commissioned a major general in the Continental Army, Sullivan played a key role in defeating an allied force of Iroquois and Loyalists along the New York frontier. He resigned from the army in 1779 and entered politics, serving as a delegate to the Continental Congress in 1781 and later as governor of New Hampshire.

572. John Barry John Barry (1745–1803), the "Father of the American Navy," was born in County Wexford, Ireland. At an early age he was a cabin boy on a ship, and by the time he was fifteen he had crossed the Atlantic and arrived in Philadelphia. By the early 1770s he was a prosperous captain in the transatlantic trade.

At the outbreak of hostilities, he joined the Continental Navy and was given command of *USS Lexington.* He soon distinguished himself by becoming the first Continental Navy captain to seize a British ship (the *Edward* on April 7, 1776). For the rest of the war he battled British warships and disrupted British communications along the Atlantic coast. One of his most important missions was to convey diplomat John Laurens to France aboard the *USS Alliance.* He also had the honor of

Commodore John Barry

bringing the Marquis de Lafayette back to France after the victory at Yorktown (1781).

After the American Revolution, he returned to his work in the merchant trade. But he soon found himself called upon to help create a permanent U.S. Navy. He became its senior captain and commanded all U.S. ships in the West Indies (1798–99). He returned to Philadelphia (1801) and remained the senior naval officer until his death in 1803. Statues in Philadelphia, Washington, and Wexford, Ireland, commemorate this distinguished commodore.

573. Richard Montgomery   Richard Montgomery (1738–75) was born in Swords, County Dublin, the son of Thomas Montgomery, a baronet and member of the Irish Parliament. He joined the

Gen. Richard Montgomery

British Army in Canada in 1756 and served for sixteen years. In 1772 he moved to New York and married into the prominent Livingston family. He was appointed brigadier general by the Continental Congress in 1775, and was second in command in the successful Montreal Expedition. He then joined forces with Benedict Arnold (not yet a traitor), and was killed leading an assault on Quebec City on December 31, 1775.

574. Sharpshooter Timothy Murphy, Hero of Saratoga   Timothy Murphy (1751–1818) was born in Pike County, Pennsylvania. He became a member of Colonel Daniel Morgan's Rifle Corps, a fierce group of sharpshooters who were deadly accurate with their aim. In the Battle of Saratoga,

the turning point in the American Revolution, Murphy's marksmanship killed two British commanders. The ensuing confusion is credited as a major factor in the American victory. Murphy became the most celebrated marksman of the war. His contributions are immortalized with a monument at Saratoga erected by the local chapter of the Ancient Order of Hibernians.

575. James Moore   Colonel James Moore (1737–1777) was born in New Hanover County, North Carolina. As the senior officer of the First North Carolina Continentals in 1776, he was given command of the rebel action to defend Moore's Creek Bridge against an army of over 1,600 Loyalists. Although his force numbered only one thousand, Moore drove the Loyalists from the field in an engagement on February 27, 1776. The Moore's Creek engagement, the first major battle of the South, is considered to have been a crucial factor in determining the early course of the American Revolution.

576. Privateer Jeremiah O'Brien   Jeremiah O'Brien (1744–1818) was born in Maine and became a staunch supporter of the Revolutionary cause. On June 2, 1775, he led a raiding party (which included his four brothers) that seized the British warship *Margaretta* in Machias, Maine. The event took place five days before the Battle of Bunker Hill and is considered the first naval battle of the Revolution. O'Brien and his brother John were soon commissioned as privateers (ship captains authorized to seize enemy ships).

577. Master Spy, Hercules Mulligan   Hercules Mulligan (1740–1825) was born in Derry, Ireland. He emigrated to New York and later attended (as a classmate of Alexander Hamilton) King's College, now Columbia University. When the British took over New York City during the American Revolution, Mulligan remained in the city as a secret agent, posing as a loyalist. He gathered vital intelligence by eavesdropping on British soldiers during their frequent meetings in his clothing store. Thanks to Mulligan, Washington received early notification of his proposed kidnapping by British agents and the British plan to invade Pennsylvania. Mulligan played the part of a Tory so well that many Americans accused him of loyalism when they returned to the city at war's end. So when George Washington returned to New York in late 1783, he made a special effort to draw attention to Mulligan's patriotic services, publicly praising him as "a true friend of liberty."

578. The Irish on the Other Side   Not everyone of Irish descent supported the patriot cause. Like their fellow colonists, most Irish fell into three rather flexible categories—loyalist, patriot, and undecided. Of the loyalists who filed for compensation, 280 were Irish (compared with 470 Scots and just 290 English).

Many Irishmen fought as soldiers in several of the Irish regiments in the British Army. Others were everyday colonists who enlisted in the King's army. At first, British Commander-in-Chief Sir Henry Clinton complained that his forces had too many Irishmen whom he considered undisciplined. But by June 1778 he had changed his mind and established two regiments—The Volunteers of Ireland and The Roman Catholic Volunteers—to be comprised of Irish deserters from the Continental Army. The two regiments were eventually merged with a total of about 300 soldiers.

It was also an Irishman who played a key role in the British surrender at Yorktown. General Charles O'Hara was a British-born officer from a family with roots in Sligo and Mayo. Overwhelmed by his defeat, Cornwallis claimed he was too ill to carry out the formal surrender. So he tapped O'Hara, his second in command, who crossed into patriot lines under a white flag and presented George Washington with Cornwallis' surrender.

579. Sgt. Thomas Hickey Plots to Kill Washington One Irishman who almost played a pivotal role in

the Revolution was Sgt. Thomas Hickey. In the summer of 1776, as the British prepared to invade New York, he hatched a plot to assassinate Gen. George Washington. His motivation seems to have been sheer practicality. He believed (correctly) that Washington's army in New York would be swept aside by the far superior British forces and (incorrectly) that the war would end soon thereafter. When the plot was exposed, Hickey was arrested along with another soldier, Private Michael Lynch. The latter was acquitted, but Hickey was convicted of mutiny and sedition and hanged on the Bowery Road before a crowd of thousands.

War of 1812

580. Commodore Thomas Macdonough   Born in Delaware, Thomas Macdonough (1783–1825) enlisted in the United States Navy at the age of sixteen. During the War of 1812, he commanded the ship *Saratoga* in the September 1814 battle against the British fleet on Lake Champlain. Macdonough's victorious leadership in this decisive battle thwarted the British goal of invading and conquering New York State and Vermont.

Commodore Thomas Macdonough

Negotiations for a peace treaty began in earnest soon thereafter. Macdonough died of tuberculosis in 1825.

581. Commodore Oliver Hazard Perry, Hero of Battle of Lake Erie   Oliver Perry (1785–1819) was born at the Perry homestead in South Kingston, Rhode Island. His father was an officer in the United States Navy, his mother an immigrant from Ireland. Perry joined the navy under

Commodore Oliver Hazard Perry

the command of his father as a young teenager. In 1813 he was sent to Erie, Pennsylvania, where he defeated a British fleet on Lake Erie. In his official report of the British surrender, he wrote his familiar quote, "We have met the enemy, and they are ours." The victory at Lake Erie made Perry a naval hero and helped ensure U.S. control of the Northwest.

582. Andrew Jackson Andrew Jackson's (1767–1845) parents immigrated from County Antrim two years before his birth in 1767. Jackson's military career began at thirteen when he served in the Revolutionary War, but reached its pinnacle during the War of 1812. Jackson won a spectacular victory over the royal forces against the British-allied Creek Indians, who were threatening the Southern frontier. In a five-month-long campaign, Jackson defeated the Creeks, the final triumph being the Battle of Tohopeka (aka Horseshoe Bend) in Alabama. His most memorable triumph was his successful seizure of the city of New Orleans. Ironically, due to the slow communications of the day, the victory occurred *after* the U.S. and Great Britain agreed to a truce. Jackson would trade on his military fame in the 1820s when he ran for president.

The War for Texas Independence

583. Davy Crockett and the Irish of the Alamo
Before 1835, Texas was part of Mexico, which itself had only recently (1821) gained its independence from Spain. The government of newly independent Mexico was wary of the expanding United States to the north, but it also wanted to attract settlers—even if they were Americans—to its northern regions. So, beginning in the late 1820s, it offered contracts to any *empressario* who, in exchange for as much as forty thousand acres of land, agreed to settle a certain number of families in Mexican territory.

Among these Texas pioneers were many Irish. Indeed the Mexican government was quite keen on Irish immigrants, reasoning their Catholic faith would strengthen their loyalty to the Mexican government. Two notable Irish *empressarios* were James McGloin and John McMullen, who in 1828 received a large land grant for the settlement of two hundred families. The next year they brought Irish families from New York, establishing the "Villa de San Patricio de Hibernia" (town of St. Patrick of Ireland) on the Neuces River's north bank. The town became the county seat of San Patricio County, Texas, after Texas independence. In 1834, two more Irishmen, James Power and James Heweston, likewise established a settlement named *Refugio* (Refuge) on the Gulf of Mexico to which they brought dozens of families directly from Ireland.

By the early 1830s, the more than twenty thousand American settlers in Texas easily outnumbered their Mexican counterparts. The Mexican government passed laws to slow the tide of American immigration, but to no avail. To make matters worse, few of these settlers exhibited much affection for the Mexican government, especially after the overbearing Gen. Antonio López de Santa Anna became President in 1833. Protest soon flourished into open rebellion, and by late 1835 the war for Texas independence was on.

In early 1836, the Mexican Army under Santa Anna moved north to reimpose Mexican control over the restive Mexican state of Texas. A Texan army was formed to stop Santa Anna, but needed time to convene. Some five hundred frontiersmen gathered in south Texas, determined to buy time for the main Texan army. Approximately 183 of the five hundred decided to occupy the

The Battle of the Alamo

Alamo in San Antonio, to delay Santa Anna's army. Three Scotch-Irish Americans, Davy Crockett, Jim Bowie, and William Barrett Travis, led the group, which included twelve Irish immigrants and other Scotch-Irish from Tennessee and Kentucky. Santa Anna's army surrounded and overwhelmed the fort in hand-to-hand combat. The battle's survivors were executed. The other faction of the Texan army, which included many settlers from Irish colonies in south Texas, was surrounded by Santa Anna at Goliad and also executed. It would fall to another descendant of Irish immigrants, Sam Houston, to avenge the fall of the Alamo in the Battle of San Jacinto.

Mexican-American War

584. The San Patricios The San Patricio Battalion of the Mexican Army was named for the emblem on its flag: St. Patrick, depicted with a harp and shamrock. The San Patricios were founded by John Riley, a British Army veteran who deserted in April 1846 before war was declared. Although legend has it that the entire regiment comprised deserters like Riley, recent research by historian Michael Hogan indicates that only about one third were deserters. Many of them had been enticed by the Mexican government's propaganda that claimed the war was a Protestant crusade against Catholicism and by its offer of land grants of 320 acres. Others were compelled by the harsh treatment meted out to Irish Catholics in American society in general, and in the U.S. Army in particular.

The unit numbered slightly more than two hundred, with perhaps as many as half being Irish-born or Irish American. The remainder were Mexican, German, and American-born. The unit earned a reputation for fierce fighting, perhaps because so many knew they faced certain execution for desertion if captured.

Still, seventy-two San Patricios were captured

when American forces overran the fortress of Churubusco. Eleven were whipped and branded with a "D," the punishment for deserting before the hostilities. Fifty others were quickly court-martialed and sentenced to hang. Twenty were hanged on September 10, 1847, in the town of San Angel. The remaining thirty were scheduled to hang in the town of Mixcoac on September 13. Their scaffold was built on a hill overlooking Chapultepec, which was about to be attacked by the U.S. Army. The San Patricios were informed that they would live until the American flag flew over the fortress. The condemned men watched hopelessly for a few hours as the Mexican defenders slowly succumbed to the American onslaught. All were hanged within an hour of Chapultepec's surrender.

In 1959 the Mexican government unveiled a memorial to the San Patricios in the Plaza de San Jacinto in San Angel. The inscription reads: "In memory of the Irish soldiers of the heroic San Patricio battalion, martyrs who gave their lives for the cause of Mexico during the unjust North American invasion of 1847."

585. General Winfield Scott Comments on His Irish Soldiers
The great majority of Irish and Irish American soldiers in the U.S. Army did not desert and earned a reputation for reliability and courage. As Gen. Winfield Scott noted two years after the war concluded:

> In Mexico, we estimated the number of persons in the army, foreigners by birth, at about 3500, & of these more than 2000 were Irish. . . . It is hazardous, or may be invidious, to make distinctions; but truth obliges me to say that, of our Irish soldiers—save a few who deserted from General Taylor . . . not one ever turned his back upon the enemy or faltered in advancing to the charge.

—Gen. Winfield Scott, July 1850

Gen. James Shields

586. James Shields
Born in Ireland, James Shields (1810–79) emigrated to Illinois at age sixteen. A Black Hawk War veteran, Shields served as a brigadier general during the Mexican War. He led a brigade of volunteer troops during the drive from Veracruz to Mexico City. Shot through the lung at Cerro Gordo in April 1847, he was breveted to major general for his conduct in that battle. His men also contributed to victories at Churubusco and Chapultepec, where he was again wounded. Shields remained with the army in Mexico until mustered out in 1848.

Shields would later rejoin the army to fight in the Civil War. He also enjoyed a successful career in politics, including election to the U. S. Senate from three different states (Illinois, Missouri, and Minnesota; see entry #329).

587. Stephen Watts Kearney
Steven Watts Kearney (1794–1848) was born in New Jersey. He joined the army in 1812 and made a career out of military service. Cited for bravery and promoted before the War of 1812 ended, he afterward chose frontier duty. During the Mexican War, he was given the vital assignment of capturing New Mexico and California. New Mexico capitulated peacefully, but in California Kearney fought and won a major battle near San Diego before marching on Los Angeles and winning the Battle of San Bernardino. A national hero as a result of his military success, Kearney spent three months settling California's political situation before returning east.

The Civil War

588. The Irish in the Civil War The Civil War provided the Irish in America with a superb, if grim, opportunity to disprove the nativist claim that they would never make loyal, patriotic citizens. More than 144,000 Irish-born served in the Union Army. In addition, tens of thousands of American-born Irish also served. Thousands ended up giving their lives for the Union and eighty-nine Irish-born soldiers would earn Congressional Medals of Honor.

One of the reasons so many Irish served in the Civil War was their relative poverty. Many Irish immigrants stepped off ships in America and were immediately confronted by Union Army recruiters offering two- to three-hundred-dollar cash bonuses for enlistment. For penniless immigrants with no specialized skills, this offer—equal to a year's pay at the beginning of the war—was too good to refuse.

Another inducement to enlistment was an appeal to nationalism. Many regiments were formed under ethnic names like Mulligan's Brigade and Corcoran's Legion. The recruiting posters often made clear that England, Ireland's historic oppressor, was sympathetic to the Confederacy. Some hoped to gain military experience that they could later use in an uprising in Ireland against British rule. Indeed, many of the most ardent Fenians of the late 1860s were veterans of the Union Army.

589. Thomas Francis Meagher Calls the Irish to Arms Thomas Francis Meagher (1823–67) participated in the Young Ireland uprising of 1848 and was

Gen. Thomas Francis Meagher

exiled to Australia by the British government. He later escaped and came to America where he assumed a leading role in the Irish nationalist movement. Famous for his oratory, he issued an inspiring call to the American Irish to fight for the Union, linking the effort to the cause of Irish freedom:

> The Republic, that gave us asylum and an honorable career—that is the mainstay of human freedom the world over—is threatened with disruption. It is the duty of every liberty-loving citizen to prevent such a calamity at all hazards. Above all, it is the duty of us Irish citizens, who aspired to establish a similar form of government in our native land. It is not only our duty to America, but also to Ireland.

Meagher soon formed the Irish Brigade. He hoped the unit's performance would raise the low standing of the Irish in American eyes and provide experienced recruits to a future Fenian uprising in Ireland.

590. Michael Corcoran (1827–63) Michael Corcoran was one of the most influential men in Irish America before the war. An Ulster native, he was forced to emigrate in 1849 when local authorities prepared to arrest him, rightly, for conducting nocturnal raids against landlords. He went to New York, where he became an Irish nationalist leader. He joined the 69th New York Militia, rising to become its colonel. He gained national recognition in 1860 for refusing to lead his regiment in a parade honoring the Prince of Wales during the regent's New York visit. When the war started, Corcoran actively recruited Fenians into the 69th, hoping to lead them back to Ireland. He was captured at First Manassas and stayed in Richmond's infamous Libby Prison until August 1862. After his release he raised five new Irish regiments, called the Corcoran Legion. They served in

Suffolk, Virginia, and in the defense of Washington before Corcoran, constantly ill since his imprisonment, died in December 1863.

591. The Fighting 69th and the Irish Brigade

Formed in 1851, the 69th New York Militia was composed solely of Irish from its inception. During the 1850s, Irish revolutionary exiles gravitated to the unit, forming most of its officer corps when the war began. The unit's exemplary performance at the first Battle of Bull Run convinced the Union to permit the formation of an Irish Brigade, with the 69th at its core.

The Irish Brigade was founded by Brigadier General Thomas Meagher in August 1861. Originally composed of the 63rd, 69th, and 88th New York regiments, the 29th Massachusetts was attached during the Peninsula Campaign to bring the brigade up to strength. Composed of anti-Irish American natives, the 29th was traded out for the Irish 28th Massachusetts after Antietam. The brigade was completed in October 1862 when the 116th Pennsylvania, also predominantly Irish, was attached.

The Brigade distinguished itself by engaging in some of the most savage fighting of the war: in hand-to-hand combat versus Wheat's Louisiana Tigers at Malvern Hill, charging the "Bloody Lane" at Antietam, charging "The Stone Wall" at Fredericksburg, again fighting hand-to-hand versus Hood's Texans at Gettysburg's "Wheatfield," and charging the "Mule Shoe" at Spotsylvania. While these battles gained the nation's respect, they also resulted in horrific casualty rates.

592. Battle of Marye's Heights, Fredericksburg

On December 13, 1862, Union forces assaulted Confederate entrenchments along a ridge known as Marye's Heights, in Fredericksburg, Virginia. Fourteen waves of attackers were sent across open fields against the fortified Confederate position. All were shattered by repeated volleys of Confederate fire. The Irish Brigade was in the third wave, and achieved international fame with the tenaciousness of their attack. Eliciting cheers from their Confederate adversaries, many of whom were Irish themselves, their attack collapsed when the Brigade's officers were felled. Of the fourteen attacks, the Irish came closest to attaining the ridge. The Brigade was permanently crippled by the 45 percent losses it sustained in the attack.

In the aftermath of the futile assault on Marye's Heights, Gen. Robert E. Lee commented on the extraordinary courage exhibited by the men of the Irish Brigade.

> Never were men so brave. They ennobled their race by their splendid gallantry on that desperate occasion. Though totally routed, they reaped a harvest of glory. Their brilliant, though hopeless assaults on our lines excited the hearty applause of our officers and men.

593. Private Miles O'Reilly

Private Miles O'Reilly authored a series of wry letters published in the *New York Herald* during the war, commenting on life in the Union army and the war's conduct. The letters were so popular that they were published in two volumes in 1864. Purportedly a member of the 47th New York Infantry, O'Reilly was actually Charles Graham Halpine (1829–68), an army officer and former journalist and poet who immigrated to America from Dublin in 1851. He served in the Irish Brigade and, restricted by his rank from criticizing the conduct of the war, created O'Reilly to voice his views.

594. George G. Meade

Lauded as the Victor of Gettysburg, George G. Meade (1815–72) rose to command the Army of the Potomac through steady, although unspectacular, service. A frustrated Lincoln had elevated to him to commander of the Army of the Potomac in 1863, having gone through several generals who proved incompetent or timid. At Gettysburg, Meade's superior force withstood Lee's offensive thrust into northern territory. But his unwillingness to pursue and destroy the retreating Confederate Army proved a major disappointment to Lincoln and led him to make Ulysses S. Grant general-in-chief with ultimate authority over all armies, including Meade's Army of the Potomac in 1864. Meade proved adept at carrying out Grant's orders, which allowed Grant to concentrate on coordinating all U.S. forces, and bringing the war to a close within a year. After the war, Meade, whose ancestors immigrated from Kerry in 1690, directed the quashing of the 1867 Fenian invasion of Canada. He died from pneumonia, complicated by old war wounds.

595. Philip Sheridan   "Little Phil" (he was 5'4") Sheridan (1831–88) was the son of Irish immigrants. A West Point graduate (1853), his aggressive fighting style during the Civil War

earned him rapid promotion. In 1864, he was given command of all U.S. cavalry. He played a key role in bringing about the eventual defeat of Robert E. Lee's Army of Northern Virginia, defeating J.E.B. Stuart, eliminating the Confederate Army of the Valley, burning Lee's food supplies in the

Gen. Philip Sheridan

Shenandoah Valley, and cutting off the routes he needed to gain more. In April 1865 at the Battle of Five Forks, he defeated Lee and forced the Confederate flight that soon ended in surrender. Years later, as commander of the Army, he formulated and enforced U.S. Indian policy in the west.

596. St. Clair Augustin Mulholland   St. Clair Augustin Mulholland (1839–1910) was born in Lisburn, County Antrim. He came to America as a child with his family and settled in Philadelphia. A member of his local militia, Mulholland helped organize the 116th Pennsylvania Infantry, a regiment that eventually joined the famed Irish Brigade. Lt. Colonel Mulholland was wounded for the first time participating in the famous, if futile, charge up Marye's Heights during the Battle of Fredericksburg. Promoted to the rank of major, he led the recapture of a federal battery in the battle of Chancellorsville (May 1863). Wounded at both the Battle of the Wilderness and Totopotomy Creek in May 1864, Mulholland returned to command in the fall of that year and stayed on for the duration of the war. In March 1865, after taking a Confederate stronghold at Boydton Plank Road, he was promoted to brigadier general. For his exceptional service in the Civil War, Mulholland was awarded the Congressional Medal of Honor.

597. Stephen C. Rowan   The family of Stephen C. Rowan (1808–90) emigrated from Ireland when he was ten. He entered the navy in 1826, entering the officer ranks nine years later. Rowan was instrumental in the acquisition of California during the Mexican War. During the Civil War, he helped pioneer the art of amphibious assault, establishing the use of naval cannonade to support troop landings at Roanoke Island, North Carolina. He cooperated with the army to capture the North Carolina coast north of Wilmington in 1862, ending the area's use to blockade-runners. He commanded the blockade vessel *USS New Ironsides* off Charleston, South Carolina, until late 1864, when he was transferred to shore duty.

598. Mathew Brady   One of the most profound innovations to affect the character of the Civil War was not related to military technology at all: It was photography. The leading practitioner of this new medium at the time of the Civil War was Mathew Brady (1823–96). Born in upstate New

York, he later moved to New York City where he learned the new daguerreotype imaging process and in 1844 opened a lavish Daguerrean Miniature Gallery on lower Broadway in New York.

Within five years Brady became one of the nation's most highly regarded portraitists. In 1849 he opened a studio in Washington, D.C., and the next year published *Gallery of Illustrious Americans*, a book featuring the portraits of twenty-four prominent individuals, including U.S. presidents, inventors, and writers. In 1858 he opened the National Photographic Art Gallery in Washington and two years later the National Portrait Gallery in New York.

When the war came, Brady assembled his team of more than thirty assistants and sent them to photograph the conflict. Initially, they mainly photographed Union officers or scenes of camp life. That changed with the battle of Antietam in September 1862. Upon hearing of the battle, Brady sent two of his assistant photographers, Alexander Gardner and James F. Gibson, to Sharpsburg. There they took hundreds of photographs of the battle's aftermath. Most focused on the thousands of fallen soldiers whose bodies littered the landscape.

Brady put the grim collection of photographs on display in his New York gallery under the title "The Dead of Antietam." Tens of thousands paraded by the exhibit in astonishment. For generations people on the home front had relied upon writers and artists to convey the scenes of conflict and carnage. Now photographers could capture such images in unprecedented detail and realism. "The dead of the battle-

Mathew Brady

field come up to us very rarely, even in dreams," commented the *New York Times*, "We see the list in the morning paper at breakfast, but dismiss its recollection with the coffee . . . Mr. Brady has done something to bring home to us the terrible reality and earnestness of war. If he has not brought the bodies and laid them in our dooryards and along streets, he has done something very like it." Americans and indeed people around the world would never look at war the same way again.

599. Bridget Divers Bridget Divers served alongside her husband in the 1st Michigan Cavalry during the Civil War as a vivandiere. These women served as nurses, color bearers, and sometimes as soldiers, although their role was intended to be noncombative in nature. Known also as Michigan Bridget, Irish Bridget, Bridget Danvers, and Bridget Devers, she fought during the war and is also believed to have worked as a nurse at the White House and as Postmistress.

Bridget earned respect from the troops, not only because her husband served in the same regiment, but for her valor as well. She mobilized her regiment under fire twice and was seen firing her weapon on several occasions. She also galloped through enemy lines during the battle of Cedar Creek. She followed her husband when he was transferred to the frontier in 1865, working as a laundress for the remainder of her life.

600. Jenny Hodgers Little is known of Jenny Hodgers (1844–1915) before the Civil War, other than the fact that she was born in Belfast, came to America as a stowaway, and settled in Belvidere, Illinois. What is known is that she disguised herself as a man and enlisted in Company G of the 95th Illinois Volunteer Infantry. Known to her fellow soldiers as Albert Cashier, Hodgers served from 1862 to 1865 without ever being detected. She fought with the regiment at Vicksburg, Red River, and Nashville, ending up in Mobile, Alabama, at the war's end. Mustered out, she returned to Illinois, where she took up farming. She lived the rest of her days under the guise of a man. The truth of her identity was discovered in 1911 when she received medical treatment for a broken leg, but the doctor agreed to keep it secret. Hodgers' story was revealed to the public when she was committed to an insane asylum at the age of seventy and officials discovered her true sex. After an official inquiry, the Bureau of Pensions in Washington declared that Jennie Hodgers was indeed Albert Cashier who had served in the 95th Illinois Volunteer Infantry. When she died in 1915 she was given a funeral with full military honors.

601. Irish Confederates Although the 144,000 Irish who served in the Union army are better known, thirty thousand Irish also served the Confederacy. They came principally from the South's cities, such as New Orleans, and formed some of the hardest fighting Confederate units. The most notable Confederate Irish units were the 1st Virginia Infantry, 10th Tennessee Infantry, Cobb's [Georgia] Legion, and the 6th Louisiana Infantry (also known as "Wheat's Tigers," after their commander). Mistrusted at first by Confederate generals who remembered the San Patricios from the Mexican War, the Irish units quickly put those doubts to rest by fighting savagely, even when facing Northern Irish units as they did at Antietam and Fredericksburg.

Like their northern counterparts, many southern Irish intended to gain combat experience for an eventual Fenian uprising in Ireland. However, the southerners also were dedicated to State's Rights ideology, seeing it as analogous to Ireland's struggle against Britain.

602. Matthew Fontaine Maury A descendant of Irish Huguenot immigrants, Matthew Fontaine Maury (1806–73) entered the U.S. Navy as a midshipman in 1825. He traveled around the world and became fascinated by oceanography, astronomy, and navigation. Upon his return he took time off to publish the first of several influential books on navigation, *A New Theoretical and Practical Treatise on Navigation* (1836). Promoted to lieutenant, he was asked to conduct a survey of the southeast coast of the United States. Concerned about the readiness of the U.S. Navy, he wrote many articles urging the creation of a naval academy. By the mid-1840s, Maury was superintendant of the U.S. Naval Observatory. There he conducted studies of oceanography and published *Wind and Current Chart of the North Atlantic* (1847) and *Abstract Log for the Use of American Navigators* (1848). His greatest work came in 1855, *The Physical Geography of the Sea,* a landmark book in oceanography that greatly enhanced navigation and cut down on travel times. When his home state of Virginia seceded in 1861, he joined the Confederate States Navy. After designing the James River defenses, he was transferred to England as a navy purchasing agent. After the war he taught meteorology at the Virginia Military Institute.

603. Stonewall Jackson Thomas Jonathan Jackson (1824–63) emerged as one of the most effective military commanders of the Confederate Army in the early days of the war. At the first battle of Bull Run in June 1861, he earned his nickname when a commander seeking to rally his troops shouted, "See, there is Jackson, standing like a stone-wall." Thereafter he became Robert E. Lee's most trusted lieutenant. He waged a brilliant Shenandoah Valley campaign from May to June 1862, striking terror into the Union for the threat he posed to Washington, D.C. Jackson later played a key role in Lee's strategy at the Battle of Seven Days, Second Bull Run, Antietam, and Fredericksburg. At the Battle of Chancellorsville in May 1863, Jackson once again flanked the Union army paving the way for a smashing Confederate victory. But in the course of battle he was mortally wounded by "friendly fire" from his own troops. His death dealt a serious blow to the Confederate cause.

604. Patrick Cleburne, "Stonewall of the West" Patrick Cleburne (1828–64) joined the 15th Arkansas as a private in 1861, and within three years was known as "The Stonewall of the West." Born in Ireland, Cleburne emigrated to the South in 1849, after a short tour in the British Army. Elected captain of the 15th after joining, he exhibited extraordinary leadership and tactical ability, resulting in a rapid rise to major general. Criticism of his commanding officer, Braxton Bragg, and his 1864 proposal to emancipate slaves willing to fight in Confederate service, halted his rise. He died leading a charge at the Battle of Franklin, November 30, 1864.

605. Robert Kennedy Tries to Burn New York Confederate spy Robert Kennedy led a team of Confederate secret agents in a plot to burn New York City. Initially, the arson attack was to occur on the eve of the 1864 presidential election. Confederates hoped the planned inferno would terrorize and demoralize the Union, leading voters to elect Democrat George B. McClellan over Abraham Lincoln. McClellan, the former Union Army general, was believed to be in favor of a cease-fire followed by a negotiated settlement between North and South. At the very least, a massive fire in New York City would seriously impair the Union war effort, as New York was the North's financial center and a major military post.

But logistical problems forced Kennedy and his fellow conspirators to delay their arson spree until after the election. On November 25, 1864, Kennedy and six others checked into separate hotels where at a prearranged time they set their rooms on fire. To allow the fires to progress without detection, the men were instructed to close the windows and doors of their rooms. Instead, it slowed the fires down by limiting their supply of oxygen. In the end the fires caused little damage and were quickly extinguished. One conspirator, however, also set fire to P.T. Barnum's Museum across the street from his hotel and it burned to the ground. Kennedy's coconspirators

escaped to Canada. He was captured and executed.

606. Michael O'Laughlin and the Plot to Kill Lincoln On June 30, 1865, Michael O'Laughlin was found guilty of conspiracy in the assassination of Abraham Lincoln. The previous January, Confederate veteran O'Laughlin hesitantly agreed to help John Wilkes Booth, a childhood friend, kidnap Lincoln and bring him to Richmond in a last-ditch effort to save the Confederacy. After two failed attempts, O'Laughlin quit. When Richmond fell, Booth decided to assassinate Lincoln instead. O'Laughlin was named as an accomplice and arrested. He was sentenced to life in prison and shipped to Fort Jefferson in the Dry Tortugas, where he died during a yellow fever epidemic in 1867.

607. Varina Howell Davis Varina Howell Davis (1826–1905) was the Confederacy's first and only First Lady. Born in Natchez, Mississippi, Varina was the granddaughter of Colonel James Kemp, an educated Irish immigrant who became a successful and respected planter in Mississippi. She married local planter Jefferson Davis when she was seventeen. Her interest in politics was whetted, not dimmed, when Davis was elected to Congress and eventually rose to cabinet status. As First Lady, she advised Davis on political matters and tried to serve as a model of strength to the women of the South as the Confederacy's economy worsened. After the war, her incessant lobbying secured Davis' release from prison in 1867.

608. Fr. Abram Ryan, Poet of the Confederacy Born in Maryland, Abram Ryan (1838–86) was ordained a Catholic priest and served as a chaplain in the Confederate Army. Following the war he served as a parish priest in several cities, including Mobile, Alabama. He began writing poetry and on May 19, 1866, his first published poem, "The Conquered Banner," appeared in the pages of the *Freeman's Journal.* The poem became an overnight sensation. It was reprinted in papers across the South and soon set to the music of a popular hymn. Its spirit and tone are captured in the last stanza:

> Furl that Banner, softly, slowly!
> Treat it gently—it is holy—
> For it droops above the dead.
> Touch it not—unfold it never,
> Let it droop there, furled forever,
> For its people's hopes are dead!

Within months it was being recited or sung everywhere from parlors to public meetings.

Published thirteen months after Gen. Robert E. Lee surrendered at Appomattox, it captured the spirit of sentimentality and martyrdom then emerging in the war-torn South. It was the first notable contribution to what came to be known as the "Lost Cause" genre of Southern literature and song. The characterization of the South's bid for independence as noble and tragic, was born.

Inspired by his success, Ryan continued to write poems in the "Lost Cause" style for the next two decades. Among the more memorable are, "C.S.A.," "The Sword of Robert E. Lee," and "The South." All touched on the now-familiar themes of heroic sacrifice by men pledged to defend their native land against a powerful, tyrannical invader. "There's grandeur in graves," reads one line, "There's glory in gloom." The similarity between Ryan's work and rhetoric, poetry, and song of Irish nationalism is striking. Not surprisingly, among Ryan's collected poems one finds several about Ireland's struggle for freedom.

Ryan was the first, but by no means the last contributor to the Lost Cause idea. In fact, the phrase Lost Cause comes from a book written by Edward A. Pollard and published a few months after "The Conquered Banner" appeared. In the decades that followed, a veritable Lost Cause industry arose, producing hundreds of books, poems, and songs, not to mention countless memorials to Confederate warriors.

Spanish-American War

609. Alfred Thayer Mahan Alfred Thayer Mahan (1840–1914), an author and naval officer, was born in West Point, New York, in 1840. Mahan's father, Thomas, was the son of Irish immigrants who had fled Ireland after the unsuccessful rising of 1798. Mahan attended the United States Naval Academy, and served in the navy for over forty years. He became president of the Naval War College in 1886, where he had been a lecturer on history and strategy. His book *The Influence of Sea Power upon History* established him as one of the world's leading authorities on naval strategy. The immensely influential book convinced many that the U.S. needed to build up its navy and establish friendly ports around the world. War with Spain provided both an opportunity to test this new navy and to acquire several territories of strategic importance, among them Puerto Rico, Cuba, and the Philippines.

610. The Rough Riders Even before the United States declared war on Spain in 1898, Theodore Roosevelt (he was a descendent of Irish immigrants from Meath and Antrim) established the first United States Volunteer Cavalry Regiment. Known popularly as the Rough Riders, it was comprised of approximately one thousand men. Recruited from the ranks of businessmen, college athletes, cowboys, and others, the Rough Riders left for Cuba and fought in the decisive battle known as San Juan Hill (which actually took place on nearby Kettle Hill). Their gallant charge up the hill earned the regiment—and its most famous member— popular adulation.

One of those

Teddy Roosevelt as a Rough Rider

who didn't come home to cheers was Colonel William "Bucky" O'Neill. Born to Irish immigrant parents in St. Louis, Missouri, O'Neill played a key role in forming the famous Rough Riders and accompanied them to Cuba in the spring of 1898. At the battle of San Juan (Kettle) Hill, O'Neill was killed by a sharpshooter. His family buried him in Arlington National Cemetery, and a number of years later a statue was dedicated to him in the plaza of City Hall in Prescott, Arizona.

611. The Decorated Irish-Born   In addition to the thousands of Irish Americans who served in the U.S. armed forces during the war, countless Irish-born men did as well. Eleven of the latter Irish-born soldiers earned Congressional Medals of Honor for their service.

World War I

612. Irish American Opposition to the U.S. Entry into the War   When World War I broke out in the summer of 1914, Irish Americans joined the rest of America in opposing U.S. involvement. For most Americans, this was simply an expression of traditional American isolationism. For Irish Americans, however, there were additional reasons, most especially the long-standing belief that whatever was bad for England had to be good for Ireland. At the very least they balked at the idea of American soldiers—no doubt many of them Irish American—being sent to die on behalf of His Majesty's empire. They rejected John Redmond's decision to pledge Irish support to the British war effort as a means to gain home rule after the war. Irish American opposition reached its apex in the months following the 1916 Easter Rising and summary executions of the leaders. Still, when the U.S. declared war on Germany in April 1917, Irish Americans set aside their nationalist ideals and cast their support to the American cause.

613. "Over There"   On April 7, 1917, as soon as he heard that America had declared war on Germany, famed songwriter George M. Cohan set about writing a patriotic song that would soon become the World War I anthem, "Over There." "I read the war headlines and I got to thinking and humming to myself," he later recalled. "Soon I was all finished with the chorus and the verse, and by the time I got to town I had a title." Finished in a single day, the song proved wildly popular, selling millions of copies of sheet music and records. Woodrow Wilson declared that it inspired American manhood. In 1940, Cohan received a Congressional Medal of Honor for "Over There" and "You're a Grand Ole Flag."

614. The Irish Brigade   The 69th New York National Guard Regiment, made famous as part of the Irish Brigade during the Civil War, once again emerged as a showcase unit of the U.S. Army. One of its members, the poet Joyce Kilmer, who was later killed in action, wrote of the inspiration behind the regiment's recruiting strategy:

> It was desired to enlist strong, intelligent, decent living men, men whose sturdy Americanism was strengthened and vivified by their Celtic blood, men who would be worthy successors to their forgotten patriots who at Bloody Lane and Marye's Heights earned the title "The Fighting Irish."

Despite Kilmer's reference to Celtic blood, the Brigade this time around was merely heavily Irish in composition, as soldiers of many ethnic backgrounds joined its ranks. Still, its two key leaders—Col. William J. "Wild Bill" Donovan and Chaplain Fr. Francis Patrick Duffy—kept alive the association with the Irish.

The 69th saw action early in France, playing an important role in battles at Lorraine, Champagne, Champagne-Marne, Aisne-Marne, and St. Mihiel, Meuse-Argonne. No regiment saw more action than the 69th and as a result, it suffered high casualty rates—644 killed and nearly 2,900 wounded out of 3,500 total men. The men of the 69th earned numerous honors and awards, including Donovan's Medal of Honor (see entry #626).

615. Fr. Francis Patrick Duffy   Patrick Duffy (1871–1932) was born to parents who fled the

Fr. Francis Duffy

Great Famine in Ireland. The third of eleven children, he studied for the priesthood at St. Joseph's Provincial Seminary at Troy, New York, and was ordained in 1896. During World War I, Duffy served as a military chaplain to the "Fighting Sixty-Ninth" Regiment of the New York National Guard. He was decorated in France and America, and became a national hero. After his death in 1932, Duffy was honored by a statue in New York's Times Square.

616. Billy Mitchell   Brigadier General William "Billy" Mitchell (1879–1936) was born in Nice, France, the son of Senator John L. Mitchell. He joined the army at the outbreak of the Spanish-American War, beginning a military career that lasted until 1926. He learned to fly airplanes in 1916 with the Signal Corps and went to Europe to observe military flying during World War I. When the U.S. entered the war, he was a key figure in forming the American air program. As a colonel he led the allied air forces in offensives at St. Mihiel and Meuse-Argonne. His exploits were carried in the popular press and he ended the war a brigadier general and a household name.

Mitchell soon became assistant chief of the Air Service and an outspoken advocate for in-

creased air power and an air force separate from the army and navy. He faced strong opposition from a conservative military establishment that saw little use for the airplane. To show the vulnerability of naval ships to air strikes, he staged dramatic sinkings in 1921 and 1922 by aircraft of seven captured German ships. He also wrote two books on the subject. Mitchell was eventually court-martialed in 1925 for his public criticisms of the War Department and navy over the issue of air training and preparedness. Found guilty and sentenced to a five-year suspension, he retired from the military instead. He spent the last ten years of his life writing and speaking on the need for improving American air power. He died in 1936 before his predictions—including one that the Japanese would attack Pearl Harbor—materialized. Many of his theories were used in WWII. He was awarded a Congressional medal posthumously in 1948 by the chief of staff of the new independent U.S. Air Force.

World War II

On the High Seas

617. Admiral Daniel J. Callaghan   Daniel J. Callaghan (1892–1942) served as President Roosevelt's naval aide at the beginning of World War II. In November 1942, after being appointed chief of staff of South Pacific forces, he took command of the cruiser-destroyer squadron that intercepted a Japanese attack against Guadalcanal. In the early-morning hours of November 13, 1942, Callaghan's cruisers launched a surprise attack on an enemy fleet south of Savo Island. Although substantially outnumbered, U.S. forces routed the Japanese. During the attack, however, a shell struck the bridge of the flagship *USS San Francisco*, killing Admiral Callaghan and 106 officers and crewmen. Callaghan was awarded the Medal of Honor posthumously.

618. Admiral Daniel V. Gallery   Born in Chicago,

Daniel V. Gallery (1901–77) had an illustrious forty-three-year naval career. A graduate of the U.S. Naval Academy in Annapolis and the U.S. Navy Postgraduate School, Gallery demonstrated exceptional skill in antisubmarine warfare during World War II. In 1942, while commanding the Fleet Air Base in Reykjavic, Iceland he earned the Bronze Star for combat operations against the U-boats. He was appointed commanding officer and assigned to the *USS Guadalcanal* in September 1943. Under his command, the *USS Guadalcanal* Task Groups sank three German submarines and captured one (U-505)—the first enemy ship seized by the navy in 129 years. The latter effort earned the Task Group a Presidential Unit Citation and Captain Gallery the Distinguished Service Medal. After the war, Admiral Gallery was appointed to numerous high-ranking positions and wrote several popular books about the navy.

619. Admiral William D. Leahy   William D. Leahy (1875–1959) was born in Hampton, Iowa. He served in the Spanish-American War and World War I, where he rose to the highest position in the U.S. Navy—chief of naval operations. He retired in 1939 and went on to serve as governor of Puerto Rico and ambassador to Vichy, France. Recalled to active duty in 1942, he became chief of staff to President Franklin Roosevelt and was one of his most trusted advisors on military matters. In 1944 he was promoted to fleet admiral, becoming one of the first officers in the U.S. military to hold a five-star rank. Leahy continued in his role as military chief of staff for President Harry S. Truman, holding the post until his retirement in 1949.

620. Fr. Joseph T. O'Callahan   Fr. Joseph O'Callahan, S.J. (1905–64), taught math and physics at Holy Cross College in Worcester, Massachusetts, before enlisting in the navy as a chaplain during World War II. His heroism during a Japanese attack of his ship, the *USS Franklin,*

earned O'Callahan the Congressional Medal of Honor—the first chaplain to receive this honor. After the war, O'Callahan returned to Holy Cross College to resume teaching. A year after his death, the navy named a ship in his honor and dedicated a memorial to him in the Medal of Honor Grove of Freedom Foundation.

621. Andrew Jackson Higgins   His motto was "The hell I can't" and it served him well. Born in Nebraska, Andrew Jackson Higgins (1886–1952) never graduated from high school. After a stint in the coast guard, he settled in New Orleans and found work in the lumber industry, eventually starting his own lumber business. His foray into shipbuilding began when he needed ships to carry the lumber he imported from around the world. Lumber and shipbuilding proved a good match and by the time the Japanese bombed Pearl Harbor, Higgins owned a major shipbuilding enterprise. One of the crafts he designed for the oil industry to explore the swamps in Louisiana prepared him well for the task of designing landing craft for World War II. Higgins also had great foresight. He anticipated the shortage of steel and the need for boats that the war would produce so he bought the entire 1939 crop of mahogany from the Philippines and stored it for future use.

When World War II broke out, the United States Navy announced a design competition for a high-speed troop transport capable of landing in shallow water. Higgins applied and so impressed the military officials with his LCVP (landing craft, vehicle and personnel) that they awarded him with a major contract. His boats transformed the nature of modern war, allowing for fast and efficient landing of soldiers and equipment along enemy shorelines. Thousands of "Higgins Boats," as they were called, made the June 6, 1944, D-Day invasion possible. By war's end tens of thousands were at work in his huge Higgins Industries complex in New Orleans. They produced 20,094 boats—more than 90 percent of the U.S. Navy fleet.

The highest and most authoritative testament to Higgins' genius came from the man who knew best. "He is the man who won the war for us," asserted General Dwight D. Eisenhower in 1964. "If Higgins had not designed and built the LCVPs, we never could have landed over an open beach. The whole strategy of the war would have been different." Higgins was all but forgotten by the general public after his death in 1952, but recent D-Day commemorations and the enormous popularity of the film *Saving Private Ryan* have given momentum to the initiative to build a National D-Day Museum in New Orleans, the seat of Higgins Industries.

622. The Sullivan Brothers   The five Sullivan brothers, Albert, Francis, George, Joseph and Madison, were born in Waterloo, Iowa, between 1914 and 1920. In 1937, George and Francis enlisted in the navy. They were followed by their three younger brothers shortly after the bombing of Pearl Harbor plunged the U.S. into war. In February 1942 all five were assigned to the light cruiser, the *USS Juneau*. After service in the Pacific, including combat actions in the Guadalcanal Campaign, they were lost on November 13, 1942, when a Japanese submarine torpedoed and sank the ship. The tragedy received

The Sullivan Brothers

extensive press coverage in the United States, resulting in a new navy policy prohibiting family members from serving together in the same ship.

The story of the Sullivan Brothers was commemorated in the patriotic film, *The Fighting Sullivans*. The Navy commemorated the Sullivans by naming a destroyer in their honor. The *USS The Sullivans* served the Navy until final decommissioning in 1965. A second *The Sullivans* was launched in 1997 and is homeported in Mayport, Florida.

In the Air

623. Colin Kelly   The first hero of World War II was Captain Colin Kelly. His bomber sunk a Japanese warship on December 9, 1941, just two days after Pearl Harbor, when the nation needed a piece of good news. Tragically, Kelly's plane was struck by enemy gunners and he died in the crash. In honor of his accomplishment, the military posthumously awarded him the Distinguished Service Cross.

624. Edward H. O'Hare   Lieutenant Commander Edward H. "Butch" O'Hare was born in 1914 in St. Louis, the son of E. J. O'Hare, a prominent businessman and attorney. He entered the military after graduating from Western Military Academy in 1933. O'Hare was assigned to VF-3, the *USS Saratoga*'s Fighting Squadron. He was awarded the Congressional Medal of Honor in 1942 for single-handedly shooting down five enemy bombers and wounding a sixth. He died on November 27, 1943, at the age of twenty-nine in the navy's first night-fighting combat mission. O'Hare International Airport in Chicago is named in honor of this WWII hero.

625. Thomas B. McGuire   Flying Ace Major Thomas B. McGuire (1920–45) was born in New Jersey. A member of the Army Air Corps during World War II, he began the war as a fighter pilot defending the Aleutian Islands off Alaska. In

March 1943 he was transferred to the Pacific to fly with the 475th Fighter Group. He shot down his first three enemy planes on August 18, 1943, and ten more over the next two months. Named a squadron commander in 1944 he continued to add to his tally of enemy kills. By January 1945 he had thirty-eight—just two short of the record set by Major Richard I. Bong. But on January 7, McGuire was killed when his plane crashed on a mission over Negros Island. He was awarded the Medal of Honor posthumously and McGuire Air Force Base in New Jersey was named in his honor.

On the Ground

626. "Wild Bill" Donovan   Born in Buffalo, New York, William Donovan (1883–1959) originally considered the priesthood, before settling into a career in law. He was in private practice as a lawyer when the U.S. entered World War I. He was appointed a major and assigned to the 69th Regiment ("The Irish Brigade") of New York. He distinguished himself as a soldier during the regiment's tour of duty in France, earning many awards and commendations, including the Medal of Honor. His fearlessness earned him the nickname "Wild Bill."

After the war he served the U.S. government as a special observer foreign and military affairs. From 1924 to 1929 he was assistant attorney general in the Justice Department. In the thirties he built a very successful law practice with the firm Donovan Leisure Newton & Irvine.

In 1940 President Franklin Roosevelt sent Donovan on a fact-finding mission

William Donovan as a soldier in World War I

to England. There he learned the intricacies of England's unconventional warfare unit and became convinced of the need for one in the U.S. In July 1941, after earnest lobbying by Donovan, Roosevelt appointed Donovan coordinator of information. During the war, his operation was renamed Office of Strategic Services, or OSS, and it presided over America's vital covert actions, espionage, and propaganda dissemination. Donovan returned to private law practice after the war and the OSS was eventually remade into the CIA.

627. Lt. Audie Murphy   Before he became a famous actor, Audie Murphy (1924–71) earned glory as a soldier in World War II. Born in Texas, he enlisted in the army in 1942. He fought in many theaters, including the Allied invasion of France, and received more decorations (twenty-eight) than any other soldier during the war. He was also wounded three times. Murphy won the Medal of Honor when in January 1945 he jumped atop a burning tank and used its .50mm gun to single-handedly repel an attack by a German force of more than two hundred. Murphy wrote about some of his wartime adventures in a bestselling book, *To Hell and Back.* After the war, he became an actor and appeared in nearly forty films, including one based on his book. He died in 1971 in a plane crash.

An Irishman on
the Other Side

628. William Joyce, aka Lord Haw Haw   Born in Brooklyn, William Joyce (1906–46) moved to Britain with his family at the age of three. In the early 1920s, the family relocated to England. As an adult in the 1930s, Joyce became an ardent fascist and founded the British National Socialist League. At the outbreak of World War II, he fled to Germany and offered his services to Josef Goebbels' propaganda office.

On September 18, 1939, the people of Britain heard for the first time Joyce's signature opening "Germany calling! Germany calling!" What followed was the first of hundreds of Nazi propaganda broadcasts touting the unstoppable advance of Hitler's legions and urging the people of Britain to see the futility of opposing them. The goal of these broadcasts was to undermine the morale of the British people and soldiers in the field. For his service to the Third Reich, Joyce was awarded the Cross of War Merit, First Class in August 1944.

His pretentious and obviously manufactured aristocratic accent earned him the derisive nickname "Lord Haw Haw."

At the end of the war, he was arrested by British soldiers and taken to London. Tried for treason, he denied the charge could be brought because he was an American citizen. But British officials were determined to hang him. They declared that an illegal British passport he obtained in the 1930s (in which he claimed Irish birth) had carried with it the obligation of loyalty to the Crown. His appeals were denied and he was hanged in January 1946.

The Cold War

629. George F. Kennan A sixth-generation Irish American from Milwaukee, Wisconsin, George Kennan (b. 1904) joined the Foreign Service a year after graduating from Princeton in 1925. He became an expert on Communist Russia in the 1930s and accompanied Ambassador William Bullitt on his trip to Moscow that resulted in the establishment of U.S.–Soviet diplomatic relations. After stints in various European posts before and during World War II, he arrived in Moscow in 1944 as minister-counselor. There he observed first hand the workings of Stalin's Communist regime.

In February 1946, the still relatively unknown diplomat in Moscow sent his famous cable outlining his views on the proper diplomatic approach the U.S. should take regarding the Soviets. He ar-

gued that Communism was inherently expansionist and that for the foreseeable future negotiations with the Soviets would not work. Instead, the U.S. should apply "counterpressure" wherever the Soviets (or any Communist group) threatened to expand. Known as the "containment" policy, it became the basis (albeit with many deviations) for American foreign policy for most of the Cold War.

Kennan became one of the nation's most highly regarded foreign policy experts and was subsequently appointed to many prestigious diplomatic assignments, including chief of policy planning at the State Department in 1947 and two ambassadorships to the Soviet Union (1952–53) and Yugoslavia (1961–63). After retirement, Kennan embarked upon a second career as an author and educator. Among his twenty books on foreign policy are *Russia Leaves the War* (1956) and *Memoirs 1925–1950* (1967). The latter won both the Pulitzer Prize and the National Book Award.

630. William Casey William Casey (1913–89) was born in Elmhurst, Queens, and attended college at Fordham and earned his law degree at St. John's University (New York). During World War II he worked in the Office of Strategic Services, the forerunner to the CIA. Even though he would spend two decades after the war becoming an authority on tax law, he never lost his interest in international affairs.

In the mid-1960s Casey became active in politics as a Republican. He worked for Richard Nixon's successful run for president in 1968 and in 1969 founded the Citizens Committee for Peace with Security, a hawkish organization supportive of Nixon's antiballistic missile program. In 1971, Nixon appointed Casey to the Securities and Exchange Commission; he later became chairman.

The high point in his career came when President Ronald Reagan tapped him to serve as

Thomas Dooley

director of the Central Intelligence Agency. Casey led the agency from 1981 to 1987, one of the most tense periods of the Cold War. He was at the center of the Iran-Contra scandal that threatened the Reagan presidency.

631. Thomas A. Dooley   A St. Louis, Missouri, native, Dr. Thomas Anthony Dooley III (1927–61) practiced medicine in Southeast Asia. His 1954 experiences as a naval officer assisting refugees fleeing from North Vietnam inspired his bestselling account *Deliver Us from Evil,* published in 1956. It was an important work for shaping American popular opinion about the character of Communism in Asia. His 1958 *The Edge of Tomorrow* described Dooley's efforts to establish St. Patrick's Hospital in Laos with a team of only five doctors. Dooley's popularity in the United States as "the jungle medic" helped garner support for his clinics and for a group he founded called Medical International Corporation (MEDICO). After his death in 1961, admirers sought to have Dooley canonized as a saint.

632. Francis Gary Powers   Francis Gary Powers (1929–77) was an air force test pilot when the CIA recruited him to fly spy missions. He flew for the U2 reconnaissance program, taking aerial photographs of Soviet military operations. In 1960, his plane was shot down, and the Soviets captured Powers and his plane. When Soviet Premier Nikita Khrushchev learned about the American spy plane, he canceled an important summit meeting with the superpowers, thus heightening tensions. Powers was tried and sentenced for

espionage, but was returned to America in a 1962 spy exchange. He never received any due recognition for his service and indeed some, in classic Cold War excess, criticized him for failing to commit suicide to avoid capture. Powers died when the helicopter he flew for a Los Angeles television station crashed in 1977. In May 2000, Powers was given a posthumous award for his service during the Cold War.

Korea

633. The Irish-Born Heroes   In February 1952, St. Patrick's Cathedral in New York City was filled to capacity. The occasion was a memorial Mass in honor of nine men killed while serving in the U.S. armed forces in Korea. What set these young men apart from the more than fifty thousand who died in the Korean conflict (1950–53) fighting for the United States was that they were all Irish-born noncitizens. As resident aliens, they were eligible for the draft. What they were not eligible for was American citizenship in recognition for their service (the law was changed in 1953 to allow for this). And so, Patrick Sheehan, John Canty, Bart Galvin, and Patrick White of County Kerry; Michael Gannon of Mayo; Michael Hardiman and Michael King of Roscommon; William Scully of Limerick; and Daniel Harrington of Cork gave their lives for a country they'd barely gotten to know and in which they had not yet become citizens. In recent years, a fellow "alien draftee," Kerry-born John Leahy, who survived his tour in Korea, has been leading an effort to have the men awarded posthumous citizenship.

634. Some Notable Medal of Honor Recipients   Among the more than one hundred Medal of Honor recipients, one finds Irish Americans well represented. Included among the many names are Lloyd L. Burke, Henry A. Commiskey, John D. Kelly, Frank N. Mitchell, Walter C. Monegan, Raymond G. Murphy, George H. O'Brien, and

Richard Shea. The official citation that accompanied Robert M. McGovern's posthumous award tells the story of their bravery:

As 1st Lt. McGovern led his platoon up a slope to engage hostile troops emplaced in bunker-type pillboxes with connecting trenches, the unit came under heavy machine gun and rifle fire from the crest of the hill, approximately 75 yards distant. Despite a wound sustained in this initial burst of withering fire, 1st Lt. McGovern, assured the men of his ability to continue on and urged them forward. Forging up the rocky incline, he fearlessly led the platoon to within several yards of its objective when the ruthless foe threw and rolled a vicious barrage of handgrenades on the group and halted the advance. Enemy fire increased in volume and intensity and 1st Lt. McGovern realizing that casualties were rapidly increasing and the morale of his men badly shaken, hurled back several grenades before they exploded. Then, disregarding his painful wound and weakened condition he charged a machine gun emplacement which was raking his position with flanking fire. When he was within 10 yards of the position a burst of fire ripped the carbine from his hands, but, undaunted, he continued his lone-man assault and, firing his pistol and throwing grenades, killed 7 hostile soldiers before falling mortally wounded in front of the gun he had silenced.

Vietnam

635. The Irish-Born Killed in Vietnam Just as in the Korean conflict, a significant number of immigrants from Ireland fought and died for America in Vietnam. In 1997 one Declan Hughes, not a Vietnam veteran himself, set out to see if any Irish-born had died in Vietnam. After three years of research, he discovered sixteen men born in Ireland who died while serving the United States armed forces in Vietnam. He found another four who died in the service of the Australian armed forces.

636. The Story of Robert Kerrey Robert Kerrey's (b. 1943) experience in Vietnam vividly conveys the sense of conflict, confusion, and tragedy many Americans experienced during and after the war. Like many Irish Americans of his generation, Kerrey volunteered for military service (1966), becoming a member of the elite Navy SEALS. He

The Vietnam Memorial

earned the Medal of Honor for executing a difficult command while seriously injured in a raid against Viet Cong forces in March 1969, an action that cost him the lower portion of one of his legs.

Kerrey returned to the United States and set about rebuilding his life. He eventually turned to politics, serving as Governor of Nebraska (1982–88) and later as its senator (1988–2000). Kerrey retired in 2000 and took a job as president of the New School in New York City. In the spring of 2001, however, Kerrey was forced by investigative reporters to admit that in one of his first actions in Vietnam, his unit had been responsible for the killing of dozens of innocent civilians. Kerrey maintained that the deaths were accidental and that he has always deeply regretted the incident. "Every person who has gone to war has struggled with the question of, did he do it right?" Kerrey said in the wake of the revelations, "and I have struggled with that question privately since February of 1969."

637. John McCain Before his political career, John McCain (b. 1936) followed in the footsteps of his father and grandfather, both admirals in the U.S. Navy. McCain became a navy pilot and volunteered for combat duty when the conflict in Vietnam began. In 1967, his plane was shot down over Hanoi. He suffered serious injuries from the crash and at the hands of his captors and was placed in a Hanoi prison. He endured over five years of unspeakable brutality, despite being offered early release on several occasions (he refused, in keeping with the war code that POWs should be released in order of capture). McCain returned home after the war, recovered his health, retired from the navy, and entered politics.

638. Col. David Hackworth During his twenty-five-year military career, Colonel David Hackworth earned over one hundred awards (including eight Purple Hearts), making him America's most decorated living soldier. During

the Korean conflict he became the youngest man in the army promoted to captain. As the youngest full colonel in Vietnam, he refused additional promotions because he felt that his combat skills would be wasted. He led the first paratroopers into Vietnam in 1965 and quickly learned the tactics of the Vietnamese. In five years of combat, Hackworth's command claimed 2,500 enemy troops, and lost only twenty-five. Frustrated by the military's handling of the war, he went on national television in 1971 and announced what no one in the Pentagon wanted to admit: "This is a bad war . . . it can't be won, we need to get out." Hackworth resigned and went into self-imposed exile in Australia. He has since become a high-profile journalist and commentator on military and national defense matters.

639. Robert McNamara, Architect of the War In 1961, President John F. Kennedy selected former auto industry executive Robert Strange McNamara (b. 1916) as his secretary of defense. He remained in the job after Kennedy's assassination, overseeing the massive buildup of American forces in Vietnam. Initially a hawk who believed in the invincibility of American military force, McNamara eventually grew convinced that Vietnam was a war America could not win. He resigned in 1968, even as many had taken to calling the conflict "McNamara's War," and became the president of the World Bank. Many years later, McNamara published a memoir, *In Retrospect: The Tragedy and Lessons of Vietnam*, in which he expressed regret for his role in the Vietnam War, but went to great pains to shift the blame for the buildup to others, especially President Johnson.

640. Tom Hayden Leads the Antiwar Movement In 1960, Tom Hayden (b. 1939) cofounded the Students for a Democratic Society (SDS), the ideals of which were formative in the New Left. Positioning themselves as a radical, even revolutionary alternative to mainstream liberalism, Hayden and his fellow SDS members took aim at civil rights, economic inequality, and corporate power. By the mid-1960s, they increasingly focused their attention on the war in Vietnam.

During the 1968 Democratic Convention in Chicago, Hayden was among the leading antiwar protestors. When the Chicago police stormed the demonstrators and the situation deteriorated into chaos, Hayden was among hundreds arrested. Tried and acquitted as one of the Chicago Seven, Hayden was one of the nation's most widely recognized antiwar spokesmen (see also entry #555 about the Berrigan Brothers).

PART VII

Culture

Symbols

641. The Harp Next to the shamrock, the second most common symbol in Irish culture is the harp. It's everywhere in Ireland, from the backs of coins to kegs of Guinness. This may seem somewhat strange, since the harp doesn't figure prominently in traditional Irish music. Prior to the subjugation of Ireland by the British in the seventeenth century, however, Irish harpists were famous throughout Europe and enjoyed a revered place in the old Gaelic order. Harpists played the music that accompanied the recitations of that other famed group in Gaelic Ireland, the poets. The harpist tradition was virtually wiped out with the plantations and Penal Laws. When a harp festival convened in Belfast in 1792, only eleven harpists could be found in the entire country. The few songs written down during that event are the only connection remaining to this once essential element of Irish culture. As with the shamrock, nationalists in the nineteenth century adopted the harp as a symbol of Irish nationhood.

642. The Shamrock Like so many aspects of Irish history and culture, to find the origin of the shamrock as a significant feature of Irish life one must go back to pre-Christian times. Ancient Celts believed the shamrock, or white clover, possessed curative powers and could foretell the weather (its leaves were said to arch upward before a storm). The word shamrock derives from the Irish word *Seamr g,* or "summer plant."

The shamrock's significance in modern times, however, comes from its association with St. Patrick. Legend has it (and all we have is legend since St. Patrick never mentioned the shamrock in his writings) that he used the shamrock to explain the mystery of the Trinity to pagan Celts by comparing the three leaves with the Father, Son, and Holy Spirit. Doubtless, some missionary, if not Patrick himself, used this unique teaching tool in the Christianization of Ireland in the fifth and sixth centuries. The practice of wearing shamrocks on St. Patrick's Day dates as far back as the sixteenth century, and perhaps earlier. The shamrocks became a symbol of Irish national identity in the nineteenth century when Nationalists adopted it as their symbol. Ironically, so too did Ulster Unionists for a time.

643. The Irish Flag Why, if they represent the clashing interests in Ireland's troubled history, are

An Irish harp

the colors green and orange in the Irish flag? Well, you might say it's the product of wishful thinking. Green has been a color associated with Ireland since the 1600s and is most likely derived (surprise) from the greenery of the Irish landscape. The color orange dates from the 1600s as the symbol of the Protestant Ascendancy. William III, also known as William of Orange, defeated Catholic James II in Ireland in 1691 to complete England's "Glorious Revolution." The Orange Order, the Protestant organization dedicated to upholding the union between Ireland (later just Northern Ireland) and Britain, dates from 1795.

The earliest proposal for uniting these antagonistic symbols in a national flag dates from the 1830s. The Young Ireland movement of the 1840s adopted the tricolor flag as a symbol of Protestant and Catholic unity. It persisted for a few decades before giving way to the green flag with a harp. It was in the aftermath of the Easter Rising of 1916 that the tricolor was revived as the emblem of militant nationalism. It became the official flag of the Irish Free State in 1922. The Good Friday accord of 1998 has come as close as any effort to making the symbolic intent of the flag a reality.

644. Leprechaun Stop right there, turn around slowly, and DROP that picture in your mind of the little guy on the Lucky Charms cereal box. That jolly little imp, and his counterparts on greeting cards, pub signs, and your Aunt Margaret's stationery, bears almost no resemblance to the leprechauns of Irish mythology. To borrow a phrase from a long-dead philosopher writing about something entirely different, they were "nasty, brutish, and short." Leprechauns were grumpy, alcoholic, insufferable elves in the employ of Irish fairies. They made shoes for fairies (hence their depiction as cobblers) and guarded their treasure which to the leprechauns' eternal frustration was revealed occasionally to mortals by a rainbow. Somewhere in the course of the Irish American experience, the leprechaun took on the characteristics of the loveable, but ultimately contemptible, stage Irishman.

645. The Blarney Stone It's both a place in Ireland and a term that means calculated flattery. The latter term originated in the late 1500s when one Lord Cormac Mac Carthaig (McCarthy), resident of Blarney Castle, faced pressure from Queen Elizabeth to renounce his ancestral claim to the castle and surrounding lands and to acknowledge that he held them only through a grant from the Crown. Rather than openly defy the formidable monarch, he pretended to accept her request, but stalled its enactment by issuing a steady torrent of flattery and kiss-uppery. After years of this oh-so-cordial runaround, an exasperated Elizabeth is reputed to have said, "This is all Blarney. What he says he never means." The term stuck and it was not long thereafter that the legend of the Blarney Stone—that those who kiss it will be granted the gift of persuasion—took hold.

646. Claddagh Ring With the explosion of interest in all things Irish in the last decade, the claddagh ring has become one of the most popular ring designs in the world. Most wearers know enough to say that it's a traditional Irish wedding ring worn with the hands pointed inward by someone who's "taken" and outward by one accepting suitors. Some continue by pointing out the meaning of its three symbols: heart (love), the hands (friendship), and the crown (loyalty).

But that much said, where does the claddagh ring come from? No one knows how the design came into being or what it meant in ancient times, though some association with the local chieftain or king seems probable. What is known is that it originated in the fishing village of Claddagh, located at the mouth of the Corrib River opposite Galway City. Sometime in the late seventeenth century, a man named Richard Joyce, who is believed to have learned the goldsmith trade while held as a slave in Algeria, began producing the

distinctive rings. The design quickly gained popularity in and around Galway and then spread across Ireland. In the late nineteenth century, Irish nationalists promoted a Fenian claddagh—the same design minus, you guessed it, the crown. Today the Claddagh ring is found on the fingers of many people who have no Irish ancestry at all.

647. The Celtic Cross The Celtic Cross so many people wear around their necks today is modeled after the extraordinary "high crosses" of Ireland. Most of these ancient relics date from the ninth and tenth century, when detailed stone carving was rare in the rest of Europe. Monumental in size and covered in intricate carvings of biblical stories and Celtic designs, they are often located on the former sites of monasteries. The most distinct feature of the Celtic Cross—the ring at the junction of the cross bars—is of uncertain origin.

Very likely it was borrowed from Celtic symbolism as ancient Celts, like many other groups, saw the circle as symbolic of life. The most famous high cross ("Cross of the Scriptures") is found at the monastic center of Clonmacnoise, which apparently was a center of stone carving.

Expressions

648. The Emerald Isle For anyone who has seen the lush greenery that dominates the Irish landscape, the reason Ireland is known as the Emerald Isle is not hard to fathom. The first known reference to Ireland as the Emerald Isle comes from a poem "Erin" by the United Irishman William Drennan in 1795. It soon became a staple expression in the romantic and sentimental poetry and song popular in the nineteenth and early twentieth century.

A Celtic Cross

649. Scream Like a Banshee   Ancient Irish folklore contains many frightening figures, but none more so than the banshee—the shrieking messenger of death. In most cases, the banshee (in Irish *Bean Si* for "female spirit") appears as an old woman with flowing white hair who weeps and shrieks as she warns of an impending death. The banshee was feared not so much for her ghostly appearance, but for her message of death. Indeed, her sorrow suggests sympathy, not evil.

650. The Luck of the Irish   Upon reflection, this may appear to be a rather absurd phrase. What sort of luck is it that brings about one thousand years of invasion, colonization, exploitation, starvation, and mass emigration? Well, this term has a happier, if not altogether positive, American origin. During the gold and silver rush years in the second half of the nineteenth century, a number of the most famous and successful miners were of Irish and Irish American birth (see entry #873). Over time this association of the Irish with mining fortunes led to the expression "luck of the Irish." Of course, it carried with it a certain tone of derision, as if to say, only by sheer luck, as opposed to brains, could these fools succeed.

651. O', Mac, Mc, and Fitz   All four terms designate one's ancestry. "Mac" is the Gaelic term for son and "Mc" is merely a shorthand version. Lord Blarney, for example, Cormac Mac Carthaig (McCarthy), was son of Carthaig. The commonly held belief that "Mc" signifies an Irish name and "Mac" a Scottish one is incorrect. Both Mac and its contraction Mc are found in the traditional Gaelic societies of Scotland and Ireland.

"O" is the Gaelic word for grandson. The apostrophe, which suggests a contraction, is a legacy of British colonialism. Misguided English bureaucrats assumed the "O" stood for the word "of" (as in "crack o' dawn") and added the apostrophe when compiling official records and census data. Over the centuries, many families dropped the O', which accounts for the existence of both

John Mackay, one of the "Silver Kings"

Sullivan and Sullivan, O'Mahoney and Mahoney, etc. In recent decades many people in Ireland, and a few in the States, have dropped the apostrophe in favor of the more traditional spelling.

"Fitz" also means "son of" but it comes from the French-speaking Normans who arrived via England in the twelfth century. It's a corruption of the French word *fils*, which means "son." Fitzgerald, therefore, means "son of Gerald."

652. American Wake   Unlike their Italian counterparts at the turn of the century, very few Irish immigrants ever returned to their homeland. This fact reflected both the turmoil and lack of opportunity in Ireland, as well as the expense and difficulty of the transatlantic voyage. Because an Irish man or woman would likely never be seen again, family and friends often held an "American wake" the night before he or she departed. Like a real wake, there was food and drink, song and dance, crying and keening. This ritual marking the "death" of an emigrant's life in Ireland gradually faded by the early twentieth century as fewer people left for America and improved communications allowed for continued contact.

653. Irish Bull   The Irish Bull was a popular form of humor at the turn of the century. Essentially, it was a quick anecdote that depended on ignorance or a confusion of terms to deliver a humorous punch line. For example: Two tired Irishmen were walking along when one exclaimed, "How much further, I'm exhausted." "It's ten miles to town," responded his friend. "Ah that's not so bad—only five miles each." Or an

Irish Bull might take the form of a single sentence, as in "She's the type of woman who'll look you right in the eye as she stabs you in the back."

As with so many Irish popular culture forms, the Irish Bull was both a celebration of Irish wit and storytelling *and* a perpetuation of the stereotype of the Irish as essentially dim-witted.

654. Murphy's Law   Murphy's Law, the observation that whatever can go wrong will go wrong, was first uttered by air force engineer Capt. Edward A. Murphy, Jr., during an acceleration tolerance experiment conducted in 1949. After discovering that all sixteen sensors attached to the test subject's body had been installed backward, Murphy declared, "If there are two or more ways to do something, and one of those ways can result in a catastrophe, then someone will do it." The quip quickly circulated among his fellow engineers and eventually made its way into trade journals and then into general usage.

655. The Life of Riley   So far as one can tell, there was no real Riley who lived a worry-free and luxurious life. Some associate the phrase with James Whitcomb Riley who wrote a good many poems about carefree boys enjoying sleepy summer days, but that's a bit of a stretch. A more likely source is the 1880s song popular on the vaudeville circuit, "Are You the O'Reilly?" It told of the great days that lay ahead when O'Reilly struck it rich—"A hundred a day will be small pay." The chorus went as follows:

> Are you the O'Reilly who keeps this
>   hotel?
> Are you the O'Reilly they speak of so
>   well?
> Are you the O'Reilly they speak of so
>   highly?
> Gor blime me, O'Reilly, you're looking
>   well.

656. In Like Flynn   There are two competing claims for the origin of this expression which means both quick success ("A timely word to the *maitre de* and we were in like Flynn") or fast friends ("I said just the right thing to the boss and I was in like Flynn"). The first attributes the term to silver screen star Errol Flynn who in his heyday epitomized the dashing and debonair Hollywood playboy. His reputation as an irresistible lady killer, both on screen and off, led to the expression "in like Flynn." A second explanation for the term argues that it originated with the Chicago political boss Michael J. Flynn. With his candidates winning year after year, Chicagoans began to use the expression "in like Flynn" to refer to any sure thing.

657. Beyond the Pale   This rather grim term takes us back to the fourteenth century Ireland and the Statutes of Kilkenny. These laws established a sweeping series of prohibitions against fraternization between Anglo-Irish colonizers and the native Irish. They also defined what became known as the Pale of Settlement (pale comes from the Latin word *palus*, or fence post) a narrow strip of land, little more than twenty miles wide in most places, running north from Waterford to Dundalk on Ireland's eastern coast. Anyone living "beyond the pale" were considered "Irish enemies" not entitled to protection under English law (see entry #52).

658. Mulligan   Sometime in the early twentieth century, golfers began to use the term "Mulligan" to describe a "do-over" shot allowed in an informal game. The earliest written reference to the term is in the 1949 *Dictionary of Sports:* "Mulligan . . . a handicap of a free shot given after a player makes a bad one." The expression most likely does not refer to a specific individual named Mulligan, but rather to the common expression for an Irish fool. The expression may have predated them, but the great team of Harrigan and Hart certainly did the most to popularize it through their string of hit musical comedies in the 1870s and 1880s known

Harrigan and Hart's Mulligan Guards

as the Mulligan Guards. So when casting about for a term to describe an allowance given for a foolish shot, Mulligan seemed an apt choice. In recent years, with the booming popularity of golf among both men and women, the term has crept into general usage to describe a do-over after any sort of flub.

659. Go the Whole Hog This expression for "to overindulge" is of uncertain origin, but more than one scholar claims it derives from the Irish nickname for a shilling—a "hog." Thus, to blow one's money meant to "go the whole hog," an expression that eventually came to mean any form of excess.

660. Yes Man This term used to describe the ultimate sycophant was first coined by famed sports cartoonist T.A.D. Dorgan. He first used it in a

1913 cartoon entitled "Giving the First Edition the Once-Over" to ridicule weak-kneed editors by labeling each a "yes-man." Years later another Irish American, Fred Allen (born John Sullivan), popularized a similar term for show business called "loyalty laughter."

661. Knock on Wood There are half a dozen competing explanations for this term and practice, but more than one expert asserts that it derives from ancient Celtic tradition. Druids considered the oak tree sacred. To summon the assistance of, or thank, a fairy or god, Celts rapped a tree trunk.

662. Lynch Law During the American Revolution, a Virginia planter and justice of the peace named Charles Lynch of Lynchburg, a town founded by his ancestors, presided over an extralegal court that dispensed summary justice to loyalists, from floggings to a few hangings. Thereafter, the term "lynch" became synonymous with vigilante justice, especially as a violent form of oppression used against African Americans and some whites from the Civil War through the 1960s.

663. Mickey or Mickey Finn This term for a doctored drink, "slip him a mickey," likely dates back to the nineteenth century, though it gained widespread recognition in the gangster movies and detective novels of the 1930s. Whatever its exact origins, it clearly derives from the association of the Irish with both drink and organized crime.

Eleven Common Words
with Irish Origins

664. galore   from the Irish *go leor,* enough, plenty

665. shanty   from the Irish *seantigh,* a run-down house

666. spree   from the Irish *spreath,* spoils taken in a raid (i.e., cattle)

667. slogan   from the Irish *sluaghairim,* a war cry (literally "army shout")

668. smithereens   from the Irish *smidirini,* fragment

669. shenanigans   from the Irish *sionnachuighim,* literally, "I play the fox"

670. spunk   from the Irish *sponc,* spirited or courageous

671. whiskey   from the Irish *uisce* and *beatha,* water of life

672. boycott   from the name of its most famous victim, Captain Charles Cunningham Boycott, who was ostracized for carrying out tenant evictions during the "Land War" of the 1880s; to shun or withhold patronage (see entries #382 and #910)

673. donnybrook   from the wild behavior associated with the annual fair at Donnybrook near Dublin, from the late fourteenth to the mid-nineteenth centuries; a brawl

674. hooligan   from a notorious Irish family named Hooligan living in the slums of London in the 1890s (and later popularized in Fred Opper's cartoon *Happy Hooligan*); a rowdy

The Nineteenth-Century Stage and Show

Roles and Genres

675. The "Stage Irishman"   The stage Irishman was a staple of American comedic theater for more than a century. He was a mishmash of stereotypes about the Irish—hilarious and fun-loving on the one hand, lazy, drunken, and violent on the other. Even though it was their culture being ridiculed, working-class Irish flocked to theaters to see the stage Irishman. By the late

Dan Bryant

nineteenth century, however, many in the emerging Irish American middle class found him both embarrassing and insulting and worked to have the character eliminated from vaudeville routines (see entry #675).

676. Minstrel Shows   The minstrel show was one of the most popular forms of entertainment to emerge in the mid-nineteenth century. While there were many variations, a typical show consisted of a group of blackfaced white minstrels who performed skits and routines based on racist caricatures of singing and dancing African American slaves.

Irish performers played a key role in the popularization and development of the minstrel show.

The acknowledged "father" of the American minstrel show was an Irishman, Thomas Dartmouth Rice, popularly known as "Jim Crow" (after his popular "Jump Jim Crow" dance routine). As an early black impersonator, he established a vogue for blackfaced minstrelsy. The original minstrel company, the Virginia Minstrels, first performed in 1843 under the leadership of Daniel Decatur Emmett, also famous for writing "Dixie" and "The Blue Tail Fly (Jimmy Crack Corn)." Virtually all the best-known companies, including Bryant's Minstrels, Campbell's Minstrels, and Haverly's Minstrels, were comprised of Irish performers. The best-known company was the Christy Minstrels, who performed on Broadway for nearly a decade, often to songs written by another Irish American, Stephen Foster.

The heyday of the minstrel show was between 1850 and 1870, at which point it was superceded by vaudeville and the variety show. Although many of its elements influenced vaudeville, and later radio and television, the main impact of the minstrel show was in its folk music and dances, much of it derived from a mixture of Irish and African styles.

677. Vaudeville Popular in the U.S. from the 1880s through the 1930s, vaudeville was characterized by ridiculous and often crude exaggeration. Its origin (and name) can be traced to a place in Normandy, France called Val de Vire, France, where in the fifteenth century satirical and humorous drinking songs were popular diversions. In urban America, vaudeville became a kind of variety show on stage, where the predominantly working-class audience could expect a series of acts by one performer or various entertainers— anything from jugglers, musicians, acrobats, and family routines, to singers, wild animal acts, ribald comedians, and scantily clad women. Many of the great Irish American performers from the early twentieth century, such as George M. Cohan, James Cagney, the Keatons, Harrigan and Hart, and Fred Allen, got their start in vaudeville.

Ethnic humor, in particular, found its way into nearly every routine. Audiences of Irish, Germans, Jews, and others flocked to the performances, despite the fact that their ethnic group would invariably come in for ridicule and parody based on widely held stereotypes. For the Irish, it was the "stage Irishman" (see entry #675) and the hopeless Irish maid who invariably brought disaster to her employer's home.

With its low admission fees and democratic approach, vaudeville was geared for the masses, not the elite attracted to "legitimate" theater. By one estimate, at its peak ca. 1900, vaudeville shows drew two million patrons a day. The advent of motion pictures and radio, coupled with the financial losses of the Great Depression, marked the rapid decline of vaudeville.

Playwrights and Producers

678. John Daly Burk Although "Irish" plays were staged in colonial America, they were written by English authors and the Irish theme was invariably pejorative stereotypes. The first noted Irish playwright in America was John Daly Burk (1772–1808), an emigrant from Dublin who arrived in Boston in 1796. Most of his plays were patriotic dramas about important chapters in American history. His most famous was his first, *Bunker Hill* (1797). It proved immensely popular and was revived continuously for the next fifty years.

679. John Brougham The first figure to produce Irish American drama was Irish-born John Brougham (1810–80). He arrived in 1842 and launched a theatrical career that produced more than one hundred scripts. Brougham performed in his productions, most of which were historical and biographical in focus. While most of his work focused on American history—one of his more popular works was *The Declaration of Independence* (1844)—he did perform as Daniel O'Connell and Fr. Theobold Mathew, the famous temperance advocate. Some of his work was rather racy, and he is seen as an early contributor to American burlesque.

680. Dion Boucicault A Dubliner who became known as the "Irish Shakespeare," Dionysius Lardner Boursiquot (c. 1820–90) began his career in theater as an actor in London in 1837. Soon, however, he turned to writing. Boucicault's second play, *London Assurance* (1841) was a major success and enjoyed revivals for the rest of the century. In 1853 he and his wife emigrated to America. He traveled and performed extensively before settling in New York City. There he wrote and debuted his most memorable plays, including *The Octaroon* (1859) and three Irish dramas, *The*

Colleen Bawn (1859), *Arrah-na-Pogue* (1864), and *The Shaughrawn* (1874). At a time when most Irish-themed productions were of the low-brow, raucous "stage Irishman" type, Boucicault's serious dramas did much to elevate the quality and status of Irish theater. In all Boucicault penned more than two hundred plays. He also lobbied for copyright laws in the U.S.

681. Dion Boucicault Observes Shortly after he completed one of his most famous plays, *The Colleen Bawn* (1860), Dion Boucicault offered the following observation on tapping into his Irish heritage.

> I have written an Irish drama for the first time in my life. The field of Irish history is so rich in dramatic suggestion that I am surprised that the mine has never been regularly opened before. I had long thought of writing a play from material gathered from my native country, but this is the first time I ever tried it. I hope that this play will lead other, greater men, of finer genius and talent than I possess, to create more Irish plays.

682. Harrigan and Hart The Irish slums of Manhattan were the landscape of Edward Harrigan's (1845–1911) imagination. Although he fled his birthplace as a teen, he would triumphantly return as the playwright and songwriter of the Irish immigrant experience. Together with his partner, Tony Hart (born Anthony J. Cannon, 1857–91), he would create entertainment over a fifteen-year partnership that rang true with Irishmen, from orphaned newsboys to overworked laborers.

Their original productions were humorous spoofs on Dion Boucicault's more serious works. But a successful lawsuit by Boucicault for libel prompted the duo to write original comedies in the emerging vaudeville style. Harrigan and Hart not only wrote their works, they performed them. Many of Harrigan's songs such as "Danny by My

Dion Boucicault playbill

Side" and "Why Paddy's Always Poor" became popular songs that remained in use for a generation. Their most popular show was the Mulligan Guard series, featuring Dan Mulligan and his hilarious encounters with fellow Irishmen and other immigrants in the tenements of New York. Later Mulligan plays took up the theme of Irish American upward mobility as Dan and his wife, Cordelia, come into sudden riches and move uptown to Fifth Avenue. Despite the best efforts of his wife, Dan never makes the cultural jump from the slums to uptown refinement—a theme repeated endlessly thereafter in Irish American literature, song, and cartoons. Harrigan and Hart had a tremendous influence on vaudeville, burlesque, and musical comedy, and on comedians like Milton Berle and Bob Hope.

683. Augustin Daly John Augustin Daly (1838–99) was one of nineteenth-century America's most successful and influential theater managers and dramatists. Born in Plymouth, North Carolina, he moved to New York City in the 1850s. He worked as a drama critic for several New York newspapers and, drawing on his knowledge of several languages, began translating and adapting many plays from French and German. His debut as manager came in 1867 with the production of his melodrama *Under the Gaslight.* Success in that and subsequent ventures allowed him to open his first theater in 1869. When that

theater burned in 1873, he established a new one named Daly's Theatre. Daly earned critical and popular praise for his noted productions of Shakespearean comedies and other original works of serious drama. Under Daly's

Augustin Daly

tutelage, two of Irish America's greatest stars, Ada Rehan and John Drew, got their start in theater. Daly continued to write and at the end of his life had written more than ninety plays.

The Performers

684. The Drews Offsetting the low comedy of Harrigan and Hart somewhat were serious Irish dramatists like Dublin-born John Drew, Sr. (1827–62). He emigrated to the U.S. with his family and had his first introduction to the theater at Niblo's Garden in New York City where his father worked. Drew debuted on the stage in the famed working-class theater district known as the Bowery when he was eighteen. But he soon gravitated toward a career in serious Irish drama. He married Louisa Lane Drew (1820–97), an English-born actress and together they managed Philadelphia's Arch Theatre. Their repertory company became one of the most famous in America for its performances of theater classics.

Given the Drew family's prominence in theater, it is hardly surprising that their children would continue the tradition. Georgiana Drew (1856–93) became an actress and in 1876 married famed actor Maurice Barrymore (see entry #692) to begin one of the most acclaimed families in show business.

John Drew, Jr. (1853–1927), likewise headed for the footlights, making his stage debut in 1873. Two years later he debuted in New York as Bob Ruggles in *The Big Bonanza*, a comedy by Irish American producer Augustin Daly. His breakthrough performance came in 1879 as Alexander Sprinkle in Daly's *Arabian Night; or Haroun al Raschid and His Mother-in-law.* Drew stayed with Daly for the next thirteen years as his star continued to rise.

In 1892 he joined Charles Frohman's company, where for the next two decades he starred in Shakespearean comedies, society dramas, and light comedies such as *A Marriage of Convenience, One Summer's Day, Much Ado About Nothing, The*

John Drew

Circle, and *School for Scandal.* His career declined after Frohman's death in 1915. Held in such high regard by his fellow actors, Drew was named lifetime president of the Players' Club, a rare honor previously bestowed only upon two men.

685. James O'Neill Famous for his stage role as Edmond Dantes in *Monte Cristo,* James O'Neill (1849–1920) emigrated from Ireland in 1854. In 1876, he joined New York's Union Square Theatre Company, where he played many demanding roles. But it was not until 1882, when he first played Dantes, that O'Neill achieved widespread fame and eventually a sizable fortune. He bought the rights to the play and performed it for the rest of his career, a total of more than six thousand performances. A 1918 automobile accident weakened O'Neill's health, and he died two years later in his Connecticut home. His son, the great playwright Eugene O'Neill, was always haunted by the feeling that his father had sold his creative soul for a safe and profitable career as a one-role actor.

686. Ada Rehan An Irish-born actress who emigrated to New York, Ada Crehan (1860–1916) took the stage name of Rehan as the result

Ada Rehan

of a printing error in her debut performance in Newark, New Jersey. A Shakespearean actress who worked with Augustin Daly's New York theater company from 1879 to 1899, she was the company's leading woman and performed memorable comedic roles in addition to successful serious performances. Her last performance was a benefit at the New York Met in 1905.

687. Barney Williams Barney Williams, whose real name was Bernard O'Flaherty, became one of the most popular Irish performers in the early antebellum period. Often accompanied by his wife, Maria Pray, he specialized in "the genuine Paddy, the true Irish peasant." Often this meant playing the stereotypical stage Irishman—a lovable buffoon who was fond of whiskey, song, dance, and fighting. A collection of his songs, *The Barney Williams Songster,* was very popular in the 1840s.

Entertainment Odds and Ends

688. Lola Montez Born in Limerick to a British father and Spanish mother, Marie Gilbert (1818–61) grew up in India and was educated in Scotland. She made her stage debut in 1843 in London as "Lola Montez, the Spanish Dancer" and soon became an international sensation as a "Spanish" dancer. She was strikingly beautiful and drew the amorous attention of many notable Europeans. Her most famous affair, with King Ludwig I of Bavaria, ultimately led to his abdication in 1848. Montez drew huge crowds during her American tour from 1851 to 1853. She later retired from dancing and became a popular lecturer on beauty secrets and heroines. She ended her days doing charity work.

689. Buffalo Bill Cody The legend and career of William Cody (aka Buffalo Bill) began on November 25, 1869, when the *New York Weekly* published the first installment of a new series: "Buffalo Bill, King of the Border Men." Author Ned Buntline, the paper explained, had gone west in search of an authentic hero and found him in the person of a twenty-four-year-old Irish American named William Cody. It was the beginning of an American legend and a career that would last more than three decades.

William Frederick Cody (1845–1917) was born in Scott County, Iowa. He left school at age twelve when his father died and tried his hand as a fur trapper, gold prospector, Pony Express rider, and Union Army scout. He later took up buffalo hunting to supply meat to the Kansas Pacific Railroad, killing over four thousand of the enormous creatures and earning his nickname. Subsequent service with the Fifth Cavalry as a civilian scout brought him many violent encounters with Sioux and Cheyenne warriors, including one where he shot and killed the Cheyenne chief Tall Bull.

Buntline's original stories caused a national mania over Buffalo Bill and made Cody a celebrity. Dozens of writers would eventually churn out more than three thousand "Buffalo Bill" dime novels. In the years that followed, Cody formed an idea for a spectacular touring show that would combine theater, circus, and rodeo for audiences starved for the legends and lore of the fast disappearing West. The result was *The Wild West* (Cody never called it a "show") which debuted in Omaha in May 1883. It proved a huge hit with audiences and Cody took it on the road and town after town brought out capacity crowds. *The Wild West* grew more elaborate every year, eventually topping out at four hundred horses and 650 cowboys, Indians, musicians, and support staff. They thrilled audiences across the U.S. and Europe with huge reenactments of cattle drives and clashes between Indians and cowboys. Over time Cody added big name stars like Annie Oakley and Sitting Bull. Cody attributed much of his success to the work of his PR man and fellow Irish American, John M. Burke.

At the height of his career, Cody was an international media superstar, earning an estimated one million dollars a year from ticket sales and endorsements for products like Winchester rifles and Stetson hats. Unfortunately, Cody blew every penny on high living and poor investments. Dire financial straits forced him to keep performing long after his skills and popularity had faded. He died in Colorado in 1917 at the age of seventy-two.

690. Patrick Gilmore When Patrick Sarsfield Gilmore (1829–92), a native son of County Galway, left Famine Ireland in 1848, he sailed along with the regiment band for which he played the cornet. He became leader of the Boston Brigade Band (later known as the famous Gilmore's Band). Gilmore was bandmaster of the 24th Massachusetts Regiment during the Civil War, and in 1863 revamped all Massachusetts' militia bands.

Patrick Sarsfield Gilmore

After the war, Gilmore became one of the world's most famous bandleaders. His signature was the "monster band" that grew to include a chorus of thousands accompanied by hundreds of instruments. In 1869 at the National Peace Jubilee in Boston he organized an extravaganza performance that included more than ten thousand participants, firing cannons, ringing church bells, and one hundred firemen beating anvils in Giuseppe Verdi's "Anvil Chorus." In 1872 he assumed leadership of the 22nd New York Regiment Band. For the next twenty years they performed across the United States and Europe and remained extremely popular right up to Gilmore's death in 1892.

Twentieth-Century
Stage and Screen

Actors and Actresses

691. Irish American Academy Award Winners

Year	Name	Award	Film
1931	Lionel Barrymore	Best Actor	*A Free Soul*
1932	Helen Hayes	Best Actress	*The Sin of Madelon Claudet*
1935	Victor McLaglen	Best Actor	*The Informer*
	John Ford	Best Director	*The Informer*
1936	Walter Brennan	Best Supporting Actor	*Come and Get It*
1937	Spencer Tracy	Best Actor	*Captains Courageous*
	Alice Brady	Best Supporting Actress	*In Old Chicago*
	Leo McCarey	Best Director	*The Awful Truth*
1938	Spencer Tracy	Best Actor	*Boys Town*
	Walter Brennan	Best Supporting Actor	*Kentucky*
1939	Thomas Mitchell	Best Supporting Actor	*Stagecoach*
1940	Walter Brennan	Best Supporting Actor	*The Westerner*
	John Ford	Best Director	*The Grapes of Wrath*
1941	John Ford	Best Director	*How Green Was My Valley*
1942	James Cagney	Best Actor	*Yankee Doodle Dandy*
	Greer Garson	Best Actress	*Mrs. Miniver*
1944	Bing Crosby	Best Actor	*Going My Way*
	Barry Fitzgerald	Best Supporting Actor	*Going My Way*
	Leo McCarey	Best Director	*Going My Way*
1945	James Dunn	Best Supporting Actor	*A Tree Grows in Brooklyn*
1948	Walter Huston	Best Supporting Actor	*The Treasure of Sierra Madre*
	John Huston	Best Director	*The Treasure of Sierra Madre*
1949	Mercedes McCambridge	Best Supporting Actress	*All the King's Men*
1952	Anthony Quinn	Best Supporting Actor	*Viva Zapata!*
	John Ford	Best Director	*The Quiet Man*
1954	Grace Kelly	Best Actress	*The Country Girl*
	Edmund O'Brien	Best Supporting Actor	*The Barefoot Contessa*
1955	Jack Lemmon	Best Supporting Actor	*Mister Roberts*
1956	Anthony Quinn	Best Supporting Actor	*Lust for Life*
	Dorothy Malone	Best Supporting Actress	*Written on the Wind*
1958	Susan Hayward	Best Actress	*I Want to Live*
1960	Burt Lancaster	Best Actor	*Elmer Gantry*
1962	Gregory Peck	Best Actor	*To Kill a Mockingbird*
	Ed Begley	Best Supporting Actor	*Sweet Bird of Youth*
1963	Patricia Neal	Best Actress	*Hud*
1967	George Kennedy	Best Supporting Actor	*Cool Hand Luke*
1969	John Wayne	Best Actor	*True Grit*
1970	Helen Hayes	Best Supporting Actress	*Airport*
1972	Liza Minnelli	Best Actress	*Cabaret*
1973	Jack Lemmon	Best Actor	*Save the Tiger*
	Tatum O'Neal	Best Supporting Actress	*Paper Moon*

1974	Art Carney	Best Actor	*Harry and Tonto*
	Ellen Burstyn	Best Actress	*Alice Doesn't Live Here Anymore*
1975	Jack Nicholson	Best Actor	*One Flew Over the Cuckoo's Nest*
1977	Jason Robards	Best Supporting Actor	*Julia*
1980	Robert Redford	Best Director	*Ordinary People*
1981	Warren Beatty	Best Director	*Reds*
	Maureen Stapleton	Best Supporting Actress	*Reds*
1983	Jack Nicholson	Best Supporting Actor	*Terms of Endearment*
	Shirley MacLaine	Best Actress	*Terms of Endearment*
1985	Anjelica Huston	Best Supporting Actress	*Prizzi's Honor*
1988	Jodie Foster	Best Actress	*The Accused*
	Kevin Kline	Best Supporting Actor	*A Fish Called Wanda*
1991	Jodie Foster	Best Actress	*The Silence of the Lambs*
1995	Susan Sarandon	Best Actress	*Dead Man Walking*
1996	Frances McDormand	Best Actress	*Fargo*
1997	Jack Nicholson	Best Actor	*As Good as It Gets*

692. The Barrymores In the 1920s, the Barrymore family of actors, John, Lionel, and Ethyl, were known as "the first family of the stage." They were the children of Maurice and Georgiana Barrymore. Maurice was born in Fort Agra, India, and began acting in London in 1872. Moving to New York in 1875, he gained immediate fame, leading to a long and successful career. His marriage in 1876 to actress Georgiana Drew,

the daughter of the famous actors, John and Louisa Lane Drew, established what became one of the most acclaimed families in show business.

The most famous of the trio, John Barrymore, became famous for his roles as a debonair leading man and his skillful performances of Shakespeare's *Richard III* and *Hamlet*. He also starred in films such as *Dr. Jekyll and Mr. Hyde* (1920), *Beloved Rogue* (1927), *Dinner at Eight* (1933), *Romeo and Juliet* (1936), and *The Great Profile* (1940). Barrymore achieved additional fame for his flamboyant lifestyle and frequently outrageous antics off screen.

Ethyl Barrymore was born in 1879. She made her theatrical debut in New York City in 1894 and went on to star in many Broadway plays. Although she made several films, her first love was the theater, as evidenced by her opening, in 1928, the Ethel Barrymore Theater in New York. By this time she began to perform for radio (and later television). She made one film with her two brothers, *Rasputin and the Empress* (1933). Her 1944 performance as a poor mother with Cary Grant earned her an Oscar for Best Supporting Actress.

Lionel Barrymore, born in 1879, became one of the most acclaimed character actors of the first half of the twentieth century. He earned critical praise for his roles in *Peter Ibbetson* (1917) and *The Copperhead* (1918), and *The Jest* (1919), but his real love turned out to be film. His performance in *A Free Soul* (1931) earned him an Oscar for Best Actor. Some of his other popular films include *Grand Hotel* (1932), *Rasputin and the Empress* (1932), *Captains Courageous* (1937), *The Valley of Decision* (1945), *Duel in the Sun* (1947), and *Key Largo* (1948). In his older years he perfected the role of the irascible grump in films such as *A Christmas Carol* (1938) and *It's a Wonderful Life* (1946).

Of the great Barrymore trio, only John had children, Diana and John Jr. Both pursued careers in acting. Sadly, Diana's promising career was derailed by alcoholism, depression, and eventually suicide in 1960. His son, John Blythe Barrymore, Jr. (b. 1932), known as John Drew Barrymore, achieved nominal success as a film actor. His daughter, actress Drew Barrymore (b. 1975), carries on the family tradition.

693. Walter Brennan   One of Americas most talented and prolific character actors (three Academy Awards for Best Supporting Actor), Walter Brennan (1894–1974) came to the profession almost by accident. Born to Irish parents in Lynn, Massachusetts, Brennan joined the army when the U.S. entered World War I in 1917. Following the service, a chance move to California to sell real estate led him to pursue roles as an extra and to work at ABC. Before long, Brennan earned small character roles in feature films and went on to play a supporting role to some of the top leading actors of his time. In all, he appeared in over a hundred films, primarily Westerns, many of them classics. He played his crusty old man trademark character in the long-running TV series *The Real McCoys* in the 1950s.

694. James Cagney   Born the son of a bartender, James Cagney (1899–1986) grew up on the tough streets of New York's Lower East Side. Drawn to the theater, he began touring with a vaudeville troupe as a song-and-dance man with his wife Frances. In the late 1920s he moved to Broadway and enjoyed critical success opposite Joan Blondell in the musical *Penny Arcade* (1929). His performance in the film version brought him to Hollywood where he subsequently won the lead role in the movie *Public Enemy* (1931). It launched his career as the classic Irish gangster and led to several more films such as *Angels with Dirty Faces* (1938), *Each Dawn I Die* (1939), and *The Roaring Twenties* (1939). Cagney broke out of the urban tough role with his Academy Award–winning performance portraying song-and-dance showman George M. Cohan in *Yankee Doodle Dandy*

(1942). Cagney made many more films over the course of his career and received the American Film Institute's Life Achievement Award (1974) and the U.S. Medal of Freedom (1984).

695. Bing Crosby   The ultimate crooner, Harry Lillis "Bing" Crosby (1903–77) enjoyed enormous popularity as both a singer and actor. In the twenties he sang with orchestras and performed in an early sound film. But his big break came in 1932 when he landed his own radio show on CBS. Popular for his smooth and relaxed style, Crosby was soon recording hit records and acting in Hollywood films. He earned an Oscar for his portrayal of a singing priest who helped solve the problems of a poor city parish in *Going My Way* (1944). He later made seven "Road"

Bing Crosby

films with Bob Hope and Dorothy Lamour. In the 1960s, Crosby continued to record and ran a successful television production company. All told, from his many endeavors he amassed one of the biggest fortunes in entertainment history.

696. Barry Fitzgerald   Comedic actor Barry Fitzgerald (1888–1961) began life as William Joseph Shields in Dublin. While working as a civil servant, he played walk-on parts at the Abbey Theatre, eventually graduating to major roles. In 1932, after a New York run with the Abbey Players, he stayed in America and began a successful stage career on Broadway. His film career began in 1936 when John Ford cast him in the film adaptation of Sean O'Casey's play *The Plough and the Stars*. He subsequently acted in supporting roles in many films, including *How Green Was My Valley* (1941) and *None But the Lonely Heart* (1944). But it was his role alongside Bing Crosby as a lovable Catholic priest in the classic, *Going My Way* (1944), that earned him wide recognition and an Oscar for Best Supporting Actor.

697. Errol Flynn   Born in Hobart, Tasmania and educated in England and Australia, Errol Flynn (1909–59) led an adventurous life both on and off the screen. He debuted in the Australian film *In the Wake of the Bounty* (1933) and two years later relocated to Hollywood. His title role in *Captain Blood* (1935) launched his career as a dashing swashbuckling star. Unfortunately, he handled his fame poorly and his alcohol abuse, drug habit, and womanizing eventually hurt his career by the late 1940s. Although he was acquitted of charges of statutory rape for having sex with a sixteen-year-old girl on his yacht, the headlines "Robin Hood Charged with Rape" did great damage to his reputation. He died in 1959 still trying to revive his career and recover his fortune.

698. Helen Hayes   At the age of five, Helen Hayes (1900–93) began a vaunted acting career that spanned much of the century and led to the sobriquet "First Lady of Theater." A native of Washington, D.C., she made her Broadway debut at the age of twenty, eventually becoming a leading player in works by Shaw, O'Neill, and Shakespeare. A versatile actor on stage and screen, her work in Hollywood earned her two Oscars, including one for her first film, *The Sin of Madelon Claudet*.

699. Buster Keaton   The star of many classic silent movies, Joseph Francis "Buster" Keaton (1895–1966) joined his family's vaudeville act at five, in violation of child labor laws. Although his parents were accused of abuse for rough stage treatment of little Keaton, he parlayed his childhood inclination for mishaps into a sympathetic character and became an accomplished acrobat.

The famous Harry Houdini gave him the nickname "Buster" after seeing the youngster fall down a flight of stairs. He acted in his first silent film in 1917 and by the 1920s he was producing, directing, and starring in his own films. Most were classic slapstick shorts featuring Keaton—"the great stone face"—as a pathetic character who wore a perpetual deadpan expression while enduring one calamity after another.

Like many stars of the silent film genre, Keaton was unable to make the jump to sound films when they arrived at the end of the 1920s. He spent most of the 1930s out of work and struggling with alcoholism, financial ruin, and marital difficulties. He made a comeback in the 1950s and 1960s as a grand old man of American entertainment.

700. Gene Kelly   Gene Kelly (1913–96), the suave and handsome dancer, actor, and choreographer, began his career on Broadway in the late thirties, eventually landing the title role in *Pal Joey* in 1940. Displaying a wonderful talent for both dance and song, he moved to Hollywood where he became the quintessential song-and-dance man, starring in such classic musicals as *On the Town, Anchors Aweigh,* and *Singin' in the Rain.* An innovator in the field of choreography, Kelly propelled dance on film in new directions and was awarded a special Academy Award for choreography for the spectacular *An American in Paris.*

701. Grace Kelly   Born into a talented Philadelphia Irish family, Grace Kelly (1929–82) epitomized glamour in a film career that included starring roles in *High Noon* and *High Society.* She was

Grace Kelly

the picture of cool detachment in three classics by Alfred Hitchcock: *Dial M for Murder, Rear Window,* and *To Catch a Thief.* In 1956 she married Prince Rainier of Monaco and disappointed her legions of fans by retiring from the screen. She suffered a tragic and premature death in a car crash on a mountain in southern France.

702. Pat O'Brien Born William O'Brien, Jr., Pat O'Brien (1899–1983) epitomized the early twentieth-century Irish American image. In his youth, he performed at Marquette University with friend Spencer Tracy and later joined him in studying acting in New York City. He made his Broadway debut in the popular 1925 production of *A Man's Man.* His breakthrough to film stardom came in his third film, *The Front Page* (1930). O'Brien achieved fame on the stage and screen in the 1930s and 1940s, most often in roles depicting Irish Americans—*Angels with Dirty Faces* (1938), *The Fighting 69th* (1940), *Fighting Father Dunne* (1948), and *The Last Hurrah* (1958). Yet his most famous performance was when he played Knute Rockne in the 1940 classic, *Knute Rockne–All American.* Over the course of his career, O'Brien received honors from Irish American groups including the John F. Kennedy Medal of the Ancient Order of Hibernians.

703. Maureen O'Hara Born Maureen Fitzsimmons (b. 1921) in Milltown, County Dublin, she was raised in a family active in singing and acting. She studied theater in England and Ireland and joined the Abbey Theatre in 1939. A year later she was in London starring in her first film *(Jamaica Inn)* and soon found herself in Hollywood, where she met the great director John Ford. Her first major role came in Ford's Academy Award–winning film *How Green Was My Valley* (1940). In the many roles she landed thereafter, O'Hara turned her feisty redhead persona into the American stereotype for Irish colleens. Many of O'Hara's films had Irish themes, most notably the ever-popular *The Quiet Man* (1952), with John Wayne. She worked with many of Hollywood's top leading men in both dramatic and comedy roles and her numerous pairings with Wayne were popular with moviegoers. O'Hara left Hollywood for St. Croix in the 1960s after marrying aviator Charles Blair, but kept a home in County Cork and maintained connections with several Irish American groups. In 1999 she was honored as Grand Marshal of New York's St. Patrick's Day Parade.

704. Gregory Peck Gregory Peck (b. 1916) originally wanted a career in medicine, but eventually found himself drawn to the theater. Born in La Jolla, California, to a mother from County Kerry, he moved to New York in the early 1940s. He won a role in *The Morning Star* (1942) and received favorable reviews. More stage productions followed until his first film roles in *Days of Glory* (1943) and *The Keys of the Kingdom* (1944). In these and subsequent films, such as *Spellbound* (1945), *Duel in the Sun* (1946), *The Yearling* (1946), *Gentleman's Agreement* (1947), and *Twelve O'Clock High* (1949), Peck gained a reputation as a skilled and conscientious actor. He won an Oscar for his performance as the compassionate Southern lawyer in *To Kill a Mockingbird* (1962). It was during the filming of *Moby Dick* (1956) in Ireland that Peck developed a lifelong affection for the country.

705. Tyrone Power Tyrone Power (1914–58) was born in Cincinnati into a theatrical family. His parents Frederick Power and Emma (Reaume) were respected Shakespearean actors. Power began acting in school and made his professional debut in *The Merchant of Venice.* After years of acting in the theater, he moved into film acting, signing a contract with Twentieth Century Fox. He quickly became a major star for his roles in many films. After service in the Marine Corps during World War II, he returned to Hollywood. His starring role in *The Razor's Edge* (1946) earned rave reviews and is considered one of his best performances, second only to that in his last film, *Witness for the Prosecution* (1957).

706. Pat Rooney Vaudeville entertainer Pat Rooney (1880–1962) enjoyed a seventy-year-long song-and-dance career in stage, nightclubs, and television. Born in New York, Rooney took to the stage at the age of twelve in an act with his sister after their father's death. He starred in stage productions, often musical comedies, and teamed with his several wives. He showed his dance skill in *Night Club,* one of the first sound films. For a time he paired with Herman Timberg in a popular Irish-Jewish act playing at New York's noted Palace Theater. Rooney remained an active entertainer until his death in 1962.

707. Spencer Tracy Born in Milwaukee, Spencer Bonaventure Tracy (1900–67) had one of the most successful careers in the history of film. Throughout his seventy-four films, he displayed tremendous versatility in roles ranging from Fr. Flanagan in *Boys Town* (1938) to Clarence Darrow in *Inherit the Wind* (1960). After serving in the navy during World War I, he returned to college where he took up acting (meeting actor Pat O'Brien in the process). In the early 1920s he began acting in New York where he caught the eye of producer George M. Cohan. Through Cohan, Tracy received both mentoring and roles in major Broadway productions. With his reputation established, Tracy went to Hollywood where he signed with Twentieth Century Fox in 1930. In his first film, *Up the River* (1930), director John Ford gave him the lead opposite Humphrey Bogart. Tracy went on to win consecutive Oscars for his roles in *Captains Courageous* (1937) and *Boys Town* (1937) and earned many more nominations in the years that followed. His romance with Katharine Hepburn, both on- and off-screen, gave his roles an extra depth and led to such wonderful movies as *Woman of the Year* (1942.)

708. John Wayne The "Duke" as he was popularly known, was born in Iowa as Marion Michael Morrison (1907–79). His family moved to California when he was still young and he at-

tended USC on a football scholarship. To make extra money, Wayne worked as a set laborer and assistant propman at the nearby Fox Studios. Soon he got his first of several small parts in low-budget Western films and serials, meeting director John Ford in the process. Wayne achieved stardom as the Ringo Kid in Ford's 1939 classic *Stagecoach.* From there Wayne went on to make over 150 films, fifteen with Ford, including *The Quiet Man* (1951), which won an Oscar. He became perhaps the most famous actor in the twentieth century and an icon of American manliness and patriotism. Although Wayne was of somewhat distant, mostly Scotch Irish heritage, he enjoyed tremendous popularity among Irish Americans who were drawn to his mixture of brash machismo and unflinching love of country.

709. Other Notable Irish American Stars of the Silver Screen

Some Recent: Warren Beatty, Ed Burns, James M. Cain, George Clooney, Brian Dennehy, Robert Downey, Jr., Harrison Ford, Jody Foster, Anjelica Huston, Bill Murray, Jack Nicholson, Chris O'Donnell, The O'Neals (Ryan and Tatum), Aidan Quinn, Jason Robards, Mickey Rourke, Meg Ryan, Susan Sarandon, the Sheens (Martin and Charlie), Emelio Estevez, Brooke Shields, and Maureen Stapleton.

Some Classics: Ed Begley, Peter Boyle, Alice Brady, Ellen Burstyn, Dennis Day, James Dunn, Mia Farrow, Ava Gardner, Judy Garland, Greer Garson, Susan Hayward, John Huston, Walter Huston, George Kennedy, Burt Lancaster, Jack Lemmon, Jack Lord, Shirley MacLaine, Dorothy Malone, Patricia Neal, Edmund O'Brien, Maureen O'Sullivan, Peter O'Toole, Anthony Quinn, Ronald Reagan, and Debbie Reynolds.

Behind the Scenes

710. Walt Disney A native of Kansas City, Walt Disney (1901–66) spent most of his boyhood on a farm in Missouri. At age sixteen he went to Chicago to study art and from 1920 to 1922 he worked in Kansas City, Missouri, where, under the pioneer animator Ub Iwerks, he made simple cartoon advertisements that were shown in movie theaters. In 1923 Disney came to Hollywood with his brother Roy and opened a small studio to create animated shorts. His first two series—*Alice in Cartoonland* (1924–26) and *Oswald the Rabbit* (1926–28)—enjoyed only modest success. But his debut of the short cartoon *Steamboat Willie* in 1928 launched an entertainment juggernaut that would branch into feature-length movies, television, and theme parks and create characters popular with children all over the world. Throughout his career he was at the forefront of animation innovation, introducing the Technicolor process in 1932 and the first full-length feature cartoon in 1937, *Snow White and the Seven Dwarfs*. In 1950 Disney launched its production on the emerging medium of television. Although originally drawn to the profession as an illustrator, Disney discovered that his true talent lay in dreaming up new characters, images, and projects and then directing the team that brought them into being. As his success grew, he did less and less of the animation.

In 1955, he opened Disneyland, in Anaheim, California, an amusement park based on the characters and themes of his studio's productions. Disney World, in Orlando, Florida, opened in 1971, five years after Disney's death.

711. John Ford Born John Martin Ford (not Sean Aloysius O'Feeney as he often claimed) in Cape Elizabeth, Maine, to parents who had emigrated from Galway, John Ford (1895–1973) became one of the most highly regarded directors in Hollywood. He arrived in California sometime around 1913, just as the film industry was taking form. He slowly worked his way into the field, going from stunt man, to actor, to assistant director. By the 1930s he was a director in his own right. His first big hit was *The Informer* (1935). The story of an IRA turncoat won Ford his first of four Oscars. His next hit was *Stagecoach* (1939), a

John Ford

film that launched the career of a young actor he discovered, John Wayne. Ford later won Oscars for *The Grapes of Wrath* (1940), *How Green Was My Valley* (1941), and *The Quiet Man* (1952). His last feature film was *Seven Women* (1965). The American Film Institute awarded him its first Life Achievement Award in 1973.

712. Leo McCarey Although Thomas Leo McCarey's (1898–1969) Irish parents urged him to pursue a career in law, fate would lead him into the film industry as a writer, producer, and director of light-hearted comedies and nostalgic romances. McCarey directed many classic films such as *The Awful Truth* (1937) and *An Affair to Remember* (1957), both starring Cary Grant. Perhaps most notable are *Going My Way* (1944), a multiple Academy Award–winning film about a priest's efforts to save his parish, and 1945's *The Bells of Saint Mary's* (1945), about a financially burdened parochial school, both starring Bing Crosby as Father Chuck O'Malley.

713. John Huston John Huston (1906–87) was born into a theatrical family—his father was the well-known actor Walter Huston. He grew up in theaters and after trying his hand at everything from amateur boxing, to riding in the Mexican cavalry, to journalism, he became a script writer in 1931. His first film was also one of his greatest, *The Maltese Falcon* (1941). He went on to make many more films with its star, Humphrey Bogart, including, *The African Queen* (1952) and *The Treasure of the Sierra Madre* (1948).

Huston developed a strong interest in his

Irish heritage. During the 1950s and 1960s, he lived in St. Clerans in County Galway with his wife and two children. He became a passionate devotee of James Joyce and his last movie (starring his daughter Angelica) was based on Joyce's short story *The Dead* (1987).

714. Mack Sennett   Film director, producer, actor was born Michael Sennett (1880–1960) in Danville, Quebec, Canada. As a young man he moved to New York where he appeared in comedic roles on Broadway and in burlesque. In 1908, sensing the potential of film, he switched to the motion picture industry and became a devoted student of D. W. Griffith, the director of *Birth of a Nation*. A cofounder of Keystone Studio, he is credited with establishing slapstick comedy in America (he got the idea from French theater and films). One aspect of slapstick he is credited with inventing is the custard pie in the face. "A pie in the face," he once said, "provided the recipient does not anticipate it, has no equal in slapstick comedy. It can reduce dignity to nothing in seconds." Sennett is most remembered for his Keystone Kops series. The routines involving a crew of hapless policemen are memorable for their humor and for their subtle, classically Irish, jabs at authority. Sennett received a special Oscar in 1937.

715. Preston Sturges   Edmund Preston Biden (1898–1959) was a Chicagoan whose maternal grandparents had immigrated to Canada from Ireland. Inspired by silent jokesters like Buster Keaton, Sturges achieved success as an actor, director, writer, and producer in the 1940s. After a failed attempt at songwriting, Sturges turned to playwriting, finding success with *Strictly Dishonorable* in 1929. Sturges' big break came in 1940 when he directed his own script (the first to do so), a political comedy called *The Great McGinty*. Other directing credits include *Never Say Die* (1939), *Sullivan's Travels* (1941), and *Hail the Conquering Hero* (1944).

716. Robert J. Flaherty   Born in Michigan, Robert Flaherty (1884–1951) grew up in Canada. From an early age he showed an interest in photography, later moving to film. Known as the "father of documentary filmmaking," his first film, *Nanook of the North* (1922), was shot during a sixteen-month stay in an Eskimo community. It earned international praise for its dramatic interpretation of the Eskimo way of life and was a major contributor to the genre of nonfiction filmmaking that emerged in the 1930s. Indeed, the term "documentary" was first coined by fellow filmmaker John Grierson who used it to describe Flaherty's film *Moana* (1926), about an isolated South Seas tribe. He went on to make several more documentaries in the 1930s and 1940s.

Entertainment Odds and Ends

717. ABIE'S IRISH ROSE   The most popular Broadway musical of the 1920s was based on a most improbable scenario—an Irish-Jewish romance. *Abie's Irish Rose* was panned by the critics as fatuous and thin, but audiences loved it. When it finally closed, it held the record for the longest-running show in Broadway history at 2,327 performances (long since surpassed). It soon became a movie (in 1929 and again in 1946) and popular radio program. Interestingly, even though Irish-Jewish marriages were very rare at the time, *Abie's Irish Rose* was only one of more than twenty films in the 1920s based on that scenario. Indeed, it's a device that persists to this day in popular sitcoms, from *Bridget Loves Bernie* in the 1970s, to *Northern Exposure* (featuring the characters Joel Fleishman and Maggie O'Connell) in the 1990s.

718. Willis O'Brien   Willis O'Brien (1886–1962) was born in Oakland, California, and worked many jobs before finding his calling in film animation. Working as a cartoonist for a San Francisco newspaper, he started making sculptures in 1913. Soon, he began experimenting with rubber, allowing his models to move. O'Brien eventually found work with Thomas Edison's Biograph Company. His animated dinosaurs in *The Lost World* (1925) was a breakthrough moment in the history of film special effects. O'Brien's most famous work was his creation of King Kong for the (1933) film of the same name.

O'Brien left a lasting impact on his field. His innovative techniques with miniatures were used for several decades. He also devised a rear-projection system that allowed live actors to appear in the mini-set. In 1950, the stop-animation techniques he developed earned him the first special Oscar awarded for special effects for his work on *Mighty Joe Young* (1949). In recent years, O'Brien has been listed as among the one hundred most influential people in filmmaking history.

719. Emmett Kelly   Emmett Lee Kelly (1898–1979) was born in Sedan, Kansas. An aspiring cartoon-

Emmett Kelly

ist, Kelly drew Weary Willie the clown, a character he was to later portray in a variety of circus troupes. In the midst of Depression-era blues, the disheveled tramp with large frowning lips and worn clothes won raucous laughter from his audiences. He became a regular feature of the Ringling Brothers Barnum and Bailey Circus in 1942 and appeared in *The Greatest Show on Earth* in 1952. Today, Emmett Kelly, Jr., delights kids of all ages as Weary Willie.

720. Shipwreck Kelly   Alvin "Shipwreck" Kelly (1885–1952) was one of the most memorable characters to emerge during the Roaring Twenties. Beginning with his first stunt in 1924

(13 hours and 13 minutes) he achieved international fame for his ability to sit for incredibly long periods atop flagpoles. No explanation has ever been given for the origin of his nickname, other than the fact that he once worked on the New York waterfront. So great was the mania surrounding his exploits that several impostors, calling themselves "Shipwreck Kelly," staged their own flagpole sitting stunts. The real Kelly topped them all by sitting on Atlantic City's Steel Pier's flagpole for seven weeks in 1930—still the record. By the end of his career, he figured he had sat on poles for over twenty thousand hours.

Ten Classic Irish American Films

721. ANGELS WITH DIRTY FACES (1938)   A classic 1930s gangster movie, *Angels with Dirty Faces* (1938) tells the story of two youngsters growing up in the slums of New York. James Cagney's Rocky Sullivan is sent to reform school, and graduates to a life of crime, while his friend Jerry Connolly (Pat O'Brien) becomes a priest. Fr. Connolly struggles to reform the young boys of the neighborhood, who adore and emulate Rocky, and tries to build a recreation center as an alternative. He and Rocky come to blows when Rocky offers stolen money as a donation to the center. Cagney gives one of his best performances as the classic Irish American thug—quite a contrast to the image he would portray in *Yankee Doodle Dandy* in 1942.

722. GONE WITH THE WIND (1939)   Although *Gone With the Wind* is set firmly in the American South, its Irish origins are solid. Scarlett O'Hara's father, Thomas, is an Irish immigrant who names his plantation, Tara, after the ancestral home of the high kings of Ireland. After Scarlett teases him for talking "like an Irishman," he admits he's proud to be Irish and imparts to her an Irish love of the land, saying, "Why, land's the only thing in the world worth working for, worth fighting for, worth dying for, because it's the only thing that lasts." As another example of their Irish and Catholic heritage, the O'Haras are twice shown saying the Rosary.

723. GOING MY WAY (1940) Like *Angels with Dirty Faces,* this film is set in a tough Irish neighborhood of New York City and features an idealistic priest who tries to help the troubled youth of his parish. But the focus here is on the relationship between two priests—Bing Crosby and Barry Fitzgerald. With superb performances and a heartwarming story, the film took three Oscars—Crosby (Best Actor), Fitzgerald (Best Supporting Actor), and Leo McCarey (Best Director).

724. YANKEE DOODLE DANDY (1942) One of Hollywood's grandest musicals, *Yankee Doodle Dandy* chronicles the rags-to-riches life of the great Irish American song-and-dance man George M. Cohan. The film marked an important turning point in the career of James Cagney who previously had enjoyed fame starring in a series of gangster movies. His performance as the ebullient Cohan put on display many of Cagney's heretofore unused talents honed in his early days in vaudeville. It also won him an Oscar for Best Actor. The movie's unbridled patriotism—opening right after the attack on Pearl Harbor—came as a needed boost to American morale. The film remains a favorite for its lively songs and fantastic dance numbers.

725. A TREE GROWS IN BROOKLYN (1945) Elia Kazan's directorial debut, *A Tree Grows in Brooklyn* (1945), is based on Betty Smith's novel about young Francie Nolan growing up in Brooklyn during the Depression. Although Smith's parents were German immigrants, she grew up with Irish immigrants and they appear consistently in her fiction. Francie's father, Johnny, is a common figure in Irish fictional families: the charming drunk, the lovable but unreliable source of songs and stories. The bittersweet coming-of-age story tracks

Francie's ups and downs, her family's poverty, her love of learning, and her father's death. Long a favorite, *A Tree Grows in Brooklyn* won two Oscars: Best Supporting Actor for James Dunn as Johnny, and a special Best Child Actress award for Peggy Ann Garner in the role of Francie.

726. THE QUIET MAN (1952) The first American movie to be filmed on location in Ireland, *The Quiet Man* (1952) has become an Irish American classic, aired at least once every St. Patrick's Day. Starring John Wayne as Sean Thornton, a native who returns to Inisfree after life as a boxer in Pittsburgh, the movie highlights the stock images of rural Ireland: thatched cottages, horse-drawn carts, turf fires, and red-haired local beauties (Maureen O'Hara). Thornton buys a picturesque cottage and courts O'Hara, but her brother disapproves of the returned

John Wayne

Yank and refuses to hand over O'Hara's dowry, without which she can't consider herself properly married. *The Quiet Man,* considered a risk by director John Ford's studio, went on to win four Oscars, including Best Director and Best Screenplay, and remains a must-see for hibernophiles everywhere.

727. THE LAST HURRAH (1958) John Ford's screen adaptation of Edwin O'Connor's book of the same name tells the story of Frank Skeffington, a thinly disguised fictional version of Boston politician James Michael Curley. Skeffington (played masterfully by Spencer Tracy) has been in politics for decades and decides to run for office one last time. He employs all the tried and true tricks of

Spencer Tracy

old-style machine politics, but finds the world has changed. However much one might quibble with O'Connor's historical interpretation of the end of machine politics, the film, like the book, highlighted the dawn of a new, more assimilated chapter in the Irish American experience.

728. THE MOLLY MAGUIRES (1970) *The Molly Maguires* is based on a real secret society of Irish coal miners in Pennsylvania in the 1870s. The group served as an unofficial union that fought mine owners for higher wages and better working conditions. In the movie, Sean Connery is Jack Kehoe, the leader of the Mollies, who forms a close friendship with newcomer James McParlan (Richard Harris) who turns out to be an informer and a detective. Over the course of the film, Harris' character identifies closely with Kehoe and the Mollies, as they terrorize the area, blowing up trains and raiding the police station and local businesses, although his true colors emerge in the end. There are great performances by Connery and Harris, a gripping historical story line, and an excellent score of Irish ballads.

729. THE BROTHERS MCMULLEN (1995) *The Brothers McMullen*, written and directed by Ed Burns, won top honors at the Sundance Film Festival in 1995. The three brothers, each unique but similar in drinking habits (they're never very far from a bottle of beer), provide a good cross-section of suburban Irish American men in the '90s. The eldest Jack (Jack Mulcahy), is a married high school coach who is resisting parenthood and his safe suburban life. Burns' character, Barry, is a cynical aspiring filmmaker and ladies' man who wants to

move to Manhattan but can't quite afford to. The youngest, Patrick (Mike McGlone), is about to move in with his Jewish girlfriend, but is held back by residual Catholic guilt. The film's low budget is evidenced by the many scenes filmed at Burns' parents' house in Long Island, but real humor and true-to-life situations give it a fresh, original voice. The film's popularity can also be attributed to the surge in interest in Irish and Irish American culture in the 1990s (see entry #256).

730. THE DEAD (1987) John Huston's final film, *The Dead* (1987), is a beautiful and loyal adaptation of James Joyce's short story. Houston directs his daughter Angelica as Gretta, Donal McCann as her husband, Gabriel, and a mostly Irish cast, including the late tenor Frank Patterson. The story unfolds over a dinner party hosted by Gabriel's relatives during which Irish politics and culture are discussed. But the most haunting scenes are the final ones in Gabriel and Gretta's hotel room. Gretta tells her husband about a boy who loved her and died when she moved to Dublin. Gabriel realizes that he has never loved or been loved as the dead youth, Michael Furey, did. The final paragraphs of Joyce's story are respectfully and effectively filmed in an unforgettable way.

Radio and Television

731. Fred Allen Fred Allen (1894–1956) was born John Florence Sullivan in Cambridge, Massachusetts. He attended Boston's public schools and worked all manner of jobs to help support himself. One of these jobs—at a public library—brought him into contact with a book on comedy. Soon he was hooked on the idea of a life in show biz. By his eighteenth birthday he was appearing with the B. F. Keith vaudeville circuit as "Freddie St. James: The World's Worst Juggler."

By the early 1920s Allen was appearing at one of New York's most famous vaudeville houses, the Palace Theater. There he met his show biz partner, Portland Hoffa, whom he married in

1927. They would form one of the most memorable husband-and-wife comedy teams of all time, second only to George Burns and Gracie Allen.

Allen's opportunity to jump from stage to broadcast studio came in October 1932 when he was hired by CBS to host *The Linit Bath Club Revue*. It was an immediate success and launched Allen on a seventeen-year career in radio. By 1939 the name of the popular Saturday night program was changed to *The Fred Allen Show*.

By far Allen's funniest and most popular feature sketch was "Allen's Alley" which debuted in late 1942. It featured Allen walking through his neighborhood encountering an incredible cast of characters, including the *very* average John Doe, a pompous poet by the name of Falstaff Openshaw, the lovable Jewish mama Mrs. Nussbaum, and a blustering Southern senator Beauregard Claghorn (the inspiration behind the Looney Tunes rooster Foghorn Leghorn).

Another well-known feature of Allen's show was his famous "feud" with Jack Benny. It began one night in 1936 when Allen made a crack about Benny's violin playing. The next week Benny retaliated in kind and the good-natured dispute was on. They played the roles to the hilt, but offstage they were very good friends.

But Allen was not merely a comedian, he was a sharp social critic and iconoclast, an antiauthoritarian in the great Irish American tradition of Edward Harrigan and Finley Peter Dunne. He delighted in puncturing the swelled egos of public figures, teasing his sponsors, and lampooning current events. "You can take all the sincerity in Hollywood," he once said, "place it in the navel of a fruit fly and still have room enough for three caraway seeds and a producer's heart."

The last *Fred Allen Show* was broadcast on June 26, 1949. Fittingly, his "enemy" Jack Benny appeared as his guest. He continued to appear regularly on *What's My Line* before his death on St. Patrick's Day 1956.

732. Gracie Allen   Grace Ethel Cecile Rosalie

Allen (1895–1964), the acclaimed wife and show business partner of George Burns, began her career as a small child in vaudeville, performing with her father, the singer and dancer Edward Allen. At fourteen she formed a vaudeville act with her sisters, but by the early 1920s she had pretty well given up her stage career and was working as a stenographer. Then she met George Burns and soon she was back on stage. The couple married in 1926 and soon gained their own radio show that ran for seventeen years. Husband-and-wife domestic humor was their stock in trade, with Burns playing the reserved straight man to Allen the airheaded chatterbox with a gift for simple wisdom. Burns and Allen made thirteen films together and later moved to television with the sitcom *George Burns and Gracie Allen Show* (1950–58).

733. Art Carney   Best known as Ed Norton from the television comedy *The Honeymooners*, Art Carney (b. 1918) appeared in many media, including *The Odd Couple* on Broadway, *The Cavanaughs* TV series, and the film *Harry and Tonto*, for which he won an Oscar in 1975. Carney built his career in radio in the 1940s, appearing on daytime dramas, mysteries, and children's shows, usually in character and doing dialect parts, before reaching the pinnacle of his career on *The Honeymooners*.

734. Jackie Gleason   After winning an amateur-night competition at fifteen, Jackie Gleason (1916–87) began a slow ascent up the rungs of the show business ladder. A native of Brooklyn, he filled a variety of occupations (including radio disc jockey and exhibition diver in the water follies) before moving to

Jackie Gleason

Hollywood in the 1940s to shoot eight unexceptional movies. He returned to New York in the late 1940s to work on Broadway. He launched a successful television career in 1950 as the host of the Dumont network's *Cavalcade of Stars*. That led to the *Jackie Gleason Show* in 1952. *The Honeymooners*, the show that made Gleason's career, began as a series of five- to ten-minute skits on the show. It eventually became the main feature and in 1956–57 Gleason created a whole season of thirty-minute episodes. Gleason won a Tony Award for his role in the Broadway musical *Take Me Along* (1959) and an Oscar nomination for Best Supporting Actor for his portrayal of pool shark Minnesota Fats in *The Hustler* (1961).

735. Ed Herlihy   Ed Herlihy (1909–99) was famous before anyone knew his name or saw his picture. As the voice of Universal Studio's newsreels shown before every movie, Herlihy informed millions of Americans about the leading news of the day, especially the events of World War II. Two years after the war, he began a long association with Kraft Foods, hosting their sponsored radio programs and later the *Kraft Television Theater* in the 1950s. Audiences never saw his face, but grew to love his friendly, assuring voice. It was Herlihy who introduced Cheez Whiz, Velveeta, and Miracle Whip to America. Once when helping a blind man cross the street at New York's Times Square, the man said, "I know you. You're the cheese man on TV." Herlihy did countless commercials for other products and later provided voiceovers for movies such as Woody Allen's *Radio Days* and *Zelig*.

736. Carroll O'Connor   Carroll O'Connor (1924–2001) was born in New York City and grew up in middle-class comfort. After serving in the marines during World War II he went to college where he fell in love with theater. Accepted at the National University of Ireland, he spent several years studying and performing in his ancestral homeland. He returned to the U.S. and began a successful career on Broadway. In the 1960s, he performed in more than two dozen films, but was still largely unknown when selected by Norman Lear to play Archie Bunker in the television comedy *All in the Family*. He played this role for thirteen seasons, winning an Emmy Award in 1972. At the time, the Norman Lear comedy sparked much controversy and debate for its treatment of social issues like race and crime. Today, however, it is seen as a path-breaking show and O'Connor's performances as Archie, the unreconstructed bigot and sexist, are hailed for their enduring quality.

737. Ed Sullivan   Ed Sullivan (1901–79) began his career in journalism right out of high school when he joined his local paper to cover weddings, deaths, and sports. He advanced quickly in the newspaper world, eventually creating the column "Little Old New York" for the *Daily News*. In that same year (1932) he joined WABC as a radio host, introducing up and coming players in the worlds of entertainment and the arts. In 1942 Sullivan moved his act to the brand new medium, television. His program, *Ed Sullivan Entertains*, eventually led to the *Ed Sullivan Show*, a program that defined television for a generation. For more than three decades Sullivan showcased the greatest names in show business as well as the occasional dancing bear and plate spinner. Much of America tuned in to catch stars such as Elvis Presley, the Beatles, and Judy Garland.

Music

The Nineteenth Century

738. Thomas Moore   For most Irish immigrants in America, the great composer of Irish music was Thomas Moore (1779–1852). A poet and friend of many of the leading literary figures of his day, Moore was born in Dublin and graduated from Trinity College in 1799. He studied law, but found his calling in writing poetry. In 1807, he published the first of many volumes of *Irish*

Thomas Moore

Melodies, collections of poems set to music by Moore and Sir John Stevenson. The songs, among them "The Harp That Once Through Tara's Halls," "The Last Rose of Summer," "Oft in the Stilly Night," proved phenomenally popular among London's aristocracy and nationalists in Ireland and America. As William H. A. Williams writes in the *Encyclopedia of the Irish in America,* "Moore's themes—love of Ireland, a powerful feeling of nostalgia, especially the strong sense of loss that permeates so many of his songs—helped to define the Irish parlor ballad for other songwriters who followed in his wake."

739. Captain O'Neill Another significant contributor to traditional Irish music was Captain Francis O'Neill (1848–1936) of the Chicago Police Department. Motivated by his love of traditional Irish music and the stirrings of the Gaelic Revival (see entries #392 and #400), O'Neill began in the 1890s to collect hundreds of Irish songs, many that had never been committed to paper. Despite not knowing how to read music, he eventually collected more than two thousand songs and published several volumes, including *The Music of Ireland* (1903), *The Dance Music of Ireland* (1907), and *Irish Folk Music* (1910).

740. Daniel Emmett A multitalented and

Capt. Francis O'Neill

largely self-taught musician, Daniel Decatur Emmett (1815–1904) was a key contributor to the phenomenally popular theatrical form known as minstrel show (see entry #676). He learned the technique of "Negro impersonation" while traveling with circus bands and eventually organized the popular Virginia Minstrels. In 1859 Emmett, a Northerner, wrote "Dixie," the song that quickly became the anthem of the South during the Civil War. Emmett's other songwriting credits include "Old Dan Tucker" (written as a teenager) and "Turkey in the Straw."

741. Stephen Foster Stephen Collins Foster (1826–64), author of classic minstrel tunes such as "Camptown Races," "My Old Kentucky Home," "Oh, Susanna," and "Old Folks At Home," was born to a Pennsylvania pioneer family that had roots in Derry, Ireland. Although he received no formal musical instruction, Foster went on to become one of the most successful songwriters in American history. In his twenty-year career, he wrote approximately two hundred songs, many of them romantic minstrel tunes that romanticized slavery and the Cotton Kingdom of the pre–Civil War South. Remarkably, he only visited the region once. Many of his most popular works were penned while working with Edwin P. Christy, one of the originators of the minstrel show.

742. The Vaudeville Era With its singular focus on urban tenement life, vaudeville (see entry #676) produced hundreds, if not thousands of songs that featured Irish American characters and situations. As with nearly everything associated with vaudeville, parody, stereotype, and ridicule run throughout the songs. A very common theme was that of wayward upward mobility, where Irish Americans are ridiculed for assuming middle-class pretensions. For example, in *Miss Mulligan's Home-Made Pie* (1885) the lady of the house nearly kills her tea guests with an inedible pie. *There Goes McManus* (1889) tells the story of an Irishman who encounters disaster at a fancy ball when his rented pants split. Other songs hit on the familiar themes of conflict with other ethnics, the dangers of hard labor, and the Irish love of fighting (*Throw Him Down McCloskey,* 1890). These raucous songs of the vaudeville era horrified the very upwardly mobile Irish that they parodied. Perhaps that explains why, despite the stereotypes and coarse images, working-class Irish Americans flocked to the theaters to hear them sung.

The Twentieth Century

743. Tin Pan Alley   In the late nineteenth century, New York City was the capital of America's popular music industry. Tin Pan Alley was the nickname for successive music publishing districts located off Broadway (the name itself is a reference to the incessant sound of pianos being played by so-called "song pluggers" demonstrating their work to publishers).

It was here that much of the "Irish" music that Irish Americans have grown to love was actually written. In contrast to the songs of the Harrigan and Hart era that took as their theme the ups and downs of Irish American life, the focus of Tin Pan Alley Irish songs shifted from the slums of America to the mythical green fields of "dear old Ireland." "My Wild Irish Rose" (1897), "A Little Bit of Heaven," "Mother Machree" (1910), "When Irish Eyes Are Smiling" (1912), and "Toore-re-loora-loora" (1912) are some of the best examples of Tin Pan Alley "Irish music." Chauncey Olcott earned much of his fame in singing such tunes. Many, of course, were written by non-Irishmen who had never set foot on the Ould Sod. "My Irish Molly O" (1907), for example, was written by the team of William Jerome and Gene Schwartz. Still, for all their commercialism and lack of authenticity, Irish American audiences loved them.

744. Chauncey Olcott   Chauncey Olcott (1860–1932) began his performing career in minstrel shows in the 1880s. When he traveled to England

in 1891, he acted in a light Irish opera, an experience that helped shape his career. Returning to America, Olcott became a star of Irish comedies and dramas, often writing plays and songs himself. He played a major role in popularizing the Tin Pan Alley vision of Ireland as a quaint land of green fields, devout Catholics, jolly pubs, and heroic nationalists. His best-remembered song is "My Wild Irish Rose."

Although Olcott enjoyed twenty years of success, his popularity declined after World War I. His business sense, however, had made him a small fortune over the years. In declining health, Olcott left for Monte Carlo, where he died of anemia in 1932.

745. George M. Cohan   George Michael Cohan (1878–1942) was a renaissance man of twentieth-century entertainment. A multitalented actor, dancer, lyricist, playwright, and producer, Cohan was once called "the best thing the Irish ever gave America." This descendant of County Cork emigrants began his career as an infant in the family vaudeville act, the Four Cohans, which became a Broadway success at the turn of the century. Having left the family act but not the family, Cohan became renowned individually as a father of the musical comedy. Though he received little critical acclaim, Cohan elevated vaudeville with its crude Irish stereotyping into a more respectable Broadway entertainment. In a career spanning nearly forty years, Cohan had a hand in eighty Broadway shows, for which he acted, wrote, composed, or otherwise contributed. Cohan single-handedly added a new dimension to Tin Pan Alley music by writing suc-

George M. Cohan

cessive American patriot songs, including "Yankee Doodle Boy," "You're a Grand Old Flag," and the World War I favorite, "Over There." The latter won him a Congressional Medal that was presented by President Franklin D. Roosevelt in 1940. Cohan, portrayed by James Cagney in the 1942 Academy Award–winning film *Yankee Doodle Dandy,* was also the subject of the 1968 Broadway musical *George M!*

Classical Performers

746. Victor Herbert Born in Dublin, Victor Herbert (1859–1924) studied and began his musical career in Germany, then moved to New York to play in the Metropolitan Orchestra and compose for the New York Philharmonic. Herbert went on to succeed Patrick S. Gilmore as the leader of the 22nd Regiment Band, conduct the Pittsburgh Symphony, and form the Victor Herbert Orchestra. Although best known for his operettas, most notably *Babes in Toyland, Mlle. Modiste,* and *Naughty Marietta,* he also wrote two cello concertos, two full-length operas, and a film score. Active in Irish politics, Herbert was the president of the Sons of Irish Freedom.

747. Count John McCormack Born in County Westmeath, Ireland, to working-class parents, John Francis McCormack (1884–1945) won first prize singing tenor at the National Irish Festival at age nineteen. Four years later, after studying in Italy, McCormack became the youngest principal tenor in London's Covent Garden. He sang in *La Traviata, The Barber of Seville,* and *Madame Butterfly.* Better known as a concert singer, McCormack was well loved for Irish folk songs like "I Hear You Calling Me." He sang in Ireland celebrating Catholic Emancipation and in 1929 was made a papal count. Although McCormack had become an American citizen in 1919, he retired in Ireland.

748. Eileen Farrell Born into a family of former

vaudevillians, Eileen Farrell (b. 1920) developed a love of music from an early age. When she was nineteen, she moved to New York City to study singing and seek performance opportunities. In 1940 she joined a studio choral group on CBS radio and the next year starred in her own show, *Eileen Farrell Sings.* It ran for six years and led to a successful singing tour that began in 1947. Widely acclaimed for her range and versatility, Farrell soon began to make appearances with some of the top orchestras and opera companies in the nation, including the New York Philharmonic and Metropolitan Opera. In 1960 she recorded an album of popular songs that earned her a Grammy.

Big Band and Jazz

749. Tommy and Jimmy Dorsey The brothers Jimmy (1904–57) and Tommy Dorsey (1905–56), musicians, composers and dance band leaders, were charismatic leaders of the swing craze that gripped the big-band era before and after World War II. Performing both together and separately (following a well-publicized disagreement over song tempo) for over forty years, they sold a combined total of 110 million records. They also appeared frequently on television and in several movies. Their bands included such luminaries as Bing Crosby, Frank Sinatra, and Glenn Miller, and they wrote hits like "I'm Getting Sentimental Over You" and "Boogie Woogie." Another star launched by the Dorseys was Helen O'Connell (1920–93), who joined the band while still a teenager and went on to a life-long career in show business.

Tommy Dorsey

750. Hoagy Carmichael   It's hard to put Hoagland Howard "Hoagy" Carmichael (1899–1981) in just one category of American entertainment. Born in Bloomington, Indiana, he developed a love of piano, especially ragtime. His first career as a lawyer was short-lived. He quit the legal profession to work as a bandleader, arranger, and composer. In 1924 Bix Beiderbecke and the Wolverines recorded his first composition, "Riverboat Shuffle." It soon became a jazz classic. Carmichael achieved even greater success in 1927, when lyrics were added to one of his melodies to become "Star Dust," one of the most popular songs ever recorded. Soon Carmichael was composing popular songs for the likes of the Dorsey Brothers, Gene Crupa, Louis Armstrong, Benny Goodman, and Jack Teagarden. These songs included "Georgia on My Mind" (1930), "Rockin' Chair" (1930), and "Lazy River" (1931). From the 1930s through the 1950s he worked in Hollywood, producing several more hit songs, including "Thanks for the Memory" (1938), "Two Sleepy People" (1939), and the Oscar-winning "In the Cool Cool Cool of the Evening" (1951). Carmichael also appeared as a character actor, often portraying himself (or someone like him) as a piano player and songwriter. In the 1940s and 1950s, he tried his hand at hosting several radio programs and a television variety show, *Saturday Night Revue.* He returned to acting in the early 1960s, with a stint on a weekly television Western and in frequent guest appearances on other television programs. Despite his great versatility, Carmichael's greatest talent lay in composing, a fact recognized by the Songwriter's Hall of Fame in 1971.

751. John McLaughlin   This acoustic-guitar virtuoso was born in England in 1942 and moved to the United States in 1969. Working with musical wizards such as Herbie Hancock, Jan Hammer, Carlos Santana, and the legendary Miles Davis, McLaughlin made a name for himself and received critical acclaim as a master of jazz-rock fusion. McLaughlin's signature style, a synthesis of the sounds of the Indian subcontinent and the West, earned him an international following. McLaughlin has served as bandleader of various musical groups, including the Mahavishnu Orchestra, Shakti, the John McLaughlin Trio, and most recently in the aptly named Free Spirits.

752. Gerry Mulligan   The names of musicians Gerry Mulligan (1927–96) performed with reads like a *Who's Who* of Jazz: Gil Evans, Chet Baker, Stan Getz, Thelonius Monk, and Miles Davis. Part of the "cool jazz" movement of the 1950s, Mulligan endeared himself to both jazz enthusiasts and musicians, finding success in his five-decade career as a baritone saxophonist, arranger, and composer. Gerald Joseph Mulligan hailed from Queens, New York, and provided music for *Luv,* a 1967 comedy about middle-class New York starring Jack Lemmon, and appeared in several movies, including *I Want to Live* in 1958 and *Bells Are Ringing* in 1960.

*Some Notable Rock and
Pop Music Performers*

753. Eddie Cochran   When Ray Edward Cochran taught himself to play the guitar at age twelve he favored country music. He switched to rock after hearing Elvis Presley and became a pioneer of the rockabilly music genre. The Minnesota native moved to Southern California in 1953 at age fifteen and started a small band. Along with Jerry Capehart, Cochran wrote songs and made demo tapes. Their big break came in 1958 with the release of the hit song "Summertime Blues." Cochran was always more popular in Britain than in America (Beatle George Harrison studied his guitar technique) and he died there in a car crash at age twenty-one while on tour.

754. Rosemary Clooney   Rosemary Clooney (b. 1928) started her career in 1945 teamed with her sister Betty singing duets on WLW Radio in Cincinnati. Discovered by bandleader Tony

Pastor, they joined his band in 1947 as the Clooney Sisters. When Betty dropped out after two years of a grueling road tour, Rosemary made for New York, where she signed a recording contract with Columbia Records. Her first hit, "Beautiful Brown Eyes," sold a half million copies in 1950, but it was her 1951 recording of the novelty song "Come On-a My House" that launched Clooney to stardom. Six more hits followed in the next two years and in 1953 she landed on the cover of *Time* magazine. She began an acting career and hosted her own television show from 1956 to 1957. Unfortunately, a collaboration with Duke Ellington and Billy Strayhorn *(Blue Rose)*, while artistically acclaimed, sold poorly. A second album of love songs with trombonist Nelson Riddle was quashed by Columbia. Add to that the growing popularity of rock and roll and Clooney's career went into steep decline, as did her personal life. The biggest blow came in 1968 while campaigning for Robert Kennedy. Standing just a few feet away from Kennedy when he was fatally shot, Clooney suffered a nervous breakdown. She eventually mounted a comeback in the mid-1970s, touring with Bing Crosby. In 1977 she teamed with former 1950s singing stars—Margaret Whiting, Rose Marie, and Helen O'Connell—to become "Four Girls Four." They toured for six years before Clooney went solo again. She continues to record and perform in concert.

755. Judy Collins Judy Collins (b. 1939) was trained a classical pianist, but found her true calling as a self-taught guitarist. She began performing in folk clubs and coffeehouses when she was twenty, covering songs by well-known stars like Bob Dylan and Joni Mitchell as well as performing those she wrote herself. In 1961, after a performance at the famed Village Gate in New York City, Collins met Jac Holzman of Elektra Records. Her first record brought her wide acclaim, but it was her second, *Wildflowers*, that truly made her a star. Her cover version of Joni Mitchell's "Both Sides Now" earned her a

Grammy nomination. Her 1972 album, *Colors of the Day*, included the hit "Amazing Grace," sung a cappella. Collins has remained an active songwriter and performer ever since.

756. Bill Haley (and the Comets) One of the founding fathers of rock and roll, Bill Haley was born in 1925 in Highland Park, Michigan. He started out as a disc jockey and aspiring Western swing star, recording his first record in 1948. In 1951 he changed styles and recorded a cover version of Jackie Brenston's rhythm-and-blues hit "Rocket 88." The record sold poorly, but prompted Haley to consider the idea of recording similar upbeat songs aimed at a teenaged audience. Before long he abandoned country music and changed his band's name to Bill Haley and His Comets. Their first hit, "Crazy Man Crazy" came in 1953. Many consider it the first rock-and-roll record to make it onto the Billboard pop charts. Haley came out with his signature song, "Rock Around the Clock" in 1954, but it only took off when rereleased a year later on the soundtrack to the film, *Blackboard Jungle*. Haley landed eight more songs on the Top 40 in the next year and toured the U.S. and Britain in 1957. By 1958, his star began to set as performers like Elvis Presley and Jerry Lee Lewis commanded the spotlight. In all Haley sold sixty million records and was inducted into the Rock and Roll Hall of Fame in 1987, six years after his death.

The Revival of Traditional Irish Music

757. The Irish American Song Traditional Irish music never quite disappeared in the twentieth century. Indeed record companies like Columbia and Victor churned out vast numbers of traditional recordings by such greats as fiddler Michael Coleman and uilleann piper Patsy Touhey. Still, by the 1930s it was clear that most Irish Americans preferred the sounds of less traditional Irish American music as performed by Paddy Noonan, Frank Patterson, Dennis Day, and Bing Crosby.

The Clancy Brothers

Some of this music retained certain traditional qualities, albeit watered down and big bandized. Other music, as exemplified by the Irish Rovers' "Unicorn," were simply novelty songs sung with an "Irish" brogue.

758. The Clancy Brothers Spark the Traditional Revival In 1959, Paddy, Tom, and Liam Clancy and Tommy Makem settled in New York City and became central figures in the burgeoning folk music scene. Playing in small clubs in Greenwich Village with other folkies like Peter, Paul, and Mary and Pete Seeger, the Clancy Brothers brought an Irish sensibility and material that eventually garnered an invitation to the *Ed Sullivan Show* in 1961. Playing to an audience of over eighty million people, they became overnight national sensations and toured relentlessly throughout the 1960s, including regular sold-out shows at Carnegie Hall. The exuberant renderings of Irish tunes were popular with audiences who frequently sang along.

The success of the Clancy Brothers launched a revival of traditional Irish music that has continued to this day. World-famous bands like the Chieftains can thank the Clancy Brothers for paving the way for their subsequent success.

Dance

759. Gene Kelly The auspicious career of Gene Curran Kelly (1913–96) as dancer, choreographer, actor, and film director began as a member of The Five Kellys—a dance troupe with his two sisters and two brothers—in Depression-era Pittsburgh. He later operated a dance studio, before moving to New York in the late 1930s. Kelly's Broadway break came in 1940 as the lead in the musical *Pal Joey*. His 1942 film debut in *For Me and My Gal* made him one of Hollywood's hottest performers. Kelly's trademark athletic dancing style and his ability to blend elements of jazz, ballet, and tap into an accessible form made him popular with both men and women. He is credited with introducing many innovations in special effects to filmmaking. Kelly's film achievements include *An American in Paris* (which won him an Academy Award for choreography), *Brigadoon,* and his most famous, *Singin' in the Rain.*

760. Michael Flatley and Jean Butler With roots in Counties Carlow and Sligo, Chicago-born Michael Flatley (b. 1958) transformed traditional Irish dance into a modern, worldwide phenomenon as the extraordinary male lead in *Riverdance* and *Lord of the Dance.* Described in *National Geographic* as a "national treasure," Flatley at seventeen became the first American to win the All-World championship in Irish dancing. In the early 1980s Flatley toured with the traditional Irish band The Chieftains. He also performed at the 1997 Academy Awards, shortly after his sold-out Radio City performances. Flatley holds the *Guinness Book* record for the most number of taps per second (recorded at twenty-eight).

Flatley's partner in *Riverdance,* Jean Butler, was born on Long Island. Butler and Flatley were part of the original seven-minute performance that gave rise to *Riverdance,* an intermission diversion, at the Eurovision Song Contest. Butler eventually left *Riverdance* to pursue other interests and in late 2000 debuted in another Irish dance production, *Dancing on Dangerous Ground,* in London.

761. Maria Tallchief The prima ballerina of the New York City Ballet from 1947 to 1965, Maria Tallchief (b. 1925) was the descendant of a nineteenth-century Osage leader from Oklahoma and an Irish pioneer woman. Maria is best known for her roles as the mythical bird-woman in Stravinsky's *The Firebird,* and the Sugar Plum Fairy in Tchaikovsky's *The Nutcracker.* She was the first American-born ballet superstar to tour Europe and Asia. A two-time winner of the annual Dance Award, she also appeared on many popular television programs.

Art and Photography

Painting

762. Three Notable Nineteenth-Century Painters Three Irish-born painters earned distinction for their work in America during the nineteenth century. William Michael Harnett (1848–92) settled with his family in Philadelphia, where he found work as an engraver. He later engaged in the formal study of art at leading schools in New York and Europe. He is best known for his still-life painting of objects such as horseshoes, pipes, guns, and musical instruments. His paintings are in the collections of America's most respected art museums, including the Metropolitan Museum of Art in New York and the Museum of Fine Arts in Boston.

Having received formal training at the Cork School of Design, Thomas Hovenden (1840–95) emigrated to America in 1863. After study at the National Academy of Design, he moved to Baltimore where he began to paint a wide range of subjects, from portraits to scenes of ordinary, everyday life. He moved to France in the 1870s and continued to study and improve his technique. Exhibitions of his paintings at the Paris Salon in 1880 elicited wide praise. Hovenden returned to America in the early 1880s. His painting of the radical abolitionist John Brown *(The Last Moments of John Brown)* is among his most famous.

John Mulvany (c. 1839–1906) came to the U.S. from Westmeath as a boy. From a humble beginning as an illustrator for Chicago newspapers, he went on to study painting in Europe. He eventually settled in Iowa and began a career painting scenes of Western life. Some of his best-known works include *The Preliminary Trial of a Horse Thief* (1876) and the monumental *Custer's Last Rally* (1881).

763. Ellsworth Kelly Born in Newburgh, New York, Ellsworth Kelly (b. 1923) studied at the Boston Museum of Fine Arts School and at the Académie des Beaux-Arts in Paris. As a painter and sculptor he became a leading exponent of the so-called "hard-edge style" of minimalist art. Kelly's first one-man show opened in Paris in 1951 and drew significant attention from critics. He returned to the United States in 1954 where he continued to paint and sculpt. By the late 1950s, he was well known in modern art circles and won commissions to do sculptures for Philadelphia's Transportation Building (1957) and the New York State Pavilion at the 1964 World's Fair.

764. Georgia O'Keeffe After traveling the country as a student and teacher of art, Georgia O'Keeffe (1887–1986) moved to New York City in 1918, where she became immersed in the life of artistic bohemia. A painter of tremendous talent, she married the photographer Alfred Stieglitz in 1924 and began traveling to New Mexico in 1929. Her love affair with the American Southwest informed much of her work.

765. John Ramage In Europe and colonial America, miniature portraits were very popular among the wealthy. One of the most accomplished miniaturists was Dublin-trained gold-smith and painter John Ramage (1733–97). He moved to New York City in the 1760s and earned a sterling reputation as a superb miniature portrait painter. Wealthy and prominent colonists sought him out, as did George Washington during his stay in New York.

Sculpture

766. Augustus St. Gaudens   The noted sculptor Augustus Saint Gaudens (1848–1907) was born in Dublin to a French father and Irish mother and

Augustus St. Gaudens

moved to the United States as an infant. Eventually settling in New Hampshire, he was regarded as one of America's finest sculptors. His works include the Robert Gould Shaw Memorial in Boston, the Charles Stewart Parnell monument in Dublin, and, at the request of Teddy Roosevelt, the design of the Liberty coins, upon which he engraved the face of a young Irish immigrant, Mary Cunningham.

767. Jerome Connor   Born in County Kerry, Jerome Connor (1876–1943) emigrated to Holyoke, Massachusetts, when he was a teenager. Connor soon ran away from home and tried all manner of jobs before landing one with a monument company in Springfield, Massachusetts. There he discovered his talent in sculpture and sought additional training at the Roycroft Institute in upstate New York. Connor opened a studio in Syracuse, New York, and soon earned commissions for statues of prominent individuals, including a marble statue of Walt Whitman and a

bronze statue of Robert Emmet for the Smithsonian Institution. His other notable works include statues of Archbishop John Carroll at Georgetown University (1912) and the *Lusitania* Peace Memorial at Cobh, Ireland—considered his master work. In all Connor produced more than two hundred works during his career.

768. James E. Kelly   One of the most prolific sculptors of the late nineteenth and early twenti-eth century, James E. Kelly (1855–1933) was born to immigrant parents in New York City. Known as "The Sculptor of American History," his first major work was *Sheridan's Ride*, a stat-uette depicting Gen. Philip Sheridan at the Battle of Cedar Creek in 1864. His other noted works include busts of Theodore Roosevelt, Count Rochambeau, and Admiral Dewey.

James E. Kelly

Major works include The Sixth New York Cavalry Memorial at Gettysburg, The William McKinley Memorial in Wilmington, Delaware, and The Soldiers and Sailors Monument in Troy, New York. Kelly also designed several highly regarded equestrian statues for Theodore Roosevelt, Gen. William T. Sherman, and Fitz-John Porter, as well as creating five panels for the Monmouth Battle monument in Freehold, New Jersey.

Patrons and Critics

769. William Wilson Corcoran   The son of Irish immigrants living in Baltimore, William Wilson Corcoran (1798–1888) started out as a dry goods merchant. After making a fortune as a banker and broker, Corcoran became a generous philanthropist. In 1869 he founded Washington, D.C.'s first art museum, the Corcoran Gallery of Art. When the collection outgrew its original home on Seventeenth Street and Pennsylvania Avenue, Corcoran commissioned a new building, where the gallery has remained since 1897. The largest private art museum in the nation's capital, the Corcoran is "dedicated to art, and used solely for the purpose of encouraging the American genius."

770. John Quinn John Quinn (1870–1924) was born in Tiffin, Ohio. A successful lawyer for many prominent individuals and businesses, he used his wealth to amass a vast collection of modern art and literature. He also served as patron to James Joyce, Joseph Conrad, and Ezra Pound, as well as scores of painters and sculptors. He secured the 69th Regiment Armory in New York for the famous 1913 modern art exhibition that brought to America the works of Vincent Van Gogh and Marcel Duchamp. In fact Quinn lent seventy-seven works from his own private collection to the show. In 1921 Quinn defended James Joyce's work *Ulysses* against charges that it was obscene.

771. James Johnson Sweeney Born in New York City, James Johnson Sweeney (1895–1966) became one of the foremost critics of modern art in the twentieth century. He graduated from Georgetown University in 1922 and studied at several other institutions. He moved to Paris where he edited the literary magazine *Transition*. Returning to the U.S. in the 1930s, he worked briefly as a journalist before becoming director of exhibitions at the University of Chicago in 1933. In 1934 he published *Plastic Redirections in Twentieth Century Art* a work which established him as a leading expert in avant-garde art. Sweeney moved to New York in 1935 to teach at New York University. Starting in 1945 he held successive positions at some of the nation's leading art institutions, including curator at the Museum of Modern Art from 1945 to 1946, director of the

Guggenheim Museum from 1952 to 1959, director of the Museum of Fine Arts in Houston from 1961 to 1968, and chairman of the executive committee of the Israel Museum in Jerusalem.

Photography

772. The Men Behind Mathew Brady Mathew Brady was Irish America's foremost photographer. He is best remembered for his portraits of famous Americans like Abraham Lincoln and Ulysses Grant and his haunting photos of the Civil War (see entry #598). But Brady did not take all the pictures that bear his name. Instead, he trained numerous photographers and sent them into the field. This was especially true of the Civil War shots. Most of his trusted assistants were Irish American. Timothy O'Sullivan is probably the best known, since he eventually opened his own

Timothy O'Sullivan's photo of Devil's Slide, Utah

studio, but others include T. J. Hines, V. T. McGillycuddy, John Moran, D. F. Barry, and T. C. Roche. Many of them went on to photograph America's westward expansion in the 1870s and 1880s.

773. David Hume Kennerly   Born in 1947 and raised in Oregon, David Hume Kennerly is one of the most acclaimed photojournalists of the twentieth century. Over the past thirty years, he has racked up numerous honors, including two first place awards in both the World Press Photo Contest and National Press Photographers Contest, an Overseas Press Club award, several Emmy Awards, twenty-five cover photos for *Time* magazine, and most important, a 1972 Pulitzer Prize for his work in Vietnam. His work for *Time, Life,* and *Newsweek* magazines have taken him to 125 countries. He has also served as White House photographer to Gerald Ford. Since 1996 he has been a contributing editor at *Newsweek.*

774. Margaret Bourke-White   Margaret Bourke-White (1904–71) was a pioneer in the newly emerging field of photojournalism. She started out as one of the first women in industrial photography in 1927 and two years later was hired as the first photographer for *Fortune* magazine. In 1930, she became the first Western photographer permitted into the Soviet Union, an experience that led to her first book, *Eyes on Russia* (1931). Henry Luce hired Bourke-White as *Life* magazine's first woman photojournalist and it was her photograph that adorned the cover of its first issue. In 1937 she gained international recognition with the publication of her second book, *You Have Seen Their Faces,* a collection of moving photographs of America during the Great Depression (written in collaboration with her future husband, Erskine Caldwell. During World War II, Bourke-White became the first female war correspondent and the first allowed access to combat zones. This allowed her to become one of the first photogra-

phers to enter and photograph Nazi death camps. Bourke-White continued in this trail-blazing manner for the rest of her professional life, traveling the world and writing four more books.

Literature and Poetry

Novelists and Short Story Writers

Raymond Chandler   Born in Chicago to immigrant parents from Waterford, he was taken to England by his mother at age nine. He became a journalist and, even though a U.S. citizen, served in the Canadian army and Royal Flying Corps during the First World War. After the war, he settled in the U.S. and prospered in the oil business. He continued to write on the side and in 1933 had his first crime story published in *Black Mask.* For his first novel, *The Big Sleep* (1939), he created a tough, streetwise sleuth named Phillip Marlowe who roamed Los Angeles' tawdry underworld. Marlowe appeared in six subsequent works like *Farewell, My Lovely* (1940) and *The Long Goodbye* (1954). His success led him to Hollywood in 1943 where he worked as a screenwriter on scripts for many films, including *Double Indemnity* (1944), *The Blue Dahlia* (1946), and *Strangers on a Train* (1951). Several of Chandler's work were turned into popular films, including the film noir classics *Murder, My Sweet* (1945) and *The Big Sleep* (1946), starring Humphrey Bogart.

775. Kate Chopin   Born Katherine O'Flaherty, Kate Chopin (1851–1904) grew up in a wealthy St. Louis family. In 1870 she married Oscar Chopin, a Louisiana planter. When he died in 1882, the young widow returned to St. Louis and took up writing professionally. Her early subjects were the Creole and Cajun people she had observed while living in Louisiana. She published her first novel, *At Fault,* in 1890, but gained greater recognition for the more than one hundred short stories she wrote, especially "Désirée's Baby" and "Madame Celestin's Divorce" (still found in many anthologies). Collections of her short stories were published as *Bayou Folk* (1894) and *A Night in Acadie* (1897). Unfortunately her greatest work, the novel *The Awakening* (1899) effectively ended her writing career. Considered a remarkable work today for its unusually frank portrayal of female sexual passion, interracial marriage, and suicide, it elicited widespread condemnation when it was published. Chopin did little writing after that and died in 1904. Her works were eventually rediscovered in the 1960s and are considered superb examples of "local color" writing.

776. James T. Farrell   James T. Farrell (1904–79) was born in Chicago into a family of fifteen children. Raised by his

James T. Farrell

grandmother, he attended the local Catholic grammar school. During high school he showed much promise as a writer, though he held many other jobs before he actually began to write stories in 1929. His most famous work, the *Studs Lonigan* trilogy, took a hard-nosed look at the bitter realities of Chicago's Irish American working class. Overall, Farrell wrote almost thirty novels in his lifetime. In addition to his fiction, he also produced a body of critical essays. Farrell never cared about what critics thought of his literary works; he wrote because he wanted to. At the age of seventy-five, Farrell died, but not before writing his own obituary.

777. F. Scott Fitzgerald   One of the great writers of the interwar years, Francis Scott Fitzgerald (1896–1940) was born in St. Paul, Minnesota, in 1896. He came east to attend Princeton, but left before graduating to volunteer for service in World War I. He published his first novel, the semiautobiographical *This Side of Paradise*, in 1920, which brought him wide recognition and wealth. That same year he married Zelda Sayre. Together they formed one of the most glamorous couples of the Roaring Twenties, known for the legendary high living and parties in New York City. Despite his success, Fitzgerald was unable to support this lifestyle with his writing which included short stories, a play, and the novel *The Beautiful and the Damned* (1922). Moving to Europe in 1924, in part because it was cheaper to live there, Fitzgerald befriended Ernest Hemingway and other expatriates of the "lost generation." There he wrote *The Great Gatsby* (1925) which earned critical praise but sold poorly. Debt-ridden and increasingly alcoholic, the couple returned to the U.S. in 1930. When his next novel, *Tender Is the Night* (1934), was a flop, Fitzgerald suffered a nervous breakdown. He recovered sufficiently to write screenplays in Hollywood from 1937 to 1940 and was at work on a novel, *The Last Tycoon* (1941), when he died of a heart attack in 1940.

Fitzgerald spent much of his life trying to distance himself from his Irish Catholic roots. None of his novels have Irish Catholic characters of note except for the Bradys in his final, unfinished work, *The Last Tycoon*. Fundamentally, he was a mixture of aspiring, self-doubting WASP and, as he once put it, "straight 1850 potato-famine Irish." He once elaborated on this point in a letter to fellow Hibernian scribe, John O'Hara:

> I am half black Irish and half old American stock with the usual exaggerated ancestral pretensions. The black Irish half of the family had the money and looked down upon the Maryland side of the family who had . . . "breeding." . . . So being born into that atmosphere of crack, wisecrack and countercrack, I developed a two cylinder inferiority complex.

778. Joel Chandler Harris   The son of a "wandering Irishman" (as he once put it), Joel Chandler Harris (1848–1908) was born near Eatonville, Georgia. As a youth he worked as a printer's assistant for a local newspaper. The paper's publisher, Joseph Addison Turner, owned a plantation that Harris visited frequently. There he became familiar with the dialect, stories, and customs of African American slaves which he would later use as the basis of his famed "Uncle Remus Stories." Harris worked as a journalist for several newspapers and in 1879 published the first of his "Uncle Remus Stories," "The Story of Mr. Rabbit and Mr. Fox" in the *Atlanta Constitution*. The feature was a hit and led to a long series of tales in which Uncle Remus, a former slave, tells stories to the son of his employer. The first collection, *Uncle Remus: His Songs and His Sayings*, appeared in 1880. These tales of Brer Rabbit, Brer Fox, and other animals draw on the folklore of African Americans and are regarded as important, if somewhat distorted, examples of authentic folklore. Harris also wrote other stories and novels about life in the South, including *On the Wing of Occasions* (1900), a collection of stories featuring Billy Sanders, the Sage of Shady Dale. From 1907 until his death in 1908 he edited *Uncle Remus's Magazine*.

779. Henry James   Without a doubt, Henry James ranks as one of the greatest American writers of the late nineteenth and early twentieth century, perhaps of all time. His Irish heritage came from his paternal grandparents. His grandfather, William James, emigrated to America from County Cavan in 1798 and married a woman of Scotch Irish descent. The fortune he made in business allowed his son, Henry Sr., and grandchildren to live lives of comfort and travel.

Henry James, Jr., was born in 1843 in New York City. Educated by private tutors until age twelve, he spent the years 1855 to 1860 traveling with his family throughout Europe. They eventually returned and settled in Newport, Rhode Island. Henry attended Harvard Law School, but left to pursue his interest in writing. His essays and critical reviews began appearing in *The North American Review* by the mid-1860s and his first novel, *Watch and Ward*, was published in serial form in the *Atlantic Monthly* in 1871. A true Anglophile, he moved to England in 1876 and settled there more or less permanently. He visited Ireland on three occasions, but found the country's poverty repugnant.

James' early novels focused on the interactions between Americans and Europeans. They include *The American* (1877), *The Europeans* (1878), *Daisy Miller* (1879), and *The Portrait of a Lady* (1881). In the second phase of his career, works like *Washington Square* (1881), *The Bostonians* (1886), *What Maisie Knew* (1897), and *The Sacred Fount* (1901) addressed psychological and social relationships. His later works continued this examination of intense psychological questions. Three of them, *The Wings of the Dove* (1902), *The Ambassadors* (1903), and *The Golden Bowl* (1904) are widely considered his best work.

780. Mary McCarthy   An incisive and caustic writer, Mary McCarthy (1912–89) began writing fiction while serving as drama critic of the *Partisan Review* from 1937 to 1948. Most popular was her 1963 novel *The Group*, which was made into a motion picture in 1966. Other works of fiction, known for their wit and intellect, included *The Groves of Academe* (1952), *Birds of America* (1971), and *Memories of a Catholic Girlhood* (1957). The latter, a work of autobiographical fiction, is considered a classic of Irish American literature. McCarthy also wrote nonfiction. Her controversial essays on the Vietnam War were first published in the *New York Review of Books* and later in two books, *Vietnam* (1967) and *Hanoi* (1968).

781. Margaret Mitchell   Born in Atlanta, Georgia, Margaret Mitchell (1900–49) studied briefly at Smith College before returning to

Atlanta, where she secured a job as journalist for the *Atlanta Journal*. In 1925 she married John Marsh and one year later, while recovering from an ankle injury, began writing a book of fiction that became *Gone With the Wind*. Published in 1936, it sold one million copies within six months. The following year it won the Pulitzer Prize. By the time of her death in 1949, more than eight million copies had been sold in forty different countries. The 1939 film version of the book was also a popular hit and won the Academy Award.

At several points in the novel and film, Mitchell made reference to her Irish heritage. The O'Haras, as the name indicates, were Irish. Scarlett O'Hara's father, Gerald (modeled after Mitchell's plantation-owning grandfather, Thomas Fitzgerald), emigrated from County Meath and named his plantation Tara, the ancient seat of Ireland's high kings. In the film we see Scarlett and her family saying the rosary and in another scene hear her father remind her that people with Irish blood like her have a strong attachment to the land.

Mitchell never wrote another novel and died in an automobile accident in 1949.

782. Flannery O'Connor   The acclaimed short story writer and novelist Flannery O'Connor (1925–64) was born in Savannah, Georgia. She grew up a devout Catholic and graduated from Georgia State College for Women (now Georgia College). From there she enrolled at the University of Iowa to study creative writing. Her first short story was published in *Accent* in 1946. *Wise Blood*, her first novel, appeared in 1952. In these and subsequent works, O'Connor set her stories in the rural south and explored powerful themes, often in unconventional ways, of faith and religious consciousness. Her collection of short stories, *A Good Man Is Hard to Find, and Other Stories* (1955), firmly established her as one of the foremost short story writers of the postwar period.

By this time she had been diagnosed with lupus erythematosus, a degenerative disease that had killed her father at a young age. Despite her illness, she continued to write, publishing many short stories and another novel, *The Violent Bear It Away* (1960). A second short story collection, *Everything That Rises Must Converge* (1965), a collection of prose pieces, *Mystery and Manners* (1969), *The Complete Stories* (1971), and a collection of her letters, *The Habit of Being* (1979) were all published posthumously.

783. Edwin O'Connor   Edwin O'Connor (1918–68) was born in Providence, Rhode Island, and enjoyed a typical, Irish American middle-class upbringing. He attended a public grade school and a Catholic secondary school before attending Notre Dame, where he majored in English. His first book, *The Oracle* (1951), sold poorly and received scant critical attention. However, his second book, *The Last Hurrah* (1956), quickly became a classic and is still considered one of the most successful political novels ever written. A thinly disguised fictional account of the life of Boston political boss James Michael Curley, it masterfully tells the story of an aged politico named Frank Skeffington and his last run for office. John Ford filmed a movie version of it in 1958 starring Spencer Tracy. O'Connor wrote several more novels that took Irish America as their underlying theme, including *The Edge of Sadness* (1961) and *I Was Dancing* (1964).

784. John O'Hara   John O'Hara (1905–70) always considered himself an outsider, a sentiment perhaps shaped by his background as an Irish Catholic growing up in a largely Anglo-Protestant American society. He was born into a prosperous middle-class family in a small western Pennsylvania mining town. After an erratic education (he was dismissed from several schools), he began a career in journalism. He published his first novel, *Appointment in Samarra* in 1935. Many consider it his best book, but others like *Butterfield*

Mary Anne Madden Sadlier

8 (1935) and *Pal Joey* (1940) achieved greater recognition and were eventually made into feature films. Other critics argue that O'Hara's finest work is to be found in his short stories, many of which appeared in *The New Yorker.* The bulk of his writings were set in and around his hometown. Sadly, O'Hara spent much of his career seeking the recognition he believed was his due—from literary award committees, exclusive clubs, etc. Since his death in 1970 there has been a revived interest in and critical appreciation of his works.

785. Mary Anne Madden Sadlier The most prolific Irish American writer in the nineteenth century was arguably Mary Anne Madden Sadlier (1820–1903). Born in County Cavan, she emigrated to Montreal in 1844. There she wrote to support herself and met and married James Sadlier, a major Catholic publisher. She had six children over the next twelve years, but never stopped writing. She contributed to the Sadlier company's Catholic magazine, *The Tablet,* and completed six novels. Her target audience was the growing Irish Catholic population in America and Canada and she soon gained a devoted readership. Her novels almost always featured Irish immigrant heroes and heroines and preached the virtues of parochial schooling, faithful obedience to Church teachings, regular attendance at Mass, and vigilance against Protestant proselytizing. The Sadliers moved to New York in 1860 and her fame grew still larger, as did her circle of high-profile Catholic friends. In all Sadlier produced nearly sixty novels and reached an audience of millions.

Twentieth-Century Playwrights

786. Philip Barry Dramatist Philip Barry (1896–1949) was born in Rochester, New York. Educated at Yale, he aspired to a career as a playwright. In 1919 he joined George Pierce Baker's 47 Workshop at Harvard, where he quickly showed a talent for writing drama. The workshop produced his play *A Punch for Judy* in 1920. While at Harvard he wrote *You and I* which ran for 170 performances on Broadway in 1923.

Barry proved a prolific writer of light, satirical comedies that often took as their subject the lives of upper-class Americans. Some of his better-known works include *White Wings* (1926), *Paris Bound* (1927), *Holiday* (1928), *The Animal Kingdom* (1932), and *The Philadelphia Story* (1939). In the 1930s, Barry tried his hand at works that focused on more serious psychological, philosophical, and spiritual issues. But *Hotel Universe* (1930), *Bright Star* (1935), and *Here Come the Clowns* (1938) were not popular with audiences, so he returned to comedy.

787. Marc Connelly Born in McKeesport, Pennsylvania, Marc Connelly (1890–1980) worked as a reporter and drama critic in Pittsburgh before moving to New York City. There he became a prominent figure in the intense literary and theatrical scene of the 1920s, joining the famed literacy group known as the Algonquin Round Table and helping found *The New Yorker* (1925). Connelly wrote radio scripts, screenplays, and drama, but his greatest success came in collaboration with George S. Kaufman on several hit plays and musicals. His 1930 play, *Green Pastures,* a dramatization of material from the folktale collection *Ol' Man Adam and His Chillun* by Roark Bradford won the Pulitzer Prize. Connelly remained an active writer for decades, writing his last play for Helen Hayes in 1977.

788. George E. Kelly Born into the same family

that later produced Grace Kelly, George E. Kelly (1887–1974) became a successful playwright, actor, and director who wrote about the peculiar traits of the American middle class. Early on he worked as an actor and writer in vaudeville. His first Broadway success came with *The Torchbearers* (1922), a witty satire of the Little Theatre movement then all the rage in the country. *The Show-Off* (1924) achieved instant status as classic American comedy and was later made into three films (1926, 1934, and 1946). Kelly's most critically acclaimed play, *Craig's Wife* (1925), was a drama that examined an upper-class woman's tragic pursuit of status and wealth. It won the Pulitzer Prize. After that, Kelly's best years of original writing were behind him. None of his subsequent plays achieved popular or critical success.

789. Eugene O'Neill O'Neill grew up in the world of drama and theater. His father, James O'Neill (1849–1920), emigrated to America from Kilkenny during the Great Famine. As an adult he gained national fame and a sizable fortune for his nearly six thousand performances as the lead in the melodrama *The Count of Monte Cristo*. Most of O'Neill's early years were spent traveling the United States while his father performed. Although O'Neill's career as a playwright clearly stemmed from this experience, he always believed his father had squandered his talent by wedding himself to a single lucrative role.

O'Neill's mother, Ella (1857–1922), was born to Irish immigrants from Tipperary and educated at exclusive Catholic schools. She was an unhappy woman who eventually became addicted to morphine, prescribed to ease her pain after giving birth to Eugene. The strained relationships in O'Neill's family formed the basis for many of his plays.

O'Neill began attending boarding schools at the age of seven, as had his older brother James, Jr. (1878–1923). He failed out of Princeton in 1907 and spent the next five years living a precarious existence as a seaman and laborer. His love of reading and theater (especially the works of Irish playwrights Yeats and Synge), however, prompted him to begin writing plays in 1913.

His first big break came in 1916 when the Provincetown Players elected to perform his play *Bound East for Cardiff.* From that point forward O'Neill's fame soared. *Beyond the Horizon* won the Pulitzer Prize in 1920, as did *Anna Christie* (1922) and *Strange Interlude* (1928). All told he produced eighteen plays in the 1920s.

O'Neill's output slowed in the 1930s to only three plays. Nonetheless, he was named the Nobel Laureate for Literature in 1936. He was most productive during this period, though, writing his great masterpieces *Long Day's Journey Into Night* (posth. 1956), *The Iceman Cometh* (1939), and *A Moon for the Misbegotten* (1943). He also wrote *A Touch of the Poet* (1935–42), and *More Stately Mansions* (1935–41).

O'Neill married three times, first to Kathleen Jenkins in 1909. They had one son, Eugene, Jr. She divorced O'Neill in 1912. In 1918 he married Agnes Boulton (1893–1968), a fiction writer. They had two children, a son Shane and a daughter Oona, who later married Charles Chaplin. That marriage ended in 1929. His third marriage in 1929 to the actress Carlotta Monterey (1888–1970) lasted until his death. He and Carlotta lived in Paris and New York during the early years of their marriage. In 1938 they moved to Tao House, where they lived in seclusion until 1943.

Long Day's Journey Into Night was not published or produced during O'Neill's lifetime. *The Iceman Cometh*

Eugene O'Neill

premiered in 1946, but its critics and audiences did not receive it well. *A Moon for the Misbegotten* had an unproductive short run.

O'Neill spent the last ten years of his life suffering from a palsy similar to Parkinson's disease. It left him unable to write and he died in a hotel room in Boston in 1953.

Poetry

790. Robert Creeley Robert Creeley (b. 1906) grew up in Arlington, Massachusetts. He went to Harvard University, but dropped out just before graduating to join the American Field Service for the remainder of the war. He returned in 1945, unsure of what to do. He developed a keen interest in jazz and poetry (the latter stimulated by poetry readings he heard on the radio). After traveling in France and Spain, he returned to the U.S. and enrolled at Black Mountain College in North Carolina, where he received his B.A. in 1955. He was invited to join the faculty and became editor of the literary journal, *Black Mountain Review*. His poems which appeared in the *Review* drew him critical praise and a following. He published a collection in 1962 entitled *For Love* and another, *Pieces,* in 1968. Heavily influenced by William Carlos Williams, Creeley's poems are known for their short and concise form.

791. Louise Imogen Guiney Louise Imogen Guiney (1861–1920) grew up in a prosperous family in Roxbury, Massachusetts. Her education consisted of private tutors and then studying at the Academy of the Sacred Heart, an elite convent school. Her genteel life disappeared when her father, an immigrant from Tipperary who had earned fame as a Union Army general, died prematurely of war wounds when she was only sixteen. By the age of nineteen, however, Guiney's poems began to appear in periodicals like the *Atlantic Monthly* and *Scribner's*. In 1884 the first of some thirty books of her poetry and prose were published. To supplement her inadequate literary earn-ings, she accepted an appointment as the postmaster in the Boston suburb of Auburndale. But protests and a boycott by local nativists over the appointment of a Catholic woman to such a prominent position caused her to resign in 1897. In 1900 she sailed to England to concentrate on her writing, where she remained until her death in 1920.

792. James Laughlin Born into a wealthy family, James Laughlin (1914–97) founded the most influential avant-garde press, New Directions, in 1936. Laughlin published the works of avant-garde writers who were either ignored or avoided by mainstream publishing houses, including Ezra Pound's *The Cantos* and William Carlos Williams's *Paterson*. In the 1940s Laughlin expanded New Directions' offerings by republishing noteworthy, out-of-print works by Henry James, F. Scott Fitzgerald, and other writers he respected. Original works by Dylan Thomas, Lawrence Ferlinghetti, Tennessee Williams, and Herman Hesse were published and sold well. Laughlin then began publishing numerous English translations of notable foreign authors like Charles Baudelaire and Octavio Paz which likewise proved successful.

Laughlin was a respected poet himself whose *Collected Poems* was published in 1992. A second volume, *Poems,* was published after his death.

793. Phyllis McGinley In the 1920s Phyllis McGinley (1905–78), a schoolteacher, began to submit some of her poetry to newspapers and magazines. Soon she was publishing poems in *The New Yorker* and other major periodicals. She quit her teaching job to work as poetry editor for *Town and Country* magazine, but soon dropped that to devote herself to full-time writing. McGinley's first book of poems, *On the Contrary,* appeared in 1934 and was an instant success. A prolific writer, she churned out several other collections, including *One More Manhattan* (1937), *Husbands Are Difficult* (1941), *Stones from Glass Houses* (1946), and *Merry Christmas, Happy New Year* (1958).

Phyllis McGinley

Because McGinley mainly focused on suburban life as her subject matter, her work is often dismissed these days as shallow and lacking in seriousness. Yet even critics concede that she was exceptionally good at writing verse, and both clever and witty. Her collection *Times Three: Selected Verse from Three Decades* (1960) won the Pulitzer Prize for poetry.

McGinley's other talent lay in writing children's literature, including books such as *The Horse That Lived Upstairs* (1944), *All Around the Town* (1948), *Blunderbus* (1951), *The Make-Believe Twins* (1953), and *How Mrs. Santa Claus Saved Christmas* (1963). She also wrote essays for popular magazines like *Reader's Digest*.

794. Frank O'Hara   Frank O'Hara was born in Baltimore, Maryland (1926–66), but he was raised in Massachusetts. After service in World War II, he entered Harvard to study music, but was soon drawn to literature, especially poetry. While there he helped establish the Poet's Theatre and published poems in leading literary journals. Moving to New York City in the mid-1950s, he discovered what would become the foundation of much of his poetry: the big city. He also immersed himself in the arts, moving from the position of information desk clerk at the Metropolitan Museum of Art to associate curator of painting and sculpture. He subsequently became an editor and contributor at *Art News*. O'Hara also tried his hand at drama and had many one-act plays produced, including *Try! Try!*

Most of all, O'Hara considered himself to be a poet. His first volume of poetry, *A City Winter, and Other Poems*, appeared in 1952, followed by *Oranges* in 1953 and *Meditations in an Emergency* in 1957. O'Hara began to draw wider public recognition in 1960 when several of his poems were included in Donald Allen's anthology, *New American Poetry, 1945–1960*. Still, only a small portion of his poetry had been published by the time of his death.

795. John Boyle O'Reilly   John Boyle O'Reilly (1844–90) was born in Drogheda, Ireland. After apprenticing at various newspapers, O'Reilly became a member of the Fenian Society, a group dedicated to Irish nationalism. Soon after joining, O'Reilly was arrested and banished to a penal colony in Australia. In 1869 he escaped to America and joined the staff of the *Boston Pilot*, the diocesan paper. He soon became editor and went on to publish many volumes of poetry, ranging from patriotic odes to lyrical ballads. In testament to the wide acclaim he enjoyed for his poetry, O'Reilly was picked to deliver a commemorative poem at the dedication of Plymouth Rock in 1889—a major honor for any writer at the time, especially for an Irishman. He died only a year later at age forty-six from an overdose of sleeping pills, though it is not known whether it was a suicide or an accident.

796. James Whitcomb Riley   James Whitcomb Riley (1849–1916) was born in Indiana. His poems published in the *Indianapolis Journal* helped launch his career as "the poet laureate of democracy." Over the course of his career, he published more than a dozen books of verse that were widely popular. His folksy, dialect poems that focused on scenes of small town and rural life ("The Old Swimmin' Hole") were beloved for their sincerity and gentle humor.

Ten Important Irish
American Works of Fiction

797. HOUSE OF GOLD, by Elizabeth Cullinan (1970)   Elizabeth Cullinan's novels and short stories have been called "Irish-American domestic fiction at its best," yet, unfortunately, she has been largely overlooked by critics and readers. Most of her work features daughters of Irish American households and accurately explores themes of Catholicism and urban lower-middle class. *House of Gold* centers around the death and wake of Mrs. Julia Devlin, a long-suffering and domineering mother of nine, whose autobiography is found by a daughter-in-law while the family is gathered at her deathbed. Reading the handwritten pages, the children remember their mother and her controlling influence on their lives as she dies. Cullinan worked at *The New Yorker* with William Maxwell and Maeve Brennan, and has been compared to both of them as well as Joyce and Chekhov.

798. THE GINGER MAN, by J. P. Donleavy

(1955) *The Ginger Man*, based on Donleavy's experiences attending Trinity College, on the GI Bill, is a comic classic. Sebastian Balfe Dangerfield, an Irish American who adopts an English accent and studies law, is at home in Dublin, although the romantic notion he had of Ireland before he arrived does not jive with the reality: poor plumbing, lack of heating and other modern conveniences, and a general atmosphere that is less than welcoming to his somewhat avant-garde ways. The reader is treated to a Joycean walking tour of mid-century Dublin, with its heavy Catholic influence, its cinemas and tea shops, and of course, its pubs. Recognized for its humor today, *The Ginger Man* was considered scandalous at the time of its publication, and was banned in Ireland for many years.

799. MR. DOOLEY'S OPINIONS, by Finley Peter Dunne

(1901) Finley Peter Dunne (1867–1936) was a journalist and editor of *Collier's* magazine who expressed opinions and analyzed current events through a cranky saloon owner with an Irish accent, Martin Dooley. Mr. Dooley's views were put forth in no fewer than nine books. In *Mr. Dooley's Opinions* in 1901, he expressed the following view

of newspapers: "Th' newspaper does ivrything f'r us. It runs th' polis foorce an' th' banks, commands th' milishy, controls th'ligislachure, baptizes th' young, marries th' foolish, comforts th' afflicted, afflicts th' comfortable, buries th' dead an' roasts thim aftherward." Dooley, with his charming brogue, could get away with social commentary on Dunne's Chicago neighborhood that the straight columnist couldn't risk. The column was hugely popular, and became embedded in American journalistic culture during its long run.

800. THIS SIDE OF PARADISE, by F. Scott Fitzgerald (1920) and BUTTERFIELD 8, by John O'Hara (1935)

Two great American writers, F. Scott Fitzgerald and John O'Hara, can be considered together here, because their works share a common distaste for the Irish American origins of their authors.

In F. Scott Fitzgerald's first novel, *This Side of Paradise* (1920), Amory Blaine climbs the ladder of American society, from prep school to Princeton and beyond. But something holds him back from becoming one of the elite that populates the quadrangles below his dormitory window. While he admires Yeats and Wilde, Blaine is "puzzled and depressed" by Joyce's *Portrait of the Artist as a Young Man.* Interestingly, Amory's rejection of his Irishness has been paralleled with Stephen Daedelus's shedding his Catholicism in Joyce's novel. In Fitzgerald's novel, a Catholic priest tells Amory to remain loyal to his Irish Catholic background: "Celtic you'll live and Celtic you'll die; so if you don't use heaven as a continual referendum for your ideas you'll find earth a continual recall to your ambitions."

John O'Hara, a disciple of Fitzgerald's, grew up in rural Pennsylvania, the son of a local doctor whose early death dashed O'Hara's dreams of an Ivy League education. In fact, O'Hara could have attended Yale, but refused since he would have had to take a part-time job. In *Butterfield 8*, the character Jimmy Malloy, sharing much with O'Hara, throws himself headlong into the noirish world of hard drink, fast cars, and fast talk. But he

F. Scott Fitzgerald admits with self-loathing that while dazzled by the glamorous WASP world of Manhattan, "I'm a Mick. I wear Brooks clothes and I don't eat salad with a spoon and I probably could play five-goal polo in two years, but I am a Mick. . . . we're not American. We're Micks, we're non-assimilable, we Micks."

801. STUDS LONIGAN trilogy, by James T. Farrell (1932–36) James T. Farrell is largely responsible for reviving Irish American fiction during the 1930s and 1940s. At a time when F. Scott Fitzgerald, John O'Hara, and Mary McCarthy were masking their Irish origins and producing New York society novels, Farrell's voice was distinctly and unapologetically Irish American. Farrell uses the working-class South Side Chicago neighborhood he grew up in as the setting for most of his books. His most famous works are the trilogy of *Studs Lonigan* novels, about a street tough who goes from adolescent dreaming and loitering to a wasted life of self-destruction. *Studs Lonigan* was made into a movie in 1960 starring Jack Nicholson and Christopher Knight (the actor who played Peter in *The Brady Bunch*).

802. THE YEAR OF THE FRENCH, by Thomas Flanagan (1979) Historical novelist Thomas Flanagan's *The Year of the French* won the 1979 National Book Award. It chronicles the 1798 rebellion of the United Irishmen, one of the bloodiest uprisings in Irish history. Wolfe Tone, leader of the United Irishmen, was counting on French support to bolster the group's troops and liberate Ireland from British rule. But the rebellion was doomed; the French force that eventually landed was far smaller than expected. Flanagan's novel brings the Rebellion to life through the character of Owen MacCarthy, a poet and "hedge school" master who taught the outlawed Gaelic language. Admirers of Flanagan appreciate his research and historical accuracy as well as the lack of romantic sentiment in *The Year of the French*, and subsequently in *The Tenants of Time* and *The End of the Hunt*.

803. FINAL PAYMENTS, by Mary Gordon (1978) Mary Gordon's first novel, *Final Payments*, was a runaway success when it was published in 1978, although it has been criticized for portraying Catholicism as an oppressive force in the lives of Irish Americans. The protagonist, Isabel Moore, lives a sheltered life, taking care of her aging and ailing widowed father, whose strictness and devoutness have had a controlling effect on her. When her father dies, Isabel is left alone and free for the first time at thirty, although she remains haunted by her father and the expectations his religion and conservatism have thrust upon her. The *Los Angeles Times* has called Gordon "the patron saint of American Irish Catholic angst."

804. ALBANY CYCLE, by William Kennedy In his Albany Cycle of novels, William Kennedy has been said to do for Albany what Joyce did for Dublin. The first installment, *Legs* (1978), chronicles Jack "Legs" Diamond, a gangster in 1930s Albany, New York. The second book, *Billy Phelan's Greatest Game* (1978), features a gambler and bookie who gets drawn into the kidnapping of a politician's son. The Pulitzer Prize–winning *Ironweed* (1983) shifts the focus to Francis Phelan, Billy's down-and-out brother who is seeking to reconcile with his past. Kennedy's novels are lauded for their grittiness, realism, and warmth. As Dean Flowers in the *Hudson Review* said, "the speakeasies and gangsters and fast talk seem immediate and legendary, with Irish-Catholic Albany as a microcosm of the thirties."

805. THE LAST HURRAH, by Edwin O'Connor

Edwin O'Connor

(1956) Edwin O'Connor (1918–68) once announced that he would like his writing "to do for the Irish in America what Faulkner did for the South." And he might have done so, if not for his premature death at the age of forty-nine. *The Last Hurrah* is generally recognized as a shrewd and humorous fictionalization of Boston mayor James Michael Curley's last political campaign. Frank Skeffington (O'Connor's version of Curley) squeezes the Democratic Tammany Hall–style political machine in a spirited attempt to win, but is beaten by a modern air-brushed candidate who goes so far as to rent an Irish setter for a television ad. The novel's humor and warmth were successfully translated to the silver screen in a 1958 John Ford film starring Spencer Tracy.

806. LONG DAY'S JOURNEY INTO NIGHT, by Eugene O'Neill (1956) As perhaps the leading American playwright, Eugene O'Neill must be included here despite the fact that he was not a novelist. O'Neill's Irish heritage was an important influence in his work, and nowhere is it more evident than in *Long Day's Journey Into Night,* which was not published until three years after O'Neill's death in 1953. The play is largely autobiographical, based on O'Neill and his parents and brother. In the play, the Tyrones are dominated by the self-centered father, James, who, like the playwright's father, was an actor. One son is an alcoholic and the other is stricken by tuberculosis, while the mother retreats from the family problems into madness and drug addiction. *Long Day's Journey Into Night* won a Pulitzer Prize in 1957.

Journalism and Commentary

Colonial Era and Nineteenth Century

807. Nellie Bly Nellie Bly (1867–1922), born Elizabeth Cochrane in Pennsylvania, began her journalism career at the age of eighteen at the *Pittsburgh Dispatch.* Taking her pen name from a Stephen Foster song about a social reformer, she quickly gained a reputation for writing about needed social reforms. Bly later moved to New York and took a job with Pulitzer's *New York World.* She won national fame for her investigative reporting, especially when she posed as an inmate to write a sensational exposé of the conditions of the insane asylum on New York City's Blackwell's Island. Later she made international headlines when in 1890 she made a round-the-world trip in 72 days, 6 hours, and 11 minutes, beating the "record" of Jules Verne's fictional Phileas Fogg in *Around the World in Eighty Days.* She married Robert Seaman in 1895 and soon gave up writing.

808. Mathew Carey Born in Dublin, Mathew Carey (1760–1839) proved himself an outspoken writer as early as 1779 when he fled Ireland after criticizing England's oppression of Irish Catholics. When he fled the country again in 1783, he did not return to France where he had met Benjamin Franklin, but instead headed for America. He never forgot his beloved Ireland, though, and continued the fight against English injustice with his impassioned writing.

In Philadelphia, Carey founded the *Pennsylvania Herald* in 1785, later expanding his publications to include magazines, books, pamphlets, and America's first Roman Catholic Bible. Among his published authors were Charles Dickens and James Fenimore Cooper.

Politically, Carey was loyal to his friend Thomas Jefferson while retaining a certain independence. In fact, many believe Carey's greatest role was as go-between for the Democratic-Republicans and the Federalists. When Carey died in 1839, his son Henry took over the publishing ventures.

See also entry #137 about other colonial era newspaper publishers.

809. Patrick Ford Patrick Ford (1837–1913), the founder and editor of the *Irish World,* the largest-selling Irish American paper in the Gilded Age, was one of the most influential Irish Americans of his day. An emigrant from Ireland during the Great Famine, he expressed an interest in radical political thought at an early age. Quite likely this stemmed from one of his first jobs: working as a printer's assistant in the offices of William Lloyd Garrison's *The Liberator,* the leading national organ of radical abolitionism. After service in the Union Army and a brief postwar stint in the South, he settled in New York City, where he founded his paper in 1870.

The *Irish World* quickly became a leading voice for radical reform—something not often associated with the Irish in this era. Ford's editorials supported movements for women's suffrage, an income tax, currency reform, land nationalization, the elimination of monopolies, and the advancement of the cause of organized labor. Not surprisingly, Ford's brand of Irish nationalism reflected his social views. He advocated both Irish independence *and* a radical transformation of Irish society. To emphasize this range of concerns beyond parochial Irish or Catholic issues, Ford changed the name of his paper in 1878 from the *Irish World* to the *Irish World and Industrial Liberator.*

Ford would go on to become an enthusiastic supporter of the Land League, especially its more radical wing led by Michael Davitt and heavily influenced by the social theorist Henry George. This irritated more conservative nationalists like John Devoy, but there was little they could do, since Ford brought in the lion's share of donations to the League.

Ford cooled his radicalism in the late 1880s, in part because he took to heart the warnings of American Catholic leaders that socialism was a godless doctrine incompatible with Catholicism. The *Irish World* remained an influential paper until the time of Ford's death in 1913, whereupon it began a slow decline, closing in 1951.

810. James McClatchy When James McClatchy (1825–84) accepted a job in 1857 as the first local editor of a new San Francisco newspaper called the *Bee,* he had no way of knowing that it was the beginning of an incredible career in journalism and a publishing dynasty. Born in Ireland, he arrived in America in 1840 and found work writing for the *New York Tribune.* When news of the gold rush arrived, McClatchy headed west. Failing to strike it rich, he returned to journalism, working as a writer and editor for several newspapers. The *Bee* originated as a combination of two failed newspapers, but it prospered almost immediately under McClatchy's guidance. Soon he bought the paper and built it up to become one of the West Coast's most influential papers. A born reformer, McClatchy was also an ardent Irish nationalist and worked on behalf of Irish causes all his life. Upon his death, McClatchy's son Charles Kenny McClatchy took the helm and began a sixty-year career as a highly respected journalist and editor. Today the McClatchy Company publishes eleven daily and thirteen community newspapers in six states with a combined average circulation of 1.35 million.

811. Thomas D'Arcy McGee Thomas D'Arcy McGee (1822–68) lived a zealous and turbulent life. Born in County Louth, he arrived in America at age sixteen. He soon landed a job writing for the *Boston Pilot,* the local Catholic newspaper. His blistering condemnation of Boston's Puritan culture and heritage earned him sharp condemnation and a return trip to Ireland. Almost immediately he became involved in the Young Ireland movement, writing for its main organ, the *Nation.* He fled Ireland in the wake of the failed uprising in 1848 and returned to New York, where he started his own newspaper called the *Nation.* Again controversy soon arose, only this time it was Archbishop John Hughes who condemned him for his criticisms of the Church. In 1850 he returned to Boston and started the *American Celt.* Veering back toward conservatism in religion and nationalism, he wrote *History of the Irish Settlers in America,* a book which extolled the Irish contribution to American history. He wrote a similar work, *The Catholic History of North America* in 1855. McGee again ran afoul of the Church when he began to urge Catholic migration out of the dismal cities of the East Coast to the frontier. In 1857, tired and broke, he moved to Canada. Irrepressible, he immediately embarked on an active career in public life, beginning with his election to the Legislative Assembly of Canada in

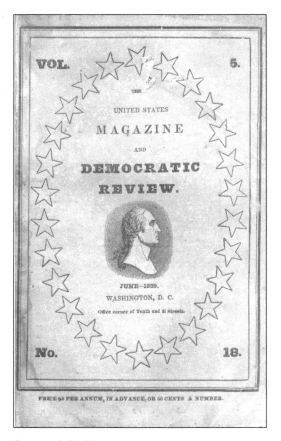

Democratic Review

1858 and subsequent appointment to several ministerial posts in several governments during the 1860s. McGee was assassinated in Ottawa, presumably for remarks made against the Fenians in the U.S. and Canada.

812. John L. O'Sullivan John L. O'Sullivan (1813–95) was the editor of *The United States Magazine and Democratic Review* in the 1840s. At the time, one of the burning national issues was westward expansion. Some Americans were reluctant to push America's frontier westward because they feared war with Mexico, the expansion of slavery into any new territories acquired, or both. John L. O'Sullivan, however, spoke for the many Americans who enthusiastically supported expansion. He is credited with coining the phrase "manifest destiny" to express the belief that expansion was a God-given inevitability and the key to nation's future greatness. The annexation of Texas, he wrote, would be "the fulfillment of our manifest destiny to overspread the continent allotted by Providence for the free development of our yearly multiplying millions." The phrase was picked up by other newspapers and soon found its way into the debates over the Texas question.

Twentieth Century

813. Jimmy Breslin Jimmy Breslin (b. 1933), the larger-than-life newspaper columnist, has chronicled New York life during a career spanning six decades. Beginning in the late 1950s as a local sports reporter, Breslin soon moved to news coverage. In 1963 he gained national attention for his coverage of the Kennedy assassination, writing a classic column in which he interviewed the man who dug the slain president's grave (giving rise to the mantra uttered by city desk editors ever since, "find the gravedigger"). In 1969 Breslin turned to writing an opinion column that came to be praised for its sharp insight and hilarious stories. In 1986, he won a Pulitzer Prize for his investigative columns that helped uncover a major political corruption scandal in New York. In addition to his newspaper columns, which have appeared in a number of publications, Breslin has written several novels, including *Table Money,* a memorable look at working-class life in Queens, New York, and a memoir, *I Want to Thank My Brain for Remembering Me,* which relates his experience of undergoing major brain surgery.

814. William F. Buckley, Jr. Son of a wealthy oilman, William F. Buckley, Jr. (b. 1925) has worn many hats in his very public career. Raised in patrician privilege in New York City and educated at top private schools, Buckley served in the U.S. Army in World War II before enrolling at Yale.

Buckley burst onto the national scene in 1951, when at the age of twenty-six, he published *God and Man at Yale,* a harsh, conservative critique of the modern university's lack of morality and principle. Recognized as a leading figure of the political conservatism, he founded *National Review* in 1955, where he served as editor and contributing writer. He later started a syndicated column (1962) and a weekly television program called *Firing Line* (1966). Beginning in the mid-1970s, Buckley has also authored a series of spy novels featuring the hero Blackford Oakes. Known for his distinctive, quasi-British accent and patrician manner, Buckley is without question the most influential promoter of conservative thought since 1950. He was instrumental in the rise of Ronald Reagan and the modern conservative movement of the 1970s and 1980s.

815. Finley Peter Dunne Born of Irish-immigrant parents in Chicago in 1867, Finley Peter Dunne loved reading and aspired to be a journalist. At age sixteen he took a job as an errand boy at the *Chicago Telegram.* For the next eight years he worked for several newspapers, slowly moving up through the ranks to become a political reporter and editorial writer. In 1893, the twenty-six-year-old seasoned scribe began writing a column commenting on politics and society.

Instead of a straightforward opinion piece, however, Dunne created a cast of fictional characters who spoke in heavy Irish dialect. Foremost was Martin J. Dooley, a saloonkeeper with an opinion on everything and everybody. Dunne used Dooley and his South Side bar to expose hypocrisy and shams in public affairs, deflate the outsized egos of politicians and robber barons, and make known the views of the "little guy." He also promoted a consistently progressive message, whether concerning women's suffrage, the right of organized labor, or tolerance toward new immigrants. Dunne gained a national following after several papers began carrying Mr. Dooley's hilarious observations of Admiral George Dewey's victory at Manila Bay in 1898.

In all Dunne wrote more than seven hundred columns, many of which were reprinted as collections in books. Many of Martin Dooley's pearls of wisdom—"Thrust ivrybody, but cut th' ca-ards"—remain part of American conversation to this day.

816. Brendan Gill Brendan Gill (1914–97) was born in Hartford, Connecticut. He was educated at Yale University and began his lifelong career as a writer for *The New Yorker* magazine in 1936. The literary community considers him one of the most influential writers of the twentieth century. He wrote fifteen books, including biographies of Frank Lloyd Wright and Tallulah Bankhead. He was passionate about art and worked to save the Grand Central Terminal in New York City. His most controversial work is *Here at the New Yorker,* which detailed life at the magazine.

817. Pete Hamill The son of Belfast immigrants, Pete Hamill (b. 1935) was born and raised in Brooklyn. He worked on the Brooklyn waterfront, enlisted in the navy, and lived for a time in Mexico before breaking into journalism in the early 1960s as a reporter for the *New York Post.* There he built a reputation as a powerful voice of liberalism, opposing the Vietnam War and supporting civil rights. He played a key role in convincing Robert

F. Kennedy to declare himself a candidate for president in 1968 and was a witness to Kennedy's assassination in June of that year. Hamill never wavered from his staunch liberalism, even as the city and political party he loved seemed to stagger in the 1970s. He also began to publish novels, many drawing on his Irish heritage and urban, working-class upbringing. His memoir, *A Drinking Life,* became a bestseller. Hamill remains a prolific writer and thoughtful commentator on public affairs.

818. William Randolph Hearst William Randolph Hearst (1863–1951) became one of the most influential figures in American journalism history. Born in San Francisco the son of a newspaper owner, Hearst went to Harvard but was expelled after two years. At age twenty-three he became "proprietor" of his father's newspaper, the *San Francisco Examiner.* From that modest beginning, he built the nation's largest chain of newspapers. Along the way, he changed the entire industry. He is best remembered for pioneering in "yellow journalism" that sensationalized news, especially stories of Spanish atrocities in Cuba in the 1890s, an effort that played a major role in pushing America into war in 1898. Hearst longed for high public office, perhaps even the presidency, and was twice elected to the U.S. House of Representatives from New York City. But his many enemies and personal scandals thwarted his runs for senate and governor. The story of Hearst's life was depicted in the landmark film *Citizen Kane,* starring Orson Wells.

819. Walt Kelly Walter Kelly (1913–73) was born in Philadelphia, but grew up in Bridgeport, Connecticut. He learned drawing from his father and after graduating high school, worked at various editing, illustrating, and cartoonist jobs across the country. It was not until 1948 that his comic strip "Pogo" first appeared in print in the *New York Star.* Set in the Okeefenokee Swamp of Georgia, the cartoon featured a varied cast of animal characters. Readers were drawn to both Kelly's humorous scenes and his political satire on topics ranging from Sen. Joseph McCarthy to the war in Vietnam. "Pogo" caught on quickly and through syndication soon became one of the most popular comic strips in America. Of his many memorable lines that have passed into common usage, the most notable is: "We have met the enemy and he is us."

820. Dorothy Mae Kilgallen Dorothy Kilgallen (1913–65) was born in Chicago and raised in Wyoming and Indiana. She discovered a talent for writing while she was in college and at the age of twenty had a byline in the *New York Evening Journal.* She moved into full-time journalism after graduation and soon became well known in New York social circles. She and her actor husband, Richard Tollmar, started a popular, gossipy talk radio program called *Breakfast with Dorothy and Dick.* The popularity of that program led to her most famous role as part of the 1960s television show, *What's My Line?* Unfortunately, she became addicted to alcohol and drugs, finally dying of an overdose in 1965.

821. Sam McClure The "muckraking" movement in American journalism is credited to Irishman Samuel Sidney McClure (1770–1851). Born in Antrim, McClure's family migrated to Illinois when he was a child. After graduating from Knox College, McClure worked for several magazines. He and his wife, Hattie, formed the first U.S. news syndicate and later *McClure's* magazine, intending to identify and correct flaws in American society. McClure's revolutionary payment method compensated journalists for their study time, which resulted in in-depth articles. The result was often exposés that enraged the subjects and attracted the "muckraking" label. The best-known example was Ida Tarbell's series on Standard Oil.

822. Anne Elizabeth O'Hare McCormick Anne Elizabeth O'Hare McCormick (1882–1954) was

Anne Elizabeth O'Hare McCormick

born to Irish parents in Wakefield, York-shire, England, and moved to Ohio as a young girl. After serving as associate editor of the *Catholic Universe Weekly,* McCormick traveled to Europe in 1920. Her regular submissions to the *New York Times* led to a position as foreign correspondent two years later. McCormick interviewed a number of leading political figures, including Hitler. Not only was McCormick the first woman to serve on the editorial board of the *New York Times,* but in 1937 she also became the first woman to win a Pulitzer Prize for journalism.

823. Mary McGrory Mary McGrory (b. 1918) was born in Boston. As a child she attended Girls' Latin School and then went on to receive a Bachelor of Arts degree in 1939 from Emmanuel College. McGrory began her journalism career as a reporter for the *Boston Herald Traveler,* and soon after became a book reviewer for the *Washington Star.* Her big break came in 1954 when she was assigned to cover the Army-McCarthy hearings. Having proved her talent as a journalist, she enjoyed top assignments thereafter, becoming one of the most prominent woman journalists of her era. McGrory has won numerous awards including the George Polk Memorial award and the Pulitzer Prize. Since 1960, her column has been syndicated nationally.

824. Edward R. Murrow Edward Roscoe Murrow (1908–65) was born in Greensboro, North Carolina. After graduating from Washington State College, he traveled extensively and held a number of jobs relating to education and foreign affairs. He got his break into the communications business in 1935 when he joined the staff of the Columbia Broadcasting System as director of education programming. In 1937, Murrow became head of the CBS European Bureau in London and won acclaim for his coverage of WWII. In the years after the war, Murrow emerged as one of the premier figures in radio and television journalism. With Fred Friendly of CBS, he established in 1947 the popular radio program on current events called *Hear It Now.* In 1951 they adapted the program to television as *See It Now.* It was on this program that Murrow had his greatest impact. In 1954, Murrow's harsh criticism of Senator Joseph McCarthy as a threat to democracy and civil liberties played a major role in ending the latter's career as an anti-Communist crusader. Murrow also pioneered in establishing the television interview program with *Person to Person,* a show that debuted in 1953 and featured conversations with celebrities and newsmakers. In 1961 Murrow left CBS to head the U.S. Information Agency, which he left in 1964 due to declining health. Shortly before his death in 1965, Murrow received the Medal of Freedom from President Lyndon Johnson.

825. Andy Rooney A kindly curmudgeon, Andrew A. Rooney is a newspaper columnist better known for the segment "A Few Minutes with Andy Rooney" on the famed investigative television news program, *60 Minutes.* His weekly takes on the irony, hypocrisy, and hilarity modern American life debuted in 1978. Audiences loved the segments for their wit and insight, and for the way they gave the hard-hitting show a light ending. On occasion, Rooney's rough-edged, politically incorrect style has sparked controversy and calls for his ouster, but in each case thousands of fans called and wrote letters in his support. Rooney has published many books, including a memoir, *My War,* of his years as a reporter for *Stars and Stripes* during World War II.

826. Mark Sullivan The son of an Irish farmer, Mark Sullivan was born in 1875 in Avondale, Pennsylvania. He became a journalist, first with the *Ladies' Home Journal* in 1904 and later as a muckraking investigative reporter for *McClure's* and *Collier's* magazines. In 1914 he became the editor at *Collier's*, but in the 1920s began a syndicated political column for the *New York Tribune* (later, *Herald Tribune*) that ran for decades. In 1926 he published the first volume of a six-volume social history of the U.S. in the early twentieth century, entitled *Our Times*.

PART VIII

Medicine
and Science

827. Some Notable Early Contributors to Medicine
Several physicians made significant contributions to the field of medicine in the colonial and early republic period. Dublin-born Dr. Samuel Clossy, for example, emigrated to New York City in 1763 and joined the faculty at Kings College (present-day Columbia University) and later cofounded its medical school. Dr. John Crawford (1746–1813) settled in Baltimore and became the first physician to introduce vaccination to America. Dr. Ephraim McDowell (1771–1830) became a renowned surgeon after he removed a twenty-pound ovarian tumor from a woman in 1809, and later performed gallstone and hernia surgery on President James K. Polk.

828. George Washington Crile, Sr. Dr. George Crile (1864–1943) was born in Chili, Ohio. He received his degree from Wooster Medical College in 1887 and performed the first successful human blood transfusion in 1906. During the Spanish-American War he studied tropical diseases and in World War I, his research included wound infection and shock. He received the French Legion of Honor in 1922. Crile cofounded the Cleveland Clinic, modeled after the Mayo Clinic. He perfected goiter and thyroid disease operations. Crile was a founding member of the American College of Surgeons, and taught at Western Reserve School of Medicine from 1900 until his death.

829. Margaret Baggett Dolan Margaret Baggett Dolan (1914–74) started her career in 1935 at the United States Public Health Service where she became an epidemiological nurse and tuberculosis nursing consultant. In 1959, Dolan became head of the Department of Public Health Nursing at the University of North Carolina's School of Public Health (1959–74). Recognized as a leading figure in public health, she was elected the nineteenth president of the American Nurses Association (ANA) in 1962, a position that led her to testify before several congressional committees and serve on a number of government advisory board. Dolan also served as the first woman president of the American Public Health Association (1973). To honor her many achievements in the field of health care, the American Public Health Association established a lectureship endowment fund in Dolan's name, shortly after her death.

830. William James Brother of the famous novelist Henry James, William James (1842–1910) earned recognition in a decidedly different field. Educated abroad, he returned to the U.S. to earn his M.D. from Harvard Medical School in 1869. He joined the faculty at Harvard, first as a lecturer in anatomy and physiology, but later switching to the philosophy department. He became increasingly interested in the emerging field of psychology and established the first laboratory in America devoted to its study in 1876. This was instrumental in gaining recognition that psychology was a discipline separate from philosophy. He helped found the American Society for Psychical Research and wrote a classic work, *The Principles of Psychology* in 1890. His *Varieties of Religious Experience* is considered a pathbreaking study into the psychology of religion. He later concentrated more on philosophy and with the publication of *Pragmatism* (1907) became a leading promoter of the theory of pragmatism.

831. Howard A. Kelly Dr. Howard A. Kelly (1858–1943), one of Johns Hopkins' "Famous Four" founding physicians, arrived at the university in 1889 after teaching at the University of Pennsylvania. He established the long-term residency program in gynecology at Johns Hopkins, which made gynecology a true specialty. Among his numerous innovations, he invented the urinary cystoscope and was among the first to use radium for cancer treatment. He founded the Kelly Clinic in Baltimore, which became a leader in radiation therapy.

832. Robert Foster Kennedy A native of Ireland, Robert Foster Kennedy (1884–1952) was a neurologist who studied medicine at Queens College and served as resident medical officer at the National Hospital at Queen Square, London. He emigrated to the United States in 1910 to accept a position as head of the clinic at the Neurological Institute in New York. The following year he achieved wide recognition as a leading neurologist when he published a study in the *American Journal of Medical Science.* The study concerned the condition where patients went blind in an eye as the result of a tumor pressing their optic nerve. That condition now bears his name. Kennedy also made advances in the understanding of multiple sclerosis and shell shock, the latter as a result of his field service in World War I. He was also an early proponent of shock treatment for severe cases of depression. After World War I he became professor of neurology at Cornell University.

833. Frank Lahey Dr. Frank Lahey (1880–1953) was born in Haverhill, Massachusetts. He taught at Harvard from 1912 to 1915 and Tufts from 1913 to 1924. In 1923 both universities established a joint chair for him. An Irish American surgeon of

Dr. Frank Lahey

worldwide fame, he utilized a team approach and pioneered trauma-reducing procedures. He was also a leader in the study and improvement of anesthesia and the team approach in diagnosis. In 1923 he opened the Lahey Clinic with three other physicians on Beacon Street in Boston. He served as president of the American Medical Association between 1941 and 1942.

834. Charles McBurney Medical pioneer Charles McBurney (1845–1913) was born in Roxbury, Massachusetts. He was considered the leading authority on diagnosing and treating appendicitis in the nineteenth century. In 1889 he discovered that appendicitis could be detected by applying pressure to a tender area near the right abdomen. This area is still known today as McBurney's Point. Five years later, the incision he made in the right lower part of the abdomen to remove an appendix became "McBurney's incision." He was also a pioneer in aseptic technique and spent much of his career at Roosevelt Hospital, which became a nationally recognized center for research and teaching.

835. Paul R. McHugh Dr. Paul McHugh (b. 1931) is one of the nation's leading authorities on the biological basis of human behavior. He was born in Lawrence, Massachusetts, in 1931 and attended Harvard Medical School. He later studied and worked at some of the leading medical hospitals in the nation, developing pioneering approaches to neuroscience. His success led to an invitation to come to Johns Hopkins University in 1975. He soon did what many considered impos-

Dr. Paul R. McHugh

sible, revive the once-vaunted department of psychiatry at Hopkins. Since 1992 he has also served as director of the Blades Center for Clinical Practice and Research in Alcoholism. McHugh has occasionally come in for criticism from some corners of the psychiatry profession for his willingness to dismiss as "psychiatric misadventures" trends like recovered memory and multiple personality disorder. Still, he is widely respected for his pathbreaking research and administrative genius. His textbook (cowritten with Phillip R. Slavney) *The Perspectives of Psychiatry* (1983) is considered by many to be the finest in the field.

836. William James MacNeven Born of Catholic parents in County Galway, William James MacNeven (1763–1841) studied medicine in Vienna, Austria. Arrested and later exiled for his role in the United Irishmen uprising of 1798, MacNeven settled in New York City. He resumed his medical practice and was soon named professor of Obstetrics at the College of Physicians and Surgeons at New York Hospital. He later moved to the Chemistry department where he established the first chemical laboratory in the state. In 1819 he published *Chemical Examination of*

Dr. William J. MacNeven

Mineral Waters of Schooley's Mountains and a second study, *Exposition of Atomic Theory of Chemistry*. He also served as coeditor of the *New York Medical and Philosophical Review*. At his death in 1841 he was acknowledged as the father of American chemistry.

837. John L. Madden Dr. John L. Madden (1912–99) was a pioneer in the field of vascular surgery. Born in Washington, D.C., to Irish immigrant parents, he graduated from George Washington University Medical School in 1937. After service in World War II, he joined the staff at St. Claire's Hospital in Manhattan where he began an extraordinary career in surgery. He was among the first in America to successfully graft arteries into patients suffering from an aortic aneurysm. Madden later developed a novel technique—electrofulguration—to remove tumors by burning them from the colon, thereby allowing a patient to avoid a colostomy. He also helped popularize modified radical mastectomy, a procedure that left part of the breast intact. In recognition of his work, Madden received many awards over his career, including the American Medical Association's Ludwig Hektoen gold medal in 1952.

838. Henry Newell Martin Irish-born doctor Henry Newell Martin (1848–96) is best known for his pioneering work in the field of physiology. After studying medicine in London and doing postgraduate work at Cambridge University under noted physiologist Sir Michael Foster, Martin left England in 1876 to head the biology department at the newly formed Johns Hopkins University in Baltimore, Maryland. Following in the footsteps of his Cambridge mentor, Martin's contributions to American medicine included new laboratory teaching methods and an evolutionary approach to zoology. Martin was also the first secretary-treasurer and a founding father of the American Physiological Society, established in 1887.

839. John Benjamin Murphy Born in Wisconsin,

John B. Murphy (1857–1916) earned his M.D. from Rush Medical College in Chicago. He became one of the most respected surgeons in America and held teaching positions at some of the nation's best hospitals and medical schools. His greatest contribution to his field was the invention of the Murphy Button in 1892, a medical device that dramatically improved a surgeon's ability to mend intestines. Because it made gastrointestinal surgery far safer, it greatly expanded the number and type of operations surgeons could undertake. Murphy later developed an improved technique for performing an appendectomy. In addition to his many honors, he was elected president of the American Medical Association (1910–11) and the Clinical Congress of Surgeons (1914–15).

840. William P. Murphy   William Parry Murphy (1892–1987) is renowned for his landmark work in treating pernicious anemia and hypochromic anemia with raw liver, together with George Richards Minot and George Hoyt Whipple. They received the coveted Nobel Prize for Physiology and Medicine in 1934 for this work.

Parry's career began when he received the William Stanislaus Murphy Fellowship and graduated from Harvard Medical School in 1922. In 1923 he began research on diabetes mellitus and other blood diseases. His work on anemia was considered outstanding. He used intramuscular injections of extract of liver to treat pernicious and hypochromic anemia and for granulocytopenia. He later held several esteemed positions at Harvard University, including Associate in Medicine and Emeritus Lecturer. He also received numerous awards, such as the Bronze Medal of the American Medical Association and the National Order of Merit and wrote *Anemia in Practice: Pernicious Anemia* (1939).

841. Joseph E. Murray   Born in Milford, Massachusetts, Joseph E. Murray (b. 1919) originally trained as a plastic surgeon. But he gradually

Dr. Joseph E. Murray

became interested in developing a treatment for kidney failure. In 1954 at the Peter Bent Brigham Hospital (today's Brigham and Women's Hospital), Murray performed the first human kidney transplant. He chose to do the operation with identical twins so as to minimize the chances that the recipient's body would reject the organ. The success of the initial operation led Murray to study the effects of immunosuppressant drugs that would allow for transplants between unrelated people. His pathbreaking research made Murray a corecipient of the 1990 Nobel Prize in medicine.

842. John Rock   Dr. John Rock (1890-1984) was a devout Catholic and daily communicant, but in 1960 he came under relentless fire from the Church hierarchy for his role in inventing the oral contraceptive, or "the Pill." Monsignor Francis W. Carney, of Cleveland, called him a "moral rapist," and hate mail poured in from all over. But Rock was a man of strong convictions and he hit the media trail to promote the virtues—moral and practical—of his invention. Soon he published a very influential book, *The Time Has Come: A Catholic Doctor's Proposals to End the Battle Over Birth Control* (1963) in which he argued that since oral contraceptives were "natural," they did not violate Church teachings. By the mid-1960s, as the Church debated the question of oral contraceptives, many—including John Rock—thought he was winning them over. But in 1968 Pope Paul VI issued *Humana Vitae* which explicitly prohibited oral contraception. Rock retired in 1971 and sought solace in the isolated hills of New Hampshire where he lived into his nineties.

Margaret Sanger

843. Margaret Sanger

Founder of the modern American birth control movement, Margaret Higgins Sanger (1879–1966) waged a successful crusade to abolish laws prohibiting publication and distribution of information about contraception. Sanger got her start in public health as a nurse working among the immigrant poor on New York City's Lower East Side. The experience opened her eyes to the interrelationship between large family size and problems such as poverty and high rates of infant and maternal mortality. She began publishing pamphlets about contraception in 1914 and two years later opened the nation's first birth control clinic. Located in the Brownsville section of Brooklyn, the clinic drew large numbers of women before being shut down by the police. Sanger served thirty days in jail for "maintaining a public nuisance." She also drew the scorn of the Catholic Church. But these incidents brought attention and supporters to her cause. Sanger later founded the American Birth Control League and served as its president for seven years. She planned the first World Population Conference in Geneva, Switzerland, in 1927, and served as the first president of the International Planned Parenthood Federation.

844. Harold J. C. Swan

Born in County Sligo, Ireland, Dr. Harold J. C. Swan (b. 1922) had doctors for parents. He studied medicine in England and moved to the United States following World War II. An expert in blood flow, he joined the staff at the Mayo Clinic in Rochester, Minnesota. From there he moved on to the University of California at Los Angeles where he developed the revolutionary technique of using catherization to treat acute myocardial infarction.

845. Henry Stack Sullivan

Henry Stack Sullivan (1892–1949) is considered by many to be one of the great contributors to the field of psychiatry in the twentieth century. Born in upstate New York, he graduated from medical school in 1917 and immediately took a job with the Medical Corps providing mental evaluations of potential soldiers. Sullivan spent most of the 1920s doing clinical research and in 1931 opened a private practice in New York City. He also began to publish studies based on his research. In so doing he proposed several novel theories of psychiatry that prompted wide debate in the field and much additional research. Most notable was his work into schizophrenia which resulted in the disorder no longer being classified as "incurable."

Mathematics and Economics

846. James M. Buchanan, Jr.

James M. Buchanan, Jr. (b. 1919), earned his Ph.D. from the University of Chicago in 1948. After teaching at several universities he settled at Virginia Polytechnic Institute and State University and there established the Center for Study of Public Choice. Buchanan has written thirteen books and countless articles on public finance, public choice, constitutional economics and economic philosophy. He was awarded a Nobel Prize in economics in 1986 for, in the words of the committee, "his development of the contractual and constitutional bases for the theory of economic and political decision-making."

847. Robert Adrian

An emigrant from Carrickfergus in Ireland, Robert Adrian (1775–1843) was the most brilliant mathematician of the early republic. He lectured at numerous schools, including the University of Pennsylvania. He is best remembered for two contributions to his field. First, he posited the exponential law of error in

1808 (subsequently proven in Germany). Second, he offered a more accurate calculation of the Earth's elliptical shape.

848. Claude E. Shannon Known as the "father of modern digital communications" and a pivotal figure in the development of information theory, Claude E. Shannon (1916–2001) was born in Michigan and earned his Ph.D. in mathematics from MIT in 1940. A brilliant mathematician, he is credited with establishing the idea that all information could be reduced to a series of 1s and 0s—the basis for digital communication and the foundation of the computer revolution. In the course of his long career, Shannon received many awards and honors, including the National Medal of Science (1966), the Institute of Electrical and Electronic Engineers Medal of Honor (1966), and the Kyoto Prize for Basic Science (1985).

849. James Tobin James Tobin (b. 1918) graduated from Harvard College and, after service in World War II, earned his Ph.D. in economics there (1947). He joined the faculty at Yale University and later served as a member of President Kennedy's Council of Economic Advisers (1961–62). He won a Nobel Prize in Economics in 1986 for, in the words of the committee, "his analysis of financial markets and their relations to expenditure decisions, employment, production and prices."

Physics

850. James W. Cronin James W. Cronin (b. 1931) was born in Chicago. He attended the University of Chicago, where he studied under the great minds of sci-

James Cronin

ence such as Enrico Fermi and Murray Gell-Mann. He earned his Ph.D. in 1955 and began research into nuclear physics at the Brookhaven Laboratory. Later he joined the faculty at Princeton. He was awarded, along with Val L. Fitch, the Nobel Prize in physics for, "the discovery of violations of fundamental symmetry principles in the decay of neural K-mesons."

Engineering

851. Christopher Colles Born in Dublin and trained as a civil engineer, Christopher Colles (1739–1816) emigrated to New York City where in 1774 he designed the city's first water system. Remarkably, it used a steam engine Colles designed himself. Unfortunately, the system was destroyed during the British invasion and occupation of New York, but its principles were revived in the water system built in 1799. Colles was a visionary who devised a plan in 1785, long before the Erie Canal (1817–25) was contemplated, to link the upper Hudson River to the Great Lakes via the Mohawk River. In 1789 he published *A Survey of the Roads of the United States of America*, the first thorough mapping of the new nation's highway system.

852. Jaspar O'Farrell Even before the Mexican American War left the U.S. in possession of California, Irish-born engineer and surveyor Jaspar O'Farrell had made his mark there. He arrived in Yerba Buena in 1843 and in 1847 was hired to correct an earlier street plan devised for what would soon be the great city of San Francisco. It was his survey that created Market Street as a major thoroughfare running diagonal to the original grid. His decision to extend streets perpendicular to Market Street running south explains why San Francisco has a somewhat disunited street grid plan. Legend has it that locals were so displeased with his revised plan that he was obliged to leave the city for a time. But good fortune smiled on O'Farrell. His street plan was accepted and soon thereafter he and his father-in-law made a major gold strike on the Yuba River. O'Farrell used the money to expand his existing ranch to sixty thousand acres. In 1858 he won a term to the state senate. Today O'Farrell's contribution to early San Francisco is remembered by O'Farrell Street.

853. William Mulholland   It is not an overstatement to say that had it not been for William Mulholland (1855–1934)—or at least the water system he built—Los Angeles today would be considerably smaller and less important a city. Born in Belfast in 1855, Mulholland spent the better part of his young adult years working aboard ships making transatlantic voyages. Eventually he emigrated to the U.S., arriving in California in 1876. He took a job with the Los Angeles Water Company as a lowly ditch tender, but spent his spare time studying engineering and hydraulics. Soon he became superintendent of the water company and instituted sweeping improvements in the system. Convinced that the city would one day soon need a newer, larger source of water, he proposed building an enormous, 240-mile aqueduct from Owens Lake in the Sierra Nevadas to Los Angeles. Construction began in 1909. In four years' time, the system of sixty-five reservoirs, twenty-seven dams, and 3,800 miles of pipe was complete. Mulholland was cheered by forty thousand revelers at the inaugural ceremonies in 1913. Unfortunately, fifteen years later one of Mulholland's dams collapsed and five hundred people were killed in the ensuing flood. He took full responsibility for the collapse, even though later studies suggested that it might not have been his fault.

Architecture

854. James Hoban   A native of County Kilkenny, James Hoban (1762–1831) worked as an architect in Dublin before coming to America in 1785. Though Hoban designed several other govern-

The White House

ment buildings in Charleston, South Carolina, and Washington, D.C., he is best known for designing the "President's Palace," or White House. He earned the prestigious commission after winning a national design competition in 1792. When British troops torched the building in 1814, Hoban also supervised the reconstruction. Hoban's design for the White House was certainly influenced by that of Leinster House in Dublin, where Ireland's Parliament currently meets.

855. Kevin Roche   Born in Dublin in 1922, Kevin Roche earned his bachelor's degree in architecture from the local branch of the National University of Ireland in 1945. Following his postgraduate studies at the Illinois Institute of Technology in Chicago, Roche joined Eero Saarinen and Associates, serving as the New York firm's principal associate in design from 1954 to 1961. Roche went on to establish his own architectural firm with partner John Dinkeloo in 1966. Some of Roche's most prominent structures include the Trans World Airlines (TWA) terminal at John F. Kennedy International Airport and the Ford Foundation Headquarters in New York City.

856. Louis Sullivan   The son of a County Cork immigrant, Louis Sullivan (1856–1924) is known as "the father of modern architecture." After brief stints at the Massachusetts Institute of Technology and the Ecole des Beaux-Arts in Paris, Sullivan settled in Chicago, a city that desperately needed his skills after the Great Fire of 1871. He joined Dankmar Adler's Chicago-based architecture business in 1879, becoming a partner two years later. Adler and Sullivan produced more than one hundred buildings during the firm's fourteen-year existence, including Auditorium Building and the Getty Tomb in Graceland Cemetery, both located in Chicago. Many of Sullivan's designs were actually built by Irish contractors and laborers. In addition to his own contributions to the field of architecture, Sullivan also influenced Frank Lloyd Wright, who worked as his chief assistant from 1887 to 1893. Sullivan's famous pronouncement, "Form follows function," came from a magazine article that he wrote in 1896.

Space Exploration

857. Neil Armstrong   Neil Armstrong (b. 1930) received his pilot's license at sixteen. He flew seventy-eight combat missions in Korea at age twenty. He joined NASA's High Speed Flight Station as a test pilot in 1955. He is one of the first two civilian astronauts selected in 1962 and served as Backup Command Pilot for the Gemini GT-5 Mission, Gemini 11, and Apollo 8. He and Pilot David R. Scott executed the first successful docking of two vehicles in space for Gemini 8. He was Spacecraft Commander aboard Apollo 11 in 1969, where he became the first human to walk on the moon.

858. Michael Collins   Born in Rome, Italy, Michael Collins (b. 1930) was the man who in 1969 piloted the Apollo 11 module that circled the moon while the first manned vehicle landed below. Three years earlier, he made two space walks as part of the Gemini 10 mission. After retiring from the space program, Collins remained active in the field. He served as Director of the

Smithsonian Institution's National Air and Space Museum from 1971 to 1978 before taking a position as vice-president of LTV Aerospace and Defense Company, Inc. In 1985 he founded his own aerospace firm. His book, *Carrying the Fire* (1974), recounts his experiences in the space program.

859. John Glenn   John Glenn (b. 1921) demonstrated his skills as a pilot in two wars. During World War II he flew fifty-nine missions. He flew sixty-three missions in Korea and shot down three MIGs. He was awarded the Distinguished Flying Cross five times. In 1957 he set a speed record from Los Angeles to New York. He joined the NASA in April 1959 as a Project Mercury Astronaut. On February 20, 1962, he flew the first manned orbital mission of the United States aboard Friendship 7. He became a United States Senator in 1974. In 1998 he became the oldest person in space aboard the space shuttle Discovery.

860. James B. Irwin   James B. Irwin (1930–91) graduated from the Naval Training Academy in 1951. In 1966 he became the Lunar Module Pilot for Apollo 15, his only spaceflight. He and a fellow astronaut were the first to use Lunar Rover 1, a car specially designed for travel on the surface of the moon. They brought back a 4.15-billion-year-old moon rock nicknamed the Genesis Rock. Irwin received numerous awards including the Distinguished Service Medal. Irwin died of a heart attack in 1991 and was buried at Arlington Cemetery with full military honors.

861. Christa Corrigan McAuliffe   Born Christa Corrigan (1948–86), she received a degree in history at Framingham State College in 1970. She earned a masters degree at Bowie State College in 1978. She taught at Concord High School in New Hampshire and became active in the community. She was chosen from 11,500 applicants for the Teacher in Space Program. This would have made her the first civilian in space. She trained at NASA's facility in Houston for 114 hours. On January 28, 1986, Challenger exploded seventy-three seconds after lift-off, killing all seven astronauts. A fellowship for distinguished teachers was established in her honor.

862. James McDivitt   James McDivitt (b. 1929) earned his degree in aeronautical engineering at the University of Michigan. In 1965 he served as Commander on Gemini 4 to evaluate prolonged effects of space flight, performance of spacecraft and procedures for crew schedules. He was the first Irish person to perform an Extra Vehicular Activity operation. In 1969 he served on Apollo 9 which was the first manned flight of all lunar hardware in Earth's orbit. They also tested the Apollo spacesuit, the first to carry self-contained life support. He later served as Apollo Spacecraft Program Manager. He retired with the rank of Brigadier General, USAF.

863. Kathryn Sullivan and Eileen Collins   The Irish American contribution to space exploration has continued in recent years with astronauts Kathryn Sullivan and Eileen Collins. Selected by NASA in January 1978, Dr. Kathryn Sullivan became an astronaut in August 1979. She served as Capsule Communicator in Mission Control for numerous Shuttle missions. During her first mission she and Commander Leestma successfully conducted a three-and-a-half-hour Extravehicular

Eileen Collins

Activity (EVA) to demonstrate the feasibility of satellite refueling. She is the first American woman to perform an EVA. In 1990 she served on the crew assigned to deploy the Hubble Space Telescope. In 1992 she was Payload Commander on NASA's Mission to Planet Earth, performing twelve experiments expected to enhance our knowledge of our climate and atmosphere.

As a child, Eileen Collins loved the idea of flying so much she saved her own money to pay for lessons. After graduating from Syracuse University in 1978, she was one of four women admitted to Air Force Undergraduate Pilot Training at Vance Air Force Base in Oklahoma. She became the Air Force's first female flight instructor (1979–1990) and was subsequently one of the first women admitted to attend the Air Force Test Pilot School. Collins was selected as an astronaut in 1990 and became the first woman to pilot a space shuttle (*Discovery*) in 1995. Her second shuttle flight occurred in 1997 and in 1999 Collins was named the first woman shuttle commander in the history of the program.

PART IX

Work, Business,
and Innovation

864. Diamond Jim Brady Diamond Jim Brady (1856–1917) earned fame both for his fortune and the flamboyant lifestyle it financed. For seventeen years he worked in all manner of jobs for the New York Central railroad, becoming an expert on the railroad industry. With this knowledge, he took a job selling railroad equipment with the firm Manning, Maxwell, & Moore. A genius at sales, he earned a fortune in commissions. He took some of this money and developed a metal cutting tool that was soon adopted industry-wide, further adding to his fortune.

Brady lived an extravagant lifestyle and became a favorite subject of the press. He was famous for wearing lots of diamonds, throwing lavish parties, and eating stupendous amounts of rich food. Brady also enjoyed keeping company with showgirls whom he showered with diamonds, of course. His generosity also extended to more serious matters. He donated $500,000 to Johns Hopkins University for a urological clinic.

Because of his voracious eating habits, Brady developed serious health problems. Even after an emergency operation at age fifty-one, Brady continued his flamboyant lifestyle. It finally caught up with him, and he died in 1917 at age sixty-one.

865. Alexander Brown One of America's first millionaires, Alexander Brown (1764–1834) was born in County Antrim, Ireland, and arrived in Baltimore in 1800. He developed a prosperous business importing in Irish linen, which he subse-

quently expanded to include commodities such as tobacco and cotton. Continued success in business allowed Brown to transform his enterprise, Alexander Brown & Sons, into a merchant banking house. He played a key role in financing Baltimore's economic development, most notably with his decision to finance the Baltimore & Ohio Railroad.

866. James Concannon James Concannon (1847–1911) is considered one of the fathers of the California wine industry. He was born in the Aran Islands and arrived in Boston in 1872 at the age of seventeen. He headed west and became a sheep farmer in Oregon. He had a talent for business and achieved success selling rubber stamps. His interest in wine led him to Livermore Valley in 1883. He planted his first forty acres with grapevine cuttings imported from France and Spain, thus establishing Con-

James Concannon

cannon Estate Vineyard. One of his early customers was the Catholic Church, which placed regular orders of sacramental wines, a tradition that kept the winery in business during Prohibition. Concannon's sons took over the winery in 1910, the year before he died. Today it is the oldest continuously run vineyard in the Golden State.

867. Elijah Craig   Born in Virginia, Elijah Craig (1738–1808) was a preacher of Georgetown, Kentucky, credited with inventing bourbon in 1788. Legend has it, he sought to create a product similar to Bushmill's whiskey that was imported from northern Ulster (where his family emigrated from). Craig originated, whether by accident or design is not known, the process of charring oak barrels to store and transport the whiskey from Kentucky to his market in New Orleans, thus producing the amber color and distinctive flavor of bourbon.

868. Michael Cudahy   Born in Callan, County Kilkenny, Michael Cudahy (1841–1910) arrived in Milwaukee in 1849. Growing up poor, he quit school at age fourteen and began working in the meatpacking industry. By 1875 the thirty-four-year-old Cudahy was a partner in the firm of Armour and Company in Chicago. He soon revolutionized his industry by applying refrigeration technology to railroad cars and warehouses, transforming meat from a seasonal to a year-round business. He later became sole owner of the Cudahy Packing Company and one of the wealthiest Irishmen in the nation.

869. Marcus Daly   A teenage-immigrant from County Cavan, Marcus Daly (1841–1900) rose from poverty to become one of America's richest men as the "Copper King" of Montana. Originally a silver miner, Daly took an assignment with a Utah mining company to investigate the potential of a silver mine in Montana. He recommended they purchase it and invested five thousand dollars of his own money. When the mine proved profitable, he sold his share for thirty thousand dollars and used the money to buy the Anaconda Silver Mine in Butte, Montana. Daly ignored others who said the mine was spent and continued to sink shafts after the silver ran out. Astonishingly, he made a huge strike—of copper, not silver—and soon became known as the "Copper King." His Anaconda Copper Company eventually became an industrial behemoth at the center of Butte, building power plants, irrigation stations, railroads, lumber mills, and banks. Daly attracted thousands of Irish miners to Butte by offering higher pay and improved industrial conditions paid for by his incredible wealth, thereby creating the most Irish town in the West. His influence extended into politics, where as a strong Democrat he used his power and money to affect national politics and was the strongest supporter of the populist William Jennings Bryan during the 1896 presidential campaign.

870. Patrick Bernard Delany   An emigrant from Kings County, Ireland, Delaney (1845–1924) became one of the most important contributors to the rapidly developing field of telegraphy. He eventually held dozens of patents for inventions and improvements in telegraph technology, including a synchronous, multiplex telegraph that permitted up to six messages to be sent simultaneously on a single wire.

871. William R. Grace   Born in County Cork, Ireland, in 1832, William Russell Grace (1832–1904) became one of the wealthiest international businessmen of his time. A trip to Peru in 1850 led to a partnership in the British shipping firm Bryce & Co. By the 1860s Grace and his brother Michael had developed the company into Grace Brothers & Co., the most powerful company trading along the western coast of South America. In 1865 Grace moved to New York City, where he established the North American office of W. R. Grace & Co. The company's success and his in-

William R. Grace

vestments in South America (including the funding of Peru's efforts in the 1879–83 War of the Pacific) made Grace a millionaire. Although he was not officially an American citizen, Grace allied himself with the Democratic Party and became the first Irish Catholic mayor of New York City in 1880 (reelected in 1882). He was active in Irish nationalist causes like the Land League in the early 1880s and helped organize a relief effort when famine threatened Ireland in 1879.

872. John R. Gregg Born in Shantonaugh, Ireland, John Gregg (1867–1948) was a stenographer who developed a phenomenally successful shorthand system. His timing was perfect as the rise of corporations and modern business practices was leading more and more businessmen to dictate letters and reports to secretaries. Gregg's fast and easy-to-learn system caught on almost immediately after it was introduced in his 1888 pamphlet, *Light-Line Phonography*. Gregg moved to the U.S. in 1893 and started the Gregg Publishing Company and the Gregg Schools. In 1902, he published *Gregg Shorthand,* the basic manuel on his method which has since been translated into Hebrew, Tagalog, Thai, Chinese, and many other languages. He also edited a monthly magazine on shorthand.

Today, the Gregg Shorthand System is the most widely used system of its type in the United States. It is taught in schools and colleges all over the country and the world.

873. "The Irish Four" aka the "Silver Kings" James Fair, James Flood, William O'Brien, and John Mackay are collectively known as the "Irish Four" or the "Silver Kings." Originally from Belfast, Fair grew up in Chicago. He headed west with the gold rush of 1849 and became one of California's leading experts in mining engineering. In 1860 he followed the silver rush to the famed Comstock Lode strike in Nevada. There he met John Mackay in 1864. Originally from Dublin, Mackay had also gone to California in

James C. Flood

1849 and became an expert in mine construction.

James Flood and William S. O'Brien (1825–78), were also drawn to San Francisco during the gold rush. They combined Flood's financial genius and O'Brien's flair for public relations to establish a successful saloon. With profits from that venture, they moved into investing and brokerage. Flood and O'Brien met Fair and Mackay and formed a partnership. In 1868, they purchased the Virginia Consolidated mine, considered by many to be a "dead" part of the famed Comstock Lode. The "Irish Four," however, extracted over $100 million worth of silver from the mine and became fabulously wealthy as a result.

874. William Kelly William Kelly (1811–88) was born in Pittsburgh, the son of a man who left Ireland because of the uprising in 1798. As a young man he entered the shipping and dry goods business and prospered. He invested in iron ore lands in Kentucky and in 1848 established the Suwanee Iron Works and Union Forge. Kelly, an inveterate tinkerer, began experimenting with new and cheaper ways to remove the carbon deposits from crude pig iron. In place of the traditional (and expensive) process of burning off the carbon, Kelly developed a pneumatic process

William Kelly

that shot cold air through the molten iron. It proved a key step in the development of steel. Kelly won a patent for the process in 1857, but went bankrupt soon thereafter. He later returned to the business, but by then found that Henry Bessemer of England had received a patent in England for a nearly identical process in 1856. It remains unclear which man deserves the title of the "inventor" of the steel-making process, but Kelly is credited with making important contributions to it. Bessemer, however, earned the lions' share of fame and profit. Kelly eventually settled his patent dispute with Bessemer and left the business of steel making.

875. Cyrus McCormick Cyrus McCormick was born in 1809, the son of Robert McCormick, who owned several businesses, including a sawmill, a distillery, and two grain mills. His father was a gifted inventor who developed several versions of a mechanical reaper, as well as several other patented devices.

By 1831, Robert McCormick's reaper had become sufficiently advanced that he and his son Cyrus began promoting it through public exhibitions at county fairs. After only minimal success, they redesigned the reaper and received a patent in 1834. Through skillful marketing and innovative policies such as allowing farmers to buy on credit and offering a money-back guarantee, the McCormick's reaper became the most popular type in the country. Sales increased from seventy-five machines in 1846 to 1500 in 1849 to more than 4,100 in 1859.

The McCormick reaper, perhaps more than any other invention in the nineteenth century, played a key role in the transformation of America from a rural nation into the world's premier industrial powerhouse. It caused a boom in agricultural production while freeing up millions of potential industrial laborers who would otherwise have stayed tied to the land.

876. Andrew W. Mellon As the man responsible for building companies like Alcoa, Gulf Oil, U.S.

Steel, and Standard Steel Car Company, Andrew Mellon (1855–1937) was one of America's true "Captains of Industry." His father, Thomas, had come from County Tyrone in 1818 at the age of five. Andrew was born one of eight children in Pennsylvania in 1855. He attended Western University of Pennsylvania and by the mid-1870s was running his father's banking and real estate business. Under his skillful guidance, T. Mellon and Sons achieved enormous growth and became the primary stockholder in many leading corporations. In 1902 Mellon changed the company's name to Mellon Bank. He married and had two sons, but was divorced in 1912.

Warren Harding appointed him Secretary of the Treasury in 1921. He held the post through three administrations until 1932. Many consider his fiscal conservatism a chief cause of the economic boom during the 1920s, but it was the same conservatism that drew criticism when the Great Depression struck in 1929. He later served as ambassador to England between 1932 and 1933.

In 1937, he donated his entire art collection, worth more than $35 million to the federal government, which established the National Gallery of Art in Washington, D.C.

877. Thomas E. Murray, Sr. When he was just nine years old, his father died, so Thomas E. Murray, Sr. (1860–1929) left school to earn money for the family. Still he managed to combine an extraordinary gift for mechanical invention with night school to eventually land a job as supervisor of a power station in Albany, New York. Company officials quickly recognized his skills and before long he was managing several additional plants in the state. In 1895 he was sent to New York City where he soon became general manager of operations. By this time, he had begun to invent new machinery and parts for electrical generators, everything from cinder catchers to safety devices designed to prevent electrocution. By the time of his death, he would have over 1,100 patents in his name, second only to Thomas Edison.

878. John Roach Born in County Cork, Ireland, John Roach (1815–87) came to America to seek his fortune at the age of sixteen. His first business venture was the Etna Iron Works in New York City. He went on to buy the Morgan Iron Works and other businesses, including a shipyard in Chester, Pennsylvania, which became the John Roach and Sons shipyard in 1859. It grew to be one of the largest ship builders in the United States, building and maintaining ships for the U.S. government and for private customers such as the Reading Railroad. Roach's son, John Baker Roach, carried on the family business after his father's death in 1887.

879. Alexander T. Stewart Alexander Turney Stewart (1803–76) is credited with establishing the first department store in America. Born in County Antrim, he opened his first dry-goods store in New York City in 1823. The business grew rapidly and in 1862 Stewart opened the largest retail store in the world, a forerunner of today's department stores. One of the keys to his success was his specialty in imported Irish lace. As his wealth grew, Stewart became a philanthropist. He found jobs for Irish immigrants and donated to the Famine relief effort. When he died in 1876 he was one of the wealthiest men in America.

Entrepreneurs and Inventors
of the Twentieth Century

880. James Casey, Clause Ryan, and Mac McCabe In the summer of 1907, nineteen-year-old James Casey decided to start a local delivery service in his hometown of Seattle, Washington. With his friend Clause Ryan, they established the American Messenger Company and soon prospered. Their slogan said it all: "best service, lowest rates." Soon they added a package delivery service for local retail stores, forming a partnership with Mac McCabe to create Merchants Parcel Delivery. They pioneered in the concept of consolidated delivery, grouping packages with similar addresses on the same truck, thereby saving time and money. As their truck fleet grew with their success, they decided to paint them a distinctive chocolate brown color. By the 1920s their company, now called United Parcel Service (UPS), had operations in Oakland and Los Angeles, California. Continued success thereafter has made UPS one of the most successful delivery companies in the world, with services to 185 countries and territories.

881. Emmett J. Culligan The founder of the world's leading producer of water treatment products was born in a small brick house in Yankton, South Dakota. Emmett J. Culligan (1893–1970) left college after two years and tried his hand at farming. After service in World War I, he landed a job with a water softening company, eventually rising to become district manager for the state of Iowa. In 1924 he started his own company, but saw it fail with the onset of the Great Depression. It was in the 1930s that he hit upon the idea of selling softened water (as opposed to water-softening equipment) to customers on a franchise basis. He started his new company, the Culligan Zeolite Company, in 1938 and soon had 150 dealers. By the 1990s the company, now Culligan International, had more than one thousand franchised dealers in the U.S. with expanding operations throughout the world and an annual revenue of $150 million.

882. Edward L. Doheny Born to Irish immigrant parents in Wisconsin, Edward L. Doheny (1865–1935) ran away from home at age sixteen to prospect for gold in the southwest. After moderate success over the course of twenty years, he found himself in the sleepy town of Los Angeles in 1892. When he learned that residents burned as fuel tons of black pitch that bubbled up from the ground, he recognized it as crude oil. He immediately leased a piece of land, sunk a well, and hit oil. Within five years he had created and then come to dominate the California oil industry. He later expanded into Mexico and was soon a multimillionaire.

Doheny is best known for his part in the infamous Teapot Dome Scandal (so-named for an oil reserve in Wyoming) which occurred during the Harding presidency. He was indicted in a scheme to bribe Secretary of the Interior, Albert Fall, in exchange for very favorable leases to oil-rich land in California. Although eventually acquitted, his name was ruined. Doheny's son was killed in 1929 and he built a library at the University of Southern California as a memorial. Edward Doheny died in 1935.

883. James Augustine Farrell James A. Farrell (1862–1943) started out at the bottom rung of the steel business in the late 1880s, working in a Pittsburgh wire factory. Despite his limited education, Farrell studied the workings of the factory until he became expert in the whole operation. Promoted to salesman, he continued to shine and moved his way into management. In 1911 he became president of United States Steel Corporation, a position he retained until 1932.

884. Henry Ford Henry Ford (1863–1947) was born on a farm in Michigan to Famine-era Irish immigrants. Always tinkering, he left the farm to begin a career as an engineer. He worked for a power company, but in his spare time designed several successful automobile prototypes. He formed Ford Motor Company in 1903 and introduced the Model T in 1908. Five years later he made industrial history by establishing the assembly line to make Model T's. Before the assembly line, it took Ford's workers 12.5 hours to complete a new car; by 1920 it took just ninety-three minutes. The speed and efficiency of the new assembly process turned the automobile from a luxury good enjoyed only by the super rich into a necessity within the grasp of middle income Americans. Between 1916 and 1927, despite inflation, the price of a Model T dropped from $345 to $290.

Henry Ford

Ford was a complex man. On the one hand, he paid his workers well and provided them with housing, schools, and recreation facilities. On the other he was fiercely anti-union and a puritan who fired workers when he learned they drank alcohol—not at work but at home! Ford also emerged in the 1920s as a prominent anti-Semite, publishing lengthy diatribes against Jews in his newspaper, the *Dearborn Independent,* writings that eventually earned the admiration of Adolf Hitler. He retracted these statements in 1927.

Despite his shortcomings, Ford was a great philanthropist and built the Henry Ford Hospital in Detroit. He left much of his estate—valued at $1 billion—to a private foundation in his name.

885. Howard Hughes Born in Houston, Texas, Howard R. Hughes (1905–76) inherited his family business, the Hughes Tool Company, when he was nineteen. By then he was a confirmed aviation enthusiast, having learned to fly at age fourteen.

Hughes transformed his family business into Hughes Aircraft Company, a multimillion-dollar operation that made him one of the wealthiest men in America. He also became active in Hollywood through his acquisition of companies such as RKO Pictures Corporation and Republic Films. He is credited with launching the careers of Jane Russell, Jean Harlow, and Paul Muni.

Hughes' love of flying and desire to create publicity for his aircraft company led him to engage in a series of famous stunts. In 1935 he set the world record for aircraft speed at 352 miles per hour. The next year, he broke the record for a transcontinental flight across the U.S. and in 1938 set a new world record for flying around the world. He then bought a controlling interest in TransWorld Airlines and built it into a major airline. During World War II, Hughes added to his growing fortune by winning contracts with the U.S. government to build military aircraft.

After several controversies in the late 1940s, Hughes became a recluse and remained so for over twenty years, living in the Bahamas, Nicaragua, Canada, England, Las Vegas, and other places. He died in 1976, while flying to the United States for medical treatment.

886. The McDonald Brothers Although Ray Kroc deserves credit for making McDonald's one of the most widely recognized companies in the world today, it was the McDonald brothers, Richard and Mac, who founded the original restaurant. They started their wildly popular eatery in 1937 in San Bernadino, California. People came for miles around for the delicious and inexpensive fare, especially burgers, french fries, and milkshakes. One day an enterprising milkshake machine salesman named Ray Kroc showed up intending to sell them more machines. Instead he hit upon the idea of franchising the restaurant across the state. The McDonald brothers were content with the very successful operation, but eventually agreed to sell Kroc the franchise rights. He opened his first franchise restaurant in Des Plaines, Illinois, in 1955. It was so successful that by 1960 there were 228 McDonald's restaurants with more on the way. Kroc bought out the McDonald brothers in 1961 for $2,700,000.

887. William Lawrence Murphy Born in Stockton, California, William L. Murphy (1876–1959) was living in a cramped one-room apartment in San Francisco with his wife when he began tinkering with a folding bed. The couple enjoyed entertaining, but their bed took up most of the apartment. In 1900 Murphy perfected his bed and applied for a patent. The Murphy Door Bed Company was born that year and soon became the leading manufacturer of folding beds. In the 1920s, as the popularity of the Murphy Bed soared, the company moved to New York City. Its fortunes rose further with the invention of the compact kitchen, which was named the Murphy Cabrinette. World War II produced a housing shortage that further benefited the company's fortunes. Murphy's son took over the business in the 1950s and guided it through a period of slack sales due to the postwar suburban housing boom. In the 1970s sales began to rise again and have continued to do so since that time. The Murphy Bed Co., as it is now known, is still a family business, run by William Murphy's grandson, Clark Murphy.

888. Thomas E. Murray, Jr. Thomas Murray's father was an industrial scientist who patented more than eleven hundred inventions during his lifetime (see entry #877). Tom Murray, Jr., was born in Albany, New York, in 1891 and raised in Brooklyn. After studying at Yale University he followed his father's footsteps and entered the field of electric and gas power. In the course of his lifetime, he demonstrated an inventive genius inherited from his father and patented over two hundred inventions of his own.

He took over the family business, the Metropolitan Engineering and the Murray Manufacturing companies, in 1929. Three years later, he was called upon to reorganize (and later merge) New York's bankrupt Interborough Rapid Transit and Manhattan Railway companies. He served in several capacities during World War II, among them arbitrating labor disputes, and received a citation from President Franklin Roosevelt.

From 1950 to

Thomas E. Murray, Jr.

1957 he played an influential role as a member of the Atomic Energy Commission. He ran for the Senate in 1958, but was unsuccessful. He and his wife, with whom he had eleven children, lived on Park Avenue in New York City.

889. Thomas Fortune Ryan Born in poverty and orphaned at age fourteen, Thomas Fortune Ryan (1851–1928) became one of America's leading financiers. He arrived in New York City in 1872, found work on Wall Street, and soon established an investment syndicate that came to dominate New York City's lucrative transportation franchises. It created the Metropolitan Street Railway Company in 1892 and a securities-holding firm, the Metropolitan Traction Company, considered the first holding company in the United States. Ryan was a secretive figure, but his ruthless dealings made him a controversial figure. His State Trust Company (1900) and Equitable Life Assurance Company (1905) were both investigated by state officials for financial irregularities. Ryan drew further scorn for his role in creating the American Tobacco Company which monopolized tobacco sales until the Supreme Court ordered its breakup in 1911. Ryan was never convicted on any of the charges brought against him and died with a fortune of more than $200 million.

Labor and
the Labor Movement
in the Nineteenth Century

890. The Arrival of the Pre-Famine Irish In contrast to those who would arrive at mid-century, many of the Irish who came during the first decades of the nineteenth century found America a place of optimism and opportunity, though their feelings were no doubt tempered by the sadness of exile. Unlike those who would flee Ireland during the Famine, these immigrants arrived to find a younger country with smaller, less tumultuous cities. They also came with greater capital and

occupational skills—fully 48 percent of Irish arrivals in 1826 were artisans (versus 28 percent unskilled).

891. Patrick Condon Observes Patrick Condon, an Irish immigrant born in Cork in 1777, arrived with his family in upstate New York in 1826. He acquired a farm and worked tirelessly to make it a success. In 1834, he wrote home, singing the praises of his adopted homeland.

> I have a fine farm free forever, no one can ask me for rent. Our family can eat their fill of bread, meat, butter, and milk any day we want all year and so I think it is better here than to stay in Ireland. Look at the English and Germans. They come here in droves every year. . . . They buy land and live like lords . . .

892. Hard and Dangerous Work Because the great majority of the Irish who arrived after 1830 lacked useful skills, most were forced to rely on the one asset they possessed in plentitude: physical strength. Irish men took up pick and shovel and performed the endless backbreaking, dangerous labor necessary to build the nation's rapidly expanding infrastructure. They excavated the foundations of new buildings, leveled land for new streets, and off-loaded ships along the waterfront. As a rule, the hours were long and the pay frequently at the level of starvation. Ralph Waldo Emerson wrote to Henry David Thoreau to express his astonishment upon learning that the Irish in Massachusetts routinely worked fifteen hours per day for fifty cents.

To make matters worse, much of this work was extremely dangerous, exposing workers to frequent injury and death. "How often do we see such paragraphs in the paper," commented an Irish American newspaper, "as an Irishman drowned—an Irishman crushed by a beam—an Irishman blown to atoms by a steam engine—ten, twenty Irishmen buried alive by the sinking of a

Irish workers laying tracks, New York City, 1880

bank—and other like casualties and perils to which honest Pat is constantly exposed, in the hard toils for his daily bread."

893. "No Irish Need Apply" In addition to hard labor, long hours, and low pay, Irish men and women also faced severe discrimination in the workplace. Tradition has it that beginning in the 1830s, Irish workers began to see signs in factories and worksites reading "No Irish Need Apply," or some such variation. Some historians claim the signs never actually existed (at least to the extent claimed), but they certainly did for women domestics because their work brought them into the homes of native-born American families. Typical was this classified ad in an 1836 newspaper:

WANTED—An English or American woman, that understands cooking, and to assist in the work generally if wished; also a girl to do chamber work. None need apply without a recommendation from their last place. IRISH PEOPLE need not apply, nor anyone who will not arise at 6 o'clock, as the work is light and the wages are sure. Inquire 359 Broadway.

894. The Irish Problem When Irish migration to America increased in the 1820s and 1830s, the Irish were more often than not viewed by American workers as undesirable competitors in the labor market. Native-born workers feared the Irish were taking their jobs, or at the very least driving down wages with their willingness to work for less. Consequently, many early labor unions refused to admit Irish workers. Some managed to gain admittance, but even then they were viewed

Sewing room at A. T. Stewart's

with suspicion and hostility. As one newspaper editorial put it in 1837:

> If they go to work at the old price [wage] the journeymen at once cry out, 'those d——d Irishmen are always ratting' and if they 'strike' the employers at once exclaim 'those d——d Irishmen are always uproarious.' So that between them all, poor Pat is treated like a football in the ring—everybody gives him a kick.
> —*The European* (N.Y.), April 6, 1837

895. The Impact of Irish Labor on the American Economy
Americans in the nineteenth century found themselves in a bind. They seemed to agree that they didn't want the Irish, but also that they couldn't do without them. The role of Irish labor in propelling forward America's industrial revolu-

tion—like that of slave labor in creating the Cotton Kingdom—was enormous. As one antebellum newspaper commented:

> America demands for her development an inexhaustible fund of physical energy, and Ireland supplies the most part of it. There are several sorts of power working at the fabric of this Republic—waterpower, steam-power, and Irish-power. The last works hardest of all.

896. Irish Women Make Up the Difference
Because Irish men earned so little, the labor of Irish women often represented the difference between survival and starvation. While some worked in the needle trades, the most common form of work for Irish women was domestic service—cooking, cleaning, and child care in a middle-class

American home. The typical Irish servant also suffered from long hours and meager earnings, but also "sneers at her nationality, mockery of her peculiarities, even ridicule of her faith," according to one observer in the 1860s. In small manufacturing cities, vast numbers of Irish women toiled as factory workers. Everywhere, Irish women who remained in the home once married took in boarders, laundry, and home furnishing work to earn desperately needed income.

897. Stereotypes

The fact that over 80 percent of Irish-born men worked as unskilled laborers and over 80 percent of Irish-born women worked as domestic servants not only left the average Irish family in poverty, it also contributed to a pervasive stereotype of Paddy the hod carrier and Brigit the laundress. It convinced many Americans that the Irish were suited mainly for physical labor.

898. Remittances, or the "American Letter"

Despite their poverty, Irish immigrants sent millions of dollars back to Ireland. Though precise statistics are not available, it is estimated that remittances to Ireland averaged more than one million dollars per year in the 1840s and rose to $10 million per year by the 1870s. The Emigrant Industrial Savings Bank in New York, founded in 1850 as an offshoot of the Irish Emigrant Society,

opened with 2,300 accounts totaling $238.56. This one bank would send more than $30 million to Ireland between 1850 and 1880. All told, it is estimated that $234 million was sent by the Irish in America to their friends and families in Ireland between 1848 and 1900. Many families in Ireland depended for their survival on what they called the "American Letter."

899. A Mixed Occupational Experience

The following chart of Irish employment in New York City in 1855 indicates three important aspects of the antebellum Irish experience. First, as the Irish dominance of jobs like laborer and domestic servant indicate, a majority of Irish immigrants in this period lacked useful skills and were forced to take hard, poorly paid work in order to survive. Second, the data from the skilled jobs tells us that the Irish are moving into the tanks of better-paid, skilled work. Third, the Irish have a long way to go before they will comprise a representative percentage of professional occupations like doctors and lawyers.

Occupations of Gainfully Employed Irish Immigrants in New York, 1855

OCCUPATION	# IRISH-BORN AND % OF TOTAL
Skilled	
Bakers	861 (23%)
Blacksmiths	1,339 (50)
Brewers/distillers	52 (14)
Carpenters	2,230 (30)
Dressmakers/ seamstresses	4,559 (46)
Ironworkers	150 (56)
Machinists	398 (23)
Masons/bricklayers	2,203 (61)
Merchants	278 (4)
Policemen	292 (25)
Printers	519 (25)
Retail shopkeepers	916 (35)

Irish stereotypes in a *Puck* cartoon

Skilled

Shoemakers	2,121 (31)
Tailors	4,171 (33)
Wine and liquor dealers	891 (55)

Professional

Doctors	113 (8)
Lawyers	40 (4)

Unskilled

Domestic servants	23,386 (74)
Laundresses	1,758 (69)
Laborers	17,426 (86)
Drivers/hackmen/ coachmen	805 (46)

Source: Robert Ernst, *Immigrant Life in New York City, 1825–1863* and N.Y. State Census of 1855

900. Labor Leaders by the 1850s With so large a percentage of Irish immigrants occupying unskilled positions, few Irish held leadership positions in the early labor movement. But by the late 1840s and 1850s, there were clear signs that Irish workers were beginning to gain influence, in part because more and more Irish were acquiring skills and moving out of the ranks of common labor. In Philadelphia in 1856, for example, J. F. Finnegan (Lithographers Society), Frank Mallon (Hatters Union), and C. C. Scanlon (Journeymen House Carpenters Association) were officers in their respective unions. In New York in 1854 it was reported that Irishmen comprised nearly all the officers of the Tailor's Trade Association.

901. Factory Workers Irish immigrants arrived just in time to supply labor for the emerging industrial revolution. By the 1830s, several mill towns were operating in New England, most notably Lowell, Massachusetts. Running on water power from rivers, these early textile factories relied initially on New England farm girls for labor. Lowell became internationally famous as a model factory town where young women lived under strict supervision, but with ample opportunities for education and wholesome activities. But as competition between factory owners grew more intense and the women became more assertive (forming a union and striking on several occasions), mill owners turned to a new, cheap, and easily exploited labor source: Irish immigrants. The speed of the transformation was astonishing. Lowell's workforce went from 8 percent Irish-born in 1845 to 50 percent in 1860.

902. Canal Diggers Many of the poor and unskilled Irish who arrived before the Famine found work building the earliest links in the emerging American transportation network. The greatest of these projects, the Erie Canal (itself the brainchild of De Witt Clinton, a descendant of Longford immigrants), was constructed largely using Irish labor between 1817 and 1825. It was a stupendous undertaking for any era—a massive trench 363 miles long across upstate New York connecting the Hudson River with Lake Erie. As this was the era before steam power, all of it was dug using manual and animal labor.

The work was dangerous and poorly paid and conditions in the camps along the canal zone atrocious. One English visitor to the canal camps near Troy, New York, wrote that the shacks of the diggers were "more like dog-kennels than the habitations of men." Hundreds died from injury or disease in the making of the Erie and other canals such as the Chesapeake and Ohio and the Illinois and Michigan, giving rise to the oft-repeated statement that the banks of America's canals are lined with the bones of stricken Irishmen.

Perhaps the most extreme evidence of this raw exploitation occurred in New Orleans in the 1830s. There, the builders of the city's New Basin Canal expressed a preference for Irish over slave labor for the simple reason that a dead Irishman could be replaced in minutes at no cost, while a dead slave resulted on the loss of more than one thousand dollars. An old song, likely exaggerating, put the death toll at twenty thousand.

> Ten thousand Micks, they swung their
>   picks
> To dig the New Canal,
> But the choleray was stronger 'n they,
> An' twice it killed them all.

Together, canal and road building, like the later railroad construction, explain why the Irish spread out so quickly across the country.

903. Irish vs. Irish: Conflict Along the Canals
Because few unions existed in the 1830s and none for unskilled construction workers, Irish immigrants often formed secret fraternal societies to militantly protect their welfare. Along the Chesapeake and Ohio Canal in Maryland, for example, Irish laborers from County Cork drove away workers who refused to join their association. When County Longford workers were brought in to undercut the Corkmen, fierce battles broke out and President Jackson sent in the army to restore order. Years later when the company refused to pay them, they destroyed their work. In the long run this spirit of collective action and solidarity among Irish workers in the 1830s provided the foundation for their successful efforts to organize into unions in the decades to come. In the short term, however, it usually did little to relieve the world of hard and poorly paid work.

904. Road Builders
Even before "canal fever" gripped America, the nation was engaged in a vast array of road-building projects, especially the National Road from Maryland to Illinois (1811–38). Like the Erie Canal, this monumental effort would be dominated by the labor of Irish immigrants. In addition to providing the bulk of manual labor, the Irish were also heavily represented as contractors. Records reveal names like

Philip McGinnis, Thomas Monaghan, Tully Gallager, and Mordecai Cochran. The latter caught the attention of one farmer who marveled at "his immortal Irish brigade, a thousand strong, with their carts, wheelbarrows, picks, shovels, and blasting tools, grading the commons, and climbing the mountainside . . . and leaving behind them a roadway good enough for an emperor to travel over."

905. Railroad Builders
Like the grim experience of canal digging, a popular saying in the era of railroad building had it that there was "an Irishman buried under every tie." Irishmen built most of the railroads in the east before the Civil War, and many of those constructed afterward. The greatest road of all, the transcontinental railroad (completed in 1867), was built by a combination of Irish, Mexican, Chinese, and German workers. The work was arduous and very dangerous, especially when sending a road through mountainous areas, and countless Irish workers perished in cave-ins and explosions; still more died of diseases that raged in the camps. Wages in the 1840s were as low as seventy cents per day and stayed low for decades to come.

As with canal digging, there were numerous incidents of gang violence, often between different groups of Irish immigrants. In one incident on the Erie Railroad in 1847, Corkonians were attacked and driven off by a gang of Far Downers. There was more at stake here than old county rivalries. In many cases, groups of workers were attacked and driven off so as to provide work for the victors. As if to emphasize this point, not long after driving off the Corkonians, the Far Downers battled a German work crew. Similar incidents occurred wherever the railroad went west, where the Irish clashed with Chinese and Mexican workers.

906. The Irish and the Transcontinental Railroad
Irish workers played a key role in building the most important railroad of the nineteenth century: the Transcontinental Railroad. From the

The Transcontinental Railroad completed

moment of the building of the first railroads in America in the 1830s, people began to dream of a railroad spanning the length of the American continent. One of the most vocal champions of the idea was Galway-born John Conness. As a member of the California legislature in the 1850s and later in the U.S. Senate, he led the way in building support for the project. The one sticking point, however, was that southerners demanded a southern route to California instead of the northern route favored in the North. The issue wasn't settled until the outbreak of Civil War.

On July 1, 1862, Congress, no longer hindered by southern opposition, passed the Pacific Railroad Act. It authorized two companies, the Union Pacific (UP) and the Central Pacific (CP), to construct a transcontinental railroad. For the most part, the CP employed the Chinese and the

UP the Irish. Several Irishmen occupied high-level positions in the project, including most especially James Harvey Strobridge. Born in Ireland, he served as the right-hand man to the CP's owner, Charles Crocker, and oversaw every phase of the construction. With enormous incentives to build their roads as quickly as possible, work went forward at breakneck speed. Conditions were harsh and the pay low, as indicated in the popular song along the Union Pacific road in the 1860s, "Poor Paddy, He Works on the Railroad":

> Then drill, my Paddies, drill—
> Drill, my heroes, drill,
> Drill all day, no sugar in your tay
> Workin' on the U.P. railway.

The last stage of the railroad's construction is

the stuff of legend. On April 28, Strobridge and his crew of mostly Chinese graders and eight Irish track layers set out to do the impossible—lay ten miles of track in a single day. The record to that point was a little more than four miles.

At Strobridge's order work began at sunup and pressed on until darkness, interrupted only for lunch. With military precision and dogged determination the workmen laid more track in one day than any before or since—ten miles and fifty-six feet. Everyone involved deserved credit for the feat, but as historian Stephen Ambrose describes it in his bestselling book, *Nothing Like It In the World, The Men Who Built the Transcontinental Railroad, 1863–1869*, the work of eight Irish track layers was particularly noteworthy. "Each man among the Irish track-layers had lifted 125 tons of iron . . . That was 11.2 short tons per man per hour. Each had covered ten miles forward and the Lord only knows how much running back for the next rail. They moved the track forward at a rate of almost a mile an hour. They laid at a rate of 240 feet every seventy-five seconds." Simply incredible.

907. Mining   The Irish were heavily represented in mining for most of the nineteenth century. As with so many other occupations which they dominated, mining was appealing because it required few prerequisite skills, besides strength and bravery. Thousands of Irish joined the national frenzy when gold was discovered in California in 1848, leaving eastern cities aboard ships headed for San Francisco. Still more joined the rush for silver and gold in British Columbia, Nevada, and Colorado in the 1850s and 1860s, and to the Klondike in the 1890s. Among the latter was one Michael MacGowan who wrote a marvelous memoir of his adventures in Irish entitled *Rotha Mor an tSaoil* or *The Hard Road to Klondike*. Another notable personality from the mining camps out west was Nellie Cashman. Born Ellen O'Kissane in Ireland, her work as a nurse and cook in mining camps from Tombstone to the Yukon earned her the nickname "angel of the mines."

While most labored as employees of large mining companies, a few notables struck it rich, most notably the so-called Irish Four who made millions mining the Comstock Lode. Gold, and later silver and copper strikes in Montana, also drew many Irish, including Cavan-born Marcus Daly whose Anaconda Copper Mine made him one of the richest men in America. Similarly, William H. Brophy struck it rich in the silver mines of Arizona, Thomas Kearns in those of Utah. Other Irishmen headed for the mining districts and made their fortunes selling food, tents, tools, and clothing to eager miners. Peter Donahue arrived in San Francisco during the rush and tried his hand at panning for gold, but soon opened a blacksmith shop. It later developed into the massive Union Iron Works. Irish Mormon Sam Brannan arrived several years before the gold rush and established a dry-goods store. At the peak of the gold rush fever in 1849–50, he pulled in more than $100,000 a month! San Francisco real estate tycoon Patrick Phelan made his initial fortune selling goods to miners.

Far less glamorous, but arguably more important to America's industrial development, was the huge coal mining industry. Here, too, the Irish played a significant role, both as miners and occasionally as mine owners. In Pennsylvania's anthracite region thousands of Irish miners toiled for meager wages in dangerous conditions. One of the wealthiest mine owners was Franklin B. Gowan, President of the Philadelphia & Reading Railroad and the man who eventually saw to it that twenty Irishmen were hanged for their alleged role in violence and murder linked to the Molly Maguires.

908. The Molly Maguires   One area of particularly bitter conflict was the coal-mining region of Pennsylvania. It was there in the 1860s that Irish miners formed a union called the Workingmen's Benevolent Association (WBA) to resist the abusive labor policies of mine bosses and the Philadelphia & Reading Railroad (headed, interestingly, by an Irishman—Franklin D. Gowan).

Some of its members also formed a clandestine labor organization known as the Molly Maguires that employed intimidation, vandalism, violence, and murder. In 1874 Gowan set out to destroy the WBA by linking it with the Mollies. Within a year, his stoking of anti-Molly sentiment resulted in more than fifty arrests and many convictions. In all, twenty alleged Molly Maguires were hanged for murder, including ten on a single day, June 21, 1877. Given the fact that many were convicted on specious evidence, it was clear that they were executed not simply for their alleged role in the murders, but also because they were opponents of big business and because they were Irish.

909. The Knights of Labor　Irish workers were instrumental in the rise of the nineteenth century's foremost labor organization, the Knights of Labor. It was founded as a secret society by seven Philadelphia tailors in 1869. Two of the men,

Robert McCauley and Joseph S. Kennedy, were Irish American.

The Knights remained a small and largely unknown organization until 1879 when Terence Powderly, the son of Irish immigrants, became its leader. Within a few short years he transformed the Knights into the first national industrial union with more than 700,000 members at its peak in 1886. Three things account for the boom in membership in the 1880s. First, facing potential condemnation by the Catholic Church (traditionally opposed to Catholic membership in secret societies), Powderly lifted the Knights' vow of secrecy in 1881 (see entry #536). Second, the Knights won several big strikes, including one by railroad workers against industrial giant Jay Gould. Third, the Knights welcomed all workers—skilled and unskilled, native-born and immigrant. It even welcomed women and African American workers—unheard of in skilled trade organiza-

The Molly Maguires

Terence Powderly

tions. This ideology of inclusiveness and solidarity was expressed in the Knights' motto—"an injury to one is an injury to all."

Irish workers by the hundreds of thousands joined the Knights for these reasons and one more: the close association between the Irish struggle for independence and the workingmen's struggle for justice. A substantial number of Irish labor activists were also members of the Land League (1879–83), the nationalist movement led by Charles Stewart Parnell that promised both independence for Ireland and land reform to relieve its oppressed farmers. Powderly himself was an active Land Leaguer, not to mention a member of Clan na Gael, a secret militant nationalist organization.

Tactics and Traditions

910. The Boycott One of the most vivid and enduring examples of the Irish influence on the labor movement was the introduction of the boycott in the early 1880s. The tactic first originated in Ireland during the Land League agitation (1879–83) as a form of social ostracization used against landlords and agents who carried out tenant evictions. In America, Irish workers transformed this social practice to inaugurate a new style of labor agitation and protest. They adapted the boycott to their new urban and industrial context. Social ostracism in rural Ireland became economic sanction in industrial America, with workers refusing to patronize offending employers.

911. Labor Day Second only to St. Patrick's Day, Labor Day is the American holiday born out of the Irish American experience. The first took place on September 5, 1882, when thousands of New York City workers took the day off to participate in festivities honoring honest toil and the rights of labor. Its immediate success testified to labor's rising power and growing sense of unity in the Gilded Age. It also exemplified the central role played by Irish workers in the labor movement of that era.

The Irish connection to the Labor Day holiday began with the founding of the organization that sponsored the event, the Central Labor Union. It had come into existence only months earlier, in January 1882, when Irish immigrant Robert Blissert called a rally of the city's workers to support the Irish nationalist movement known as the Land League. Toward the end of the rally they approved a motion to form a local labor federation to promote the interests of workers. Even as the Land League disintegrated in mid-1882, the CLU grew rapidly, reaching fifty-six member unions with eighty thousand members by summer's end.

It was also an Irishman who first proposed the idea of establishing in early September "a festive day [for] a parade through the streets of the city." Yet the precise identity of that Irishman remains a mystery. Some accounts say it was Peter "P.J." McGuire, General Secretary of the United Brotherhood of Carpenters and Joiners (and future cofounder of the AFL), who proposed the idea at a May meeting of the CLU. Others argue that it was machinist Matthew Maguire, who deserves the title "Father of Labor Day." Official bragging rights aside, both Irish American labor activists played crucial roles in establishing the Labor Day holiday.

After the months of preparation, the chosen day—September 5, 1882—finally arrived. Fittingly, workers had selected as the parade's first Grand Marshal, an Irishman named William G. McCabe, a popular member of Local No. 6 of the International Typographers Union. No one knew how many workers would turn out. Few could expect their employers to grant them a day off.

At 10 A.M. a parade of only a few hundred

The First Labor Day Parade, New York City, 1882

began slowly moving up Broadway. Soon its ranks swelled as union after union fell into line from side streets. As they walked, workers held aloft signs with messages such as "Labor Built this Republic. Labor Shall Rule It"; "Less Work and More Pay"; "To the Workers Should Belong All Wealth"; and "Strike with the Ballot." Some workers wore their traditional work uniforms and aprons, others dressed in their holiday best for the occasion. Many craft organizations pulled wagons that displayed their handiwork.

After moving up Fifth Avenue, past the opulent homes of tycoons like Vanderbilt, Morgan, and Gould (and a few of the Irish upper class, like dry-goods millionaire A. T. Stewart and shipping magnate William R. Grace), the grand procession of five thousand or more terminated at Forty-second Street and Sixth Avenue. There participants boarded elevated trains—extra cars had been added to handle the anticipated crowds—for a

short ride to Wendel's Elm Park, at West Ninety-second Street and Ninth Avenue, for a massive picnic that drew twenty-five thousand.

With such an impressive start, the idea of an annual "Labor Day" and parade quickly gained popularity among labor activists and organizations across the country. By 1887 five states made Labor Day an official holiday for state employees and hundreds of cities and towns held festivities. Finally, in 1894—just a dozen years after the first celebration in New York—President Grover Cleveland signed into law a measure establishing Labor Day as a holiday for all federal workers.

Some Notable Nineteenth-Century Labor Leaders

912. Leonora Barry   Leonora Kearney Barry (1849–1923) was born in County Cork and emigrated to the United States in 1852. She became a school teacher, married and had three children. When her husband died in 1880, she began working in a clothing factory. Wages and conditions were appalling and she soon joined a local chapter of the Knights of Labor. She quickly demonstrated her leadership abilities and was named in 1886 to the post of general investigator for the Knights' women's department. She served in that capacity for four years, touring the country, writing reports, and giving speeches. She resigned in 1990 to marry Obediah R. Lake (hence her later nickname, "Mother Lake"), a newspaper printer from St. Louis. For the rest of her life she remained active in causes related to women's suffrage, temperance and other social reform movements.

913. Mother Jones   Mary "Mother" Harris Jones (1837–1930) was born into a poor farming family in rural Cork. Her father, Richard Harris, emigrated to the United States first and sent for his family in 1850. Jones became a teacher and later a dressmaker, before marrying George Jones, an iron molder, in 1861. Living in Memphis, Tennessee, the couple had four children. All four died along with Jones' husband in a devastating yellow fever epidemic in 1867. Jones returned to Chicago and reestablished herself as a dressmaker. Again tragedy struck when her business was consumed in the Great Fire of 1871.

In the years of toil that followed, Jones grew increasingly concerned about the growing gap between the rich people for whom she worked and the poor people with whom she lived. She joined the Knights of Labor and took to active organizing. The first strike she was involved in occurred in Pittsburgh, against the Baltimore and Ohio Railroad in 1877. The local government's decision to call in the state militia, an action that led to a bloody riot, appalled her and pushed her to take up labor activism full time.

So began her long career as a labor agitator. For the rest of her life she traveled the country,

Mother Jones

from trouble spot to trouble spot, organizing unions, leading strikes, and giving inspirational speeches. She was especially active among railroad workers and miners. By the late 1890s she was one of the most well-known figures in the labor movement, and one of its most controversial. Small in stature, she stood large in the eyes of both the workers she served and the employers she chastised.

In 1905, she spoke at the founding convention of the International Workers of the World (IWW) and in 1913 she played a key role in the Ludlow Colorado Copper Mine strike. That event led her to testify in several Congressional hearings on the conditions of labor. Throughout her career she was repeatedly arrested and confronted with threats against her life.

Jones always attributed her fearlessness and radicalism to her Irish heritage. "I was born in revolution," she once said, referring to her childhood in Ireland during which took place Daniel O'Connell's crusade and the Young Ireland rebellion.

She was ninety-one years old when she worked her last strike. The "Angel of the Mines" died at age ninety-four in 1930. In his eulogy the Rev. J. W. McGuire said, "Wealthy coal operators and capitalists throughout the United States are breathing sighs of relief . . . Mother Jones is dead."

914. Denis Kearney and Frank Roney   The two most prominent Irish American labor leaders on the West Coast were Denis Kearney (1847–1907) and Frank Roney (1841–1923). Both men were born in Ireland. Kearney arrived in San Francisco in 1868 and Roney in 1875.

Kearney rose to prominence as head of the Workingmen's Party in large measure by fanning the flames of anti-Chinese racism among his largely Irish constituents. "The Chinese Must Go!" was his slogan and on several occasions he instigated attacks on the Chinese settlement in San Francisco. Kearney's efforts culminated in Congress passing the Chinese Exclusion Act of 1882, which banned all future immigration from China to the United States until World War II.

Frank Roney was a better educated and more thoughtful labor organizer. An iron moulder by trade, he worked hard to organize unions. In 1885 he established the Federated Trades of the Pacific Coast, an umbrella organization that acted as the central labor federation for the city. Significantly, Roney broke with Kearney in 1878 on the Chinese issue. He feared that Chinese immigration was lowering wages, but resisted the temptation to blame them. Instead, he worked to improve conditions for those Chinese already in the city and for legislation to limit future immigration. It was not the progressive stand on the Chinese issue, but one far more tolerant than Kearney's.

915. Florence Kelley Born in Philadelphia, Florence Kelley (1859–1943) studied at Cornell University and then the University of Zurich. It was there that she was influenced by Fredrich Engels' Socialist writings. When she returned to the United States, she joined Jane Addams and other women reformers at the Hull House. When she discovered children working on garments in nearby tenements, she began working tirelessly to get child labor laws passed, eventually moving to New York to become the director of the National Consumers League. She was responsible for labels that certified clothing was not made with child labor. Throughout her life, she continued working relentlessly for better labor conditions for women and children, even though she suffered personal tragedies such as the death of her daughter. Florence Kelley was also partly responsible for the

creation of juvenile courts. Her death in 1943, left behind a living legacy for women and children today.

916. Kate Kennedy Fights for Women's Rights Irish women also headed West during the gold rush. One notable example was Kate Kennedy (1827–90). Born in Meath, she fled the Famine with her sisters and went to New York. Tales of California gold enticed them, however, so they headed West to pursue new lives for themselves. Kennedy began teaching in San Francisco in 1857, but when she was promoted to the position of principal in 1867, she was assigned a salary lower than that of her male counterparts. In response, she waged a campaign to end the practice of paying women less than men

Kate Kennedy

for equivalent work. As a result of her efforts, the California legislature passed an antidiscrimination law in 1874, ensuring equal pay for women. Word of Kennedy's success reached famed women's rights activists Susan B. Anthony and Elizabeth Cady Stanton who later honored her with a visit when they traveled to San Francisco. In the years that followed, Kennedy became active in San Francisco's labor movement, joining the Knights of Labor and speaking frequently at labor rallies. She won a second court battle (and five thousand dollars in back pay) in the late 1880s when she successfully contested her demotion to a lesser job. Kennedy's labor and women's-rights legacy lives on today, as a school in the Mission District of San Francisco bears her name.

917. P. J. McGuire Peter J. McGuire (1852–1906)

emerged in the late 1870s as one of the nation's most important labor activists. Born to Irish immigrant parents in New York City, he left school at age eleven to earn money for the family. Eventually he learned carpentry and attended classes at Cooper Union where he met many radicals. He became a socialist in the 1870s, joining the First International in New York City. McGuire was a gifted speaker and a natural leader. In 1882 he founded the United Order of Carpenters and Joiners and was elected its first general secretary.

That same year, either he or another Irish American named Matthew Maguire proposed that workers in New York establish a Labor Day holiday and parade, thus inaugurating an annual tradition that spread across the country (see entry #911). In 1886, after growing dissatisfied with Powderly's leadership of the Knights, McGuire cofounded, with Samuel Gompers, the American Federation of Labor. Like many Irish American labor activists, his early radicalism gradually faded in favor of a more conservative "bread and butter" unionism focused on skilled workers and basic issues like wages, hours, and job security.

918. Kate Mullaney Born in Ireland, Kate Mullaney (ca. 1845–1907) was one of three thousand women working in the commercial laundries of Troy, New York. They worked twelve- to fourteen-hour days for three to four dollars per week in brutal conditions, suffering from intense heat, chemicals, and burns from irons. In February of 1864, nineteen-year-old Mullaney organized nearly three hundred other women to form the Collar Laundry Union, one of the nation's first all-female unions. Almost immediately, Mullaney led the women out on strike against Troy's fourteen commercial laundries for higher wages and better conditions. One week later, the owners relented and agreed to a series of wage increases. By 1866, Kate Mullaney and her fellow women were earning fourteen dollars a week.

Mullaney remained active in labor organiz-ing. In 1868, she attended the national convention of the National Labor Union (predecessor to the Knights of Labor) in New York City and was appointed Assistant Secretary and National Organizer for Women, becoming the first woman appointed an officer in a national labor union.

919. Hugh O'Donnell In the late nineteenth century, steelworkers were among the best-organized and highest-paid industrial workers in America. Their union, the Amalgamated Association of Iron and Steel Workers, was one of the most powerful in the nation. Andrew Carnegie, the undisputed king of the steel industry, decided in 1892 to break the union's power. With their contract set to expire on June 30, 1892, Carnegie left for an extended European vacation. He placed his top manager, the fiercely antiunion Henry Clay Frick, in charge of the negotiations for a new contract. Frick took the expected hard line and when no agreement was reached, locked the workers out.

The leader of the locked-out workers was Hugh O'Donnell. Bright and charismatic, O'Donnell was chosen by his fellow steelworkers at a post-lockout mass meeting as head of the Advisory Committee. O'Donnell organized committees to provide workers and their families with food. He also stationed workers outside the factory gates to prevent replacement workers from entering.

To gain control of the factory, Frick tried to fill it with armed Pinkerton agents. Seeking to avoid the workers stationed outside the factory gates, Frick tried to float the agents in via barge (the factory was situated along a riverbank). No one knows who fired first, but gun fire broke out as soon as the barge appeared. By day's end three Pinkertons and seven workers lay dead in one of the most infamous incidents of labor violence in American history. The workers won the battle that day, but soon lost the war as the state militia showed up and gave Frick the protection he needed to restart the factory. By November, the strike was over.

For his troubles, O'Donnell was blacklisted for life in the steel industry. Tried three times on three different charges relating to the strike, he gained acquittal in each case. He eventually ended up in Chicago working as an editor for a weekly Chicago newspaper.

920. Leaders of Agrarian Protest Irish activism in the cause of economic reform was not confined to the urban industrial workforce. Although the great majority of the Irish in America avoided agriculture (the 1870 census showed only 15 percent of Irish immigrants as farmers), their presence was felt in the leadership of the era's tumultuous farmers' movements. Oliver Kelley founded the Grange in 1867 as a farmer's association dedicated to ending the isolation of the American farmer and increasing the exchange of useful information. When an economic depression struck in 1873, the Grange was transformed into a political movement. Within two years, Granger Parties gained control of numerous Midwestern state governments and enacted some of the earliest regulations of abusive corporations, banks, and railroads.

The successors to the Grangers were the Populists who championed many of the same causes. One of their most effective organizers was Mary Elizabeth Lease (1853–1933), who compelled distressed farmers to unite to "raise more hell and less corn."

Even more influential was Populist leader and social reformer Ignatius Donnelly (1831–1901). Born in Philadelphia and trained as a lawyer, he moved to Minnesota in 1856 to establish "Nininger City," a combination real estate venture and cultural utopia. When this plan failed, Donnelly became involved in politics. At first a member of the Republican Party, his liberal tendencies led him to join the Independent Anti-Monopoly Party in the 1870s and to found the Populist Party in 1891. He became one of the movement's most renowned orators and organizers. Unfortunately, Donnelly not only blamed banks and railroads for the plight of the American farmer, but also Jews.

Labor and the
Labor Movement in the
Twentieth Century

921. Irish America on the Rise By the turn of the century, Irish Americans were nearly equal to native-born Americans in terms of occupational status. Like their native-born counterparts, about two thirds of Irish Americans worked in industry or transportation, and only 15 percent worked as unskilled labor. Upon closer inspection, however, one finds that Irish Americans held far fewer professional positions compared to native-borns, but a disproportionately high number of skilled jobs that tended to pay well and be unionized. For example, Irish Americans in 1900 constituted 7.5 percent of the male workforce, but held one third of plumber, steamfitter, and boilermaker jobs and one fifth of those in brass working, stone cutting, and leather tanning.

Evidence also indicates that by 1900 the Irish had also broadened their hold on municipal jobs, continuing to dominate police and fire departments, but now also moving into jobs as clerks, engineers, inspectors, and for women as teachers and nurses. These jobs did not pay particularly well, but they did provide steady income.

Finally, through the growing network of Catholic colleges and expanding public education system, the Irish in America began to make significant inroads into the professions, especially law and medicine.

Despite these indications of an overall economic rise by the Irish, several qualifications need to be made. First, a hard core—about 15 percent—of Irish men remained in poorly paid, unskilled work in 1900. Second, even though the trend was for the Irish to move into better occupations, they did so at a rate slower than other immigrant groups. Many historians suggest this was due to the Irish penchant for taking jobs that were

Irish American Nurse Elizabeth O'Donnell

safe and secure (i.e., municipal jobs) over riskier work in the private sector or jobs that required higher education. Others noted that the Irish had very high rates of property ownership, usually a house, a decision that no doubt placed a burden on family members to find employment early to contribute to the household income. Third, the trend of "west was best" (see #199) continued well past the turn of the century. That is, the farther west the Irish settled, the higher their socioeconomic standing. For example, while two thirds of Boston's Irish-born held unskilled jobs in 1890, less than a third did so in Chicago.

922. Irish American Women The position of Irish American women workers likewise improved by 1900. Only 19 percent of Irish American women labored as domestics. Highly educated, Irish American women instead moved into jobs as secretaries, stenographers, telephone operators, nurses, and teachers. In the case of teaching, Irish American dominance of that profession was unmistakable. In most cities, Irish American women made up between 20 and 30 percent of the teachers. None of these jobs paid high wages, but for Irish American women, they carried with them the intangible benefits of professionalism and respectability.

923. The Labor Movement in the Early Twentieth Century America entered the twentieth century with its industrial power ranked first in the world and its unions ever more firmly in the control of Irish leaders. By 1910 nearly half the 110 member unions of the AFL were led by Irish-born or Irish

American men. Overwhelmingly they represented a constituency that was non-Irish, reflecting both Irish upward mobility and vast immigration from Eastern and Southern Europe.

Though buffeted by war, depression, and antiunion policies of employers, union membership rose from nearly one million in 1900 to more than five million in 1920. Irish union leaders were known for their oratory, organizing skills and tough negotiating tactics, but also for pursuing the moderate ideological course laid down by AFL founder Sam Gompers. Known as "pure and simple" unionism, it shunned radicalism and stressed high wages, shorter hours, and job security. Such a policy often ran afoul of the interests and outlook of more radical Jewish, Italian, and Slavic workers. Still, as the careers of William Z. Foster and Elizabeth Gurley Flynn attest, not all Irish American labor leaders were conservative (see entries #934 and #935).

924. The Church and the Labor Question The Catholic Church remained staunchly antiradical and anti-Socialist, but the rights of Catholic workers to organize into unions was firmly established. So too was the right of priests to speak more freely on social and labor issues. Father John A. Ryan emerged as a leading spokesman for economic justice with the publication in 1906 of *A Living Wage*. In this and subsequent works he summoned the authority of Pope Leo XIII's *Rerum Novarum* and other teachings to call for social security, a living minimum wage, public housing, and a more equitable tax system. In 1911 he authored Minnesota's minimum wage bill that became law in 1913.

925. The Pivotal New Deal Years The American labor movement entered a new phase with the stock market crash of 1929. Many of the gains of the last two decades, both material and institutional, were swept aside by the economic earthquake known as the Great Depression. "The only thing the unions can do during these times," observed Pulp and Paper Workers union President

John Burke, "is hang on and . . . try to save our organization."

But the crisis of the Depression turned out to be a moment of opportunity for American labor. In Washington, D.C., Senator Robert Wagner of New York (son of an Irish mother) successfully pushed for landmark labor legislation granting workers the right to organize, elect their representatives and to strike, boycott, and picket, as well as prohibiting unfair practices by employers like blacklisting. This led to a flurry of labor union activity and the reemergence of the industrial union movement that had died with the Knights of Labor in the 1880s. The Congress of Industrial Organizations (CIO) committed itself to unionizing mass production workers in key industries like automobile, appliance, and rubber manufacturing. When it broke from the AFL in 1936, it was led by Irish Americans John Brophy as Director and James B. Carey as secretary-treasurer. One of the CIO's vice-presidents was Mike Quill, a radical Irish immigrant and former IRA member who founded the heavily Irish Transport Workers Union in 1934.

926. The Communism Issue During the 1940s and 1950s, as Senator Joseph McCarthy waged his crusade against domestic Communism, organized labor felt the sting of the Red Scare. Many Irish American union leaders, either out of personal anti-Communism or public pressure, purged radicals from their ranks and supported similar purges of radical unions from AFL and CIO. Mike Quill, for example, had allied himself with the Communists in the CIO, shocked the organization in 1948 when he adopted an outspoken anti-Communist position. For this Quill and others earned praise from the Catholic Church and the Irish American middle class, but also the animosity of more radical union leaders.

927. Corruption While some Irish American labor leaders became negatively associated with union conservatism, others came to symbolize growing union corruption. In 1953 the AFL suspended the International Longshoremen's Association, headed by Joseph Patrick Ryan, for its corruption and links to organized crime. Tony Boyle, who succeeded John Lewis as president of the United Mine Workers, was later indicted for corruption.

928. Declining Union Membership The 1950s were the glory days of the American labor movement. Wages were high, strikes were rare, and union membership reached its historic highpoint with 39 percent of the American workforce enrolled. The AFL and CIO reconciled their differences and joined forces once again under the leadership of Irish American George Meany.

But the harmony, strength, and Irish leadership would soon dissipate. In the coming decades union membership declined steadily, especially among groups like the Irish who occupied many of the traditional trades most affected by American de-industrialization. By 1990, a mere 12 percent of the American workforce was in a union. Moreover, the one area of the economy where union organization was growing—public sector jobs like teachers—were no longer the province of the Irish.

In areas where the Irish remained prominent, the cultural habits and traditions that had once made their unions extraordinarily successful, now ran up against the civil rights movement and new standards of fairness. For example, the Steamfitter's Union, long known for its tradition of Only Irish Need Apply (or, more specifically, only Irish who could point to a blood relative already in the union), found itself subject to lawsuits and government

George Meany

scrutiny by the Justice Department for refusing to consider minority applicants for apprenticeships. Construction trades, and municipal police and fire departments were buffeted by similar challenges.

929. Irish American Prosperity

As the fortunes of organized labor declined after 1955, those of Irish Americans rose precipitously. Irish Americans, by the 1970s and 1980s, were far removed from the world of their parents and even further removed from their grandparents. They were more suburban, better educated, more cosmopolitan, more wealthy—even more Republican.

Some Notable Twentieth-Century Labor Leaders

930. Fr. John Corridan

Father John Corridan (1911–84) was the model for the "waterfront priest" in the classic movie *On the Waterfront*. Portrayed by Carl Malden as a Kerryman who blended with the rough New York longshoreman crowd, Corridan fought corrupt unions on the piers of New York and applied Christ's teachings to longshoremen's lives. His work led to the creation of the Waterfront Commission formed to rid the docks of criminal activity. Some of Corridan's supporters met with violence from opposition forces.

931. Leonora O'Reilly

Leonora O'Reilly (1870–1927) was born into a family steeped in labor radicalism. Her father died when she was young, so she was raised by her mother, a garment worker and political radical. At only age sixteen she founded the Working Woman's Society, a trade union and mutual aid society. In 1897 she organized the first women's local of the United Garment Workers of America. Six years later she contributed to the founding of the New York Women's Trade Union League. O'Reilly's skill as an orator and determination drew thousands of women into the labor movement. She was also prominent in the women's suffrage movement, the Henry Street Settlement House, and the NAACP.

932. Philip Murray

Born in Scotland, the grandson of Irish refugees of the 1798 Uprising, Philip Murray (1886–1952) is best known for his part in organizing labor unions for coal miners and steelworkers. He was born in Scotland. Educated in Catholic schools in Scotland, he worked with his father in the coal mines beginning when he was ten years old. His father instilled in him a strong commitment to the principles of trade unionism.

The family moved to the mining district of Pennsylvania in 1902. Murray lost his job as a miner after a fight with a supervisor. After that, he became a full-time union organizer. In 1912 he was elected to the United Mine Workers executive board. He became a trusted ally of John Lewis and together in 1920 they were elected vice president and president of the UMW respectively. They steered the UMW through tough times in the 1920s and became staunch supporters of the New Deal in the 1930s. Murray was appointed by President Roosevelt to the Labor and Industrial Advisory Board of the National Recovery Administration. He worked with Lewis to establish the Congress of Industrial Organizations (CIO) and took over as president when Lewis resigned in 1940. Two years later Murray became president of the United Steelworkers of America. He retained the presidencies of both organizations until his death in 1952. A devout Catholic, Murray was drawn to the social teachings of liberal clerics like Fr. John A. Ryan. He also believed in racial equality and was a member of the NAACP.

933. Mary Kenney O'Sullivan

Mary Kenney O'Sullivan (1864–1943) forged a career as a union and women's rights activist. Born to Irish immigrants in Missouri, she became a dressmaker and later found work in a printing and binding factory. Relocating to Chicago, she continued work in several binderies. With help from settlement house workers at Hull House, she helped organize the Chicago Women's Bindery Workers' Union. Her success as an organizer drew the attention of the

Elizabeth Gurley Flynn

American Federation of Labor which appointed her its first woman general organizer in 1892. That same year she teamed with Mary Kehew to establish the Union for Industrial Progress, an organization dedicated to studying factory working conditions and recommending reforms. She moved to Boston in 1894 after marrying the labor editor at the *Boston Globe*, and continued her work, organizing workers in the rubber, shoe, laundry, and garment industries. In 1903 she cofounded the Women's Trade Union League and took an active role in its work to enact progressive labor laws and to organize workers. In 1914 the state of Massachusetts hired her as a factory inspector for the Division of Industrial Safety, a post she held for the next twenty years. In recognition of her work, O'Sullivan became the first Irish American woman to have her portrait hung in the Massachusetts State House.

934. Elizabeth Gurley Flynn   Elizabeth Gurley Flynn (1890–1964), one of America's foremost radicals in the early twentieth century, was born in the Bronx into an Irish immigrant family. Her parents were ardent Irish nationalists and socialists and she received a thorough education in both from an early age. As Flynn put it in her autobiography, *Rebel Girl,* "My ancestors were immigrants and revolutionaries from the Emerald Isle. . . . There was an uprising in each generation in Ireland, and forefathers of mine were in every one of them. . . . Before I was ten, I knew of the great heroes—Robert Emmet, Wolfe Tone, Michael Davitt, Parnell, and Jeremiah O'Donovan Rossa."

By the time she was twenty-one, she was a member of the International Workers of the World and one of its most influential speakers and strike organizers. Of her speaking, the novelist Theodore Dreiser wrote of her first attempt: "It was in January last [1906] that she made her first appearance up the lecture platform and electrified her audience with her eloquence, her youth, and her loveliness." In the 1920s she cofounded the American Civil Liberties Union and worked for the release of anarchists Nicola Sacco and Bartolomeo Vanzetti, who had been convicted of murder. She suffered a nervous breakdown after they were eventually executed in 1927.

After recovering, she moved to New York City from Oregon. She joined the American Communist Party and spent her last twenty-seven years working tirelessly for the party and its principles. She was jailed for sedition from 1954 to 1957 under the Smith Act and in 1961 was voted head of the party. She left for Moscow and died there in 1964. The Soviets gave her an elaborate state funeral.

935. William Z. Foster   William Foster (1881–1961) was a leading early-twentieth-century radical and labor organizer. Growing up in an Irish working-class ghetto of Philadelphia, Foster became a union organizer at the turn of the century for the IWW. In 1918 he led a successful AFL drive to organize the Chicago meatpackers. Later that same year, he and another Irish American labor activist, John Fitzpatrick, organized thousands of steelworkers (few of whom were Irish) who in late 1919 would engage in the largest industrial strike to that time. In 1921 he joined the Communist Party and ran as its candidate for President in 1924, 1928, and 1932. He died in Moscow.

936. Margaret Haley   Born in Joliet, Illinois, Margaret Haley (1861–1939) grew up in Chicago. She became a teacher in 1876 and worked in several of the city's public schools. She became an early member of the Chicago Teachers' Federation, founded in 1897, and was named a CTF district vice president in 1900. One year later she retired from teaching to become a full-time business agent for the union. Almost immediately, she won a dispute with the Chicago Board of Education over the latter's refusal to deliver on promised salary increases. Haley lobbied state officials on a wide range of education issues, winning passage of a state pension plan for teachers (1907) and a state tenure law (1917).

Haley also had an impact at the national level. In 1904 she became president of the National Federation of Teachers and rebuilt it into a formidable organization. From this platform she successfully prodded the influential National Education Association to focus its attention away from colleges and toward grade school teachers. When the American Federation of Teachers was founded in 1916, Haley worked as an organizer.

Throughout her life, Haley involved herself in a wide range of progressive causes beyond education. She was a passionate advocate of women's suffrage, child labor legislation, and various political reforms.

937. George Meany

George Meany (1894–1980) was born in the Bronx, the grandson of immigrants who left Ireland in 1853. Raised in the Bronx, he followed in his father's footsteps and became a plumber. He soon became active in the plumbers' union and through skill and pure ambition worked his way up the ranks, culminating in his election in 1952 as president of the AFL. Three years later he oversaw the reunion of the AFL and Congress of Industrial Organizations (CIO). He became the new organization's president and remained in the post until one year before his death in 1980.

During his long tenure as president of the AFL-CIO, Meany lobbied against corruption in labor and became a civil rights advocate, helping to pass the Civil Rights Act of 1964. He worked with Presidents from Eisenhower to Carter. He was instrumental in getting Medicare started, along with the Occupational Safety and Health Act of 1970.

938. John Mitchell

John Mitchell (1870–1919) knew the hard life of the coal miner firsthand. His father was killed in a mining accident when he was a child and he entered the mines at age twelve. Living in Illinois, he joined the local chapter of the United Mine Workers of America in 1890. He rose up through the ranks to become a member of the UMW's state executive board by 1897. After playing a prominent role in the union's first national strike that year, he was elected national vice president in 1898 and almost immediately assumed the presidency at age twenty-eight. Mitchell's reputation among workers soared in 1902 when he successfully organized thousands of Pennsylvania coal miners and won a prolonged strike that drew the intervention of President Theodore Roosevelt. But the rest of the decade brought defeats in Colorado and West Virginia, resulting in bitter criticism of his leadership by more radical members of the union. He resigned the UMW presidency in 1908, but continued to work for industrial harmony. For the remainder of his life, Mitchell wrote articles for magazines and lectured across the country on labor issues.

939. Mike Quill

Born in Kerry and a veteran of the Irish Civil War, Mike Quill (1905–66) came to New York at nineteen and found work in the New York subway system. In 1934 he was among a group of IRA veterans who helped form the Transport Workers Union; he was elected president of the heavily Irish union a year later. As leader of the TWU for over thirty years, Quill succeeded in creating one of the nation's strongest unions and winning better conditions, hours and wages for its members. He also played a role in the national labor movement, gaining election to the national executive board of the Congress of Industrial Organizations (CIO) in 1938. He remained active in the CIO for decades. Quill also ran for public office, gaining election to the City Council in New York in 1937 on the American Labor Party ticket. He was reelected in 1943 and 1945. Quill's last major act was to declare a TWU strike on January 1, 1966, paralyzing the city. He died of heart failure only four weeks later.

940. Secretaries of Labor With the Irish so prominent in both politics and the labor movement, it was only a matter of time before one served as secretary of labor. The first was Maurice J. Tobin, the former two-term mayor of Boston and governor of Massachusetts. He was tabbed by President Truman in 1948 and served until 1953. A fellow Irishman, Martin Durkin, succeeded him for a brief stint in 1953. James P. Mitchell held the office for most of Eisenhower's two terms (1953–61). Oddly enough it was John F. Kennedy that broke the string of Irish secretaries of labor. Peter Brennan later served from 1973 to 1975 and Raymond Donovan from 1981 to 1985.

PART X

Sports

941. Gaelic Football This Irish version of football goes back centuries, originally involving whole parishes competing in all-day matches on fields running for miles. In 1884 the Gaelic Athletic Association was formed to formalize the game's rules, eliminate some of its more violent elements, and oversee competition.

The game they settled upon involves two sides of fifteen players who square off for two thirty-minute periods. Players are allowed to advance the ball only by dribbling it with their hand or foot, or punching or punting it forward toward their opponent's goal. Points are scored by putting the ball between the goalposts and over the crossbar (one point) or putting it between the posts and under the bar into a net (three points).

942. Hurling and Camogie A traditional Irish field sport, hurling is played by two teams of fifteen players who use sticks called "hurleys" to swat a ball to a goal. The official rules of the game were established in 1884 by the newly formed Gaelic Athletic Association. The hurley is a thirty- to thirty-seven-inch-long stick made from ash wood with a broad end called the "bas." The ball, called a slitter, has a cork center and a leather cover. The object is to catch the slitter on the blade of the hurley, carry it, and hurl it into the goal. Regulation hurling is played on a field measuring 90 yards by 150 yards. Championship and league matches last sixty minutes.

Camogie is the female version of hurling. The game is unique to Ireland and is one of the fastest field games in the world. Every hurling and

Hurling

camogie team has a goalkeeper, six defenders, two mid-fielders and six forwards. There are two methods of recording scores: a "point" when the ball is played over the crossbar, and a goal when it is played over the goal line between the posts and under the crossbar. Every year Inter County and Inter Clubs compete to reach the All-Ireland Championship, played on the first Sunday in September. The winning team receives the O'Duffy Cup.

943. The Gaelic Athletic Association The GAA, founded in Thurles, Co. Tipperary, in 1884, was formed to foster traditional Irish sports. By providing an alternative to the English games of rugby, soccer, and cricket, the GAA hoped to instill national pride in young Irish generations and reduce "foreign" or English influences. The association had strong political connections to the Fenians and the Irish Republican Brotherhood.

From its inception, the GAA looked to the American Irish for financial and general support. In 1888, an "American invasion" was devised to raise funds by bringing Irish players over for a series of matches in New York, Boston, Philadelphia, and other northeastern cities. Irish immigrants were grateful to see the games, but the trip was not profitable. Indeed, a third of the forty-five-man Irish team ended up staying in the U.S., draining talent from Ireland.

The popular Irish games of hurling and Gaelic football had been played in New York and other cities since the 1850s. Throughout the 1880s and 1890s, many teams composed of players from particular counties in Ireland competed in New York, usually in Celtic Park, Queens. In Chicago, there were fifteen clubs with two thousand members when that city's branch of the GAA was formed in 1893. However, it was not until December 1914 that the "GAA of the U.S." was formed in New York.

In 1928, the GAA opened a park of its own, Innisfail, in the Bronx. Today, the park, renamed Gaelic Park, continues to host American GAA teams. Players are generally recent immigrants and first-generation Irish Americans.

Baseball

944. The Irish Presence Players of Irish birth and origins played a key role in the popularization of the "national pastime." They were drawn to it, myths about Abner Doubleday aside, because baseball was fundamentally an urban sport and Irish Americans a fundamentally urban people. The Irish were also quite poor, another factor that has contributed to one group or another dominating a particular sport. While many Irish-born players excelled at the game, the great majority of the Irish involved were born in the U.S. By the 1890s, at least one third of professional baseball players were of Irish origin. Another tabulation on

KELLY, RIGHT FIELD, BOS

King Kelly

1915 found eleven of baseball's sixteen managers were likewise Irish.

945. Nineteenth-Century Standouts With so many Irish Americans playing professional baseball in its early decades, it's not surprising that many of the game's earliest stars were of Irish ancestry. Mike "King" Kelly, for example, helped the Chicago Nationals win five championships in the 1880s. He led the league in batting in 1884 and 1886 and was a legendary base stealer, giving rise to the expression, "slide, Kelly, slide." "Big" Ed Delahanty (one of five brothers who made the big leagues) posted a whopping career batting average of .346 and even hit four home runs in a single game. Roger Connor was the home run king of the so-called "deadball era," with 192 round trippers over his career to go with twelve seasons with a batting average over .300. Joe Kelley was a standout left fielder for the Baltimore Orioles in the 1890s. He hit over .300 in twelve consecutive seasons, including .391 in 1894. Pitcher Tim Keefe won 342 games in fourteen seasons, twice winning more than forty games in a single season. He is credited with inventing the changeup. Pud Galvin became baseball's first three-hundred-game winner and pitched more innings (5,959) and complete games (641) than anyone but Cy Young.

946. The Catchers

Roger Patrick Bresnahan Roger Patrick Bresnahan, a tough guy who paradoxically pioneered the use of safety equipment in professional baseball, in 1945 became the first catcher elected to the Baseball Hall of Fame. The Toledo, Ohio, native went by his nickname "the Duke of Tralee," after the hometown of his family, Tralee, County Kerry, Ireland. His career soared in 1901 after he began playing for manager John McGraw, a fellow stocky and pugnacious Irishman. Bresnahan's legacy are the shin guards used by modern catchers. He fashioned his from a set of cricket shin guards after one too many foul balls struck him behind the plate.

Mickey Cochrane   Baseball fans in one unsanctioned contest voted Mickey Cochrane the sixth-best baseball catcher of the twentieth century. He was officially elected to the sport's Hall of Fame in 1947. Gordon Stanley Cochrane was born in Bridgewater, Massachusetts, and died in Lake Forest, Illinois. Cochrane batted .320 for his career and excelled behind the plate, but also possessed a spirit that gave him exceptional leadership qualities. "Black Mike" was the spark of the Philadelphia Athletics' championship teams of 1929 to 1931 and as player-manager he later directed the Detroit Tigers to two league championships and a World Series title. A beaning in 1937 ended his playing career.

947. The Infielders
Mark McGwire   A modern-day sultan of swat, Mark McGwire hit seventy home runs in 1998 to break Roger Maris' single-season record of sixty-one set back in 1961. He did so in a back and forth race with Chicago Cubs star Samy Sosa (who ended the season with sixty-six home runs) that was not decided until the final game of the season. McGwire, along with Ken Griffey, Jr., is considered a likely candidate to challenge baseball's all-time career home run record of 758 set by Hank Aaron.

Eddie Collins   In his first full season in 1909 with Connie Mack's Philadelphia Athletics, Eddie Collins set the tone for the rest of his remarkable twenty-five-year career, posting a .346 average with sixty-seven stolen bases. He went on to hit over .340 in ten different seasons for a lifetime batting average of .333.

Joe Cronin   Joe Cronin had it all—great bat, great glove, great legs. He hit over .300 eight times and collected more than one hundred RBIs in each of eight seasons as well. Cronin was league MVP in 1930 when he posted a .346 average with 126 RBI.

948. The Outfielders
Hugh Duffy   Hugh Duffy was a brilliant outfielder for the Boston Beaneaters as well as one of the hardest hitters in the game during his era. He assembled a string of ten straight .300-plus seasons, and in 1894 he batted an all-time record .438 while leading the National League in doubles (fifty) and home runs (eighteen).

Max Carey   Known as an excellent hitter and basestealer, Max Carey hit .300 in six different seasons and led the league in steals in ten straight seasons. In 1922 he stole fifty-one bases and was caught only twice. Carey was also a superb fielder and still holds several defensive records for center fielders.

949. The Pitchers
Nolan Ryan   One of the hardest throwers in baseball history, Texan Nolan Ryan was elected to the sport's Hall of Fame in 1999 by winning 99 percent of the vote from sports writers. Pitching baseballs at one hundred miles per hour, Ryan set numerous records, including most strikeouts (5,714), most no-hitters (seven), most games with fifteen or more strikeouts (twenty-six), and most strikeouts in a single season (383). The "Ryan Express" never showed signs of slowing down and became the only pitcher to strike out sixteen or more batters after the age of forty, accomplishing the feat three times.

Don Sutton Along with Nolan Ryan, Don Sutton was one of the greatest pitchers in recent baseball history. Playing most of his career for the Los Angeles Dodgers, he racked up 324 wins versus 256 losses (ERA 3.26). His greatest asset was his consistency. He won fifteen games or more for eight consecutive seasons (1969–76). He was inducted into the Hall of Fame in 1998.

Ed Walsh Certainly the most astounding statistic in Ed Walsh's career is his lifetime ERA of 1.82. Maybe the fact that he threw the spitball when it was still legal had something to do with it. Regardless, he was one of the most dominant pitchers of the early twentieth century. In 1908 he went 40–15, with a 1.42 ERA.

950. Notable Team Owners Charles Comiskey (1858–1931) was the son of an Irish politician in Chicago. He began baseball playing with Milwaukee as third baseman and later won four league titles (1885–88) as player-manager for the St. Louis Browns of the American Association. After his playing and managing days were done, Comiskey bought a team in Sioux City, Iowa, and moved it to Chicago, naming them the White Stockings. He later helped organize the American League. During his thirty-one years as owner, Comiskey's White Sox (as they were eventually called) won four championships. Despite the "Black Sox" scandal of 1919, when his players threw the Series for $10,000, Comiskey was elected to the Baseball Hall of Fame in 1939.

Walter O'Malley (1903–79) began his career as an attorney, but later moved into banking where his investment skills led him to become a millionaire. He was an attorney for the Brooklyn Dodgers until 1950 when he purchased the team. Two years after his Dodgers won their only World Series, O'Malley became one of the most hated men in sports (at least in New York) when he relocated the team to Los Angeles. But O'Malley was a visionary. He recognized before most people the extraordinary future growth in the West, especially California, and seized the opportunity to move his team there. It must also be said in his defense that the Dodgers had very poor attendance records in the mid-fifties and negotiations with the city for a new stadium eventually collapsed.

The new Dodger Stadium opened in 1962. Since that time O'Malley's Dodgers have won six National League championships and two World Series. In 1970 he handed over control of the team to his son Peter. He received the first Busch Award for his work in the baseball industry in 1975 and died in 1979.

In more recent times, Charlie Finley built a dynasty with his Oakland Athletics in the early 1970s, winning World Series in 1972, 1973, and 1974.

951. The Legendary Managers Among the many successful Irish American managers, two stand out in particular: Connie Mack and John McGraw. Connie Mack (1862–1956), born Cornelius McGillicuddy, was an average player in his career 1884 and 1899 (lifetime batting average of .249). He is most remembered for his forty-nine seasons as manager of the Philadelphia Athletics (1901–50) in which he won nine American League pennants and five World Series. Mack was elected to the Baseball Hall of Fame in 1937—thirteen years before he retired!

With a lifetime batting average of .334 compiled over a sixteen-year career, John McGraw (1873–1934) would most likely have made the Hall of Fame for his record as a player. But he is probably better known for his career as one of baseball's greatest managers. After managing Baltimore for three seasons (as a player-

Connie Mack

manager), he took the helm of the New York Giants in 1902 and stayed on for thirty-one years. He guided the Giants to a World Series victory in 1905, earning him the nickname "Little Napoleon" for his reputation as a demanding manager. In the next few decades, his teams won ten league pennants and three World Series championships. McGraw's 2,840 victories as a manager ranked second only to the great Connie Mack. He retired as manager and was elected to baseball's Hall of Fame in 1937.

952. Casey of "Casey at the Bat"   Ernest L. Thayer's 1885 poem about the "Mighty Casey" has long been a favorite of baseball fans. But just who was that Casey? Several real Irishmen, including Boston shortstop Tim Casey and Philadelphia pitcher Daniel Michael Casey, claimed they were Thayer's inspiration (the latter Casey even hit the vaudeville circuit as the "real" Casey). Many others, not necessarily named Casey also claimed the honor. Finally, in 1935, Thayer revealed that his inspiration for the fictional Casey had come from a high school classmate, a "big Irishman" named Daniel H. Casey who once threatened to beat him up. Even those who can't recall the whole poem, usually remember the final stanza:

> And somewhere men are laughing,
> And somewhere children shout,
> But there is no joy in Mudville—
> Mighty Casey has struck out.

Sportswriters and Sportscasters

953. TAD Dorgan   Thomas Aloysius Dorgan, or Tad, as he was known by sports fans across the country, was born in San Francisco in 1877. His natural talent for sketching landed him a job as a cartoonist and illustrator for the *San Francisco Bulletin*. William Randolph Hearst wooed him to the *New York Journal* in 1902 where he focused on sports, especially his first love, boxing. His sketches of athletes, particularly fighters, and daily cartoons were widely syndicated in papers across the country. Dorgan is best remembered for the many expressions he invented, such as the superlatives "the cat's meow" and "the cat's pajamas" and the exclamation "For crying out loud!" He also added several slang terms to the American lexicon, including "hot dog," "hard-boiled" (a tough guy), and "cheaters" (eyeglasses).

954. Jimmy Cannon   A tough and opinionated New York sportswriter and essayist during the mid-twentieth century, Jimmy Cannon viewed sports as an extension of show business. He also covered World War II for *Stars & Stripes*. He was at times a progressive, writing of African American boxing champion Joe Louis well before the civil rights movement: "Louis is a credit to his race—the human race." He wrote of Babe Ruth: "He was a parade all by himself, a burst of dazzle and jingle, Santa Claus drinking his whiskey straight and groaning with a bellyache caused by gluttony." He was inducted into the National Sportscasters and Sportswriters Hall of Fame in 1986.

955. John Kieran   Born in the Bronx in New York City, John Kieran held several blue-collar jobs before working as a sportswriter for the *New York Times* in 1915. After brief stints at competing newspapers during the 1920s, Kieran returned to the *Times* in 1926. His "Sports of the Times" column was the first to carry a byline in the paper's history. Kieran's wide-ranging knowledge led to a ten-year run as a panelist on a radio program called "Information Please" from 1938 to 1948. Kieran also wrote several books on nature, including the award-winning *Natural History of New York City*. He was inducted into the National Sportscasters and Sportswriters Hall of Fame in 1971.

956. Charles Louis McCarthy   Radio sports broadcaster "Clem" McCarthy called the Kentucky Derby, other prestigious races, and boxing title matches for NBC Radio from 1929 to 1947. Known for his signature "rrrracing fans" raspy voice and staccato delivery, he was inducted into the American Sportscasters Association Hall of Fame in 1987. The son of a horse dealer and auctioneer, he knew horses and horse racing. He is remembered for miscalling the winner of the 1947 Preakness, a mistake he corrected moments after the race where fans blocked his view of the final seconds. Clem covered the legendary rematch between Joe Louis and Max Schmeling in 1938. He was inducted into the National Sportscasters and Sportswriters Hall of Fame in 1970.

957. Vin Scully   Vin Scully has one of the most recognizable voices in this history of American sports broadcasting. He began his career in 1950 with the Brooklyn Dodgers under the tutelage of the legendary Red Barber. He followed the team when it moved west in 1958. In the years that followed, Scully began to broadcast baseball games on national radio and television, including the playoffs. Over the course of more than fifty years behind the microphone, Scully has had the good fortune to broadcast some of the greatest moments in baseball history, including four no-hitters by Sandy Koufax, Hank Aaron's 715th home run, Maury Wills' 104th stolen base, and Kirk Gibson's dramatic home run in the first game of the 1988 World Series. He was named the 1982 winner of the Baseball Hall of Fame's Ford Frick award for outstanding broadcaster and in 1991 was inducted into the National Sportscasters and Sportswriters Hall of Fame.

Football

College

958. Notre Dame, the "Fighting Irish"   The nickname of America's most storied college football team tells us a lot about the Irish American experi-

ence. On the one hand, the Irish in America suffered from the stereotype that they were prone to fighting and violence. On the other, American society worshipped competitiveness and a fighting spirit. Thus, in taking the name the "Fighting Irish," Notre Dame managed to take a negative stereotype about the Irish and transform it into an American virtue. To the extent that it helped Americans see the Irish as fighters on the gridiron and not in the streets, it was a positive development.

The precise origin of the term is impossible to determine. Sports journalists in the early twentieth century sometimes used the adjective "fighting" when describing the team, but that was hardly unique to Notre Dame. It seems to have become an unofficial nickname after World War I and was sanctioned by the school in 1927. Even though many of the team's players were not Irish (some weren't even Catholic), Knute Rockne defended the name: "They're all Irish to me. They have the Irish spirit and that's all that counts."

959. Frank Leahy   When Notre Dame hired Frank Leahy as head football coach in 1941, he had very big shoes to fill. As one of Knute Rockne's former players, he knew the standard of excellence, and was by all accounts successful. Leahy, who called his players "lads," was respected as a superb, focused coach. He won five national championships in his eleven seasons and his career record of 87–11–9 was comparable to Rockne's

105–12–5 and he did best Rockne's longest winning streak. In the postwar period, as corruption tarnished many collegiate football programs, Leahy maintained the Fighting Irish's reputation as scandal-free. When Leahy began

Frank Leahy

to suffer health problems in 1953 related to his relentless work habits, he retired. His two immediate successors, both former Notre Dame standouts, fared poorly.

Professional

960. Some Early Stars

Paddy Driscoll   Born in 1896, Paddy Driscoll became one of the early stars of professional football. As a speedy quarterback for the Bears, he could do it all—run, pass, and even kick. In fact, he was a superb punter and field goal kicker and once drop kicked four field goals in one game (still a record). He was inducted into the Hall of Fame in 1965.

Ed Healey   The first player ever sold (1922) to another team, Ed Healey went on to a storied career with the Chicago Bears. George Halas called him "the most versatile tackle ever." He was inducted into the Hall of Fame in 1964.

Ray Flaherty   He was one of the most successful (80–37–5) and influential coaches in the early years of football. As coach of the Boston and later Washington Redskins (1936–42), he won four Eastern Division titles and two NFL championships. Later, as coach of the New York Yankees, he won two AAFC divisional titles. Two of his most important innovations were the behind-the-line screen pass and the use of a two-platoon system (one for rushing and another for passing).

Before becoming a coach, he played for the Los Angeles Wildcats, New York Yankees, and New York Giants and was named All-NFL in 1928 and 1932. He was inducted into the Hall of Fame in 1976.

961. George Connor   He was an All-American at Holy Cross College and Notre Dame and in a sterling career with the Chicago Bears (1948–55) he was named All-NFL five times. Incredibly, he earned three of his All-NFL distinctions at different positions—offensive tackle, defensive tackle, and linebacker. Credited with being the first big and agile linebacker, he was inducted into the Hall of Fame in 1975.

962. Art Donovan   Service in World War II (plus four years at Boston College) made Donovan a rookie at age twenty-six in 1950. The imposing defensive tackle was named All-NFL from 1954 to 1957 and played a key role in the Colts dominance in the 1950s. He was the first Colt inducted into the Pro Football Hall of Fame in 1968.

963. Mike McCormack   In his first season (1951) with the New York Yanks, McCormack made the Pro Bowl (he played in five more). A two-way player, he excelled at both defensive middle guard and offensive tackle. After a stint in the army interrupted his career (1952–53), he was traded to the Browns. In 1954 he was the player who stole the ball that set up the Browns touchdown to win the Championship. He retired in 1962 and was inducted into the Hall of Fame in 1984.

964. Frank Gifford   Frank Gifford has enjoyed two successful careers—first as a professional football player, and then as a sportscaster. Playing for the New York Giants, Gifford was an All-Pro selection four times, the NFL MVP in 1956, and the NFL Pro Bowl MVP in 1959. When he retired from football, he pursued sportscasting, working for major networks, most notably appearing on *ABC Monday Night Football*. Gifford has written about his experiences in and knowledge of football in four books to date.

965. Bill Walsh   At the helm of the remarkable San Francisco 49ers in the 1980s was coach Bill Walsh. Totally committed to the 49ers, Walsh has at times served as coach, general manager, and/or president. During his career, Walsh coached two players who are among the best to play their positions—quarterback Joe Montana and receiver Jerry Rice. He is known as an unpredictable and tactical genius with a calm demeanor who was ex-

tremely demanding of his players, yet sensitive to them as a team and as individuals.

966. Art Rooney One of the creators of the NFL, Art Rooney purchased the Pittsburgh Pirates (the future Steelers) for $2,500 in race-track winnings in 1933. His passion for horse racing was legendary. One weekend in 1936, he took $500 to the races and left with $300,000! Not one to waste money, he applied his earnings to his shrewd business dealings.

For decades, Rooney watched the Steelers lose until the 1970s, when they became a football powerhouse, winning the Super Bowl in 1975, 1976, 1979, and 1980. True to his team, Rooney stayed on as chairman until his death at age eighty-seven.

Basketball

College

967. Ned Irish Long before there was the professional basketball and the NBA, there was college basketball, Madison Square Garden, and Edward S. "Ned" Irish (1905–82). A sportswriter and basketball enthusiast, Irish was hired in 1931 by MSG to stage an annual college basketball triple-header featuring six teams from the New York area. The immediate success of the event led to an expanded schedule of double-header matches. The Garden soon became the nation's leading arena for the game and Ned Irish its leading promoter. Under his guidance, both the National Invitation Tournament (1938) and NCAA championship (1939) began at the Garden and were held there annually for decades to come. Irish was subsequently inducted into the Basketball Hall of Fame in 1964.

Professional

968. Some Early Stars
Stretch Murphy: (1907–92) At 6'6", Charles

"Stretch" Murphy was professional basketball's first "big man." In college he teamed with John Wooden to make Purdue a national powerhouse (1926–30). Murphy was noted for his defense and for perfecting the outlet pass that powered Purdue's innovative running game. After college he played briefly for the ABL Chicago Bruins (1929–30) and Independent League Indianapolis Kautskys (1930–33).

"Poison" Joe Brennan: Joseph Brennan (1900–89) enjoyed a stellar seventeen-year professional career, playing in many of the upstart leagues of that era. Among his highlights, Brennan led the Metropolitan Basketball League in scoring in 1922 and guided his Brooklyn Dodgers team to Met League championships in 1922 and 1923. He later joined the all-Irish Brooklyn Visitations and led them to ABL championship 1929, 1931, and 1935.

Robert McDermott: One of the first great shooters of the early game, Bobby McDermott (1914–63) played sixteen seasons for eight teams in four leagues. He was a seven-time NBL All-Star, five-time NBL MVP (1942–46), and led the Fort Wayne Zollner Pistons to three straight World Tournament titles (1944–46).

969. Ed Macauley "Easy" Ed Macauley (b. 1928) played ten seasons in the NBA, dividing his time between the St. Louis Hawks (1949–50 and 1956–59) and Boston Celtics (1950–56). Macauley's nickname derived from his fast and graceful moves to the hoop. His greatest years were with the Boston Celtics in which he teamed with fellow Hall of Famers Bob Cousy and Bill Sharman, considered one of the greatest scoring trios in NBA history. In the course of his career, he was named an NBA All-Star seven times and won one NBA championship (1958, St. Louis).

970. Dick and Al McGuire Richard (b. 1926) and Albert McGuire (1928–2001) are the only brothers elected to the Basketball Hall of Fame. Dick McGuire played twelve NBA seasons with the New York Knicks and Detroit Pistons during which he was named an NBA All-Star seven times. He led the league in assists in 1950 and piloted the Knicks to three consecutive NBA championships (1951–53). As a player, he was known as "Tricky Dick" for his lightning fast moves, slick passing, and uncanny ability to find an opening. He later coached both the Pistons and Knicks.

Dick McGuire's younger brother Al made his mark in coaching college basketball. First with Belmont Abbey and then with Marquette University, McGuire established himself as one of the game's great motivators and teachers. He led Marquette to eleven consecutive postseason tournament appearances, including the NIT (1970) and NCAA (1977) tournament championships. The latter victory was the last game he coached. He later became a highly respected analyst for televised basketball.

971. Bill Bradley Long before he entered politics, Americans knew Bill Bradley as a star basketball player. At Princeton University, he was a three-time All-American forward and the focus of the best-selling book by John McPhee, *A Sense of Where You Are* (1965). Bradley helped the U.S. to a gold medal at the 1964 Olympic Games and was voted college player of the year by the National Association of Basketball Coaches in 1965. Bradley graduated in 1965, but opted to study at Oxford University rather than enter the NBA. In 1967 he signed with the Knicks and played for ten seasons, winning two NBA Championships. In 1983, six years after his retirement, he was elected to the NBA Hall of Fame.

972. Rick Barry After leading the nation in scoring in his senior year at the University of Miami, Rick Barry (b. 1944) joined the NBA's San Francisco Warriors and won the Rookie of the Year award (1966). Barry jumped from team to team and between the NBA and the short-lived

American Basketball Association (ABA) long before free agency, a habit that brought him criticism for his alleged lack of loyalty. What Barry did not lack was talent and the statistics from his professional career attest to this: twelve-time All-Star (NBA and ABA), NBA scoring leader in 1967, and NBA Finals MVP in 1975. Barry was known throughout his career as tough competitor and a superb free-throw shooter—his 89.3 percent from the line is still second best in NBA history. After retiring in 1980, Barry became a television basketball analyst and then a minor league coach. In 1987, he was inducted into the Basketball Hall of Fame.

973. Kevin McHale Kevin McHale (b. 1957) played twelve seasons with the Boston Celtics (1980–93) and was a key component to the team's dynasty in the mid-1980s. Teamed with Larry Bird and Robert Parrish, he was part of one of the greatest frontlines in NBA history. Considered one of the great pivot players at the low post, he was named to seven NBA All-Star teams and twice grabbed the NBA's Sixth Player award. McHale helped lead Boston to three NBA championships (1981, 1984, and 1986). He was inducted into the Basketball Hall of Fame in 1999.

974. The Commissioners Walter J. Kennedy began as a public relations director for the Basketball Association of America and continued in that capacity when it merged with the NBA. Kennedy became commissioner in 1963 and presided over the emergence of the NBA as a major professional sport, negotiating its first television contract and orchestrating the expansion from nine to eighteen teams.

Maybe it was destiny—Larry O'Brien was born in Springfield, Massachusetts, the birthplace of basketball and the home of the National Basketball Association's Hall of Fame. After a career in politics as a presidential advisor and Postmaster General, O'Brien became commissioner of the NBA in 1975. He served nine years, retiring in 1984. Not long thereafter, in recognition of his contribution to the league, the NBA named its championship trophy in honor of Larry O'Brien.

Ice Hockey

975. Not Many Americans Until very recently, professional hockey claimed very few American-born stars. Indeed, a check of the Hockey Hall of Fame finds only two American-born players out of 218. Only one of them, Joseph Mullen, is Irish American.

Still, given the enormous number of Canadians who claim Irish ancestry, it's not very surprising to find a large number of Canadian-born Hall-of-Famers with Irish roots. Consider the following Canadian-born Hall of Famers:

King Clancy	Frank McGee
Alex Connell	Billy McGimsie
Bill Cowley	George McNamara
Jack Darragh	Paddy Moran
Bill Durnan	Buddy O'Connor
Moose Goheen	Lynn Patrick
Red Kelly	Kenny Reardon
Ted Kennedy	Fred Scanlan
Lanny McDonald	Marty Walsh

976. Joe Mullen One of only two American-born players in the Hockey Hall of Fame, Joe Mullen (b. 1957) was born in New York City. He starred at Boston College before joining the St. Louis Blues. Over the course of eighteen NHL seasons, Mullen became the first American-born player to tally more than a

Joe Mullen

thousand career points. In stints with St. Louis, Calgary, Pittsburgh, and Boston, Mullen scored forty or more goals and had forty or more assists in six seasons. He also won the Lady Bing Trophy for sportsmanship in 1987 and 1989.

Figure Skating

977. Nancy Kerrigan Winner of the silver medal for women's figure skating in the 1993–94 Winter Olympics, Nancy Kerrigan captured international sympathy when she was injured by an attacker hired by her competitor Tonya Harding prior to the 1994 National Championships. Kerrigan's injured knee threatened to cancel her Olympic performance. A world-class figure skater, she was considered a serious competitor for Olympic gold before the spiteful injury. She had won bronze at the 1992 Winter Olympics and a gold medal at the 1993 National Championships. Her tenacity to compete and capture the silver medal won worldwide admiration for the skater supported by her father and legally-blind mother.

978. Peggy Flemming A native Californian, this figure skater born in 1948 captured the only American gold medal along with the American public in the 1968 Winter Olympics, the first games to be televised. Peggy was the figure skating world champion three times from 1966 to 1968 before winning Olympic gold. In the public eye as a skater by age twelve, Peggy is credited with sparking public interest in a sport that was devastated by a plane crash that killed the entire U.S. figure skating team along with Peggy's coach. Following her competitive years, she became an on-air analyst for ABC Sports for more than eighteen years.

979. Dorothy Hamill The fourth American woman to win an Olympic gold medal, figure skater Dorothy Hamill took gold on Valentine's Day in the 1976 Olympics at Innsbruck, Austria. Her wedge hairstyle was copied nationally and called an important fashion statement by *Life* magazine. From Connecticut, Dorothy was a two-time World Silver medalist in 1974–75 and a three-time U.S. National Champion. She joined professional skaters and in 1993 bought the Ice Capades, which she later sold. She originated a maneuver known as the "Hamill Camel" and was inducted into the U.S. Figure Skating Hall of Fame in 1991 for her accomplishments.

Boxing

980. Early Champs: Yankee Sullivan and John "Old Smoke" Morrissey In 1851 Irish-born "Yankee Sullivan," also known as James Ambrose and Frank or Francis Murray, claimed the title of heavyweight champion of America when his rival Tom Hyer retired. In 1853 he fought John "Old Smoke" Morrissey. The bout turned into a brawl and Sullivan lost his title to Morrissey by decision. Sullivan died mysteriously—perhaps by his own hand—in 1856 in a San Francisco prison, charged with ballot-box stuffing.

John "Old Smoke" Morrissey (1831–78) was born in Tipperary County, Ireland. After coming to the United States as a boy, he honed his fighting skills on the streets of Troy, New York. His success and his nickname were due to sheer power, bravery, and tolerance for pain. After winning the heavyweight championship from Yankee Sullivan in 1853, Morrissey opened casinos in San Francisco and New York City and a racetrack in Saratoga, New York. His popularity won him influence in New York politics and seats in the U.S. House and Senate.

981. John L. Sullivan In the twentieth century, many an Irish American who had never been within a thousand miles of South Bend, Indiana, lived and died with the fortunes of Notre Dame's football team. They identified with the team as a symbol of their own struggles and aspirations. In the late nineteenth century, Irish Americans didn't

John L. Sullivan

have Notre Dame football to identify with, but they did have John L. Sullivan. Born in 1858 into the tough Irish neighborhood of Roxbury in Boston, he rose in the 1880s to become the world's most successful bare-knuckled boxer, defeating some two hundred opponents. What his fans loved most about him, apart from his extraordinary skills, was the audacious way he proclaimed his invincibility. "The bigger they are," he famously quipped, "the harder they fall."

Sullivan's greatest contest came in July 1889 when he fought Jake Kilrain for the world championship. The fight took place in Mississippi, one of the few states that placed no regulations on bare-knuckled boxing, and lasted seventy-five rounds before Kilrain's corner threw in the towel. Sullivan entered semiretirement after that and toured the country as a celebrity and aspiring actor. But hard drinking and high living left him broke and desperate. On September 7, 1892, though overweight and out of shape, he battled and lost to the next Irish star of the ring, "Gentleman" Jim Corbett. Though he never fought again, Sullivan remained a celebrity the rest of his life.

982. Jim Corbett "Gentleman Jim" Corbett (1866–1933) knocked out John L. Sullivan to become world heavyweight boxing champion in 1892. This victory, won with padded gloves, ended the era of bare-knuckle boxing and the London Prize Ring Rules. Corbett was known not for brute strength but for a "scientific" approach involving innovations in timing and quick thinking in the ring. Out of the ring, his debonair manner earned him his nickname and brought some much-needed respectability to the sport. When his boxing career ended, Corbett went on to act in the theater and in movies and to write his autobiography, *The Roar of the Crowd.*

983. Jack Dempsey   Following in the footsteps of the great Irish American heavyweights John L. Sullivan and "Gentleman Jim" Corbett, Jack Dempsey (1895–1983) became one of boxing's most powerful hitters, reigning as champion from 1919 to 1926. Originally from Colorado, Dempsey left home at sixteen, traveling and fighting throughout the West before ascending the ranks as a master of the quick knockout. At a time when boxing held true mass appeal, Dempsey's fights attracted thousands of fans, including over 100,000 people who watched his last fight at Soldier Field in Chicago. Dempsey lost this classic fight to Gene Tunney (another Irish American) when Tunney survived the infamous "long count" knockdown in the ninth round, eventually winning the fight on points.

984. Gene Tunney   Known as Gene Tunney or by the nickname "the Fighting Marine," James Joseph Tunney (1897–1978) was born in New York City and began his boxing career while serving in World War I. He won the world heavyweight title in 1926, easily defeating the popular Jack Dempsey. In a controversial and legendary 1927 rematch, Tunney won by decision, thanks to a referee's long count. When his career as a fighter ended, Tunney became a businessman and writer, author of *A Man Must Fight* (1932) and *Arms for Living* (1941). His son John V. Tunney served as a U.S. senator in the 1970s.

985. Italian and Jewish Fighters with Irish Names   The image of the Irish boxer was so powerful in the late nineteenth century that many aspiring non-Irish pugilists took Irish "ring" names. They believed, quite correctly, that their chances of getting better bouts and higher placement on fight cards depended on their appearing Irish.

In 1905, fresh off its successful campaign to rid American theater of the "stage Irishman" character, the Ancient Order of Hibernians announced a campaign against what it termed "the nefarious custom of criminals, pugilists, and the abandoned and submerged tenth of society adopting Irish names, both Christian and surnames." Still, it was the 1930s before Italian and Jewish fighters ceased the "nefarious" practice.

Golf

986. John McDermott   Born in Philadelphia in 1891, he started out learning the game as a caddy. In 1909, aged eighteen, McDermott competed in his first U.S. Open Championship and finished forty-eighth. In 1910 he finished in a tie for first, but lost in the playoff. He tied again in 1911, but won the playoff. In a game still dominated by golfers from England and Scotland, McDermott was the first American-born player to win the U.S. Open. He repeated as champion in 1912.

987. Bobby Jones   Robert (Bobby) Tyre Jones, Jr. (1902–71) is still regarded as one of the best golfers in the history of the game. As an amateur, he won the U.S. Open four times, the U.S. Amateur four times, and the British Open three times. He was the first golfer to win the U.S. and British Opens in the same year (1926). He is also the only golfer to win what was then the "grand slam" of golf, the open and amateur titles in the U.S. and Britain in 1930. He retired that same year and became a lawyer.

988. Ben Hogan   Ben Hogan (1912–97) is considered to be one of the three best golfers in the sport's history. Born in Dublin, Texas, to Irish descendants, he began caddying at a young age. By the time he turned seventeen, he was playing golf professionally. After World War II, he returned to the links, winning two PGA titles (1946 and 1948), and the U.S. Open (1948). In 1949, he was involved in a serious auto accident, and people wondered if he'd

Ben Hogan

ever walk again. He not only walked, he played again, winning three more U.S. Opens (1950, 1951, and 1953), two Master's tournaments (1951 and 1953) and the British Open (1953). His victory in the 1950 U.S. Open, coming just sixteen months after the auto accident, is considered by many to be one of the gutsiest performances ever in professional sports.

989. Sam Snead One of the greats of the game, Sam Snead was born in Hot Springs, Virginia. "Slammin' Sammy," as his fans called him, won three Masters tournaments (1949, 1952, 1954) and three Professional Golfers' Association (PGA) titles (1942, 1949, 1951). His one disappointment in an otherwise brilliant career was his inability to win the U.S. Open—he finished second four times. At his retirement, Snead had more PGA tournament victories (eighty-four) than any golfer in history.

990. Women Golfers of Note While women's professional golf enjoys ever-growing popularity these days, it started many decades after the men's game was firmly established. Thus the Ladies Professional Golf Association's Hall of Fame was established in 1964 and it was eleven years before its first member met the qualifications for induction—ten years on the tour and at least thirty tournament victories, including two majors. Two of the greatest golfers in the game are Pat Bradley (b. 1951) and Patty Sheehan (b. 1956). Bradley became the twelfth player inducted into the LPGA Hall of Fame in 1991. Over her career, she has won all four majors on LPGA tour and been named LPGA Player of the Year twice (1986 and

1991). In 1993, Sheehan became the thirteenth inductee. Among her thirty-plus wins are three LPGA titles (1983, 1984, and 1993) and two U.S. Opens (1992 and 1994).

Tennis

991. Jimmy Connors Born in Belleville, Illinois, his mother, Gloria, a tennis teacher herself, began instructing him when he was three. His family was never rich, he's been called a "blue-collar battler" by columnists, and he doesn't talk much about his Irish heritage. On the court, he stood out for his petulant behavior, and his amazing list of accomplishments. They include: 133 singles titles, including eight Grand Slams of Tennis. In the 1970s, he was ranked number one for 159 weeks, which is the longest-running number-one ranking in men's tennis. Connors is credited with bringing tennis back into widespread popularity in the 1970s.

992. John McEnroe Born in Germany in 1959, John McEnroe's family carries strong Irish Catholic roots that he mentions often. Tennis became his passion at an early age, he was playing in local New York club tournaments by the time he was eight. In 1977 he became the youngest player to advance to the men's semifinals in Wimbledon's history. His career closely parallels Jimmy Conners. McEnroe has ninety career singles titles, including seven Grand Slams and thirteen senior titles, and held the number-one ranking for 170 weeks, taking the record away from Connors. He was also ranked the best doubles player for another record 257 straight weeks.

993. Maureen Catherine Connolly Known as "Little Mo," in 1953 Connolly became the first woman to win the grand slam of tennis—Wimbledon, and the U.S., Australian, and French Opens. Born in San Diego in 1934, she started playing tennis at the age of ten. In 1947, she won the girls' fifteen-and-under title in the Southern

California Invitational. She became the youngest female ever to win the National Junior Championship in 1949 (and again in 1950). In 1951 Connolly won the women's singles title at the U.S. Open in New York and became a favorite with the media. She repeated as U.S. Open champion in 1952 and also won at Wimbledon. In the year following her Grand Slam season in 1953, she won for the third time at Wimbledon and second time at the French Open. But a serious leg injury later that year while horseback riding abruptly ended her career. Connolly stayed active in tennis, mainly as an instructor. In 1968 she was elected to the National Lawn Tennis Hall of Fame.

Track and Field

994. James E. Sullivan   One of the founding fathers of modern American track and field, James E. Sullivan (1862–1914) grew up committed to the idea that athletics built character and health. He was a reformer who actively promoted the idea of building parks and playgrounds in cities to provide the maximum opportunity for sports. Seeking to establish a national organization that would establish uniform rules and standards for athletic events and rigorously enforce rules of conduct and sportsmanship, Sullivan founded Amateur Athletic Union (AAU) in 1888. It became the leading organization of its kind and greatly expanded the field of amateur athletics. In recognition of his service to amateur sport, Sullivan was named director of St. Louis Olympic Games in 1904. The James E. Sullivan is presented annually, in the words of the AAU, "to the athlete who has not only achieved athletic excellence, but who has exhibited leadership, character, sportsmanship and the ideals of amateurism."

995. Early Irish American Olympians   At the first modern Olympic Games, held in Athens in 1896, two Irish Americans from Boston turned in standout performances in track and field. James Brendan Connolly won the triple-jump, while Thomas Burke took the gold medal in both the 100-meter and 400-meter dashes. Four years later Irish-born John Flanagan (a U.S. citizen) and won the gold medal in the hammer throw. He repeated as champion in the 1904 and 1908 games. Joining Flanagan in the winner's circle in 1904 was another Irish-born member of the U.S. team, Martin Sheridan, who won gold in the discus throw (James Mitchell, also born in Ireland, won the silver). Sheridan repeated as champion in 1908. That was also the year Irish-born Johnny Hayes won gold in the marathon. In the 1912 games, Patrick McDonald (born County Clare) won gold in the shot-put, while Matthew McGrath (Tipperary) took gold in the hammer throw.

Subsequent Irish and Irish American Olympic gold medal winners in track and field include: Patrick Ryan (1920: hammer throw), Daniel Kinsey (1924: 110-meter hurdles), Thomas "Eddie" Tolan (1932: 110-meter and 200-meter dashes), Parry O'Brien (1952 and 1956: shot-put), Harold Connelly (1956: hammer throw), William Toomey (1968: decathlon).

996. Jim Ryun   Born in Wichita, Kansas, Jim Ryan (b. 1947) enjoyed a career as one of America's premier milers. He achieved national recognition as a high school track and field star, setting the record for the mile (3:55.3) in 1963 that still stands. In college at the University of Kansas, Ryun won three National AAU one-mile titles and five national collegiate titles. He participated in the 1964, 1968, and 1972 Olympic games, winning a silver medal in the 1500 meter run in 1968. Hopes for a gold medal in 1968 were dashed by a bad case of mononucleosis. At the height of his career, Ryun held the world record in the mile, 1500 meters, and 880 yards. In retirement Ryun turned to politics and serves in the House of Representatives. In 1980, Ryun was inducted into the USA Track & Field Hall of Fame.

997. John Kelley   A fixture at the Boston Marathon for more than sixty years, John Kelley

(b. 1907) enjoyed perhaps the longest career in running in American history. Born in Worcester, Massachusetts, Kelley was an eleven-time National AAU champion in four events and made the 1936, 1940, and 1948 Olympic teams. His greatest chance for a medal was in 1940, but the Olympics were canceled that year due to the outbreak of World War II. From 1931 to 1992, Kelley ran in sixty-one Boston Marathons, winning it twice (1935 and 1945). He was eighty-five years old when he ran in his last marathon. In 1980, Kelley was inducted into the USA Track & Field Hall of Fame.

Athletic Odds and Ends

998. Jack Kelly Jack Kelly (1889–1958) was an Olympic champion and father of Grace Kelly, the late Princess of Monaco. Born to Irish immigrants, and the youngest of ten children. He began his rowing career in 1909, and by 1913 had won over nine races. In 1919 and 1920 he was the national single sculls champion, which led him to the 1920 Olympics in Antwerp, Belgium. There he won the singles and doubles competitions in the same day. In the 1924 Paris Olympics he won the singles and doubles again. After his rowing career came to a close, he became a successful businessman and Democratic Party leader.

999. Paul Morphy By the time he was ten years old, Paul Morphy (1837–84) was playing chess with some of the best players in his hometown of New Orleans. At age twenty he burst onto the international scene, traveling to Europe and beating all the best chess players but

Paul Morphy

one, who refused to play him. He even played blindfolded and won! He became the acknowledged "chess master" of the world before the term was used or recognized. But chess was hardly a way to make a living in the mid-nineteenth century, so Morphy eventually dropped it and took up law. He worked as a lawyer in New Orleans until his death.

1000. William Muldoon Born in Belfast, New York, William Muldoon (1845–1933) enjoyed one of the most storied and varied careers in sports. After working as a bouncer, longshoreman, and cab driver, he joined the New York City Police Department. In 1876 he organized the Police Athletic Association. He won a national championship in wrestling and even toured Japan with a team of American wrestlers. He retired from the police in 1900 and opened a saloon. But he was drawn to the idea of establishing a fitness center for businessmen. Soon he had a long client list of wealthy New York tycoons eager to "get into shape" at his upstate athletic compound. He counted among his most famous patrons U.S. Presidents, William Howard Taft and Theodore Roosevelt. Muldoon is credited with developing the concept of a health spa and with inventing the medicine ball.

1001. Michael Phelan Many billiards fans consider Michael Phelan (1817–71) the "Father of American Billiards." He emigrated from Ireland, and settled in New York. In 1850, he wrote the first American book on billiards, *Billiards Without Master*. He also became the first American champion, winning a tournament in Detroit for $15,000. He held many inventions and patents in the world of billiards, including cushion and table designs. He was the first to add diamonds to the table to aid in aiming. He established a billiards equipment manufacturing company that eventually (through mergers) became the Brunswick Corporation, still the largest American billiards manufacturer.

select bibliography

Barnes, John. *Irish-American Landmarks: A Traveler's Guide*. Detroit: Gale Research Group, 1995.

Bernstein, Iver. *The New York City Draft Riots: Their Significance for American Society and Politics in the Age of the Civil War*. New York: Oxford University Press, 1990.

Birmingham, Stephen. *Real Lace*. New York: Harper & Row, 1973.

Brown, Thomas N. *Irish-American Nationalism, 1870–1890*. New York: J. B. Lippincott Co., 1966.

Burchell, R. A. *The San Francisco Irish, 1848–1880*. Manchester: Manchester University Press, 1979.

Cahill, Thomas. *How the Irish Saved Civilization: The Untold Story of Ireland's Heroic Role from the Fall of Rome to the Rise of Medieval Europe*. New York: Nan A. Talese/Doubleday, 1995.

Clark, Dennis. *Hibernia America: The Irish and Regional Cultures*. Westport: Greenwood Press, 1986.

_____. *The Irish in Philadelphia: Ten Generations of Urban Experience*. Philadelphia: Temple University Press, 1973.

Connolly, S. J., ed., *The Oxford Companion to Irish History*. New York: Oxford University Press, 1998.

Coogan, Tim Pat. *The Troubles: Ireland's Ordeal, 1966–1996 and the Search for Peace*. Boulder: Roberts Rinehart Publishers, 1997.

Demeter, Richard. *Irish America: The Historical Travel Guide*, Volumes I–II. Pasadena: Cranford Press, 1997.

Dezell, Maureen. *Irish America, Coming into Clover: The Evolution of a People and a Culture*. New York: Doubleday, 2001.

Diner, Hasia R. *Erin's Daughters in America: Irish Immigrant Women in the Nineteenth Century*. Baltimore: Johns Hopkins University Press, 1983.

Dolan, Jay P. *The American Catholic Experience: A History From Colonial Times to the Present*. New York: Doubleday & Co., 1985.

_____. *The Immigrant Church: New York's Irish and German Catholics, 1815–1865*. Baltimore: Johns Hopkins University Press, 1975.

Dolan, Terrence Patrick. *A Dictionary of Hiberno-English*. Dublin: Gill & Macmillan, 1999.

Doyle, David Noel and Owen Dudley Edwards, eds. *America and Ireland: The American Identity and the Irish Connection*. Westport: Greenwood Press, 1980.

Duffy, Sean, ed., *The Macmillan Atlas of Irish History*. New York: Macmillan, 1997.

Ellis, John Tracy. *American Catholicism*. Chicago: University of Chicago, 1956.

Erie, Steven P. *Rainbow's End: Irish-Americans and the Dilemmas of Urban Machine Politics, 1840–1985*. Berkeley: University of California Press, 1988.

Ernst, Robert. *Immigrant Life in New York City, 1825–1863*. New York: Columbia University Press, 1949.

Foster, R. F. *Modern Ireland, 1600–1972*. New York: The Penguin Press, 1988.

Glazer, Nathan and Daniel P. Moynihan, *Beyond the Melting Pot*. Cambridge, Mass.: M.I.T. Press, 1963.

Glazier, Michael, ed., *The Encyclopedia of the Irish in America*. Notre Dame: University of Notre Dame Press, 1999.

Golway, Terry. *For the Cause of Liberty: A Thousand Years of Ireland's Heroes*. New York: Simon & Schuster, 2000.

_____. *The Irish in America*. New York: Hyperion, 1997.

_____. *Irish Rebel: John Devoy and America's Fight for Irish Freedom*. New York: St. Martin's Press, 1998.

Greeley, Andrew M. *The Irish Americans: The Rise to Money and Power*. New York: Harper & Row, 1981.

_____. *The Most Distressful Nation: The Taming of the American Irish*. Chicago: Quadrangle Books, 1972.

Griffin, William D. *The Book of Irish Americans*. New York: Random House, 1990.

_____. *A Portrait of the Irish in America*. New York: Macmillan, 1983.

Handlin, Oscar. *Boston's Immigrants: A Study In Acculturation*. Cambridge: Harvard University Press, 1941.

Hennessey, James. *American Catholics: A History of the Roman Catholic Community in the United States*. New York: Oxford University Press, 1981.

Herm, Gerhard. *The Celts*. New York: St. Martin's Press, 1977.

Holland, Jack. *Hope Against History: The Course of Conflict in Northern Ireland*. New York: Henry Holt, 1999.

Ignatiev, Noel. *How the Irish Became White*. New York: Routledge, 1996.

Keneally, Thomas. *The Great Shame and the Triumph of the Irish in the English-Speaking World*. New York: Doubleday, 1999.

Kenny, Kevin. *The American Irish: A History*. New York: Longman, 2000.

_____. *Making Sense of the Molly Maguires*. New York: Oxford University Press, 1998.

Kinealy, Christine. *A Death-Dealing Famine: The Great Hunger in Ireland*. London: Pluto Press, 1997.

Knobel, Dale T. *Paddy and the Republic: Ethnicity and Nationality in Antebellum America*. Middletown: Wesleyan, 1986.

Laxton, Edward. *The Famine Ships: The Irish Exodus to America*. New York: Henry Holt, 1996.

Leyburn, James G. *The Scotch-Irish: A Social History*. Chapel Hill: University of North Carolina Press, 1962.

Llywelyn, Morgan. *The Essential Library for Irish Americans*. New York: Tom Doherty Associates, 1999.

McCaffrey, Lawrence J., ed. *Irish-American Nationalism and the American Contribution*. New York: Arno Press, 1976.

_____. *The Irish Diaspora in America*. Washington, D.C.: Catholic University Press, 1976.

Meagher, Timothy J. *Inventing Irish America: Generation, Class, and Ethnic Identity in a New England City, 1880–1928*. Notre Dame: University of Notre Dame Press, 2000.

Miller, Kerby. *Emigrants and Exiles: Ireland and the Irish Exodus to North America*. New York: Oxford University Press, 1985.

_____ and Paul Wagner. *Out of Ireland: The Story of Irish Emigration to America*. Washington, D.C.: Elliott & Clark, 1994.

O'Connor, Thomas H. *The Boston Irish: A Political History*. Boston: Northeastern University Press, 1995.

O'Hanlon, Ray. *The New Irish Americans*. Niwot: Roberts Rinehart Publishers, 1999.

Padden, Michael and Robert Sullivan. *May the Road Rise to Meet You: Everything You Need to Know about Irish American History*. New York: Penguin, 1999.

Ryan, Dennis. *Beyond the Ballot Box: A Social History of the Boston Irish, 1845–1917*. Madison: Fairleigh Dickenson University Press, 1983.

Shannon, William V. *The American Irish*. New York: Macmillan, 1963.

Shaw, Richard. *Dagger John: The Unquiet Life and Times of Archbishop John Hughes of New York*. New York: Paulist Press, 1977.

Werner, M. R. *Tammany Hall*. New York: Greenwood Press, 1928.

Wittke, Carl. *The Irish in America: A Political and Social Portrait*. Baton Rouge: Louisiana State University Press, 1956.

photo credits

American Irish Historical Society   3, 8, 9, 11, 16, 18, 21, 23, 24, 27, 28 (both), 30, 31, 34, 38, 40, 42, 47, 50, 51, 53, 54, 66, 69, 98 (both), 101, 102, 107 (both), 110 (both), 113 (right), 117 (left), 121, 122, 127, 129, 130, 132, 133, 135, 137, 139, 140, 141, 142, 144, 145, 146, 149, 150, 151, 152, 153, 155, 169, 175, 176, 177, 183 (top), 185, 189 (right), 198, 199, 200, 201, 203, 204, 206, 212, 215, 223, 225, 228, 229, 231, 232, 233 (both), 248 (both), 249, 255 (right), 269, 279 (bottom), 290, 291 (bottom), 295, 299, 305

Author's Collection   81, 91, 308, 311

Boston Public Library   87, 89, 104, 115, 188, 191, 197, 238, 241, 243, 244, 245, 246, 250, 258, 262, 281, 294

California Historical Society   291 (top)

Concannon Vinyards   289

Department of the Navy, Naval Historical Center   214

George Meany Archives   312

Irish Echo   86, 159, 161, 164, 167, 253, 319

Johns Hopkins University Medical School Archives   279 (top)

Lahey Clinic Archives   278

Library of Congress   48, 71, 77, 108, 119, 120, 207, 210, 218, 226, 234, 255 (left), 256, 266, 283, 302, 307, 320, 322, 329, 333

Museum of the City of New York   57, 59, 64, 83, 297

NASA   285

National Museum of Ireland   5

New York Public Library   37, 62, 68, 79 (both), 117 (right), 183 (bottom), 298, 304, 306

Nobel Prize Museum   280, 282

Pittsburgh Penguins Archives   328

Tamiment Collection, New York University   314

University of Notre Dame Archives   113 (left), 179, 182, 189 (left), 217, 237, 261, 264, 267, 272, 324

University of Texas Institute of Texas Cultures   74, 202, 331

index

Page numbers of illustrations appear in italics.

about the author

EDWARD T. O'DONNELL is a professor of American history at Holy Cross College in Worcester, Massachusetts. He is the author of numerous articles and essays about Irish American history, including a weekly history column for the *Irish Echo*. He lives with his wife and four daughters in Holden, Massachusetts. Please visit his website at www.EdwardTODonnell.com.

March 2002